REPORTING
THE CAMPAIGN

*This is Volume 22 in a series of studies
commissioned as part of the research program
of the Royal Commission on Electoral Reform
and Party Financing*

REPORTING THE CAMPAIGN
ELECTION COVERAGE IN CANADA

Frederick J. Fletcher
Editor

Volume 22 of the Research Studies

ROYAL COMMISSION ON ELECTORAL REFORM
AND PARTY FINANCING
AND CANADA COMMUNICATION GROUP –
PUBLISHING, SUPPLY AND SERVICES CANADA

DUNDURN PRESS
TORONTO AND OXFORD

© Minister of Supply and Services Canada, 1991
Printed and bound in Canada
ISBN 1-55002-118-4
ISSN 1188-2743
Catalogue No. Z1-1989/2-41-22E

Published by Dundurn Press Limited in cooperation with the Royal
Commission on Electoral Reform and Party Financing and Canada
Communication Group – Publishing, Supply and Services Canada.

Canadian Cataloguing in Publication Data

Main entry under title:
Reporting the campaign

(Research studies ; 22)
Issued also in French under title: Sous l'oeil des journalistes.
ISBN 1-55002-118-4

1. Electioneering – Canada. 2. Press and politics – Canada. 3. Elections –
Canada. I. Fletcher, Frederick J. II. Canada. Royal Commission on Electoral
Reform and Party Financing. III. Series: Research studies (Canada. Royal
Commission on Electoral Reform and Party Financing) ; 22.

#29.95

HE8689.7.P6R46 1991   324.7'3'0971   C91-090534-7

Dundurn Press Limited
2181 Queen Street East
Suite 301
Toronto, Canada
M4E 1E5

Dundurn Distribution
73 Lime Walk
Headington
Oxford, England
OX3 7AD

CONTENTS

TABLES

FOREWORD

THE ROYAL COMMISSION on Electoral Reform and Party Financing was established in November 1989. Our mandate was to inquire into and report on the appropriate principles and process that should govern the election of members of the House of Commons and the financing of political parties and candidates' campaigns. To conduct such a comprehensive examination of Canada's electoral system, we held extensive public consultations and developed a research program designed to ensure that our recommendations would be guided by an independent foundation of empirical inquiry and analysis.

The Commission's in-depth review of the electoral system was the first of its kind in Canada's history of electoral democracy. It was dictated largely by the major constitutional, social and technological changes of the past several decades, which have transformed Canadian society, and their concomitant influence on Canadians' expectations of the political process itself. In particular, the adoption in 1982 of the *Canadian Charter of Rights and Freedoms* has heightened Canadians' awareness of their democratic and political rights and of the way they are served by the electoral system.

The importance of electoral reform cannot be overemphasized. As the Commission's work proceeded, Canadians became increasingly preoccupied with constitutional issues that have the potential to change the nature of Confederation. No matter what their beliefs or political allegiances in this continuing debate, Canadians agree that constitutional change must be achieved in the context of fair and democratic processes. We cannot complacently assume that our current electoral process will always meet this standard or that it leaves no room for improvement. Parliament and the national government must be seen as legitimate; electoral reform can both enhance the stature of national political institutions and reinforce their ability to define the future of our country in ways that command Canadians' respect and confidence and promote the national interest.

In carrying out our mandate, we remained mindful of the importance of protecting our democratic heritage, while at the same time balancing it against the emerging values that are injecting a new dynamic into the electoral system. If our system is to reflect the realities of Canadian political life, then reform requires more than mere tinkering with electoral laws and practices.

Our broad mandate challenged us to explore a full range of options. We commissioned more than 100 research studies, to be published in a 23-volume collection. In the belief that our electoral laws must measure up to the very best contemporary practice, we examined election-related laws and processes in all of our provinces and territories and studied comparable legislation and processes in established democracies around the world. This unprecedented array of empirical study and expert opinion made a vital contribution to our deliberations. We made every effort to ensure that the research was both intellectually rigorous and of practical value. All studies were subjected to peer review, and many of the authors discussed their preliminary findings with members of the political and academic communities at national symposiums on major aspects of the electoral system.

The Commission placed the research program under the able and inspired direction of Dr. Peter Aucoin, Professor of Political Science and Public Administration at Dalhousie University. We are confident that the efforts of Dr. Aucoin, together with those of the research coordinators and scholars whose work appears in this and other volumes, will continue to be of value to historians, political scientists, parliamentarians and policy makers, as well as to thoughtful Canadians and the international community.

Along with the other Commissioners, I extend my sincere gratitude to the entire Commission staff for their dedication and commitment. I also wish to thank the many people who participated in our symposiums for their valuable contributions, as well as the members of the research and practitioners' advisory groups whose counsel significantly aided our undertaking.

Pierre Lortie
Chairman

INTRODUCTION

THE ROYAL COMMISSION'S research program constituted a comprehensive and detailed examination of the Canadian electoral process. The scope of the research, undertaken to assist Commissioners in their deliberations, was dictated by the broad mandate given to the Commission.

The objective of the research program was to provide Commissioners with a full account of the factors that have shaped our electoral democracy. This dictated, first and foremost, a focus on federal electoral law, but our inquiries also extended to the Canadian constitution, including the institutions of parliamentary government, the practices of political parties, the mass media and nonpartisan political organizations, as well as the decision-making role of the courts with respect to the constitutional rights of citizens. Throughout, our research sought to introduce a historical perspective in order to place the contemporary experience within the Canadian political tradition.

We recognized that neither our consideration of the factors shaping Canadian electoral democracy nor our assessment of reform proposals would be as complete as necessary if we failed to examine the experiences of Canadian provinces and territories and of other democracies. Our research program thus emphasized comparative dimensions in relation to the major subjects of inquiry.

Our research program involved, in addition to the work of the Commission's research coordinators, analysts and support staff, over 200 specialists from 28 universities in Canada, from the private sector and, in a number of cases, from abroad. Specialists in political science constituted the majority of our researchers, but specialists in law, economics, management, computer sciences, ethics, sociology and communications, among other disciplines, were also involved.

In addition to the preparation of research studies for the Commission, our research program included a series of research seminars, symposiums and workshops. These meetings brought together the Commissioners, researchers, representatives from the political parties, media personnel and others with practical experience in political parties, electoral politics and public affairs. These meetings provided not only a forum for discussion of the various subjects of the Commission's mandate, but also an opportunity for our research to be assessed by those with an intimate knowledge of the world of political practice.

These public reviews of our research were complemented by internal and external assessments of each research report by persons qualified in the area; such assessments were completed prior to our decision to publish any study in the series of research volumes.

The Research Branch of the Commission was divided into several areas, with the individual research projects in each area assigned to the research coordinators as follows:

F. Leslie Seidle	Political Party and Election Finance
Herman Bakvis	Political Parties
Kathy Megyery	Women, Ethno-cultural Groups and Youth
David Small	Redistribution; Electoral Boundaries; Voter Registration
Janet Hiebert	Party Ethics
Michael Cassidy	Democratic Rights; Election Administration
Robert A. Milen	Aboriginal Electoral Participation and Representation
Frederick J. Fletcher	Mass Media and Broadcasting in Elections
David Mac Donald (Assistant Research Coordinator)	Direct Democracy

These coordinators identified appropriate specialists to undertake research, managed the projects and prepared them for publication. They also organized the seminars, symposiums and workshops in their research areas and were responsible for preparing presentations and briefings to help the Commission in its deliberations and decision making. Finally, they participated in drafting the Final Report of the Commission.

On behalf of the Commission, I welcome the opportunity to thank the following for their generous assistance in producing these research studies – a project that required the talents of many individuals.

In performing their duties, the research coordinators made a notable contribution to the work of the Commission. Despite the pressures of tight deadlines, they worked with unfailing good humour and the utmost congeniality. I thank all of them for their consistent support and cooperation.

In particular, I wish to express my gratitude to Leslie Seidle, senior research coordinator, who supervised our research analysts and support staff in Ottawa. His diligence, commitment and professionalism not only set high standards, but also proved contagious. I am grateful to Kathy Megyery, who performed a similar function in Montreal with equal aplomb and skill. Her enthusiasm and dedication inspired us all.

On behalf of the research coordinators and myself, I wish to thank our research analysts: Daniel Arsenault, Eric Bertram, Cécile Boucher, Peter Constantinou, Yves Denoncourt, David Docherty, Luc Dumont, Jane Dunlop, Scott Evans, Véronique Garneau, Keith Heintzman, Paul Holmes, Hugh Mellon, Cheryl D. Mitchell, Donald Padget, Alain Pelletier, Dominique Tremblay and Lisa Young. The Research Branch was strengthened by their ability to carry out research in a wide variety of areas, their intellectual curiosity and their team spirit.

The work of the research coordinators and analysts was greatly facilitated by the professional skills and invaluable cooperation of Research Branch staff members: Paulette LeBlanc, who, as administrative assistant, managed the flow of research projects; Hélène Leroux, secretary to the research coordinators, who produced briefing material for the Commissioners and who, with Lori Nazar, assumed responsibility for monitoring the progress of research projects in the latter stages of our work; Kathleen McBride and her assistant Natalie Brose, who created and maintained the database of briefs and hearings transcripts; and Richard Herold and his assistant Susan Dancause, who were responsible for our research library. Jacinthe Séguin and Cathy Tucker also deserve thanks – in addition to their duties as receptionists, they assisted in a variety of ways to help us meet deadlines.

We were extremely fortunate to obtain the research services of first-class specialists from the academic and private sectors. Their contributions are found in this and the other 22 published research volumes. We thank them for the quality of their work and for their willingness to contribute and to meet our tight deadlines.

Our research program also benefited from the counsel of Jean-Marc Hamel, Special Adviser to the Chairman of the Commission and former

Chief Electoral Officer of Canada, whose knowledge and experience proved invaluable.

In addition, numerous specialists assessed our research studies. Their assessments not only improved the quality of our published studies, but also provided us with much-needed advice on many issues. In particular, we wish to single out professors Donald Blake, Janine Brodie, Alan Cairns, Kenneth Carty, John Courtney, Peter Desbarats, Jane Jenson, Richard Johnston, Vincent Lemieux, Terry Morley and Joseph Wearing, as well as Ms. Beth Symes.

Producing such a large number of studies in less than a year requires a mastery of the skills and logistics of publishing. We were fortunate to be able to count on the Commission's Director of Communications, Richard Rochefort, and Assistant Director, Hélène Papineau. They were ably supported by the Communications staff: Patricia Burden, Louise Dagenais, Caroline Field, Claudine Labelle, France Langlois, Lorraine Maheux, Ruth McVeigh, Chantal Morissette, Sylvie Patry, Jacques Poitras and Claudette Rouleau-O'Toole.

To bring the project to fruition, the Commission also called on specialized contractors. We are deeply grateful for the services of Ann McCoomb (references and fact checking); Marthe Lemery, Pierre Chagnon and the staff of Communications Com'ça (French quality control); Norman Bloom, Pamela Riseborough and associates of B&B Editorial Consulting (English adaptation and quality control); and Mado Reid (French production). Al Albania and his staff at Acart Graphics designed the studies and produced some 2 400 tables and figures.

The Commission's research reports constitute Canada's largest publishing project of 1991. Successful completion of the project required close cooperation between the public and private sectors. In the public sector, we especially acknowledge the excellent service of the Privy Council unit of the Translation Bureau, Department of the Secretary of State of Canada, under the direction of Michel Parent, and our contacts Ruth Steele and Terry Denovan of the Canada Communication Group, Department of Supply and Services.

The Commission's co-publisher for the research studies was Dundurn Press of Toronto, whose exceptional service is gratefully acknowledged. Wilson & Lafleur of Montreal, working with the Centre de Documentation Juridique du Québec, did equally admirable work in preparing the French version of the studies.

Teams of editors, copy editors and proofreaders worked diligently under stringent deadlines with the Commission and the publishers to prepare some 20 000 pages of manuscript for design, typesetting and printing. The work of these individuals, whose names are listed elsewhere in this volume, was greatly appreciated.

Our acknowledgements extend to the contributions of the Commission's Executive Director, Guy Goulard, and the administration and executive support teams: Maurice Lacasse, Denis Lafrance and Steve Tremblay (finance); Thérèse Lacasse and Mary Guy-Shea (personnel); Cécile Desforges (assistant to the Executive Director); Marie Dionne (administration); Anna Bevilacqua (records); and support staff members Michelle Bélanger, Roch Langlois, Michel Lauzon, Jean Mathieu, David McKay and Pierrette McMurtie, as well as Denise Miquelon and Christiane Séguin of the Montreal office.

A special debt of gratitude is owed to Marlène Girard, assistant to the Chairman. Her ability to supervise the logistics of the Commission's work amid the tight schedules of the Chairman and Commissioners contributed greatly to the completion of our task.

I also wish to express my deep gratitude to my own secretary, Liette Simard. Her superb administrative skills and great patience brought much-appreciated order to my penchant for the chaotic workstyle of academe. She also assumed responsibility for the administrative coordination of revisions to the final drafts of volumes 1 and 2 of the Commission's Final Report. I owe much to her efforts and assistance.

Finally, on behalf of the research coordinators and myself, I wish to thank the Chairman, Pierre Lortie, the members of the Commission, Pierre Fortier, Robert Gabor, William Knight and Lucie Pépin, and former members Elwood Cowley and Senator Donald Oliver. We are honoured to have worked with such an eminent and thoughtful group of Canadians, and we have benefited immensely from their knowledge and experience. In particular, we wish to acknowledge the creativity, intellectual rigour and energy our Chairman brought to our task. His unparalleled capacity to challenge, to bring out the best in us, was indeed inspiring.

Peter Aucoin
Director of Research

PREFACE

IN MODERN DEMOCRACIES, election campaigns are contested to a large degree in the media. From the days of the openly partisan press to the contemporary multi-media environment, political leaders have relied upon mass media to mobilize electoral support. While the right to vote freely and the credibility of the ballot process are central to democracy, the conduct of campaigns and the flow of information to voters are also important. If campaigns are perceived to be conducted unfairly, the entire electoral process may become suspect. Concern for the legitimacy of the system is one of the primary reasons that most democracies have enacted regulations dealing with aspects of electoral communication. These regulations cover a wide range of media activities, including campaign advertising, election broadcasting and even some aspects of news and public affairs.

The Commission's research program on mass media and elections examined the major developments in electoral communication in Canada and other democratic countries in recent decades, in the context of electoral reform. The research studies were designed to cast light on major aspects of election media, whether amenable to regulation or not. Effective regulation requires an understanding of the entire system of campaign communication.

The results of the research program provided background for the Commission's report. Whatever their substantive focus, the studies examined issues such as fairness in electoral competition and public confidence in the electoral process, issues that are central to electoral reform. Some studies examined central elements in the campaign communication system, while others assessed its effectiveness in meeting the information needs of voters and the communication needs of parties. Several projects considered alternative forms of communication that might contribute to improved information for voters. The studies examined campaign media in the larger sense, including partisan advertising, free broadcast time, candidate communication strategies, new communication technologies and news and public affairs coverage, among other topics.

Research dealing directly with mass media and elections is reported in volumes 18 through 22. Volume 16, on opinion polling, and Volume 17, on the attitudes of Canadians toward the electoral system, also deal with campaign communication, but include material on other subjects as well. Taken together, the seven volumes provide a comprehensive overview of the issues of campaign communication.

The studies reported in Volume 22 examine aspects of journalistic practice in election coverage in Canada. The studies deal with the views of journalists regarding ethical and practical issues in election coverage; the relationship between parties and candidates on one hand, and news media on the other; the question of the accountability of the print media; the coverage of minor parties; problems of stereotyping of and access for minorities in election coverage; and the impact of new technologies on election coverage. The studies were intended to cover a number of topics not amenable to direct regulation.

William Gilsdorf and Robert Bernier examine aspects of journalistic practice during election coverage, with special attention to the amount and kind of campaign information provided by the news. The study is based primarily on interviews with political journalists and reflects their concerns about campaign coverage and estimates of likely future changes. It also provides a useful summary of scholarly research on campaign coverage and contrasts the working theories of practitioners with the observations of scholars and other critics. Jean Charron traces the development of the relationship between politics and the media in Quebec since 1945, with emphasis on the decline of the partisan press and shifts in the use of the media by politicians. The study provides a good sense of the uneasy relationship between candidates and journalists. Christopher Dornan picks up this theme and argues that as the press increasingly becomes recognized as an independent participant in the political process, it should become an object of public scrutiny and commentary. Because external accountability poses a threat to traditional press freedom, Professor Dornan calls instead for a more self-critical approach from within news organizations. Robert Hackett examines media coverage of minor parties, contrasts practices in Canada with those in other countries and argues that a market-driven approach to campaign communication produces significant inequalities for new and smaller parties. The study provides a careful content analysis of the coverage of minor parties during the 1988 campaign, at both the national and community levels, supplemented by interviews with journalists and officials of minor parties. The study suggests a number of policy options designed to ensure that the campaign debate is as democratic as possible.

Eileen Saunders examines the obstacles to participation in the campaign debate faced by minorities through case studies of the portrayal of persons with disabilities and visible minorities in the 1988 campaign coverage. She discusses the actual and potential role of the media in developing an adequate level of public understanding about the concerns of these groups. To reduce marginalization and stereotyping, she suggests improving the representation of these groups in the media and sensitizing journalists to the issues. Issues of stereotyping in election coverage are examined further in the study by Gertrude Robinson and Armande Saint-Jean, "Women Politicians and their Media Coverage," published in Volume 6.

In order to provide an empirical basis for their analysis, many of the authors examined the 1988 campaign. The studies were conducted in late 1990 and early 1991. The authors thus had the benefit of various works on the 1988 campaign but also faced the problem of reconstructing events some two years after they occurred.

Although varied in focus and method, the studies provide a wide range of perspectives on Canadian journalistic practice in election coverage. They report the views of journalists, party officials, advocacy groups and media critics and, in some cases, compare them with the findings of content analysis. For the most part, the studies deal with aspects of election communication not amenable to direct regulation, but they provide important suggestions for self-directed reforms as well as for further research.

The studies reported here will be of interest not only to students and scholars examining the mass media and/or election campaigns, but also to media practitioners and others concerned about fairness, accountability, ethics and representation. These studies have implications beyond election campaigns but the issues raised in this volume in the narrower context of elections may stimulate consideration of the broader issues of media practice.

The Commission's research program on mass media and elections drew on the expertise of a wide range of communication scholars and political scientists in addition to those whose work is published in these volumes. Their assistance is greatly appreciated. Among those who participated as peer reviewers and advisers, several deserve special recognition: Peter Desbarats, Dean of the School of Journalism at the

University of Western Ontario; David Taras, University of Calgary; Holli Semetko, University of Michigan; and Marc Raboy, Laval University. The research program also benefited from the advice of individuals from the parties and the media: John Coleman, President, Canadian Advertising Foundation; Terry Hargreaves, Elly Alboim and Colin MacLeod of the CBC; Geoffrey Stevens, political columnist; Lynn McDonald, sociologist and former MP; and others who prefer to remain anonymous. On behalf of the authors and the Commission, I must also acknowledge our debt to the practitioners from the media and the parties who attended our seminars or agreed to be interviewed and provided much valuable assistance and advice.

The administration of the research program depended heavily on the work of Cheryl Mitchell, who served as my assistant from the inception of the program, and our research assistants at York University: Catherine Bolan, Claudia Forgas, Marni Goldman, Todd Harris, Sharon Johnston and Sheila Riordon. We were also assisted most ably by the Commission staff. Peter Constantinou and Véronique Garneau had particular responsibilities for research in this area. The staff of the Department of Political Science, the Faculty of Arts, Calumet College, and the Faculty of Environmental Studies at York University were very accommodating.

The authors themselves deserve special acknowledgement for their willingness to try to meet tight deadlines, complicated by their normal academic responsibilities, and in particular to respond with cheerfulness and despatch to our requests for revisions. The conscientious peer reviewers were of major assistance to the authors and ourselves in preparing these studies for publication.

The unfailing good humour and encouragement of Peter Aucoin, the Director of Research, made an important contribution to the work. It was a privilege to work with the Commissioners, whose willingness to bring their experience to bear on the most esoteric of formulations was an inspiration. Pierre Lortie's overall direction and, in particular, his suggestions for research and incisive comments on various drafts made a vital contribution, which is reflected in these research volumes as well as in the Final Report of the Royal Commission. Working with the other research coordinators was a genuine pleasure. Richard Rochefort and his staff were crucial in bringing these studies to publication.

On a personal note, I wish to thank my wife and frequent collaborator, Martha Fletcher, for encouraging me to undertake this task, which I have found very rewarding, and for her direct advice on many aspects of the work, as well as for bearing more than her share of the burden of domestic management. My son, Frederick, reminded me that work, however important, must be balanced with other aspects of life but also that the future of the democratic process is worth working for.

Cheryl Mitchell brought dedication and skill to the work and must have an ample share of the credit for whatever contribution the research program has made. Catherine Bolan coordinated the substantive editing of this volume and assisted in the editing of one of the chapters. For errors in design and execution, however, I remain responsible.

Fred Fletcher
Research Coordinator

REPORTING
THE CAMPAIGN

1

JOURNALISTIC PRACTICE IN COVERING FEDERAL ELECTION CAMPAIGNS IN CANADA

William O. Gilsdorf
Robert Bernier

INTRODUCTION

ELECTORAL CAMPAIGNS HAVE become media events. Increasingly, the voter is removed and/or insulated from the practice and process of campaigns, forced to become a passive observer and consumer of prepackaged messages and news reports. Where once the site of the contest might have been in the mind of the voter, the first line of struggle has now shifted to the contest between the journalist and the candidate's advisers for control of the campaign agenda and the interpretation of events and statements. At best, the voter is left with a strategic decision of where to place her or his vote, based on the predigested information provided by the candidate or the journalist.

Since the 1960s, political candidates and their strategists have started adapting to the realization that media use and control are essential to effective campaigning. By 1988, all three of the major parties were devoting the major share of their expenditures to strategies of advertising and media manipulation. Media organizations have similarly assigned large portions of their budgets to election coverage. Along with the routine coverage of government (part of what several have labelled the permanent campaign), election campaigns are still seen as coveted assignments by reporters and editors, and as major sites of legitimation and credibility for media institutions.

The importance of the media as key players in the Canadian political process is now generally recognized. At an earlier time, party organization and word of mouth were the primary sources of campaign information; but first the newspapers and then the electronic media became the source of choice for those Canadians who were active and interested in politics. Television and, occasionally, radio have also become the principal source of information for the increasing number of Canadians who are at the margins of political participation.

Because of the real and perceived importance of the media in the conduct of election campaigns, it is important for research to go beyond the examination of the content of election coverage to examine the nature and process of journalistic practice, including the relationship between party and media. As will become evident to the reader from our review of previous research on Canadian elections, there has been relatively little examination of the assumptions, routines, standards and constraints that influence the practices of journalists and their organizations during campaigns. In fact, journalistic practices in Canada generally have not been the subject of systematic research; we have only the anecdotal accounts and memoirs of retired journalists.

This study intended to fill that gap by clarifying and exploring the nature and development of journalistic practices in covering elections in Canada. We begin with an overview of the research on journalistic practice in election coverage in Canada, in order to put our work in perspective and make clear our own assumptions concerning the nature and significance of journalistic activity during and between elections.

The second and third sections of the study are analyses of election journalism as a practice that is grounded and evolves in the context of the resources, constraints and operating procedures of Canadian news organizations. This discussion takes the form of a summary of interviews with Canadian print and broadcast journalists. An effort has been made to present patterns in journalistic practices and point out notable exceptions. These two sections cover English and French media practice separately, in that order.

Journalistic practices have, in our view, become institutionalized in Canada; that is, they are determined by the resources of and constraints on news organizations and by established procedures for covering social events, political or otherwise, that have evolved over the years. As we discuss journalistic practices in the second section of this study, we shall try to situate our discussion within a historical examination of the evolution of the procedures of election journalism in Canada. Here we hope to highlight what we believe are the major changes that have taken place in the French and English media's coverage and analysis of election issues since 1979 (and, in some cases, earlier).

Throughout each of these discussions, we shall be drawing upon interviews that we conducted with political journalists in French and English media outlets across Canada. Our study concludes with some generalizations and recommendations concerning journalistic practice as it has evolved and is evolving in the context of Canadian elections.

The Goals of This Study

Our broad aim is to examine election journalism as a routine but evolving practice. Journalistic practice, we believe, is being transformed in relation to a number of broad factors in Canada: changing technologies; new political parties; new party strategies and methods of political organization; new balances of power and influence within and among media organizations; and new forms of professional organization and practice among political journalists.

Within the evolving professional milieu, we believe that campaign journalists are faced with a set of institutionalized but flexible constraints. Like journalists everywhere, they must work with limited budgets; they struggle for time and space in which to present their work; they accomplish that work within the bounds of established organizational traditions and routines; and they negotiate these routines in an often adversarial (and always uneasy) relationship with their political sources. Canadian election journalists must cope with all these factors. But, in our view, the contexts in which journalists cover elections in Canada are not just a fixed set of constraints; they are also conditions of possibility. That is, journalists can and sometimes do react to changing circumstances with new strategies for covering campaigns. They may tell their stories in conventional ways within conventional formats, but they can and often do reflect upon and modify these conventions in light of changing circumstances; and even if they do not, they must apply some degree of skill to work effectively. In other words, we believe that journalistic practice influences the news business and the coverage of election issues in particular. Furthermore, we believe that journalistic practice influences the course of campaigns and the results of the vote.

Journalistic Practices and the Coverage of Elections in Canada

The literature on journalistic practices and the coverage of elections in Canada has focused on a number of themes. Some authors have noted that Canadian journalists have not simply responded to changing political events but have searched for new ways (with varying degrees of coherence and success) of telling campaign stories. There is a good deal of evidence to suggest that Canadian political journalists tend to rely on tried and true narrative themes in their election reporting – to the point of developing blind spots with respect to "unusual developments" in "unusual campaigns" (Fletcher and Everett 1989). The media's overwhelming focus on the Free Trade Agreement to the exclusion of all other issues in the 1988 federal election is a frequently cited case in point (Frizzell et al. 1989).

At the same time, these and other studies suggest that our political journalists periodically recognize the problems associated with conventions and routines and that they work with varying degrees of success to change them. In this country, political journalists have been particularly aware of the importance they attach to national issues, the leader tours and the use of polls to make sense of the campaign. Self-criticism in these cases – such as it is – has certainly been encouraged by criticism from outside the profession. Nevertheless, actions do not always match words. Journalists have been promising to shift their focus from the leader tours since the 1979 election at least. They have shown some sign of doing so since then. The fact that Canadian journalists discuss these patterns, periodically find them problematical and modify them at least to some degree suggests that election journalism involves more than simple efforts to satisfy the demands of the information market, of "political masters" or even of technological change.

Serious academic research on Canadian elections has been going on for 30 years. John Meisel, of Queen's University, published the first book of studies on an election, *The Canadian General Election of 1957* (Meisel 1962). Meisel continued to study voting behaviour in subsequent elections, publishing volumes on the 1962 and 1965 elections.[1] For the 1974, 1979 and 1980 elections, the National Election Study was extended by a team of political scientists at the University of Windsor and Carleton University. Their work resulted in two volumes of analyses: *Political Choice in Canada* (Clarke et al. 1979) and *Absent Mandate* (Clarke et al. 1984).

Although the volume that Meisel published in 1962 contained an article on media coverage, it was not until the 1974 election study that questions began to be asked about media coverage. Along with the extensive interviews of voters, the 1974, 1979 and 1980 studies also included a content analysis of selected newspaper coverage. In *Absent Mandate*, the major conclusions concerning public interest in the campaign were as follows:

- The importance attached to television by the public ... make[s] it the ideal medium from the point of view of political parties and politicians trying to get their messages across to the voters (Clarke et al. 1984, 289).
- Public perceptions of the most important issues in election campaigns are closely related to the agenda of discussion that is set by the country's communication media and, through these media, by the politicians on the campaign trail (ibid., 84).
- Patterns of election news coverage give evidence to arguments that the power to set election agendas is largely the prerogative of politicians and the media (ibid., 87).
- Content analysis of coverage of the 1974, 1979 and 1980 elections ... confirm[s] the point that ... coverage has a decidedly national focus, and stories emphasizing the leaders' behaviour constitute one of its major components (ibid., 118).
- In both 1979 and 1980, much of the leader coverage had a distinctly negative tone (ibid., 119).

A series of national election studies confirmed these observations and added others. Exploring the further implications of the national focus of election coverage, Fletcher (1987) found that the media's preoccupation with national leaders, political parties and issues during the campaign leads them to neglect local candidates. Furthermore, media focus on the three major parties and their leaders is often at the expense of minor parties and other groups and tends to favour incumbency. Fletcher notes that recent shifts in voter preference suggest that campaigns themselves are increasingly significant. This is evident in voter volatility in recent election campaigns, where nearly 60 percent of voters have been willing to change their voting preference (ibid., 345). In the 1984 election, nearly half the voters reported making their vote decision during the campaign (ibid., 355).

Fletcher lists several ways the media push national issues to the forefront: televised leaders debates, emphasis on party leaders and the use of national opinion polls. In 1979 and 1984, the leaders debates were an important feature of the campaign and were heavily reported in the media. In Fletcher's sample of daily newspapers, party leaders were mentioned far more frequently than any other political actors. Media-initiated polls proliferated during these campaigns, with an increase in national polls during the four elections that were held between 1974 and 1984.[2]

The 1988 federal election was the subject of studies that examined the role of television more closely, especially the televised leaders debates, as well as the impact of new technologies on party strategy and the responses of voters to campaign information. Frizzell et al. (1989), for example, caution that although it is true that the media, particularly television, are the channels through which voters get most of their information, their influence can be overestimated. These authors' analysis of data from the 1988 campaign showed the following: the media gave roughly equal exposure to leaders and parties; although free trade was the major issue reported by the media, its impact was deemed by researchers to be largely neutral; and newspaper and broadcast coverage (in the sample) were strikingly similar. According to the authors, an even greater influence than that of journalists may be the election debates, when the leaders speak directly to the voters and can have a profound impact on public opinion. In the 1988 leaders debates, for example, the media did not pick a winner until the polls began to react to the public's response. "It was apparent that the public had been moved by images, and the media hastened to adopt this view of events" (ibid., 79).

In the second edition of *Absent Mandate,* Clarke et al. reported that as people increasingly rely on television as a source of political information, media images become the reality for much of the public, and televised leaders debates are now a "fundamental part of campaign strategy" (1991, 101). Two-thirds of respondents reported having watched leaders debates in 1984 and 1988. The importance of debates in shaping the images of leaders is evident in the coverage they receive in the press and in news broadcasts, and in their use in party campaign commercials. Because the debates in 1984 and 1988 took place early on in the campaign, they most likely "provided the backdrop to much of the media coverage and interpretation which followed" (ibid., 103).

However, the authors claim that the extent to which debates affect voting is generally modest and in most cases statistically insignificant. For example, although voters considered John Turner's performance in 1988 to be superior to that of his opponents, only small effects on voting were found: respondents who saw at least one of the debates were slightly more likely to vote Liberal than those who saw neither of the debates. Much of the same pattern held in 1979 and 1984, where the effects of the debates on voting behaviour were, at best, small. Clarke et al. (1991) conclude that although debates between party leaders on television are more important than ever in the dynamics of the campaign, it would be a mistake to conclude that they can shift a large number of votes.

In their study of the 1988 campaign, Johnston et al. (1992) found that the televised leaders debates "clearly punctuated" the campaign.

For a brief period directly following the debates, free trade opponents who saw the debates were more likely than nonviewers to say they would vote Liberal (ibid.). Although the Liberal surge in popularity produced by seeing the debate was direct and unmediated, the authors noted a second surge, which was most likely achieved through "propagation" (the social contagion achieved through media reports) and through poll results and word of mouth. This study is especially useful as it examines not only voter preferences but also the process leading to the outcome through a series of intertwining media influences throughout the campaign. The interaction of polls, television and advertising created a changeable dynamic in the information environment in 1988. For example, the authors suggest that the televised leaders debates, along with public opinion polls on the debates, combined to create "bandwagon" and "strategic voting" patterns that could have accounted for the Liberal rise and NDP drop during the campaign. They also examined the impact of advertising, in particular third-party advertising in the latter part of the campaign, noting that the shift in voter preferences during the last week coincided with the "crescendo" of advertising. This might have been a factor in turning the free trade support into Conservative votes (ibid.).

In yet another perspective on media and voter preference, MacDermid (1991) studied the patterns of media consumption among respondents in National Election Studies between 1965 and 1988. He found that a significant number of Canadians pay little attention to the media's political coverage: only about 40–50 percent of the 1988 respondents attentively followed campaign news on television and in the newspapers. Media consumption also differs according to socio-economic variables such as sex, age and education: the most active participants are middle-aged, better-educated males who have higher than average incomes. Media messages are quite likely to be picked up by interested partisans, with the effect of reinforcing their existing political opinions.

Although there has been much debate over the issue of media bias, MacDermid (1991) argues that those who are most open to media messages are also the most likely to be able to detect bias. Given that the media are virtually the sole source of information for voters, the narrow range of political awareness, combined with the dominance of certain methods of communication such as television, give cause for concern. MacDermid suggests that more effort should be given to extending political messages to ensure that a broad diversity of viewpoints and methods of communication is being imparted to voters.

Methodological approaches to studying the role of the media in election campaigns date back to Qualter and Mackirdy (1964), whose "The Press of Ontario and the Election" was published in John Meisel's *Papers on the 1962 Election*. That initial paper was the first of what has become the dominant form of political media research in Canada, namely, content analysis of election coverage. It concerned itself with variables such as space allotment, the positioning of content and the positive or negative nature of party coverage. This was followed by research with a similar methodology in the 1970s. Researchers at the University of Windsor (Wagenberg and Soderlund 1975; 1976) looked at the 1972 and 1974 elections, considering variables of newspaper chain ownership. Whereas the earlier Qualter and Mackirdy analysis had revealed very favourable treatment of all parties, the later research showed a decided trend toward negative coverage. Interestingly, the Wagenberg and Soderlund studies showed a great similarity in the emerging issue agenda, regardless of the ownership pattern.

Fletcher followed in somewhat the same tradition of content analysis. However, he broadened his concerns to examine "the contest waged by the parties and then leaders to determine the issues ... [and] to manage events so that the news coverage will come out as close to their preferred version of events as possible" (Fletcher 1981a, 125–26). This combination of party strategy and content analysis of newspaper and broadcasting coverage permeates much of Fletcher's later work and that of others such as R. Jeremy Wilson and William Gilsdorf.

Wilson (1980–81), like Fletcher, analysed the content of both newspapers and television network news broadcasts. Like a number of researchers in the United States, he concluded after the 1979 and 1980 election campaigns that "horse-race commentary" dominated the coverage. Television contributed strongly to this, with its focus on the party leader tours, a general process that he felt undermined some principles that are fundamental to a democratic system.

The content analysis tradition culminated in what was clearly the most thorough and extensive project organized to study media coverage, beginning with the 1979 election and extending through the 1980 Quebec referendum and the 1980 and 1984 elections. Four researchers at the University of Windsor – Walter C. Soderlund, Donald Briggs, Ronald Wagenberg and Walter Romanow – systematically collected and analysed selected newspapers and radio and television news broadcasts for factors of space and time allotment, thematic content and commentary on parties and leaders. The Windsor Group extended their method in studies for the Royal Commission on Newspapers (1981) and the Caplan-Savageau Task Force on Broadcasting Policy

(1986). The results of their election studies have been synthesized and presented in the only book by academics to appear in Canada focusing exclusively on media election coverage: *Media and Elections in Canada* (Soderlund et al. 1984).

Their approach was derived from theories of gatekeeping and agenda setting, which concern themselves with media content from the perspective of the sender rather than the receiver. Gatekeeping is the process of information selection by decision makers in the media, such as editors, reporters and publishers; agenda setting is the cumulative result of these gatekeeping processes. From this perspective, the authors are able to focus on "how content is selected from the social environment and the consequences of that selection process" (Soderlund et al. 1984, 31).

Soderlund and his colleagues were concerned about the implications, for the democratic process, of a number of the patterns that they observed. One such trend, negative campaigning, has increasingly been a feature of news reporting and political advertising. This is particularly evident in the print media, where a more confrontational style of reporting has had the effect of detracting from policy analysis, while at the same time the tabloid sector of the industry has led the trend away from serious reporting. In the electronic media, where news reporting tends to be very limited in length, reporters and editors are more likely to respond to the dramatic elements of the electoral process than to the "humdrum" of fact-oriented debate. This emphasis on "attack and counterattack" in media coverage creates a negative atmosphere and emphasizes competitive elements over the more substantive issues (Soderlund et al. 1984, 131). The authors expressed concern that the generally critical comments about politicians by the media encourage public mistrust of them.

Two other trends in political coverage which the authors questioned were the reliability of the media's interpretation of public opinion polls and the "Americanization" of Canadian elections, in which the emphasis on the leadership parallels trends in the United States.

The authors' latest work further examined the developing patterns of political coverage and investigated the implications of polls more deeply. Drawing on 1984 federal election campaign data, they found that the media's preoccupation with public opinion polls represented a shift away from focusing on party leadership, which previously had been the most important focus in campaigns apart from the parties themselves (Wagenberg et al. 1988). Polls were mentioned in 2 percent more newspaper items than was leadership (ibid., 121). This was the first time this had happened in political coverage in Canada, and it led the authors to believe that the pre-eminence of polls, combined with the status of television debates, reveals a growing tendency to equate campaigns with horse-races. One consequence of horse-race journalism is that "what may now be influencing voting decision is less where the parties stand on substantive matters than whether they are deemed likely to win or lose" (ibid.). Polls, the authors concluded, are a real source of influence on voting behaviour, and the media emphasis on polls during the 1984 campaign was a significant factor in the election outcome.

There are two recent works on the news media and journalistic practices in Canada. One is Peter Desbarats' *Guide to Canadian News Media* (1990). Desbarats, a former journalist and now dean of the School of Journalism at the University of Western Ontario, provides a look at the structure and process of the Canadian news media. Included is an insightful chapter on political journalism. Desbarats notes that two developments have transformed the relationship between media and politics in Canada in recent years: the emergence of television as the primary and most persuasive information source, and the introduction of public opinion polls as a determining factor in political strategy. Although the assumption is that media do influence political opinion and voter preferences, Desbarats argues that there is little hard evidence to support this assumption. Instead, the role of the media may be that of an agenda setter: although the media may not be able to tell people what to think and may not be able to change their political views, they can influence what people think about by setting the agenda for public discussion (ibid., 149–50). The media, politicians, media consultants and journalists, however, behave as if media are in fact influential, and this assumption seems to be shared by voters, who are always ready to blame the media for whatever current problems affect their political system.

The other recent work on the news media is David Taras' book, *The Newsmakers* (1990). Combining several research strategies, especially interviews with key party and media personnel, Taras covers a number of issues related to this study and the mandate of the Commission: the rising influence of television, the effects of advertising, and the increased reliance of media and parties on polls. He argues that the media set agendas and consequently have an effect on political outcomes. As a result, politicians have changed their strategies and behaviour to meet the challenges presented by the new media environment. Taras' most important points are summarized below.

First, polls were found to be influential in shaping party strategy, sometimes in combination with other new technologies such as direct mail. For example, by indicating where the undecided voters are – by region, income, ethnic group and age – the polls permit the parties to target their messages. In 1988, upon identifying undecided voters, the Conservatives launched a campaign of strategically timed letters and phone calls; their computerized direct-mail system reached about 200 000 voters in 40 ridings (Taras 1990, 186). Second, extensive third-party advertising in 1988 suggests that nonparty advertising will become increasingly prevalent, particularly if the "right" of interest groups to wage an election campaign parallel to that of the parties becomes more established (ibid., 227).

Third, Taras' exploration of the modern media in democratic elections raises several implications for the electoral process: emphasis on visual material may be detrimental to substantive political events and developments; journalists now have the principal responsibility to evaluate, interpret and frame the contexts for the actions of political leaders; media focus on the "politics of personality" at the expense of parties; and media and technology have contributed to the erosion of political parties by replacing their communication and information functions with public opinion polls, professional consultants and advertising.

As has been apparent, there are few academic studies of election coverage practices produced in French-speaking Canada, with the exception of a couple of content analyses done for the Canadian Radio-television and Telecommunications Commission (CRTC) in the 1970s. There has been some limited analysis of the coverage of the 1980 referendum and several examinations of journalistic practices in wider political contexts. Robert Bernier's *Le Marketing gouvernemental au Québec: 1929–1985* (1988) focuses on the marketing practices of the Government of Quebec, and his recent book, *Gérer la victoire? Organisation, communication, stratégie* (1991), is based on a comprehensive survey of party strategists following the 1988 federal election. Bernier made several important findings on party strategists' use of the media during election campaigns. In 1988, the Conservatives and, to a lesser extent, the Liberals exhibited their capacity to modify the content of their ads in response to new developments in the campaign in very short time lapses, a practice seen as becoming institutionalized in electoral marketing schemes. This trend is fundamentally tied to the extent and quality of a party's human and financial resources, reducing the chances of less established parties to communicate with voters in this way. Bernier also reported on the increasingly sophisticated relationship between politicians and journalists, which was evident in the way party "spin doctors"[3] influenced the press to declare a winner of the leaders debates, when journalists were initially reluctant to do so.

Other works produced in French Canada include a few graduate theses and articles on the Quebec press gallery (Charron and Normand 1984; Cantin 1981; Lesage 1980; Wright 1979; Canada, Canadian Study 1980). Additional comment on relevant francophone research is contained in the section on the French media.

A number of journalists, some of them very experienced in political coverage, have published books and films on election campaigns with insight into party strategy and relations with the media. Clive Cocking, a freelance journalist, travelled with the media in the 1979 campaign, recording his impressions of their conduct (Cocking 1980). Largely anecdotal and lacking an analytical frame of reference, the book is nevertheless useful for its comments on "pack" behaviour and the pressures on journalists. Peter Raymont, a freelance film, television and radio documentarist, followed the same 1979 campaign, focusing on four journalists: Mark Phillips, then of CBC-TV; Richard Gwyn, columnist for the *Toronto Star*; Jim Munson, then of Standard Broadcast News; and Doug Small, then a reporter for Canadian Press. His resulting documentary, *History on the Run* (1980), reveals much about the daily routine of reporters and the various forces constraining their coverage. Dalton Camp – former president of the PC party, later a columnist and commentator, and adviser to the prime minister – gathered together his observations on the 1979 campaign in *Points of Departure* (1979). One of the book's subtexts is the relation between media and party personnel. Emerging common journalistic story lines are signalled by chapter headings like "The Death Watch" for the Liberal campaign and "The Wimp Watch" for the Clark tour.

The 1984 election produced a commentary on media practice and influence in Mary Anne Comber and Robert Mayne's *The Newsmongers: How the Media Distort the Political News* (1986). Comber and Mayne are not journalists (both have been or are consultant/policy analysts for branches of the federal government), but their work has been included here because of their critique of the media. The virtue of the book is its very readable text and its presentation of a number of negative assessments of the media that need to be considered by anyone concerned about the influence of mass media on the political process. The subtitle of the book indicates the clear and almost unflinching condemnation of the ways in which media practitioners have interfered with, manipulated and distorted the effective functioning of government.

Writing from the point of view of party activists, Comber and Mayne (1986) raise a number of important concerns. The central thesis of the book is that a new, more opinionated form of journalism has distorted political coverage to the extent that reporters are featured more than political leaders. As a result, the authors argue, Canadians are being deprived of vital political information, because political news is based more on hype than on substance. Rather than the "instant analysis" by reporters and editors, they argue that more news should feature statements by politicians and officials, without the editing which often overwhelms the intended message. For example, the 1984 coverage of Brian Mulroney and John Turner consisted primarily (in 88 percent of cases) of reporters describing and commenting upon the views and actions of the leaders, or of reactions by others.

Among other things, Comber and Mayne (1986) argue that political coverage should emphasize credible rather than instant analysis, and should focus more on ideas than on personalities. The effect would be to let citizens make their own assessments, perhaps through "fewer but longer clips," more facts and fewer opinions. Despite a few methodological concerns, the authors raise a number of important issues and provide input from a different perspective on the debate regarding political news coverage.

The Canadian literature on election coverage and journalistic practice has focused on another major theme that we pursue at length in this study: the relationship between journalists and their sources at election time. Studies by Gilsdorf (1981a, 1981b, 1990) suggest that when covering campaigns, Canadian political journalists allow themselves to be manipulated by political strategists and at the same time struggle to control issue agendas in a variety of ways. Drawing on Zolf (1973), Gilsdorf describes this negotiation of control as a "dance of the dialectic," in which politicians manipulate journalistic routines to convey their message and in which journalists counter – albeit somewhat tentatively – with a partial revision of routines to avoid such manipulation.

The emergence of the new "adversarial" journalism in the 1979 federal election campaign is perhaps a case in point. By 1979, party strategists had perfected the one-staged-event-per-day campaign, feeding on the media's desire for prepackaged regularly scheduled information concerning the major political parties and their leaders. By most accounts, journalists both took the bait and countered with a variety of new strategies, such as investigative issue coverage and reportage of media events *as* media events, in order to circumvent that manipulation (Reader's Digest Foundation and Erindale College 1981; Gilsdorf 1981a, 1981b; Fletcher 1981b). The 1979 campaign thus saw the further institutionalization of the staged campaign in Canada and also the emergence of a new type of adversarial journalism to cope with that institutionalization (see Fletcher 1988 and Frizzell et al. 1989 concerning the uneven development of this trend in Canadian election reporting). The tension

between stasis and change is a prevalent theme in the Canadian literature on election coverage, one that we pursue in this study.

Finally, a great deal of the literature has focused on the impact of
journalistic practice on the Canadian electoral process. Some studies
have looked at how the media have influenced party strategies and
affected voter volatility in the Canadian context (see, for example,
Gilsdorf 1981a, 1981b, 1990; Fletcher 1975, 1981a, 1981b, 1988; Frizzell
and Westell 1985; Frizzell et al. 1989; the comprehensive election studies
published by the American Enterprise Institute after the 1974, 1979,
1980 and 1984 elections: Penniman 1975, 1981, 1988). Others examine
how the Canadian media go beyond the mere transmission of information and communicate to their audience a sense of the possibility of
involvement in the campaigns and in politics in general (Gilsdorf 1981b).
That is, they help constitute their audience as citizens, as a Canadian
(or at least regional) public. These studies suggest that we are living in
the age of the mediated campaign. Journalistic practice has fundamentally, and probably irredeemably, become part of the process that
it is meant to be about. In this study, then, we try to clarify and explore
this theme, to examine whether and in what ways journalistic practice
has itself become an institution of the Canadian electoral campaign.

Methods

The information for this study comes from a variety of sources. First,
we surveyed the literature on election coverage in Canada (most of
which is cited above). Second, we drew upon tapes and transcripts
from our own previous studies of campaigns (some of which have been
analysed in Gilsdorf 1980a, 1980b, 1981a, 1981b, 1990). Third, specifically for this study, we conducted a new set of interviews averaging
one hour each (a total of 69 journalists representing a total of 40 different
media organizations, plus two academics and five party representatives, from across Canada). The focus of the research was on news operations. Although resources and time did not permit attention to public
affairs units on radio and television, nor a detailed treatment of radio,
we tried not to lose sight of the vital contribution to election campaign
discourse of such programs as "The Journal," "La Pointe," "W5,"
"Morningside" and a number of similar programs. These programs
provide a fuller examination of issues and controversies than is possible
on the news, but they generally operate within the same set of informal
rules and practices. It should also be noted that their primary audience is the politically attentive group that is already relatively well
informed and less susceptible to persuasion. Therefore, most party
strategists regard the news programs as being much more important.

In any case, major revelations on the public affairs shows are usually reflected in subsequent news coverage. Radio is important to specific audience subgroups, but unfortunately little is known about its effects.

This research was conducted in November and December 1990 at newspaper and broadcast organizations in St. John's, Halifax, Charlottetown, Moncton, Fredericton, Quebec City, Montreal, Ottawa, Winnipeg, Regina, Calgary, Edmonton, Vancouver and Victoria. In these interviews we questioned working journalists on a range of subjects: their focus of coverage and use of formats; their basic staff assignments; their use of wire sources; their constraints; their innovations; and the self-perceived weaknesses of their work. The findings are summarized in the next two sections and in appendix A. They have, to a substantial degree, informed the conclusions and recommendations of this study. We are grateful to the many journalists who took the time to explain their work to us with such patience.[4]

ENGLISH-CANADIAN JOURNALISTIC PRACTICES, 1988 FEDERAL ELECTION

This section has two main objectives: to describe journalistic practices in covering the most recent federal election, especially as recounted by the reporters, editors and producers whom we interviewed, and to point out the key changes that have occurred in coverage practice over the past four or five elections, identifying trends where significant. Election coverage as practised in the French media is described in the following section. The final section of this study will then summarize our major conclusions and recommendations.

Organizing Structures

What immediately becomes apparent is the break between the "national" press and the "regional" press in terms of organizing structure during the election. Much of this seems to be driven by coverage priorities, resources, and by some sense of what the audience wants to read or hear. The "national" press are those who maintain regular Ottawa-based press bureaus as part of the Parliamentary Press Gallery. While a few of the "regional" press have a correspondent in the gallery (*Winnipeg Free Press*, the western *Sun* chain, etc.), the "national" press have several personnel, who are able to cover a variety of Ottawa happenings, even to the point of having an informal "beat" system in some cases. The "national" press is almost exclusively made up of the television and larger radio networks, the major news and wire services, and bureaus representing newspapers (and *Maclean's* magazine) based in Toronto, Ottawa or Montreal. At the time of the federal election, the "national" press reassigned most of their Ottawa bureaus to election coverage (often positioning their editorial and assignment desks in Toronto for English-speaking Canada). The Ottawa staff were often supplemented by additional personnel for local and regional or special-issue coverage. Election-night coverage involved most of the news organization.

Typically, the "national" press organized a special election desk with one or more editors. Besides Canadian Press, the most extensive seemed to be CBC television, followed by CTV, the *Toronto Star* and the *Globe and Mail*. Each of these had staff assigned to follow the Conservative, Liberal and NDP leader tours, staff assigned to special-issue and/or special-feature coverage (which became almost an exclusive look at free trade), staff assigned to riding coverage (local or regional in the case of the newspapers), and one or more journalists available for analysis and comment. Because it was the most extensive, a closer look at the organization of CBC television might be helpful. This discussion is drawn from a paper based on observation and interviews during the 1988 election (Gilsdorf 1990), an excerpt from which is presented in appendix A.

The CBC had as many as 12 teams (usually a reporter, producer and three technicians) assigned either full- or part-time to election coverage. During the period of observation, there was a team with the leader of each of the three major parties, four teams doing stories on regional "battlegrounds," and teams doing special pieces on party advertising, the Reform Party, other minor parties, humorous moments in the campaign, and an examination of the proposed Value-Added Tax (to become the GST). In addition, David Halton was available for explanatory pieces and discussions with the anchor. Apart from the teams with the leaders, the pieces were slated for the Sunday election specials or to be used on "slow news days." The teams on the leader tours prepared weekly round-ups as well as their daily coverage.

The key actors at the CBC – all men – were the executive producer of news specials, the Ottawa bureau chief and assignment editor, "The National" editor, the anchor of "The National," the writer/editor and additional support personnel. Their roles were as follows (see, generally, Gilsdorf 1990):

Executive Producer of News Specials and Election Coverage This executive had the final word on most decisions with respect to the nightly coverage and the four hour-long Sunday specials. "Over the previous summer the Executive Producer had produced a paper outlining the election coverage plan and started negotiations ... to assure the unit that normally they would have at least six minutes each night on the National for election coverage" (Gilsdorf 1990).

Assignment Editor, Ottawa Bureau Chief Clearly second in command, this journalist was involved in all aspects of the coverage and had several major functions: day-to-day strategy; keeping in touch with top party strategists; keeping the coverage teams informed about the progress of the campaign, particularly developments they might not hear about (summarized in a daily report); computerization of campaign data (including a database on the positions taken in the past by the major parties and leaders) and material for election-night coverage; hands-on editing of reports; and planning future reports.

"The National" Editor This person had primary responsibility for monitoring and editing stories as they developed, keeping in regular contact (on average three calls per day) with field producers. He was also responsible for logistics.

Anchor for "The National" Peter Mansbridge was heavily involved in the coverage, personally editing and often rewriting much of his copy. He drew on his own sources within the parties and participated in planning and editing, with special attention to the Sunday-night specials, for which he had a major on-camera role. He conferred regularly with the Ottawa bureau chief. They were the main authors of the controversial report broadcast 19 October alleging that there was a move to oust John Turner as Liberal leader in mid-campaign. Mansbridge served as reporter for that story, which was prepared in-house to preserve secrecy and to protect the teams on the leader tours from backlash.

Writer/Editor The 1988 campaign was the first in which the special election team had a senior writer full time.

Additional Personnel The special election unit included two assistant editors, who handled much of the heavy telephone traffic, and several production assistants. Two senior producers worked on the election specials. In total, there were about 75 persons involved full time with the special unit, not including the personnel setting up the election-night coverage.

As this overview makes clear, the CBC devoted substantial resources to the campaign coverage. Its most experienced journalists were deeply involved and it took its responsibilities seriously. Nevertheless, its key people insist that the CBC is a news operation, with a responsibility for telling the campaign story, and not an organization devoted to political education.

Other "national" press had basically similar organizations, but with fewer personnel than those required by CBC television. For example, CTV had only four-person production teams (eliminating a video editor), and it collapsed a number of its special-issue units when it concluded that free trade seemed to be the only issue. The *Toronto Star* did not have a special election desk but did manage its coverage from Toronto, assigning reporters to the leaders on a rotating basis to prevent isolation in a single leader tour "cocoon." The Montreal *Gazette*, though generally committed to leader coverage, shared that responsibility with the Southam News Service to save expenses. All other Southam papers relied on the news service to provide daily leader coverage, except when a leader tour entered their own coverage region. When that happened, locally based reporters were assigned for as long as the leader remained in the area.

This was one of the distinguishing features of coverage organization for the "regional" papers. The coverage priority in terms of staff assignment was local and regional election activity. Wire services provided accounts of the leader tours. Numbers of staff varied, from the two-person news staff of the *Winnipeg Sun* to the two political reporters (usually concerned with provincial coverage but reassigned to cover the federal election) of the Fredericton *Gleaner*, and to more extensive staff assignments by papers like the *Winnipeg Free Press* and the Vancouver *Province*. At the *Province* the election team was composed of the assistant city editor, the city editor (both obviously responsible for assigning and editing more than just election coverage), four full-time reporters (to cover ridings, local issues and the leader tours when present locally), and usually three or four freelancers and a photographer as needed. On average, at least six persons per day would be covering some aspect of the election.

There have been some notable changes since earlier elections. For example, Doug Small recounted (in what may be a little journalistic hyperbole) that when he was covering the NDP for the Canadian Press in the 1972 election, he rode in the back seat of the car and helped carry the luggage for Mrs. Lewis, wife of the leader. He, himself, was the entire press entourage. The size and scope of all three leader tours and the number of press assigned to cover them had greatly increased by the 1979 election. Although there has always been a difference between "national" and "regional" organizations in terms of resources and coverage priorities, the split between the two over the importance of daily leader coverage and the necessary staff assignments to accomplish it seems more pronounced. Some of this is also reflected in staff available for nonelection coverage of federal politics.

Another notable change is the further questioning by "national" news organizations of the necessity to have staff assigned to the leader tours. National news organizations are beginning to combine resources and assign staff for limited time periods (such as the last week of the election) and to rely more heavily on the wire services. The French-language press signalled much of this concern in its organization of coverage in the 1984 election. The reasons for this change are varied but relate to increased cost, responses to the manipulation and control of the press by party strategists at the federal level, and a cynicism about the importance of the daily feed or "Gainesburger," as it was called.

Since 1979, election organizations at both the national and regional levels have begun to isolate personnel to concentrate on issue analysis or election overview. Some of this was in response to what the media felt was overt manipulation by the Liberals in the 1974 election when they released position papers or announced new programs just before news deadlines, allowing no time for critical assessment. Since 1979, journalists have been more and more concerned about the lack of regional coverage and issue analysis (see Fletcher 1981a, 1981b, 1988; Gilsdorf 1980a, 1980b, 1981a, 1981b). One action taken has been the structuring of issue analysis into the coverage. For example, since 1979, CBC-TV has adopted a policy of being both a "conduit" for parties and a critic of their actions. Another strategy has been to encourage reporters to combine analysis with their reporting of events.

The Role and Style of the Journalist

"La tribune de la presse" rather than the English term, "press gallery," might better connote some of the respect (or majesty) that a few polit-ical reporters assume they have and others wish they had. The gallery plays an important role in making public the legislative and govern-mental process: "The competition between a government anxious to look good and parties striving to reveal its feet of clay is central to parliamentary government, but it is an empty ritual without an audi-ence. Thus the gallery is a necessary part of the system through which the legislature performs its primary function of making the govern-ment accountable for its actions" (Fletcher 1980, 248). During elections this role of constituting an audience becomes crucial, though new tech-nologies of communication that are just beginning to be used by Canadian federal parties may make even this function unnecessary. The close symbiotic relationship between press and political party makes the boundaries of the press's role very ambiguous.

In the minds of many journalists interviewed for this study, scep-ticism about politicians has led to a more aggressive (one stated even "mean spirited") and critical press corps. They felt there was increased freedom, encouraged by editors, to analyse and critique politicians, their positions and behaviour. Many journalists also expressed concern about the growing cynicism (and less romanticism) which they felt and observed in others toward politicians and political institutions. On the organizational level, one rather general response was to assign less experienced journalists to follow the leaders and to utilize more experienced journalists for analysis. At the same time, many respondents noted that, in general, political journalists covering the 1988 election, as compared to earlier elections, seemed to be the brightest and best trained.

After careful observation of and interviews with political journalists during the 1979 and 1980 campaigns, Gilsdorf (1981a, 1981b) concluded that the following role perceptions and operative assumptions were common (though not very well defined in the minds of journalists):

- that the media should be a "watchdog" or at least a sometime adversary of politicians;
- that good reporters are sceptical of politicians and their statements;
- that the media have the right to define the issue agenda of the campaign on the basis of what the politicians say and do and what journalists perceive the reader to be interested in;
- that the media have a right of access to candidates, especially party leaders;
- that campaigns are the most exciting part of the political process and that assignment to cover the leaders carries the most prestige; and
- that most journalists deny that campaigns have much effect or that the media have any influence on election outcomes.

There were few differences from these earlier conclusions in our current assessment of journalists' perceptions of their role and style. It was something of a surprise to see the frequency with which journalists described themselves as adversaries (albeit more aggressive ones than in 1980), reasserted the need to remain sceptical, resented how little control they felt they had over the election agenda (though feelings on this seemed much stronger than in 1980) and reasserted their right of access to candidates on behalf of the public.

Campaigns still seem to represent one of the "big stories" in the lives of political reporters, and to be involved in covering an election generally brings excitement. The 1988 election proved to be especially exciting for many because it was, in their view, one of the few elections when the campaign seemed to have an impact on the final outcome – when, in fact, the final outcome was even in some doubt at times during the campaign.

A final note on autonomy and reporters: in general, reporters felt that they had a great deal of freedom about what to write and even some control over assignments. The continual process of negotiation (and sometimes conflict) over assignment and content that was observed by Gilsdorf (1990) at CBC television seemed to be reflected in the reports of other journalists interviewed for this study. It suggests that within the commonly held framework of what political news is, within the constraints assumed by journalists and within the "vocabulary of precedents" stemming from previous campaigns (Ericson et al. 1987), reporters have a relative amount of autonomy to practise their journalism as professionals.

Coverage Priorities

There is both discrepancy and agreement between what journalists told us were the coverage priorities in 1988 and what the available content analyses of coverage reveal. Journalists respond that there was a decreasing emphasis on leadership as an issue and item of coverage in 1988. However, according to the content analysis conducted at Carleton (Frizzell et al. 1989), leadership received the greatest focus on television (almost 63 percent of all items on CBC, almost 58 percent on CTV and 72.5 percent on Global) and at least 20 percent or more in print coverage. This is fairly consistent over the last four elections, based on content analyses of others (see Frizzell and Westell 1985; Soderlund et al. 1984; Fletcher 1981a, 1981b, 1988; and confirmed in a study by Gilsdorf in 1980a).

Journalists claimed that there was an increase in analysis and contextual reporting in 1988. This is confirmed by the Carleton study for the CBC when analysis of "The Journal" and the "Sunday Report" is included. For print, the number of straight news stories declined from 73 percent in 1984 to 61 percent in 1988, with a corresponding increase in backgrounders and commentary.

Policy issues were the focus of 37 percent of all items, an increase of 11 percent from 1984. The bulk of this coverage was devoted to the free trade issue, which accounted for 58 percent of all issue coverage, according to the Carleton study. It seems likely that the increased attention given to policy issues was primarily a result of the conflictual nature of the issue and the efforts of key players, and not the result of a shift in journalistic priorities.

A trend, which was first observable in the 1979 election but seemingly increased in 1984 and is still part of the permanent set of coverage priorities, is the emphasis on the campaign process. The Carleton study notes that 38.9 percent of all newspaper items in 1984 and 29.1 percent in 1988 focused on the campaign process itself. The figures for television must be at least that high. This form of coverage included items on strategy, backroom manipulation (the famous CBC-TV story on the plot against Turner), campaign colour, campaign events like the debates and items assessing the "horse-race."

Journalists almost unanimously agree that the smaller parties received the coverage they deserved – proportional to their perceived popular appeal. A few felt that the Reform Party should have been watched more closely. All agreed that the next campaign will see a minimum of five parties covered. If there are to be changes in the treatment of minor parties and special interest groups, it will require a change in news criteria.

The balance between national, regional and local coverage has not been assessed in the literature. Some earlier studies of nonelection coverage have confirmed a heavy emphasis in the "national" media on covering events in Ontario and Quebec, with all other provinces receiving marginal treatment. This differs during elections primarily because the leader tours, which receive a great deal of attention, are organized to give the appearance of a more truly national campaign (though it is still the belief of some of us that central Ontario constitutes the prime target audience because of the number of swing ridings located there). Since 1979, a frequently mentioned self-criticism of most journalists is that their coverage failed to emphasize local and regional coverage sufficiently. Comments for this study revealed no exception. Only a few of the journalists at regional newspapers, especially at the perimeters of the country, felt that local and regional coverage was adequate. Regional coverage may increase in the next election, since regionally based parties appear to be about to play major roles.

In sum, coverage priorities seem to have changed over the past four elections, except for the focus on leadership, which remains strong. Issue coverage increased in 1988, as did analysis and background reports. Regional coverage and minor party coverage may increase in the next election because of a realignment in party allegiance. Investigative stories that went beyond the exposure of a campaign strategy, perhaps with the exception of the "Mansbridge affair," were almost totally absent in 1988. We believe that general coverage priorities are not established by the media or by individual journalists but that they flow from a set of constraints, especially time and resources, from established practices and formats, and from effective news management by the parties.

Coverage Formats

As will be discussed later, television is universally acknowledged to be the preferred medium of party strategists because studies tell them that it is the most trusted medium, reaching the largest audience, especially swing voters. Campaigns are therefore heavily orchestrated to satisfy the requirements of television. Newspapers have responded to the dominant role of television with a number of format and stylistic changes, including the following (as identified by our interviewees from the print media).

Stories are now "light, tight and bright." They are shorter and often more fragmented – that is, broken down into a series of mini-stories. "Brighter" seems to mean that they convey more campaign colour or that copy will give way more often to a picture or a computer-produced graphic (often used for poll results). Special graphic logos are now attached to the special election sections of the paper or even attached to each election story in order to catch the reader's eye. Short and punchy menus of what is inside the paper may appear on the front page. Even headlines may be in a different colour or in a larger typeface. Stories are "lighter" in the sense that there seems to have been a steady supply of "election notebooks," morsels of inside gossip and information "heard on the campaign trail." The 1984 campaign, with its emphasis on personalities and the foibles of the leaders, was apparently the high-water mark for this style and format. Even writers at the Canadian Press acknowledge that they are now expected to supply "more colourful, more folksy and anecdotal pieces."[5]

At the same time, because of television's emphasis on the visual – and often more entertaining or more emotional – aspects of the election, many newspapers have attempted to "try for a broader view of the events and the issues than before, providing both the 30-second clip plus everything around it." As mentioned earlier, some papers were searching for and encouraging more background or analytical pieces. Rearranging coverage priorities to follow the leaders less and "cover the grass roots more" made increased analysis more possible. As has been the case in past elections, major dailies continued to do large "take-outs" on important issues or on candidate profiles. Many also continue to do weekend reviews – expected of Canadian Press but abandoned for this election by the *Globe and Mail*.

Elections still seem to be given a general priority over most other "big" stories by all the media. All the newspapers we contacted except one had a special election section of a minimum of one page daily and often several pages. As one journalist told us, "The fight for space was won by shorter, more concise stories." Space on the front page was still a matter of competition with other news items and other editorial priorities.

Both radio and television journalists could count on time available on each of the key newscasts. The CBC television election coverage unit had a basic understanding that there would be time on each "National" for at least one piece on each of the leaders, and often time for an additional election item, depending on the news of the day. CTV often had an item on each of the leaders, but there was no commitment to broadcast a leader piece each night. Compression of stories, caused by limited time, is one of the reasons why the "30-second clip" of a leader, which was more prevalent in the 1979 election, had given way to the "12-second sound bite." Leader stories on television still had a high priority given to visual interest, to the latest development, and to showing the camera and reporter as very much in the midst of the campaign event. Closing "stand-ups" with active, visual surroundings, hecklers or other disturbances, ambient sound, and so on, were the norm. On the other hand, pieces that were not about the leaders showed less concern for the visual, though the narrative of conflict was frequent, especially when covering the issue of free trade.

The changes in style and format, especially for the print media, seem to represent a trend over the past four elections. With the print media's concerns for readership in the competition among all media for advertising, the trend to "light, tight and bright" is undoubtedly a fixture in most print media's future political coverage, with the exceptions noted above, as it is for all news and feature coverage. The assumption is that most voters prefer the quick read. At least most journalistic organizations and their personnel seem to have this notion of the audience and are prepared to cater to it.

Doris Graber (1991) examined audience estimations of media organizations in the United States and found that journalists plan their coverage according to what they think the audience wants. Overwhelmingly, planners perceive that attention spans for news items are short. The longer, more detailed newscasts on public television are "shunned" for the more entertaining regular news programs, dubbed "infotainment." In exploring the consequences of these assumptions on political coverage, Graber found that while both print and broadcast media prefer to report on a narrow range of issues with opposing views, television coverage of policy issues is more limited than that of newspapers. Issues are often presented in "snippets," while events tend to be fragmented and barren of context. Yet television news has become the primary source of election information for the majority of people, ranking well ahead of newspapers. (This is also the case in Canada, where MacDermid (1991) found that recent trends in elections show increased attention to television news and the diminishing importance of radio and newspapers as a source of campaign information.)

Graber suggests that the fast-paced approach to election news has a profound impact on voter education. For example, to keep audiences through fast-paced news, television compresses the usual election story into 60–120 seconds. These stories are simple, thematic and graphic, with little depth of reporting and analysis. Furthermore, she suggests that this approach spills over into other aspects of the campaign, such as advertising. Media expectations of what audiences want in their news coverage mean that "stories lack the necessary context that would help the voter determine how important a particular quality or issue is in relation to the job that the incumbent will have to perform." MacDermid's (1991) observation of the Canadian situation has led him to argue that democracy can be better served by extending the methods and content of political coverage in an effort to reach a more varied audience.

Influences on Coverage Practices

This portion of our study represented an important area in the minds of our journalist respondents. We identified five categories of influences on election coverage practice: relationships with the parties; media influence on one another; technology; polling; and primary constraints.

The Influence of Relations with Parties and Party Strategists

Along with the influence of television, this topic received the most comment by journalists. There were frequent complaints and concerns expressed about access, control of the election agenda and attempts to manage the interpretation of events. The right of access to candidates, especially to the leaders, seems to be assumed by most journalists, who see it as fundamental to their societal role. To one degree or another, all party strategists want some control over access and the leader in order to minimize damage and maximize favourable coverage. The further ahead the leader and party are in the polls, the more control is exerted. Such was the case with Clark and the Progressive Conservatives in 1979, Trudeau and the Liberals in 1980, Mulroney and the Progressive Conservatives in 1984, and Mulroney for the beginning of the 1988 campaign. Journalist resentment about restricted access was increased by the fact that access was often granted first to television, then to the *Globe and Mail* and then to the "national" press – all before the "regional" press. Many journalists from the regions expressed strong feelings about being shut out by the parties and crowded out by the "national" media whenever the leader tours travelled into their territory.

In addition to problems of access, the journalists complained about too much control of the election agenda by party strategists. Several noted an increase over the past several elections of "political technocrats," especially for the Conservatives and NDP. While there may be controlled access to the leader or to key ministerial candidates, journalists have easy access to those aides that are now fashionably labelled "spin doctors." The press seems to have a schizophrenia about these aides. Journalists recognized and were cynical about the role of "spin doctors" in the campaign, yet confessed to having been influenced by them at one time or another, particularly after the televised debates. As aware as most journalists are, it seems unlikely at first glance that they would permit themselves to be influenced by "spin doctors" or by the host of other services and comforts provided on the tour. Yet, given the constraints that reporters face, the general repetitiveness of a leader tour and the inexperience of many of the reporters assigned to cover the leaders in the 1988 election, it is easy to see how coverage might have been influenced.

News organizations and individual journalists coped with their frustration over controlled access and agenda in several ways. Cynicism seemed to be one route for many individuals, manifested in a critical reporting style that often focused on strategic rather than substantive elements in the campaign. Organizational efforts included frequent contact between editors and those in the field, by phone, fax or computer link-up. Several organizations in addition to CBC television used internal, written communiqués to provide reporters with information from outside the leader tours. Other organizations set up pooled or rotation systems for reporters covering the leader. The most frequent and effective protection against leader control was to shift the priority of election coverage from the leaders to the regions, to policy issues, to non-mainstream sources, or to background and analytical stories.

The Influence of Other Media

The increased influence of television in the way campaigns are conducted and covered elicited a great deal of comment. As late as 1959, the electronic media were not allowed to be regular members of the Parliamentary Press Gallery. By 1979 (some say even earlier), television was already recognized by the parties as the most important medium. Events, press conferences, policy issue releases and issue agendas were all designed to give priority to television. Journalists we interviewed still blamed television for the entertainment focus in campaigns and campaign coverage. Organized images became standard fare. Politicians were coached to speak in editable sound bites (apparently a particular problem for Trudeau). Television events like the debates and campaign advertising became crucial in the 1988 campaign. In fact, events staged for or on television have been consistently cited by journalists as most of the significant happenings in the last four elections (see Fletcher 1981a, 1981b, 1988; Gilsdorf 1980a, 1980b, 1981a, 1981b; Frizzell and Westell 1985; Frizzell et al. 1989). For ongoing and developing stories such as leadership conventions, and for question periods and nonelection events such as Meech Lake, journalists confessed to using television as a primary source for their own stories. Perceived competition with television seems less of a factor with the "regional" press than with the "national" press. However, in all cases, as has already been discussed, coverage practices, coverage priorities and coverage format and style have all been changed in the print medium, with television cited as the largest influence.

In a reversal, some electronic journalists acknowledged that print influenced their own coverage practices. This was confirmed by Gilsdorf's observation of CBC-TV during the 1988 election (Gilsdorf 1990). Nationwide newsstand and computer access to the *Globe and Mail* affects assignment, editorial and interpretative decisions. The one journalist most frequently cited as influencing other journalists was Jeffrey Simpson, the *Globe*'s Ottawa columnist. In addition to his regular column, he was seen weekly on CBC television, and both these media were nationally distributed and readily available to other journalists, whether "regional" or "national." The CP wire was easily accessible on computer and was frequently consulted to check leads, breaking or developing stories, and opposing comment or interpretation.

Related to the interaction of print and the electronic media is the issue of the influence of competition among the media. Other than the already recounted concerns about the impact of television, there was surprisingly little mention of concern for the competitor or for "beating the competition" in the coverage of an election story. In the days of his observation at CBC, Gilsdorf saw very little direct monitoring or concern about what CTV or Global were doing in their coverage. It is still apparent that despite the lack of direct monitoring, coverage priorities are quite similar so as to not be "scooped" by the competition.

Journalists more frequently raised concerns about the influence of the "pack." Of less concern in local or regional coverage generally, this seemed to become a factor in the leader tours or when a tour entered a regional medium's territory. The pack's influence seemed to be greatest when the tour became boring, when there were substantial numbers of the press who did not understand French or when there was uncertainty about the lead to a story. In general, concerns about competition or pack influence seem to have lessened in this past campaign compared to previous ones.

The Influence of Developments in Technology

The most visible difference to anyone accompanying reporters in their campaign coverage was the change in the equipment and technology for recording, filing, researching and editing stories. In 1979 the CBC was the first to use electronic newsgathering equipment (CTV still relied on filmed records of campaign events), but it is now standard for all the television networks. As mentioned earlier, in 1988 the CBC had portable editing suites available for several of its field teams, eliminating the necessity for locating available facilities for editing at an accessible affiliate. In 1979 a few portable, computer-driven word processors were being used by print reporters. By 1988 they were standard, with capacity for instant filing via the nearest telephone or via portable cellular phone (still a little unreliable if there was static interference or in the absence of a satellite uplink). Satellite uplinks, if available, also made possible almost instantaneous filing of television and radio stories. A number of the electronic media organizations such as CTV and Broadcast News have the assurance of portable satellite links for the next election.

Perhaps the biggest improvement has been the availability of computers for information storage and retrieval. Many news organizations now have the ability to research stories more easily or even to assemble them from catalogued footage, as in the case of the CBC. Visualization through the use of computer graphics has been heavily used by both television and the print media. Our respondents credited computers with having made many improvements in our political news coverage. For example, they have been "a liberating force allowing more stories, more time for developing stories and facilitating their delivery." This liberating force has "permitted more critique," improved "the quality of writing" and allowed for "more comprehensive stories" and "more thoughtful reporting." Computers have "increased the potential coverage area," a real advantage for regional papers with remote areas to cover. As well, along with the increased speed of filing, they have narrowed the period of grace for parties between campaign promises and criticism. Print is better able to compete with the electronic media on breaking stories. Electronic newsgathering, both computer-based and recording/editing equipment, allows for easier changes in stories at the last minute.

There were, however, some disadvantages to the heavier reliance on computers and word processors. The increases in speed were often negated by breakdowns or interference. Several respondents noted that political news seemed to die more quickly, with a shorter shelf life because of the demand for something new. A number of journalists complained that word processing made it easier for them to "play around" with their stories, often causing a loss of spontaneity or coherence. A number of journalists associated the use of computers with more fragmented and shorter stories, often to the detriment of informative journalism. There is also some evidence that the increased use of computers and other forms of electronic newsgathering limits the ability of the journalist or organization to be self-reflexive. The pressure seems to mount for more immediate "here and now" coverage and for a greater number of stories.

Reporters credited satellites and cellular phones with improving the frequency and quality of the connection with editors. It was easier for electronic media to go live at certain events that were close to deadline, or for print reporters to file directly to the printshop in special instances. Pieces could now be prepared and filed in time for noon deadlines. Problems with the time zones – a special problem in a linear country like Canada – were somewhat mitigated by the improved speed of recording and filing.

The Influence of Polling

There is still division among journalists as to the desirability of the publication of polls or the commissioning and use of polls by media organizations. However, this division was less noticeable than after the 1984 election, despite the dramatic increase in the number of published polls: there were 24 published polls in the 1988 election, double the number of 1984 (Frizzell et al. 1989, 95). Some journalists felt that polls influenced the voter negatively, perhaps even discouraging turnout in constituencies where the result seemed apparent. Others argued that polls allowed people to vote strategically.

In terms of coverage practice, many journalists were concerned about the publication of polls without suitable explanation of methodology, sample size and appropriate context. "Regional" journalists felt that most polls were largely irrelevant sources of information about their coverage areas, because samples were too small to convey reliable insight or prediction. They felt that the publication of polls was mostly relevant for the "national" media, though most admitted that the results would still be published by their papers or stations, but would be given less prominence.

Some journalists were also disturbed that media organizations commissioned their own polls. These journalists felt that the use of polls and their subsequent publication became a substitute for "solid" reporting and that they led to lazy journalism and an increased emphasis on the "horse-race" aspects of the campaign. Others, who were in the majority, argued that the use and commissioning of polls led to better journalistic practice by increasing the organization's knowledge, by providing research backup to stories, and by facilitating the targeting of key issues and key contests.

Despite the concerns expressed about the use of polls, an over-whelming majority of the journalists we interviewed were opposed to any form of regulation or law governing the publication of polls. Those who did favour some controls urged either self-regulation or limited control in the last week or ten days of the campaign. All those in favour of some form of control (less than one-third) came from regional news organizations, none of which sponsored their own polls.

Primary Constraints and Their Influence

Journalistic practice, as in the case of other professional practices, must function in a context of both facilitating and constraining factors. Constraints, while most often serving to block or limit options, can often be challenged, negotiated with or altered. Writing more gener-ally from a sociological perspective on social actors and social action, Gaye Tuchman comments: "More traditional sociologies ... characterize the activities of men and women as products of their socialization to norms derived from objective characteristics of the social structure. Tersely put, they argue that society creates consciousness. In contrast, recent interpretive sociologies ... hold that the social world provides norms that actors invoke as resources or constraints as they actively work to accomplish their projects" (Tuchman 1978, 182).

We would agree with Tuchman that "the two processes occur simul-taneously." Although this section deals with the perceived constraints that shape the journalist's world, it is equally true that the practice of journalists helps shape and construct the social world that they report on and must work within, including those same constraints. The following is a list of constraints, in order of frequency of mention, that journalists experienced in the 1988 election campaign:

- access to party leaders and information;
- control and management of coverage by party strategists;
- emphasis on the single issue of free trade;
- priority given to television;
- reporter cynicism;
- expense and limited value of leader tours;

- almost total dependence on wire services for leader reports (regional newspapers);
- changes in format and demands for increased coverage;
- resources (money and personnel);
- time and/or space available;
- influence of the pack mentality;
- technology and resulting effects;
- diminishing credibility of the political system;
- reporters with a limited sense of political history; and
- stories becoming event-driven.

This list of constraints and their order of appearance can be contrasted with a similar list drawn up by Gilsdorf after his research on the 1979 and 1980 campaigns (Gilsdorf 1980b, 21):

- lack of resources, meaning lack of adequate staff and money;
- lack of adequate time and/or space for broadcast and publication;
- difficulties in maintaining perspective, especially in the leader tours;
- for print, the higher priority given to television by political parties, especially in 1979;
- reporters only talking to reporters and politicians (some elements of pack journalism);
- time zones, especially eastern deadlines while in the West;
- prescribed formats, especially for television and the Canadian Press;
- only writing about issues that were selling;
- ambiguity in the organization about commitment to election coverage and roles of individuals;
- the lack of continuity and linking of stories;
- fatigue and monotony: caught in the unvarying ritual of the campaign;
- prisoners of time and the rush of campaign events, resulting in a lack of perspective and reflection;
- limited contact with files and accessible information for background for stories and for verifying statements; and
- in 1980, the feeling of some that they were constrained by a general disinterest by voters, especially in Quebec.

What is most surprising is the change in priority assigned to the constraints of time and space and the available resources. Media organizations have either made more substantial commitments to election coverage or journalists have adjusted expectations to the realities of practice. It should also be noted that there was no mention of electoral regulations as a constraining force, though many journalists expressed the need for controls on third-party advertising. These lists should serve to highlight journalists' perceptions of what constrains or limits their ability to achieve the ideal in election coverage. Many journalists have resigned themselves to living with some constraints, while other constraints (such as time and space) are continually being negotiated.

Media Self-monitoring and Self-reflection

An important concern for us was the degree to which journalists are monitoring and reflecting on their own practice at election time. It seems to us that, in any healthy profession, there should be demonstrated concern for self-assessment – examining the nature and effectiveness of working assumptions, priorities, routines and product. We were not encouraged by what we learned from the 50 journalists (representing 29 different media organizations) that we interviewed in English-speaking Canada.

Self-monitoring

Of the 29 institutions, only six indicated that their organization had any kind of formal post-mortem, while 13 stated explicitly that they had none. Several of the journalists from organizations where there was a post-mortem felt that it was wasted and would soon be forgotten. Ten organizational representatives said that they had regular ongoing assessments, usually of a weekly nature, during the campaign, and four said that there was careful discussion before the election was called about what the shape and nature of the coverage would be. Several felt that the regular contact between the reporter/producer in the field and the editor back home was sufficient to ensure the monitoring and self-correction required for effective coverage, but many felt that more self-monitoring, even on a formal basis, was necessary.

Self-reflection on Campaign Coverage after the Election

When asked either to respond to frequent criticisms advanced by academics regarding campaign coverage or to indicate what they personally felt about their coverage practices, journalists had several typical responses. The most frequently mentioned concern was the growing cynicism in the press corps. Although many lauded the increased intelligence and training of political reporters and the fact that fewer seemed intimidated by politicians and that the press corps was more aggressive, there was still a concern that political reporting needed to be more critical and analytical. There were several journalists who disagreed, feeling that this past election demonstrated a healthy increase in critical reporting. As expected, a number felt that they submitted to party control of the agenda more than was necessary or desirable. One interesting response was that media organizations tended to overcover the things they could plan for and undercover the "real" news, which occurred in unplanned ways. It is an observation that makes sense to us and could be said generally about political reporting.

In response to the stated criticisms (see table 1.1 and the interview format in appendix B), most agreed that there was too much focus on the leaders and not enough attention paid to the party "team"; there was

Table 1.1
Responses of English-language journalists to 10 critiques
(Yes/No/NR*)

1. The media place too much emphasis on leaders and not enough on issues.		
Yes: 78%	No: 17%	NR: 4%
2. The media do not focus enough attention on each party's team.		
Yes: 37%	No: 43%	NR: 20%
3. The media pay too much attention to the "horse-race."		
Yes: 52%	No: 22%	NR: 26%
4. The media place too much emphasis on entertainment or visually exciting coverage.		
Yes: 35%	No: 26%	NR: 39%
5. The media pay too much attention to colour and trivia at the expense of issues and analysis.		
Yes: 22%	No: 43%	NR: 35%
6. The media engage in too much critical reporting and not enough straight reporting of leaders' statements, party platforms, etc.		
Yes: 17%	No: 63%	NR: 20%
7. There is too negative a tone to media coverage generally.		
Yes: 11%	No: 59%	NR: 30%
8. The media pay too much attention to personal foibles and gaffes of leaders and not enough to their potential as leaders of the government.		
Yes: 30%	No: 35%	NR: 35%
9. The media do not pay enough attention to the issues raised by minor parties and interest groups during the campaign.		
Yes: 20%	No: 59%	NR: 22%
10. The media do not provide enough analysis of key elements of party platforms by nonpartisan experts.		
Yes: 35%	No: 28%	NR: 37%
Total interviews = 48		

*NR = no response.

a split on whether there was too much attention to the "horse-race," with some feeling that it was a critical and uncertain element of the 1988 campaign; most agreed that there was too much focus on the entertainment aspects of the campaign, including campaign trivia; most did not feel that there was too negative a tone in the coverage, though most commented with concern about the negative advertising; as well, most felt that there was far less reporting on the personal foibles and gaffes of leaders as compared to 1984, which was characterized as the personality campaign; as mentioned, almost all felt there was not enough challenge to the party campaign agendas; almost all felt there was enough attention to minor parties and the issues they raised ("they got the attention they deserved"); and, finally, many still felt the need for more regional coverage – a trend that had already begun in the 1988 election.

THE ELECTORAL MEDIA COVERAGE IN FRENCH-SPEAKING CANADA
Research on media coverage of elections in Quebec has been carried out over the last 15 years, focusing on a number of different areas.[6]

Latouche (1977) noted that during the Quebec election of October 1973 the daily newspapers gave importance to pretty well the same topics (see note 6). In his study on media coverage of the 1980 referendum, Tremblay (1984) deduced that newspapers had given more importance to political sparring than to the content of information on the white paper. Jean Crête of Université Laval identified the same phenomenon during the 1981 provincial election: "In total, government policies were referred to a little less frequently (5 279 references) during the campaign than were strategies, invective and miscellaneous topics, which are found under the category 'other' in Table 2 (5 960 references)" (Crête 1984, 106).

As for Michel de Repentigny, he concluded in a study on the presentation of current events by the press that "journalists or press agencies are not always better prepared than their readers for describing the strict information content of a surprise event. As deadlines are quite inevitable, they must of course fall back on a few well-established platitudes or rely on explanations or interpretations by official actors who are often hardly better prepared to comment on the surprise event: the election of the Parti Québécois is an example of this" (de Repentigny 1989).

Moreover, with the exception of Jacques Benjamin (1975) and Robert Bernier (1991), few Quebec researchers have studied the strategies and tactics adopted by political parties in election campaigns to promote their leaders and influence media coverage to further their campaign objectives. As far as relations between politicians and the media are concerned, a study by Charron and colleagues, covering the period between 1945 and 1990, reviews the evidence gathered by previous studies, and concludes that "journalists, like all social actors, are part of an evolving society and see political and social realities from a perspective that is neither neutral nor free of the influence of their own social status" (Charron et al. 1991, 22).

The purpose of the present study is to synthesize comments gathered from 21 journalists and managers from the French-language print and electronic media regarding the organization of and changes to election coverage during the 1988 federal election. Two academics and three politicians were also interviewed for this study. The interviews were held between 26 October and 16 November 1990. Most respondents insisted on confidentiality. We shall also try to see, first, if there is a correspondence between the researchers' prior observations and those of the journalists and, second, what influence certain psychosocial factors had on the way election coverage was handled.

The 1988 Election Campaign

The three main federal political parties that took part in the general election of the fall of 1988 had, to various degrees, planned their election operations on the basis of a marketing management approach aimed, inter alia, at controlling the environment in which their leaders moved. On 31 August 1988, a confidential document on the Liberal leader tour confirmed the importance given by organizers to the leader's movements in a context in which they were trying to steer journalists' attention toward him.

The media relations section of the campaign manual for Conservative candidates, entitled *L'Aide de camp*, reminded candidates that "the media representative is also a voter equipped with a megaphone and is an important tool in manufacturing your image." According to Michel Cogger, who was co-chair of the Conservative party's national campaign, "the *Aide de camp* is one of the most important tools of our campaign in Quebec." This document proved to be an invaluable campaign manual, since it included a communications plan, a guide for designing polls, a methodology for writing speeches and advice on using telemarketing techniques. The *Aide de camp* contained a numbered appendix marked "confidential," which contained a copy of the Conservatives' national and Quebec communications strategy along with the communications strategy for the leader's tour.

When the election writs were issued on 1 October 1988, the Conservative strategy was to present Brian Mulroney as a statesman capable of anticipating and managing change (Bernier 1991). His leader tour was organized so that it was presented within a structure of controlled images (Benjamin 1975) in which daily events were planned on the basis of their media impact and on the basis of deadlines, while print journalists were kept at a distance (Frizzell et al. 1989). For example, the prime minister began his day under the light of the cameras by visiting a business that was in favour of free trade without discussing the content of the agreement; at noon he spoke to a Chamber of Commerce or a meeting of businesspersons; and in the evening he spoke to a partisan gathering. Journalists complained to people in the prime minister's entourage about the focus of the campaign, and Brian Mulroney then became a bit more accessible to the media early in the third week. It was the "spin doctors" who became aware of the level of dissatisfaction on the campaign plane.

During this time, the Liberal campaign was unfolding in a state of anarchy, and the Liberal leader's inability to give an exact cost of his daycare program, when speaking at a press conference in Montreal on 5 October, made newspaper headlines. At the same time, the refusal by federal Liberal organizers in Quebec to approve the nomination papers of candidate William Déry in the constituency of Saint-Laurent caused a crisis in the Liberal organization, an event whose repercussions in the Quebec press gave substance to the image of a party being undermined from within. The night of 19 October the CBC devoted four and a half minutes of "The National" to a report by Peter Mansbridge on the attempted putsch against the Liberal leader. The depth of this report and the care with which it was presented gave it a degree of credibility. However, the report met with serious reservations in academic, journalistic and political circles, since the CBC's journalists did not appear to have tried to verify their information with the Liberal organizers in question before broadcasting it.

According to Elly Alboim, chief of the CBC's Parliament Hill bureau, the events in the report came from 13 different information sources, and each of them was corroborated by at least two other independent sources (Bernier 1991). In addition, the presentation on screen of a document that the authors of the report did not have in hand was to raise much criticism. The document was supposed to be a copy of the memorandum sent to Turner by Liberal party strategists (Frizzell et al. 1989, 82).

A few days later, the leaders debates were held in the studio of Ottawa's CJOH in a climate in which the three parties' "spin doctors" were trying to manipulate journalists' perceptions of the performances of their respective leaders.

According to Graham Fraser (1989, 282), a journalist from the *Globe and Mail*, the "spin doctors" had an influence on certain anglophone

journalists during the French-language debate. This could be attributed
to the unilingualism of certain journalists and to the fact that the English-
language radio press included interviews held after the debates in their
reports.

During the English-language debate, the journalists present also
paid great attention to the comments of the "spin doctors" (Lee 1989).
However, the journalists who acted as panellists in the English-language
debate, as well as some of their colleagues from the electronic media who
had not been exposed to the "spin doctors"' propaganda, hesitated to
declare a winner in this confrontation (Frizzell et al. 1989). The results
of polls produced during the following days would determine the
winner. The sharp and emotional exchange between Turner and
Mulroney, which only lasted a few minutes in the first round of the
third and final hour of the English-language debate, would be the televised image engraved in viewers' memories, because the television
networks – and later the Liberals after their legal battle with the three
networks – turned it into a 30-second television advertisement.

The election campaign really began after the debates, and its only
real issue was the consequences of free trade for Canada's economic and
political sovereignty. The Conservatives' tour was speeded up, and the
number of daily events was increased to cover the regions of the country in which the Conservative electorate was being eroded.
The prime minister became more aggressive and was forced to explain the
content of the Free Trade Agreement to the press and to the electorate.
After the debates, journalists could see the cohesiveness of the Conservative
organization in the field, as well as the intensification of the "spin doctors"'
activities on the campaign plane, who insisted, among other things, that
their internal polls were valid (interview with Pierre April, 1989).

Brian Mulroney's unplanned encounter on the free trade issue with
three hecklers in front of journalists in Victoria was favourable to him
and, according to some observers, increased his credibility with the
press. The gathering of 4 000 Conservative supporters in Quebec's Patro
Roc Amadour on 11 November was a decisive media event for the
Conservatives in both Quebec and Ontario, as it made the news on
several television networks. Conservative strategists have confirmed that
the event was organized strictly for the media. Moreover, PC publicists
in Quebec were to base a two-minute free-time political broadcast on
that event.

The massive intervention by the business community after the
debates, particularly the pro–free trade national advertising campaign,
escaped judgement by the press because it was aimed directly at the
electorate through paid advertising, mainly in newspapers. The high

degree of credibility that representatives of the business community enjoyed with the Canadian electorate during that period (*Maclean's/ Decima* 1988) leads us to believe that, after the debates, the election campaign became a battle over the credibility of the various positions on free trade. In the months leading up to the election, a significant number of Québécois and other Canadians claimed to be unfamiliar with the content of the agreement.

The Organization of Election Coverage
The structure of a press organization set up as a general election approaches depends on the type of medium (electronic or print), on its financial and technical resources, on its size and on its mission as an information medium. For the purposes of this study, we will describe the structure and function of the 1988 federal election campaign coverage apparatus at the disposal of Radio-Canada in Montreal, the TVA network, Montreal's daily newspaper *La Presse* and Trois-Rivières' *Le Nouvelliste*.

Radio-Canada Television, Montreal
Radio-Canada's coverage plan – most aspects of which were implemented – was revealed around the Montreal election bureau. As established before the writs were issued, the bureau was to consist of a campaign director, Pierre Jomphe, two assignment editors who shared the coverage schedule, one journalist (Daniel Lessard) to analyse the campaign and another (Michel Morin) who was to be responsible for economic analyses and was to be called upon when needed to cover free trade. Two journalists (Gérard Jolivet and Lise Tremblay) were to be responsible for news briefs. Logistical coordination was to be provided seven days a week by two production assistants. Furthermore, an editor was to be responsible for reading press releases and assisting the assignment editors. A film librarian was to be responsible for receiving and filing all the footage that had been shot. Finally, a resource person was to be in charge of keeping the daily schedule and informing the journalists of their daily assignments.

The leader tours were to be covered by three teams, each consisting of five people: a journalist, a director, a sound technician, an editor and a camera operator. The management of the election desk was to provide for rotation of the journalists assigned to the tours so as to avoid biases toward the leaders and parties. This took place only once, however, instead of the two times planned for.

The election bureau's staff was set to go into action as soon as the election writs were issued, and 20-second news briefs on the progress of the election were to be broadcast from Monday through Friday at a rate of three or four per newscast (interview with Claude Saint-Laurent in 1988).

The difficulties related to coverage of the leaders by Radio-Canada television were greater in the fall of 1988 than in the 1984 election. According to Claude Saint-Laurent, this can be attributed to the appearance of a new generation of television news programs, such as "Première édition" (which was broadcast over the entire network), two broadcasts by the television news service, and the one-hour magazine program entitled "Montréal ce soir." Election campaign reports were to be included in these news programs, and "Montréal ce soir" was to take charge of local campaign coverage (interview with Claude Saint-Laurent in 1988). The election bureau could not guarantee daily reports on all three leaders. However, according to Claude Saint-Laurent, "balanced coverage must obviously be ensured, but nothing should prevent us from handling a clip when we consider it appropriate" (ibid.).

Coverage outside Quebec was to be handled by national correspondents: Julie Miville-Deschêne and Normand Lester in Ontario, Louise Beaudoin in Manitoba and Saskatchewan, George Trémel in Alberta and British Columbia, and James Bamber in the Atlantic provinces. Also, journalists assigned to the National Assembly in Quebec City were to cover the federal campaign in Quebec.

Radio-Canada television was to avoid suggesting thematic orientations during the 1988 campaign, because its role is not one of provoking debate. It is interesting to note what the news director stated as the campaign approached: "Already in the pre-campaign, the press in general seems to be following an agenda set by the present government. Let me remind you of the fairness that should characterize our activities and that, as in the past, we will have guidelines which we must observe closely" (interview with Claude Saint-Laurent in 1988). In conclusion, the director of the election bureau suggested that "the stories about party leaders should not, with occasional exceptions, run longer than 1 minute 30 seconds, and that thematic reports should not last longer than 2 minutes 30 seconds" (ibid.). Moreover, certain changes were to be made during the campaign to the coverage plan put forward by Radio-Canada.

Radio-Canada Moncton

Radio-Canada television in Moncton carried out regional coverage of the campaign focused on New Brunswick and the other Atlantic provinces. A single journalist covered the Atlantic provinces for Radio-Canada television during the federal election campaign. This situation affected the quality of his work, as the many trips he had to make prevented him from concentrating in depth on the reports or questioning the information disseminated by the political parties. Radio-Canada Moncton did not have an election desk. The time zone question was of concern to news organizers in the Atlantic provinces, as Radio-Canada Moncton had to shut down its transmitters in northern New Brunswick to prevent Quebec from picking up its broadcast signal on election night. Some Radio-Canada staff members in Moncton suggested that voting hours be shortened to adjust to the country's time zones so that election night would begin at the same time (real time) everywhere in Canada.

Télé-Métropole Montréal

Télé-Métropole Montréal's election desk consisted of the following staff:

- one election desk coordinator;
- one person responsible for feeds, who managed the time slots needed to send visual material back to the network (he was at work from 7:00 AM to 11:00 PM);
- one resource person responsible for communicating with journalists regarding content and for preparing the following day's schedule;
- one researcher working on election-night coverage, who was responsible for a daily report on the broadcasting of election news;
- three journalists assigned to the leader tours with three teams, each consisting of a journalist, a camera operator and a sound technician (the three journalists and their teams stayed with the same leader throughout the campaign; there was no rotation); and
- two journalists who covered the electoral districts of greater Montreal.

One journalist analysed the important events of the campaign twice a week; this type of news report varied in length from 1 minute 30 seconds to, at times, 2 minutes. The coverage of electoral districts was included in the news bulletin. During the election, two stories on the regions were produced by the following stations affiliated with the TVA network: Quebec City (four stories), Chicoutimi, Rimouski, Carleton sur Mer, Rivière-du-Loup (for Radio-Canada, TVA and Quatre saisons), Sherbrooke, Hull and Rouyn. Each station of the TVA network sent two stories to Télé-Métropole during the campaign. These stories varied in length from 1 minute 25 seconds to 1 minute 35 seconds.

La Presse (Montreal)

The daily newspaper *La Presse* set up an election desk to cover the 1988 federal election. Sixteen journalists covering the issues, polls, news briefs and the electoral districts were assigned to this desk. The three major parties were given equal coverage. Alan Frizzell and colleagues noted that 60.7 percent of *La Presse*'s reports came from Quebec coverage of the federal election (Frizzell et al. 1989). The smaller parties were covered in news briefs. Innovations in 1988 were to concentrate coverage on the free trade issue at the expense of constituency coverage, the traditional method of election coverage. *La Presse* had already begun to reduce coverage by electoral district in 1984. The space allotted to coverage of the 1988 federal election represented an average of four pages per day, distributed as follows:

- an exclusive story on the front page (photographs and text, news of the leaders);
- the bottom of page B1 devoted to the best analyses;
- coverage on the editorial page;
- coverage of the three leaders in the middle of the paper; and
- political news briefs, page B4: "Bref et local Montréal."

La Presse did not give priority to covering the leaders, given the immediacy of that type of news. The Canadian Press wire was used for news briefs from outside Quebec. By the end of the campaign, *La Presse* had devoted 225 pages to election coverage, including its summary of election results.

La Presse's election desk had a budget of $170 000, which covered expenses incurred in its operations, i.e., the salaries of the journalists, airplane tickets for the tour and all related expenses. After the leaders debates, the paper decided to set up a task force of journalists to analyse the consequences of free trade for several sectors of Quebec industry, and on election night *La Presse* produced a special section that was the work of 60 journalists and photographers.

Le Nouvelliste (Trois-Rivières)

The coverage team consisted of two coordinators and five journalists. The journalists were responsible for covering the political activities of candidates in the six federal electoral districts in the heart of the Quebec region, that is, the districts of Saint-Maurice, Trois-Rivières, Champlain, Berthier–Montcalm, Richelieu and Lotbinière. The two coordinators, who were also journalists, took part in the coverage of some political events and were in charge of running election news production meetings.

Le Nouvelliste's coverage was basically regional in nature. When the three party leaders toured the heart of the Quebec region, the paper covered reactions to their presence.

The intention of *Le Nouvelliste's* management was to set its own pace in this campaign. It decided on the press coverage to be given to the candidates and their activities. Journalists from the Trois-Rivières daily met with every candidate from the region to allow them to give their views on regional issues. The paper put greater emphasis on issues it had introduced and on exclusive reports.

Influences on Election Coverage

Numerous factors influence the content and format of coverage: the relationship between politicians and journalists, election marketing techniques, competition between media, polls, deadlines, the instantaneous nature of computerized communications and the need felt by journalists of the print and electronic media to keep a check on themselves as far as news content is concerned.

Most of the journalists interviewed for this study noted that technological changes have had an impact on the substance and form of reports. For instance, journalists now connect their computers directly to the press wire. The effect of the introduction of this new communications tool has been that election desk managers have required increased production from journalists in the field. This fact, in combination with a full campaign schedule on the leaders' planes, made it impossible for journalists to go into the content of their statements in greater depth.

Moreover, the quality of election coverage, especially in the electronic media, appears to have fallen as a result of the control and manipulation of the media by the party organizations. Journalists are in danger of being manipulated when they go on a leader tour. Some electronic journalists even gave their reports from locations chosen by the organizers of the Conservative tour. According to one veteran journalist, the media were manipulated during the 1988 federal election because they had neither the budgets nor the expertise to resist the power of the organization set up by the Conservatives in the field. In spite of themselves, journalists often become prisoners of circumstances that threaten their objectivity. In the period following the leaders debates, the organizers of the prime minister's tour laid on five events per day, leaving journalists little time to prepare their reports. Techniques for packaging the leader on tour, especially those used for the prime minister, were part of a predetermined strategy (Bernier 1991) with events planned for television. This operation enabled the

organization to control the content and image of televised information. For their part, the Liberals wanted to control access to their leader
and his image, but they were less effective in doing so than the
Conservatives were. The New Democrats were less concerned about
managing their leader's image.

In another connection, some journalists are opinion leaders, and
they sometimes influence the tone of their colleagues' coverage. Finally,
polls appear to affect election coverage. After the leaders debates, the
media awaited the results of polls before confirming that one of the
candidates had been victorious. According to Fletcher and Everett, election coverage of the campaign was profoundly influenced by the polls
(Fletcher and Everett 1989).

Post-election assessments of election coverage, which were carried
out by some news organizations, revealed that the content of information handled by journalists often depends on messages that the political parties want to send and are therefore lacking in analysis.

The Psychosocial Dimension of Influences on Election Coverage[7]

Researchers have investigated the hypothesis that statements from the
business community influenced the perceptions of the electorate and
the press regarding the desirability of the Free Trade Agreement. In
December 1987, more than 70 percent of Québécois and 80 percent of
Canadians questioned considered themselves ill-informed on the content
of the Free Trade Agreement (Léger and Léger 1987; Gallup 1987). This,
along with Michel de Repentigny's comments that journalists are not
always better prepared than readers to describe the content of a news
item, leads us to suggest that the electorate and the press took the
"peripheral route" in using the information provided by the business
community on the benefits of free trade. This hypothesis is based on the
elaboration theory developed by the American social psychologists
Richard Petty and John T. Cacioppo (1986).

The nature of the persuasion process depends on the probability that
the receiver will undertake to "elaborate" information he or she is given
for purposes of persuasion. "Elaboration" here means the thought
process set in motion by persuasion.

Petty and Cacioppo have developed two models of elaboration,
namely, the central and peripheral routes, which they describe as paths
taken by the receiver in the persuasion process. The central route is one
by which the receiving individual embarks upon an intensive thought
process focused on the real relevance of the arguments or information
presented. Thus, if we seek to persuade someone of the need to support
the Free Trade Agreement, the individual in question might scrutinize

the arguments relevant to that issue, such as the content of the agreement itself, the benefits and drawbacks for the Canadian economy and its labour force, and its consequences for Canada's political sovereignty.

The peripheral route is one by which the receiver does not pay full attention to the arguments or information directly relevant to the issue but instead looks for indirect clues about their validity. For example, on the free trade issue people might, for various reasons, not form their opinions on the basis of information concerning the substance of the issue but on the basis of indirect indicators such as the credibility of the people who support the agreement and arguments of a purely emotional nature. At the time in question, the business community was perceived by the Canadian and Quebec electorate to be the most credible source of information on the free trade issue (*Maclean's /* Decima 1988).

Factors Influencing the Choice between the Central and Peripheral Routes

The central and peripheral routes are two extremes; between them are numerous other routes combining the two approaches. There are two main factors influencing the choice of a central route over a peripheral route: the individual's motivation and his or her ability to deal with the issue (Petty and Cacioppo 1986, 20–21).

Among the factors affecting motivation, the most important are without question a person's degree of involvement and need to know. People are more likely to choose the central route if they are actively involved in an issue. However, most Canadians were unfamiliar with the content of the agreement, and many candidates found it difficult to promote an agreement whose effects included unknowns (and still include unknowns today). The ability of the public, some candidates and journalists to deal with the free trade issue was in large part related to how much they knew; however, little information was available, aside from government and business propaganda.

Furthermore, the many studies carried out by unions and opponents of the agreement warning of its threat to the country's economy were the subject of a few articles, but nothing more, in the Quebec media. Finally, most Quebec daily newspapers came down in favour of free trade in their editorials the day before the election.

Changes in Election Coverage

The computerization of communications between journalists in the field and the newsrooms of the print and electronic media has without question been one of the major changes in the coverage of election events. The parties' tactics for influencing the content of reports have been refined over the last 10 years. The leaders' campaign staff have become increasingly familiar with media operations. Coverage of the leaders is more selective at Radio-Canada; the Crown corporation has not, in the past, hesitated to present three reports on the leaders every day, even if the comments were repetitive.

Coverage of this election by the French-language print and electronic media was dominated by the free trade issue, whereas in 1984 it focused on the leader and on the need to renew the country's sense of direction. It is still too early to describe the numerous in-depth reports produced by the print media in the fall of 1988 as a structural trend, since they were related to the sudden emergence of an election issue that revolved around the impact of free trade on the country's economic and political sovereignty.

Since 1984, the daily newspaper *La Presse* has paid less attention to coverage of electoral districts in order to direct its efforts, inter alia, to election issues, in-depth reports and exclusive news reports. Since 1980, Radio-Canada has rotated its journalists assigned to the leader tours (though Télé-Métropole has not done likewise). It is some years since Radio-Canada introduced an election desk to broadcast a block of election news, which previously had been the subject of daily negotiations depending on the needs of the moment.

Financial resources, the broadcast time factor for the electronic media and the space factor for the print media are still major constraints on election coverage.

Journalists' Perceptions of Election Coverage

Table 1.2 represents the positions of the interviewed French-language journalists regarding criticisms directed at the media with respect to election coverage during the 1988 federal election.

Most of the respondents were of the opinion that the media place too much emphasis on the leaders and not enough on the issues of the campaign. Most of them felt that the electronic media pay too much attention to the "horse-race" aspect of the election, to sensational coverage and to image, at the expense of analysis. However, they deny that their reports are too critical and that they do not refer to statements by the leaders and presentations of election platforms. Nevertheless, they acknowledge that the coverage generally focuses on the blunders of the leaders and not enough on their ability to become heads of government. Finally, they are of the opinion that the key planks of the parties' election platforms are not subjected to sufficient analysis by nonpartisan experts.

Table 1.2
Responses of French-language journalists to 10 critiques
(Yes/No/NR*)

1. The media place too much emphasis on leaders and not enough on issues.		
Yes: 67%	No: 19%	NR: 14%
2. The media do not focus enough attention on each party's team.		
Yes: 62%	No: 29%	NR: 9%
3. The media pay too much attention to the "horse-race."		
Yes: 57%	No: 24%	NR: 19%
4. The media place too much emphasis on entertainment or visually exciting coverage.		
Yes: 43%	No: 38%	NR: 19%
5. The media pay too much attention to colour and trivia at the expense of issues and analysis.		
Yes: 57%	No: 29%	NR: 14%
6. The media engage in too much critical reporting and not enough straight reporting of leaders' statements, party platforms, etc.		
Yes: 29%	No: 57%	NR: 14%
7. There is too negative a tone to media coverage generally.		
Yes: 28%	No: 52%	NR: 20%
8. The media pay too much attention to personal foibles and gaffes of leaders and not enough to their potential as leaders of the government.		
Yes: 47%	No: 33%	NR: 20%
9. The media do not pay enough attention to the issues raised by minor parties and interest groups during the campaign.		
Yes: 38%	No: 52%	NR: 10%
10. The media do not provide enough analysis of key elements of party platforms by nonpartisan experts.		
Yes: 48%	No: 38%	NR: 14%
Total interviews = 21		

*NR = no response.

SUMMARY AND RECOMMENDATIONS FOR IMPROVING THE QUALITY OF ELECTION CAMPAIGN COVERAGE

Major Conclusions

The description, analysis and conclusions of this study are derived largely from the self-reporting of 69 journalists, representing 40 media organizations across Canada, as contained in hour-long interviews based on a similarly structured format. In addition, two academics and five party representatives were interviewed. The results were integrated with a number of previous research studies done by the authors of this study and with those of others concerned with media practices in the coverage of election campaigns.

The conclusions might have been more comprehensive had time permitted direct observation or a content analysis to verify the journalists' observations. As is usual in studies of this kind, radio has been underexamined as compared to print, though we made a point of interviewing representatives of all of the major radio networks. Electronic media have been studied largely at the network level only.

In general, our research confirms what has been learned about journalistic practice in studies of several past elections, with updates from the most recent federal election. As we look at the trends indicated by this study, we are both optimistic and pessimistic about the creation of a knowledgeable electorate. While a number of media organizations seem to be replicating the coverage practices of the past, there are a few that are reflective, innovating on past practice in order to function more autonomously and effectively. Our major conclusions are listed below.

1. There is too much control by political parties.
Not surprisingly, and despite a decline in assigning journalists to cover the leader tours, there is widespread concern (supported by content analysis) about the focus on party leaders and the resultant control of the election agenda by party aides. Party aides have increased in technical sophistication and are often influential in news interpretation and analysis. Journalists appear to lack the resources, time, expertise and institutional will to resist as effectively as is needed. Parties can control, to some degree, the depth of analysis through scheduling and through emphasis on media events or "photo opps" designed for television. Party control has been facilitated by the increase in number and sophistication of "political technocrats," most of whom are attached to the party leader's entourage. The journalistic establishment has not kept pace with this growth. Concerns about party control have been voiced over the past six or seven elections at least and seem equally spread over English- and French-speaking Canada. The consequence of this control is that there is too little autonomy for journalists and that there is increased opportunity to narrow the frame for political discussion to centre on the self-interest of mainstream political élites.

2. There is a trend toward increased regional emphasis.
With the exception of a few "national" media, there is a clear movement in organizations away from assigning resources to cover the leader tours and toward regional and local coverage. This is the major new finding. Although most of the media still regularly carry daily updates on the activities of the leaders, often provided by news services, even

this practice seems to be more selectively employed. There is a beneficial consequence of this in that the field of political discussion is widened to the peripheries of the country, focusing on more localized interests, but it could also weaken debate about national issues.

3. There is a widening split between regional and national media.

Many media organizations are now content to leave the commissioning of polls and the coverage of the leaders to the organizations that have active bureaus in the Parliamentary Press Gallery and are usually based in Toronto, Montreal or Ottawa. This has both beneficial and problematic consequences. Although it may make sense to divide the focus of coverage and may increase local coverage, it also serves to centralize or base national coverage in the centre of the country, further widening the gulf between centre and periphery. An informal "pecking order" seems to have emerged that privileges the "national" media to the increasing resentment of the "regional" press. This is a factor that is mainly applicable to the English media. Because of the concentration of the French-speaking reading audience in Quebec, the press there necessarily assumes both a "national" and a local mandate.

4. Coverage formats and style have become "lighter, tighter, brighter."

With the exception of the *Globe and Mail, Le Devoir* and some public-affairs programming such as "The Journal" and "Le Point," this is true for both print and electronic media and for both French and English press. The trend can be attributed to several factors: the influence of television on the conduct of campaigns, the perceived need to capture a less attentive audience (perhaps influenced by television consumption habits), and several of the new technologies that make it possible for easier and more immediate filing. The trend is evident in both the form and content of stories. The resulting compression and "glitzing" of the material provides shallower and more fragmented coverage, resulting in an even less attentive and perhaps more volatile electorate. A more positive interpretation would suggest that journalists are active in the search for new ways of telling old election stories.

5. Reporter styles are more cynical and more aggressive.

While acknowledging that younger reporters are brighter and more educated, journalists rate themselves and their colleagues as being much more cynical. This is true for both French- and English-speaking Canada. Cynicism, when matched with an increased aggressiveness, may lead to less informed, negative, "cheap-shot" journalism. Frequent comment about the loss of respect for political leaders and political organizations signals the kind of cynicism that could invade political reporting and seriously erode the institutional fabric of the country. Closer and more specialized content analysis is necessary to confirm the degree to which this self-reported cynicism has revealed itself in political coverage.

6. Journalists generally feel they have sufficient autonomy within their own organizations.

Although journalists are subject to a number of constraints and routine coverage practices, there still seems to be a healthy amount of negotiation between editor and reporter as to the direction, tone and focus of coverage. Reporters feel that they have adequate freedom to explore coverage options. This might be an expected recourse for reporters. However, interviews with reporters and then with editors, as well as the limited direct observations available, seem to support this conclusion. On the other hand, coverage of the leaders by less experienced journalists with increased autonomy – a practice of several organizations – may have left room for increased influence by the party and other factors.

7. To the detriment of other policy issue coverage, the single issue of free trade dominated the 1988 election.

As was obvious to even the most casual observer of the last election, the emphasis on free trade reversed a trend away from the coverage of policy issues and the focus on leadership and personality, which had marked earlier campaigns (though leadership remained a major focus of coverage). Much of the coverage was influenced by the media's association of free trade with important advocacy groups and the parties either for or against, and the insistence within the media on balancing only these two viewpoints. As a result, much of the coverage was presented in the "selling" mode or in a context of conflict, neither of which helped an electorate understand and explore such a complicated issue. We are also convinced that most journalists had as little understanding of the issue as most voters during much of the campaign. We doubt that there has been sufficient structural change in the way media organizations approach election coverage to ensure that a variety of policy issues will be investigated in the next election. Despite the efforts of several organizations to maintain issue-analysis teams (CBC-TV, *La Presse*, etc.), we believe that the preponderance of coverage was greatly influenced by the strategy of the opposition parties and influential interest groups (both of which were primary sources for journalists) to concentrate on free trade.

8. The continued development of new technologies brings mixed results to the quality of election coverage.

Technology that enables reporters to file more easily and with greater speed has the advantage of immediacy. It also appears to increase pressure on journalists to file more frequently, to highlight the immediate "here and now" of the campaign, to cover in less depth and possibly to fragment coverage. New technologies help journalists resist the manipulation of parties while they are on a leader tour by keeping them in more frequent contact with editors, information sources and research data banks.

9. Poll coverage and the commissioning of polls by the media has changed election coverage.

While there is division among journalists as to the benefits of media polls, there is a clear indication that coverage has changed as polls become stories in themselves. It is a major way in which the media become participants in the campaign beyond their normal role of reporting. Polls do provide valuable research bases for some media organizations, but they are inadequately reported on by many. The fact that their numbers have doubled since the 1984 election clearly added to the amount of "horse-race" coverage – which a number of journalists argued should be the basis of election coverage anyway.

10. Access to politicians and party control have replaced resources and time as the major constraints facing journalists, except among the French-speaking press.

This was one of the surprises that resulted from our interviews of English-speaking journalists. It suggests the need for the development of new strategies by media organizations and the development of new assumptions and structures of coverage practice. It may also reveal a disparity between the resource bases of English- and French-language media organizations. Limited access, together with the obvious resentment of journalists about control by party "technocrats," could have an increasingly detrimental effect on the political process. Wider participation in campaign operation may be more limited and may also appear to be more closed. We are already reading of widespread disillusion with political leaders and institutions. The narrowing of access and the resentment that it breeds can only increase feelings of cynicism and apathy. There is evidence that the increased cynicism about political institutions has already spread to attitudes about the media, which are still our primary source of information about political candidates, parties and issues.

11. Access to the media for minor parties and issue-based groups was satisfactory for most journalists.

Very few journalists felt that there was insufficient access for non-mainstream groups, though this view was not shared by representatives of these groups. Although it is clear that the next election will see as many as five parties being covered, this change is the result of popular support for two new parties and is not a result of reframed assumptions, policies or structures of election coverage practice, though it may force some changes. In order to challenge the agendas of the major parties more effectively and to ensure the entry of fresh ideas in the electoral process, we feel that this presumption of parties receiving "the coverage they deserve" needs to be re-examined.

12. Few media organizations systematically self-monitor and reflect on their coverage practice.

We believe that any vital profession or organization, including our own, should continually evaluate its own practice. We also recognize that the normal pace and stress of media organizations make this difficult and often result in the assignment of self-assessment to a low priority. As has been affirmed in our previous studies, the occasion of our interview was often the first time that there was concentrated, formal assessment. There were several exceptions, particularly the CBC, which even initiated a conference at Queen's University to reassess all election coverage after the 1988 campaign, in addition to its own internal audit. One of the results of the lack of systematic assessment is that old patterns of coverage are repeated, along with the routines and constraints that both frustrate journalists and limit the quality of coverage.

13. Several media organizations and journalists are serious about their own coverage practices and are concerned about the quality of election information that reaches the voter.

Despite the general lack of self-assessment and despite the growing cynicism and other concerns noted above, we encountered a number of journalists who feel that the coverage of elections is one of the most important assignments they have. They see themselves as professionals who are doing important work for the political well-being of this country.

Recommendations

Although most of the issues of journalistic practice discussed here are beyond the reach of state action, they constitute an important context for the work of the Commission. We hope that journalists will respond directly to our observations and recommendations and that these will be viewed as constructive attempts to improve the democratic process by increasing voter information and participation.

For journalists and media organizations, we recommend increased efforts to self-monitor coverage systematically, to develop new strategies to cope with party control and manipulation, to improve research databases and internal communication, to reassess priorities that privilege immediacy and the excitement of the horse-race, to widen coverage beyond the issue of leadership (a legitimate issue) and thus encompass a number of policy concerns, to re-evaluate the legitimacy of perceived constraints, to increase access for non-mainstream and non-élite voices, to commission polls that are methodologically sound and then report fully on both the methods and results, and to struggle against cynicism by exploring new relationships with politicians and political institutions. These are difficult tasks for any profession or organization with established practices, standards and constraints. They require both the willingness and the available time to challenge assumptions that seem natural and are taken for granted.

The Commission may wish to consider making the following suggestions and recommendations that might facilitate certain changes in journalistic practice.

1. Encourage pool coverage for leader tours, thus freeing resources for other coverage.
News and wire services, plus a representative of radio and a team representing all the television networks, would be responsible for providing coverage to all the media. This would free resources for alternative coverage, as well as freeing the media from many of the restrictions of party control. Policy releases by the parties could follow other normalized channels. This is a model that is often used in times of war or special events coverage, though the Gulf War coverage illustrates the negative possibilities. However, if media organizations do not develop alternative coverage practices and rely heavily on the provisions of the pool coverage, there could be increased party control.

2. Encourage greater access to the media for minor parties, citizens' groups and social movements.

3. Provide more opportunities for candidates to speak for themselves, reducing the incentive to attempt to manage the news.
The shrinking sound bite and the adversarial style of journalism tend to distort the communication priorities of the parties without providing any sustained assessment of their views. We think that both are required for effective election coverage.

4. Consider limiting the coverage of polls in the final days of campaigns, and require full disclosure of the results and methods of published polls which claim to be scientific.

5. Encourage the media to organize or participate in self-assessments of the basic practices and assumptions of election coverage.

6. In particular, encourage media self-assessment regarding the political consequences of increased cynicism and lack of substantive analysis in campaign coverage.

7. Encourage the commissioning of additional long-range research (incorporating observation, interview and content analysis) into journalistic practices during and between elections.

Although this recommendation might appear self-serving, it is apparent from the limitations of this study – and the time constraints that of necessity faced researchers for the Commission – that long-range research on the various media, on new technologies, and on voters and their information levels needs support and encouragement. The absence of broadly based electronic media archives in this country makes content research difficult, especially when not planned before an election.

APPENDIX A
DESCRIPTIVE EXCERPT OF OBSERVATION OF CBC-TV

Within the election unit, the primary observation was concentrated on workers at the centre of activity (or at the top when a more standard hierarchical model was chosen). My observations confirmed that there was an awareness of hierarchy, usually evidencing itself through the resolution of conflict. Among the central players there was constant negotiation, give-and-take, testing and exchange of ideas. When conflict was not resolved, usually the pressure of time would lead to its resolution in the direction of bureaucratic hierarchy. The key actors (all men) and their roles, briefly described below, were: the executive producer of news specials, the Ottawa bureau chief and assignment editor, "The National" editor, "The National" anchor, writer/editor and additional support personnel.

Executive Producer of News Specials (and Election Coverage)
He had organizing authority and control over the nightly coverage and the four hour-long specials. On a host of decisions from story lines to subject choices to editing decisions, he had the final word, especially if there was disagreement. His style was to encourage suggestions, and several times he made decisions against his own preference in favour of a suggestion of one of his producers

because, in his words, "many have been here for seven years and we have to continue to function as a team."

There was a very close working relationship with the second in command, the Ottawa bureau chief, who was brought to Toronto for the duration of the election. The two of them had worked closely together for the previous four federal elections and for the Quebec referendum and a number of provincial elections. Together they had thrashed out coverage policy and fought numerous internal battles for air time and resources within the corporation. Over the previous summer the executive producer had produced a paper outlining the election plan, had started negotiations for time on "The Journal" (which was refused), and had then begun the process which resulted in the decision to create four Sunday-night specials, to commission two extensive electoral polls, and to assure members of the unit that normally they would have at least six minutes each night on "The National" for election coverage. "The National" management reserved the right to pre-empt this implicit understanding if other news seemed more important.

Assignment Editor, Ottawa Bureau Chief

He was clearly second in command (as evident by the way he was consulted and listened to by almost everyone). He never seemed to have a clear title in the ad hoc, specially created unit, even though he had a clear title within the normally functioning bureaucracy of the CBC. Involved in all aspects of the coverage, he had several major functions. Clearly the day-to-day strategist, he was constantly in touch with top advisers in each of the three parties. Closely attached to this function was the one that he assumed for keeping coverage teams informed about the progress of the campaign, particularly what was happening in areas outside the immediate experience of the reporting team. Along with "The National" editor, he produced the GONIF (General OverNight Information File), an insider's information report containing what he thought were key issues and campaign developments and summaries of coverage by other media outlets. Originating in the 1979 election, the GONIF had become very sophisticated. It was a fairly complex intelligence report and represented important organizational knowledge. It was not intended for publication but was designed as a means of informing units about all party strategy and standings and of providing context and background. Less clear is the role the GONIF might have played in establishing themes for coverage, especially of individual leader tours, or providing story hooks or angles, or even increasing the fascination with leader campaign strategy that seems to have played such a large role in election coverage during this past decade. GONIF, which means "thief in the night" in Yiddish, was distributed to field teams and key personnel most nights during the campaign and must have lived up to several aspects of its Yiddish name, giving CBC an information edge over the competition.

Another major role of the Ottawa bureau chief was that of team specialist on the computerization of data relevant to the campaign (and the politics of the major parties between elections). The computer had gradually assumed a larger role in CBC's election coverage in each election since 1979. By 1988, with the mainframe located in Toronto, it had become the repository for enormous amounts of data on each of the parties, on each of the ridings and on all of the candidates. Researchers had been given the job of coding all of the footage shot by the various election teams and entering it into the mainframe so that it was available to reporters searching for footage to support a story. In addition, production teams located anywhere in the country with access to a CBC tieline could call up previous positions of any of the party leaders for comparison in preparing a story. Riding profiles were available for analysis and prediction. These, of course, were regularly updated with information from the CBC's own polls. The ultimate use of the computer in the election was on the night the polls closed, as selected key ridings were used to call the election outcome.

Because of his computer expertise, the Ottawa bureau chief assumed responsibility for training and orchestrating much of the rehearsal for election-night coverage. It was necessary to prepare a complex team of regional analysts to enter results as they were phoned into the computer and to make the information and appropriate interpretations available for on-air commentators and control room graphic operators (another very sophisticated computer-driven technology).

Finally, the Ottawa bureau chief was very active in the editing process for specific stories, often working directly with producers or reporters. He was a key planner in projecting ahead what stories might be needed for both "The National" and the Sunday specials. Because of the pivotal and critical role that he played within this election team, he was a constant consultant to other team members, especially "The National" anchor, most producers, "The National" editor and the executive producer for election coverage.

"The National" Editor

He was the primary person responsible for the monitoring and basic editing of stories from the field as they developed. On an average of three times per day, he was in telephone contact with a member of the field team, usually the field producer, though occasionally the actual reporter. This was especially true of the teams that were following the leaders, since there was the agreed-upon expectation that each night there would be stories on "The National" about each of the leader tours, unless the party leader had done nothing in public that day. In general, "The National" editor was the main person on the team tracking stories as they developed each day, though by 6 PM he had usually turned over the editing, rewrite and tracking process to the regular election unit writer.

A second major function of "The National" editor was his responsibility for handling all the logistics for each of the teams in the field. He assigned all the Toronto-based crews and conferred with either the Ottawa bureau chief or the executive producer about which of the other teams was available for other stories, such as those with regional focus or specific issue analysis. Logistic management meant determining available crews and equipment, available feed lines to get stories back to a CBC outlet and then fed to Toronto, or it might even have meant chartering a plane because of the time factor and no available uplink. He was the one responsible for warning local station affiliates across the country that a crew would be in at a specified time for editing a piece, thereby assuring that an edit suite would be available. At other times, with his chief competitors CTV and Global, he coordinated access to feed lines or mobile units.

Because of his knowledge of where crews were and what crews, facilities and equipment were available, and because of his regular contact with field producers, "The National" editor became a major communication link, both internally and externally, for the entire election unit. He was able to update teams on leader tours as to what the other leaders were saying or doing within the previous hour so that they could attempt to get the leader or his staff to respond. At the least, this enabled reporters in the field to have the possibility of a special angle or context for their stories. Along with the GONIF, "The National" editor's regular contact was a way of preventing complete isolation (sometimes referred to as the "cocoon effect") for a team that was confined to covering the same leader tour for several days. Another way of overcoming the isolation was for the CBC to rotate field teams on the leader tours. This was done somewhat irregularly in the last election. A major shift of teams assigned to cover the leaders occurred for four days after the debates among the leaders. Teams returned to their original tours and then were switched for another week before returning to their original assignments.

"The National" editor fulfilled another linking function by keeping the leader tours informed of which personnel would be on the plane or bus at which time. A final linking function was provided by his serving as the primary liaison with "The National" news team. He met regularly with the senior producer for "The National" and normally represented the team in the two daily assignment and line-up meetings.

He fulfilled additional communication functions by being the primary person responsible for briefing other media personnel, especially foreign journalists, a number of whom came to Canada for the last week of the election. This provided him with extensive gatekeeping and agenda-setting power as he briefed foreign journalists on the key issues (as he and the CBC team saw them) even to the extent of providing a cassette of key visuals (e.g., the "key" moment in the English debate showing a triumphant Turner and a prime minister who had lost his cool). In the four days that he was being observed for this study, he had contacts with CBS, NBC and PBS, all from the United States.

The CBC had as many as 12 teams committed either full-time or part-time to coverage of the election. In most cases, a team was composed of five members: producer, reporter, cameraperson, audioperson and editor. This had been the average contingent since the 1979 election, when CBC was the first in Canada to use electronic newsgathering. The editor was not always present in 1979, having been leap-frogged ahead to prepare for editing. By 1988, the CBC had portable editing suites available for some of its teams in the field, giving it another technological advantage. During the week I was observing at the CBC, the teams were as follows: a team assigned to each of the three leader tours; separate teams doing stories on four regional "battlegrounds" (the use of military metaphors in news units could be another study); British Columbia, Ontario, Quebec and Newfoundland (already completed); special pieces by separate teams on the upcoming media blitz, the western Reform Party, other minor parties, humorous moments in the campaign, and an issues piece on the Value-Added Tax (to become the GST). In addition, David Halton, presumably requiring a team less often, was continually available for "talkbacks" (exchanges with the anchor either done live or live to tape) and other commentary analysis pieces. Many of the teams other than those covering the leader tours were preparing pieces that would appear on the Sunday specials or on the slower news days of the weekends. Those covering the leader tours were often expected to prepare weekly wrap-up pieces on the tours that would be part of the Sunday shows.

In addition to these functions, "The National" editor regularly monitored the Canadian Press wire, which he had available on his desktop terminal, for stories on the campaign and as a way of verifying leads. He also scanned the major daily newspapers, from which he prepared a daily digest of articles and cartoons that he felt would be of interest to members of the election unit and "The National." Parts of the digest became his contribution to the GONIF.

The Anchor for "The National"

Five nights a week this was Peter Mansbridge, and on Friday and Saturday it was Knowlton Nash. Mansbridge was much more implicated in election coverage, having been part of the team along with the executive producer and the Ottawa bureau chief since 1977, and having functioned as the reporter who covered Joe Clark and the Conservative party tour during the 1979 election. His office was almost next to the executive producer's and therefore was part of the space for the election unit. Although he usually did not arrive until after midday, he was quickly absorbed into many of the consultations about developing or future stories and was an important part of the 1:30 PM general "National" line-up meeting. Although there was a writer assigned to preparing the lead-ins that he was to read for each story, he personally vetted and often rewrote much of his copy. Possessing some of his own sources within the political parties, he was part of the preparation of a number of stories, including some of the editing decisions for the Sunday-night election specials.

He and the Ottawa bureau chief consulted with each other often and were the two main authors of the most controversial piece that the CBC did during the election: the report on the attempted or considered coup to oust John Turner as leader of the Liberals. Mansbridge took the unusual route of becoming the reporter for that story, stepping aside from his usual role as anchor for "The National." The story, broadcast on 19 October, was kept very much in-house with almost all field units unaware of plans to broadcast it. The following night, there was a lengthy GONIF, explaining to the troops the basis and source of the story and justifying the secrecy on the grounds that they and their credibility were being protected.

Writer/Editor

This was the first election in which the special election unit was able to have a writer who ranked high in the editorial hierarchy of "The National." His exclusive role was to vet campaign stories and prepare the lead-in copy for "The National" anchor seven days a week. Perhaps to assure continuity and communication between "The National" and the election unit, the regular line-up editor for "The National" was assigned to the team for the period of the campaign. In any event, the permanent assignment of a writer exclusively for election stories ensured that the election unit was spared the continual fight for time on "The National" that had characterized the 1980 and 1984 elections. As the writer was a visible part of the regularized bureaucratic order and was familiar with the normal routines of "The National," he was a reassuring link for both units that the special ad hoc, semi-autonomous election unit would function smoothly in conjunction with the more permanent "National" unit. This proved to be a false assumption, contributing to some of the confusion and conflict that developed over the content of "The National" during the first day it was being observed for this study.

Additional Personnel

Housed directly within the space set aside for the election unit were two assistant editors, who sat directly behind the Ottawa bureau chief and "The National" editor and were responsible to them. They answered the phone (which seemed to ring every two minutes) when either of their "bosses" was occupied, ran down video cassettes and personnel, did research or obtained it for stories being prepared, and generally filled in where needed. There were several production assistants, one of whom reported directly to the executive producer, accompanying him whenever he went to the control room to oversee a taping or when he had to do a nonelection special. This assistant was the only woman I observed as being part of the central election unit. There were a number of female producers and reporters in the field, however. At least two in-house senior producers responsible to the executive producer and part of his permanent "specials" team occupied nearby offices and were involved in planning and producing stories for the election specials. In total, there were at least 75 persons involved full-time with the special unit, not counting the personnel responsible for the setup and operation of election night coverage.

In order to give the reader a bit of the flavour of the ambiance, an excerpt from my summary field notes is given below. It was dictated during the trip back to Montreal after the four-day visit:

How would you describe the culture in this? Well, it is certainly a culture of frenzy, of quick decision, of operating under the stress of time (and too much to do), feeling like you are part of something that's really important for the country, participating along with the politicians in the process. It's a bit of a culture of chaos, certainly a sort of organized chaos, a kind of mix of quasi-secrecy in which people speak furtively on phones or in short-hand messages to one another, and openness, in which this unit is easily willing to be examined – doesn't seem to hide anything, certainly not from me. It's a culture of group decision making and group examination, mixed with a sense of relative personal autonomy where people certainly feel that they can manage an entire area themselves and not have to worry.

To this end, it should now be added that there was continual negotiation and often conflict or disagreement. Time played a critical role in resolving disagreement over the selection or content of stories where most often the person lower in the hierarchy either agreed or dropped the issue, having said his or her piece. During the period of my observation at the CBC, there was one instance of conflict that clearly touched interpersonal feelings and seemed to be a matter of team solidarity and perceived mutual support. It took most of a day for the surface traces to disappear, and the issue never was clearly resolved. It should be emphasized that communication was often in incomplete sentences, with information exchanged on a "need-to-know basis," as one assistant editor put it – or, more accurately, on a "Don't tell me any more than I need to know" basis. There was constant interruption by telephone or by personnel wandering in from other areas or by shouts from one office or desk to another. Discussions longer than two minutes at any one time were rarely observed, though often the threads of a previous discussion would be picked up and continued until the next interruption. Most long-range planning (looking ahead beyond the immediate day or as far as the next week) took place in this form or on the run. Most discussion revolved around the "here and soon to be now." Acquiring the communication patterns and the culture and ambiance seemed to be part of the socialization process into the organization.

APPENDIX B
SAMPLE INTERVIEW QUESTIONNAIRE, FALL 1990
Interview Schedule for Reporters/Editors/Producers

Respondent name and title: _____

Date and place of interview: _____

Preamble: We are engaged in a study of changes and patterns in election coverage and campaigns over the past two decades. The purpose of our interview is to obtain the observations and recollections of experienced and well-informed reporters/editors on a number of key questions, for research commissioned by the Royal Commission on Electoral Reform.

1. **Perhaps we could begin by discussing your own involvement with election campaigns.**

   • How many elections have you covered (or have been involved in the coverage)? (get dates)

• Describe the various responsibilities you have had.

• What was your role in 1988?

2. **How do you see the role of the media in campaign coverage? What changes have you observed?**

• Have there been changes in the way new organizations organize their coverage? Prepare for the campaign?

• (Print only) Is there a change in partisan bias in the coverage?

• Have you seen changes in the way reporters approach campaign coverage? In their attitudes? (more critical reporting)

• Have you noted any changes in formats? Styles of presentations? The balance of issue pieces v. leader pieces?

• Have the technological changes had much impact on content and style of reporting? Examples.

• What about the priority given to election coverage? Have you had to fight for time and/or space?

• Has the quality of coverage been rising or falling? Examples. What factors do you think account for change?

• Do you think the media have had more or less influence in recent campaigns than in the past on: voter choice, party campaign behaviour?

• Which media are most influential (radio, television, newspapers) re: public, party strategists, other media?

• Have there been important changes in issues? In the way they are presented/framed? If Yes, what accounts for the changes?

3. **Relationships with the parties:**

• What would you say have been the major changes in the ways the parties run their campaigns? How have these changes affected coverage? Are the parties better or worse at getting their message across?

• Have you noted any trend with respect to the way leaders are presented?

• Have you noted any change in the priority given to party platforms? In the way they are presented?

• What is the trend with regard to the priorities given to the various media?

• Changes in party tactics in seeking to manage (manipulate) media coverage?

• Any changes in the way campaign staff related to the media?

• Have there been changes in the primary sources of information upon which reporters rely?

4. **Internal processes of news organizations/the planes:**

   • To what extent is coverage monitored during the campaign? Do reporters get regular feedback? On what dimensions? Changes?

   • Are priorities pre-established by the hierarchy or by give-and-take? Changes?

   • Any special guidelines re: format, frequency of filing, length, focus, tone, etc. Changes?

   • Are there opinion leaders among the political reporters who influence the coverage re: tone, format, etc. who have been the most influential in your experience? Examples of influence?

   • Would you support banning the publication (or taking) of party preference polls after the writs are issued, as a number of commentators have suggested?

   • Would you support any other form of regulation of such polls?

5. **The 1988 campaign. Now some more specific questions about the 1988 campaign:**

   • Was the coverage different from 1984 in any major ways that we have not discussed?

   • What was the basic structure of coverage? Reporters/teams assigned?

   • Was there a post-mortem in your organization? If so, what issues were discussed? Would you have changed anything?

   • What were the primary constraints on how well you could do your job in 1988? Re: resources, competition, access, space, time, filing facilities, poll results, finances, past or previous relations of parties, technology?

   • Were there some key issues? Pivotal events?

6. **Finally, there have been a number of studies critical of the media coverage in 1988 (and recent elections generally). How would you respond to the following criticisms?**

   • Too much focus on leaders and not enough on issues.

   • Not enough attention to each party's "team."

   • Too much need for entertainment or visually exciting coverage.

   • Too much attention to colour and trivia at the expense of issues and analysis.

   • Too much critical reporting and not enough straight reporting of leaders' statements, party platforms, etc.

   • Too negative a tone to the coverage generally.

   • Too much attention to personal foibles and gaffes of leaders and not enough to their potential as leaders of government.

- Not enough attempts to challenge the agendas of the parties and to raise issues of concern to significant segments of the electorate that parties are avoiding.

- Not enough analysis of key elements of party platforms by nonpartisan experts.

- Do you have any general comments on these points? Areas you would like to see improvement in?

7. **Final questions:**

- We now seem to be in the era of the permanent election campaign. To what extent has this altered political coverage between elections? What are the major differences between election coverage and political coverage between campaigns?

8. **A little personal data that will be kept confidential:**

- Do you personally identify with any of the federal parties?

- Did you vote in 1988?

Thank you.

NOTES

This study was completed on 30 December 1990.

We wish to acknowledge the special help of the following in the preparation of this study: Marie Bourbonnière, Dan Fontaine-O'Connell, Joy Forrester, David Hogarth, Paul Landon, Louise Lavoie, Jenepher Lennox, Dan Maher, Diane Moffat, Sylvie Nadon, Bushra Pasha, Ray Straatsma.

In this study, quoted material that originated in French has been translated into English.

1. Still active as a researcher and commentator on elections, Meisel has more recently shared the interests of researchers such as ourselves on the role of the media in election campaigns. In his commentary on the 1984 election, "The Boob-Tube Election: Three Aspects of the 1984 Landslide" (Meisel 1985), he identifies the television debates and the media interpretation of their significance that followed as being decisive in that election.

2. Findings by Kay et al. (1985) support Fletcher's observations. In the 1984 election, more than two-thirds of adult Canadians watched the televised leaders debates. Also, voter volatility resulted in the Liberals holding less than half their 1980 votes (ibid., 19–20).

3. The "spin doctors" were political advisers and strategists who tried to slant journalists' perceptions of their leaders' acts and words during and after the debates.

4. With few exceptions, we have treated journalist comment without attribution. A number of journalists requested anonymity, and we extended it to almost all of them because of the limited time available for summarizing the results of our interviews.

5. "Light, tight and bright" does not apply to all the media. The *Globe and Mail*, *Le Devoir* and *Maclean's* (because of its format) have attempted to counter this trend with more in-depth coverage.

6. On the changing relationship between political parties and the press, see Benjamin 1979; on the role of the media in the political process, see Martin 1988, Y. Gagnon 1980, Sauvageau 1979, Lesage 1980, and Lachapelle and Noiseux 1980; on the treatment of written information during election campaigns, see Latouche 1977 and Crête 1984; on the treatment of written information during the referendum, see Tremblay 1984; and on the treatment of televised information, see Caron et al. 1983.

7. The section on the psychosocial dimension of the influences on election coverage is essentially taken from Bernier (1991).

BIBLIOGRAPHY

Altheide, David L. 1976. *Creating Reality: How TV News Distorts Events.* Beverly Hills: Sage Publications.

Attalah, Philip, and Will Straw. 1981. "Representational Features of Media Coverage in the Quebec Referendum Campaign." Working Papers in Communications. Montreal: McGill University.

Benjamin, Jacques. 1975. *Comment on fabrique un premier ministre québécois.* Montreal: L'Aurore.

———. 1979. "Pouvoir politique et médias au Québec." *Communication information* 3 (1): 67–77.

Bennett, W.L., L.A. Gressett and W. Haltom. 1985. "Repairing the News: A Case Study of a News Paradigm." *Journal of Communications* 33 (Spring): 50–68.

Bernatchez, Jean. 1984. *Qui influence les médias? Bibliographie sélective sur les relations entre les journalistes et les sources d'information institutionnelles.* Quebec: Université Laval, Groupe de recherche en information et communication.

Bernier, Robert. 1988. *Le Marketing gouvernemental au Québec: 1929–1985.* Montreal: Gaëtan Morin.

———. 1991. *Gérer la victoire? Organisation, communication, stratégie.* Boucherville: Gaëtan Morin.

Black, Edwin R. 1982. *Politics and the News.* Toronto: Butterworths.

Blais, André, and Jean Crête. 1982. "La Presse et la politique municipale dans deux villes du Québec." *Politique* 2:41–67.

Bourgault, Jacques. 1977. "L'Attitude des mass-media vis-à-vis du gouvernement québécois." *Études internationales* 8:320–36.

B.R. (Journalist). 1971. "L'Information au Québec: De la politique à la consommation." *Socialisme québécois* 21–22:79–108.

Breed, Warren. 1954–55. "Social Control in the Newsroom: A Functional Analysis." *Social Forces* 33:326–35.

Briggs, E.D., et al. 1980. "Television News and the 1979 Canadian Federal Election." Windsor: University of Windsor.

Brown, Richard M. 1979. "The Gatekeeper Reassessed: A Return to Lewin." *Journalism Quarterly* 56:595–601.

Bruck, Peter A. 1981. "The Social Reproduction of Texts: On the Relations of Production/Product in the News Media." Working Papers in Communications. Montreal: McGill University.

———. 1984. "Power Format Radio: A Case Study of Canadian Current Affairs Radio." Ph.D. diss., McGill University.

Camp, Dalton. 1979. *Points of Departure*. Ottawa: Deneau and Greenberg.

Canada. Canadian Study of Parliament Group. 1980. *Seminar on the Press and Parliament: Adversaries or Accomplices?* Proceedings of a seminar held in the Quebec National Assembly, 18–19 April. Ottawa: Queen's Printer.

Canada. Royal Commission on Newspapers. 1981. *Report*. Ottawa: Minister of Supply and Services Canada.

Canada. Senate. Special Committee on Mass Media. 1970. *Report*. Ottawa: Queen's Printer.

Canada. Task Force on Broadcasting Policy. 1986. *Report*. Ottawa: Minister of Supply and Services Canada.

Canadian Broadcasting Corporation. 1982. *Journalistic Policy*. Ottawa: CBC.

Cantin, Hélène G. 1981. "La Tribune de la presse du Parlement de Québec." Doctoral diss., Université de droit, d'économie et de sciences sociales, Paris.

Caron, André H., Chantal Mayrand and David E. Payne. 1983. "L'Image politique à la télévision: Les Derniers jours de la campagne référendaire." *Revue canadienne de science politique* 16:473–88.

Charron, Jean. 1986. "Le Pseudo-événement de contestation comme stratégie d'accès au médias: Une Étude de cas." Master's thesis, Université Laval.

———. 1989. "Relations between Journalists and Public Relations Practitioners: Cooperation, Conflict and Negotiation." *Canadian Journal of Communication* 14 (2): 41–54.

Charron, Jean, and Jean-François Normand. 1984. *Journalistes de la Tribune de la presse et la réforme parlementaire à l'Assemblée nationale.* Quebec: Fondation Jean-Charles Bonenfant.

————. 1985. "La Tribune de la presse et le système parlementaire." *Bulletin de la Bibliothèque de L'Assemblée nationale* 15 (1): 1–20.

Charron, Jean, Jacques Lemieux and Florian Sauvageau, eds. 1991. *Les journalistes, les médias et leurs sources.* Montreal: Gaëtan Morin.

Clarke, Deborah. 1981. "Second-hand News: Production and Reproduction at a Major Ontario Television Station." In *Communication Studies in Canada,* ed. Liora Salter. Toronto: Butterworths.

Clarke, Harold D., Jane Jenson, Lawrence LeDuc and Jon Pammett. 1979. *Political Choice in Canada.* Toronto: McGraw-Hill Ryerson.

————. 1984. *Absent Mandate.* Toronto: Gage.

————. 1991. *Absent Mandate: Interpreting Change in Canadian Elections.* 2d ed. Toronto: Gage.

Cocking, Clive. 1980. *Following the Leaders: A Media Watcher's Diary of Campaign '79.* Toronto: Doubleday.

Comber, Mary Anne, and Robert S. Mayne. 1986. *The Newsmongers: How the Media Distort the Political News.* Toronto: McClelland and Stewart.

Connell, Ian. 1978. "Television News and the Social Contract." *Screen* 20 (1): 17–27.

Crête, Jean. 1984. "La Presse quotidienne et la campagne électorale de 1981." *Recherches sociographiques* 25 (1): 103–14.

Crosbie, John. 1981. "Politics and the Media: Is the Public Well Served?" In *Politics and the Media,* ed. Reader's Digest Foundation and Erindale College. Toronto: Reader's Digest.

Cuthbert, Marlene. 1980. "Canadian Newspaper Treatment of a Developing Country: The Case of Jamaica." *Canadian Journal of Communication* 7 (1): 26–31.

Cuthbert, Marlene, and Vernone Sparkes. 1978. "Coverage of Jamaica in the U.S. and Canadian Press in 1976: A Study of Press Bias and Effect." *Social and Economic Studies* 27 (2): 204–20.

Davey, Keith, and Jacques Bouchard. 1981. "The Anatomy of a Campaign: Federal Elections and the Referendum (a) Backroom Planning." In *Politics and the Media,* ed. Reader's Digest Foundation and Erindale College. Toronto: Reader's Digest.

DeBonville, Jean. 1977. *Le Journaliste et sa documentation. Sources d'information et habitudes documentaires des journalistes de la presse quotidienne francophone du Québec.* Quebec: Université Laval, EDI-GRIC.

Demers, François. 1982. "Le 'Mauvais esprit,' outil professionnel des journalistes." *Communication information* 4 (3): 63–76.

———. 1988. "L'Accès au médias pour les causes impopulaires. Le cas du Rassemblement populaire de Québec, de 1977 à 1981." *Communication information* 14 (2): 85–108.

de Repentigny, Michel. 1981a. "Le Discours de presse: ... Le Discours de qui?" *Communication information* 4 (1): 46–59.

———. 1981b. "L'Élection du Parti Québécois en novembre 1976: Axiologie du discours de presse." In *Communication Studies in Canada*, ed. Liora Salter. Toronto: Butterworths.

———. 1981c. *La Presse au Canada et sa vision des problèmes d'importance internationale.* 1 (Nouvel ordre de la communication 6). Paris: Unesco.

———. 1989. "Sur certains modes de representations de l'actualité dans la presse." In *Les Savoirs dans les pratiques quotidiennes*, ed. Claire Belisle and Bernard Schiel. Paris: Éditions du Centre nationale de la recherche scientifique.

Desaulniers, Jean-Pierre, and Philippe Sohet. 1979. "Les Actualités télévisées ou la parade du soir." *Communication information* 3 (1): 7–26.

Desbarats, Peter. 1981. *Newspapers and Computers: An Industry in Transition.* Vol. 8 of the research publications of the Royal Commission on Newspapers. Ottawa: Minister of Supply and Services Canada.

———. 1990. *Guide to Canadian News Media.* Toronto: Harcourt Brace Jovanovich, Canada.

Dion, Léon. 1964. "The Election in the Province of Quebec." In *Papers on the 1962 Election*, ed. John Meisel. Toronto: University of Toronto Press.

Donohew, Lewis. 1967. "Newspaper Gatekeepers and Forces in the News Channel." *Public Opinion Quarterly* (1): 17–27.

Dornan, Christopher. 1983. "The Illusions of Understanding: The Notion of Explanation in the News Columns of the Daily Press." Working Papers in Communications. Montreal: McGill University.

Dunsky, Menahem, and Jerry Grafstein. 1981. "The Anatomy of a Campaign: Federal Elections and the Referendum (b) Massaging the Message." In *Politics and the Media*, ed. Reader's Digest Foundation and Erindale College. Toronto: Reader's Digest.

Elliott, Philip. 1970. *The Making of a Television Series.* New York: Vintage Books.

Epp, Roger. 1984. "The Lougheed Government and the Media: News Management in the Alberta Political Environment." *Canadian Journal of Communication* 10 (2): 37–65.

Epstein, Edward Jay. 1973. *News from Nowhere.* New York: Vintage Books.

Ericson, Richard V., Patricia M. Baranek and Janet L. Chan. 1987. *Visualizing Deviance: A Study of News Organization.* Toronto: University of Toronto Press.

———. 1989. *Negotiating Control: A Study of News Sources.* Toronto: University of Toronto Press.

Farquharson, R.A. 1952. "Canadian News Has an American Accent." *Neiman Reports* 6 (1): 7–9.

Fisher, Gordon. 1981. "Does the Concentration of Ownership Hurt Political Reporting?" In *Politics and the Media,* ed. Reader's Digest Foundation and Erindale College. Toronto: Reader's Digest.

Fishman, Mark. 1980. *Manufacturing the News.* Austin: University of Texas Press.

Fletcher, Frederick J. 1975. "The Mass Media in the 1974 General Election." In *Canada at the Polls: The General Election of 1974,* ed. Howard Penniman. Washington, DC: American Enterprise Institute for Public Policy Research.

———. 1980. "The Crucial and the Trivial: News Coverage of Provincial Politics." In *The Government and Politics of Ontario,* ed. D.C. MacDonald. Toronto: Van Nostrand Reinhold.

———. 1981a. "Appendix: The Contest for Media Attention: The 1979 and 1980 Federal Election Campaigns." In *Politics and the Media,* ed. Reader's Digest Foundation and Erindale College. Toronto: Reader's Digest.

———. 1981b. "Playing the Game: The Mass Media and the 1979 Campaign." In *Canada at the Polls, 1979 and 1980: A Study of the General Elections,* ed. Howard Penniman. Washington, DC: American Enterprise Institute for Public Policy Research.

———. 1987. "Mass Media and Parliamentary Elections in Canada." *Legislative Studies Quarterly* 12:341–72.

———. 1988. "The Media and the 1984 Landslide." In *Canada at the Polls, 1984: A Study of the Federal General Election,* ed. Howard Penniman. Washington, DC: American Enterprise Institute for Public Policy Research.

Fletcher, Frederick J., and Robert Everett. 1989. "An Unusual Campaign." *Content* (Jan./Feb.): 7–8.

Fletcher, Frederick J., and D.F. Gottlieb. 1981. "The Media and the Political Process." In *Canadian Politics in the 1980's,* ed. Michael Whittington and Glen Williams. Toronto: Methuen.

Fletcher, Frederick J., with David V.J. Bell, André Blais, Jean Crête and William O. Gilsdorf. 1981. *The Newspaper and Public Affairs.* Vol. 7 of the research publications of the Royal Commission on Newspapers. Ottawa: Minister of Supply and Services Canada.

Fraser, Graham. 1989. *Playing for Keeps: The Making of the Prime Minister.* Toronto: McClelland and Stewart.

Frizzell, Alan, and Anthony Westell. 1985. *The Canadian Federal Election of 1984: Politicians, Parties, Press and Polls.* Ottawa: Carleton University Press.

Frizzell, Alan, Jon H. Pammett and Anthony Westell. 1989. *The Canadian Federal Election of 1988.* Ottawa: Carleton University Press.

Fulford, Robert, et al. 1981. *The Journalists.* Vol. 2 of the research publications of the Royal Commission on Newspapers. Ottawa: Minister of Supply and Services Canada.

Gagnon, Lysianne. 1980. "Comme si la Tribune de la presse était un coin dans un aquarium." *Le 30* 4 (1): 11–12.

Gagnon, Yves. 1980. "Les Quotidiens québécois et le référendum: Analyse commentée." *Communication information* 3 (3): 170–81.

Gallup. 1987. Survey conducted by Gallup between 4 and 7 November 1987 on the Free Trade Agreement. *Le Droit*, 19 November.

Galtung, A., and M. Ruge. 1965. "The Structure of Foreign News." *Journal of Peace Research* 21:64–91.

Gans, Herbert. 1979. *Deciding What's News.* New York: Pantheon.

Gieber, Walter. 1956. "Across the Desk: A Study of 16 Telegraph Editors." *Journalism Quarterly* 31:423–32.

Gieber, Walter, and Walter Johnson. 1961. "The City Hall 'Beat': A Study of Reporter and Source Roles." *Journalism Quarterly* 38:284–97.

Gilbert, Marcel. 1971. "L'Information gouvernementale et les courriéristes parlementaires au Québec." *Revue canadienne de science politique* 4:26–51.

Gilsdorf, William. 1980a. "The Liberal Party and the Media in the 1979 Canadian Federal Election: Some Preliminary Thoughts." In *Recherches en communication*, Vol. 1. Montreal: Université de Montréal.

———. 1980b. "The Structure of Media Coverage in the 1979 and 1980 Conservative Elections." Paper presented at the annual meeting of the Association for Education in Journalism, Boston.

———. 1981a. "Getting the Message Across: The Communication Strategy of the Federal Liberal Party in the 1979 and 1980 Canadian Federal Elections." In *Communication Studies in Canada*, ed. Liora Salter. Toronto: Butterworths.

———. 1981b. "Mediated Politics: Thoughts on the Relationship of Media to the Political Communication Process in Canada." Paper presented at the second annual meeting of the Canadian Communication Association, Halifax.

————. 1990. "The Organizing Processes of the CBC-TV National Election Unit in the 1988 Canadian Federal Election." Paper presented at the annual conference of the Canadian Communication Association, Victoria.

Gitlin, Todd. 1980. *The Whole World Is Watching.* Berkeley: University of California Press.

Gold, William, and Dalton Camp. 1981. "Deciding the News in Print: What's the Test?" In *Politics and the Media,* ed. Reader's Digest Foundation and Erindale College. Toronto: Reader's Digest.

Golding, Peter. 1981. *Mass Media and Social Change.* London: Longman.

Golding, Peter, and Philip Elliott. 1979. *Making the News.* London: Longman.

Graber, Doris A. 1991. "The Mass Media and Election Campaigns in the United States of America." In *Media, Elections and Democracy,* ed. Frederick J. Fletcher. Vol. 19 of the research studies of the Royal Commission on Electoral Reform and Party Financing. Ottawa and Toronto: RCERPF/Dundurn.

Gurevitch, Michael, Tony Bennett, James Curran and Janet Woollacott, eds. 1982. *Culture, Society and the Media.* London: Methuen.

Hackett, Robert A. 1983a. "Decline of a Paradigm: The Concepts of Bias and Objectivity in Media Studies." Edmonton: University of Alberta.

————. 1983b. "The Spectrum of Labour and Business on National TV News." *Canadian Journal of Communication* 10 (1): 5–50.

Hall, Stuart. 1973. "The Determinations of News Photographs." In *Manufacture of News,* ed. Stanley Cohen and Jock Young. Beverly Hills: Sage Publications.

————. 1985. "Significance, Representation and Ideology: Althusser and the Post-Structuralist Debates." *Critical Studies in Mass Communication* 2 (2): 91–114.

Hall, Stuart, Ian Connell and Lynda Curti. 1979. "The Unity of Current Affairs Television." In *Cultural Studies,* No. 8. Birmingham: University of Birmingham, Center for Cultural Studies.

Hall, Stuart, David Hobson, Andrew Lowe and Paul Willis. 1980. *Culture, Media and Language.* London: Hutchinson.

Hall, Stuart, Charles Critcher, Tony Jefferson, John Clarke and Brian Roberts. 1978. *Policing the Crisis: Mugging, the State and Law and Order.* London: Macmillan.

Hallman, Eugene, P.F. Oliphant, R.C. White and Leonard Kubas. 1981. *The Newspaper as Business.* Vol. 4 of the research publications of the Royal Commission on Newspapers. Ottawa: Minister of Supply and Services Canada.

Hart, Jim A. 1963. "The Flow of News between the United States and Canada." *Journalism Quarterly* 40 (1): 70–74.

Hartley, John. 1982. *Understanding News*. London: Methuen.

Hébert, Gerard, et al. 1981. *Labour Relations in the Newspaper Industry*. Vol. 5 of the research publications of the Royal Commission on Newspapers. Ottawa: Minister of Supply and Services Canada.

Ichikawa, Akira. 1978. "Canadian–U.S. News Flow: The Continuing Asymmetry." *Canadian Journal of Communication* 5 (1): 8–18.

Janowicz, Morris. 1975. "Professional Models in Journalism: The Gatekeeper and the Advocate." *Journalism Quarterly* 52:618–26.

Johnston, Richard, André Blais, Henry Brady and Jean Crête. 1992. *Letting the People Decide: Dynamics of a Canadian Election*. Montreal and Stanford: McGill-Queen's University Press/Stanford University Press (forthcoming).

Johnstone, John W.C. 1976. *The News People*. Urbana: University of Illinois Press.

Joseph, Ted. 1982. "Existing Decision-Making Practices on Daily Newspapers in Canada." *Canadian Journal of Communication* 8 (2): 65–68.

Judd, Robert P. 1961. "Newspaper Reporters in a Suburban City." *Journalism Quarterly* 38:35–42.

Kay, Barry J., Steven D. Brown, James E. Curtis, Ronald D. Lambert and John M. Wilson. 1985. "The Character of Electoral Change: A Preliminary Report from the 1984 National Election Study." Paper presented at the Canadian Political Science Association annual meeting, Montreal.

Kelly, Fraser, and Desmond Morton. 1981. "Television: Does the Image Affect Reality?" In *Politics and the Media*, ed. Reader's Digest Foundation and Erindale College. Toronto: Reader's Digest.

Kline, Stephen. 1981. "National Perspective and News Bias: A Comparison of National News Broadcasts." *Canadian Journal of Communication* 7 (4): 47–70.

Knight, Graham. 1982a. "News and Ideology." *Canadian Journal of Communication* 8 (4): 15–41.

———. 1982b. "Strike Talk: A Case Study of News." *Canadian Journal of Communication* 8 (3): 61–79.

Kubas, Leonard. 1981. *Newspapers and Their Readers*. Vol. 1 of the research publications of the Royal Commission on Newspapers. Ottawa: Minister of Supply and Services Canada.

Lachapelle, Guy, and Jean Noiseux. 1980. *La Presse quotidienne. Québec: Un Pays incertain. Réflexions sur le Québec post-référendaire*. Montreal: Québec/Amérique.

Laliberté, Raymond. 1976. "Du Journaliste et des divers pouvoirs." *Communication information* 1 (3): 231–42.

Laplante, Laurent. 1980. "Informer ou manipuler." In *Dans les coulisses de l'information: Les Journalistes*, ed. F. Sauvageau et al. Quebec: Québec/Amérique.

Latouche, Daniel. 1977. "Le Traitement de l'information en période électorale. I. Le Contenu de l'information. II. L'Orientation de l'information." *Communication information* 2 (1): 1–30; 2 (2): 191–206.

Lee, Robert Mason. 1989. *One Hundred Monkeys.* Toronto: MacFarlane Walter and Ross.

Léger and Léger. 1987. Survey conducted by Léger and Léger on 11 October and 15 October 1987 on the Free Trade Agreement. See *Le Devoir,* 24 October.

Lesage, Gilles. 1980. "L'Information politique à Québec. De Duplessis à Lévesque: Les Journalistes au pouvoir?" In *Dans les coulisses de l'information: Les Journalistes*, ed. F. Sauvageau et al. Quebec: Québec/Amérique.

MacDermid, R.H. 1991. "Media Usage and Political Behaviour." In *Media and Voters in Canadian Election Campaigns*, ed. Frederick J. Fletcher. Vol. 18 of the research studies of the Royal Commission on Electoral Reform and Party Financing. Ottawa and Toronto: RCERPF/Dundurn.

Maclean's/Decima. 1988. "The Voters Reflect." 5 December, 19.

McNell, S. 1979. "Intermediary Communications in the International Flow of News." *Journalism Quarterly* 56:116–25.

Martin, Louis. 1988. "Le Role des médias dans le processus politique." *Communication information* 2 (3).

Meisel, John. 1962. *The Canadian General Election of 1957.* Toronto: University of Toronto Press.

———. 1975. *Working Papers on Canadian Politics.* Montreal: McGill-Queen's University Press.

———. 1985. "The Boob-Tube Election: Three Aspects of the 1984 Landslide." In *The Canadian House of Commons: Essays in Honour of Norman Ward,* ed. John C. Courtney. Calgary: University of Calgary Press.

Meuller, Claus. 1973. "Class as the Determinant of Political Communications." In *The Politics of Communication: A Study of the Political Sociology of Language, Socialization and Communication,* ed. Claus Meuller. Oxford: Oxford University Press.

Murphy, James E., and Kuang Tsui Sunshine. 1980. "Comparative Coverage of a 'Conflict' in Canadian and U.S. Newspapers, 1978." Paper presented at the annual meeting of the Association for Education in Journalism. Southern Illinois University, Carbondale.

Nolan, Michael. 1981. "Political Communication Methods in Canadian Federal Election Campaigns 1867–1925." *Canadian Journal of Communication* 7 (4): 28–47.

Peers, Frank W. 1969. *The Politics of Canadian Broadcasting, 1920–1951.* Toronto: University of Toronto Press.

———. 1979. *The Public Eye: Television and the Politics of Canadian Broadcasting, 1952–1979.* Toronto: University of Toronto Press.

Penniman, Howard, ed. 1975. *Canada at the Polls: The General Election of 1974.* Washington, DC: American Enterprise Institute for Public Policy Research.

———. 1981. *Canada at the Polls, 1979 and 1980: A Study of the General Elections.* Washington, DC: American Enterprise Institute for Public Policy Research.

———. 1988. *Canada at the Polls, 1984: A Study of the Federal General Election.* Washington, DC: American Enterprise Institute for Public Policy Research.

Pepin, Marcel, and Geoffrey Stevens. 1981. "Prospects and Proposals." In *Politics and the Media,* ed. Reader's Digest Foundation and Erindale College. Toronto: Reader's Digest.

Petty, Richard E., and John T. Cacioppo. 1986. *Communication and Persuasion, Central and Peripheral Routes to Attitude Change.* New York: Springer-Verlag.

Porter, Brian. 1984. "Foreign News Flow in Canada's Smaller Press." Ottawa: Carleton University.

Qualter, T.H., and L.A. Mackirdy. 1964. "The Press of Ontario and the Election." In *Papers on the 1962 Election,* ed. John Meisel. Toronto: University of Toronto Press.

Raboy, Marc. 1984. *Movements and Messages: Media and Radical Politics in Quebec.* Trans. David Homel. Toronto: Between the Lines.

Raymont, Peter. 1980. *History on the Run.* National Film Board documentary.

Reader's Digest Foundation and Erindale College, eds. 1981. *Politics and the Media.* Toronto: Reader's Digest.

Rivet, Jacques. 1979. *Grammaire du journal politique, à travers Le Devoir et Le Jour.* Montreal: Hurtubise HMH.

Robinson, Gertrude Joch. 1974. "Twenty-five Years of Gatekeeping Research." Montreal: McGill University.

———. 1980. "The Referendum on Quebec Television: A Semiotic Approach to Television News Analysis." Montreal: McGill University.

————. 1983. "Foreign News Conceptions in the Quebec English Canadian and U.S. Press." *Canadian Journal of Communication* (9) 3: 1–32.

Robinson, Gertrude Joch, and Vernone Sparkes. 1976. "International News in the Canadian and American Press: A Comparative News Flow Study." *Gazette: International Journal for Mass Communication Studies* 22:203–18.

Romanow, W.I., and Walter Soderlund. 1978. "The Southam Press Acquisition of the Windsor Star: A Canadian Case Study of Change." *Gazette: International Journal for Mass Communication Studies* 24:255–70.

Romanow, W.I., W. Soderlund, D. Briggs and R. Wagenberg. 1982. "Media Agenda Setting in the 1979 Canadian Election: Some Implications for Political Supports." In *Political Support in Canada: The Crisis Years,* ed. Allan Kornberg and H.D. Clark. Durham: Duke University Press.

Romanow, W.I., et al. 1980. "Media Agenda Setting in the 1979 Canadian Federal Election: A Case Study for the Critic of Mass Media." Paper presented at the annual meeting of the Association for Education in Journalism, Boston.

Romanow, W.I., et al. 1981. "Newspaper Coverage of the 1979 Canadian Federal Election: The Impact of Region, Language and Chain Ownership." Paper presented at the annual meeting of the Canadian Communication Association, Halifax.

Romanow, W.I., et al. 1982. "Electronic Media Coverage of Canadian Elections: A Comparison of the 1979 and 1980 Campaigns." Paper presented at the Canadian Political Science Association and the Canadian Association of Applied Social Research, Ottawa.

Roshco, Bernard. 1975. *Newsmaking.* Chicago: University of Chicago Press.

Samuelson, Merrill. 1962. "A Standardized Test to Measure Job Satisfaction in the Newsroom." *Journalism Quarterly* 39:285–91.

Sauvageau, Florian. 1979. "Les Médias et la campagne référendaire: Role exigeant 'mission impossible'?" *Cahiers de recherche éthique* 7:57–68.

Sauvageau, Florian, and Simon Langlois. 1982. "Les Journalistes des quotidiens québécois et leur métier." *Politique* 1 (2): 5–39.

Scanlon, Joseph. 1968. "The Sources of Foreign News in Canadian Daily Newspapers." Ottawa: Carleton University School of Journalism.

————. 1970. *A Study of the Contents of 30 Canadian Daily Newspapers.* Ottawa.

————. 1974. "Canada Sees the World through U.S. Eyes: One Case Study of Cultural Domination." *Canadian Forum* 54: 34–39.

Scheer, Chris J., and Sam W. Eiler. 1972. "A Comparison of Canadian and American Network Television News." *Journal of Broadcasting* 16 (Spring): 159–64.

Schroeder, Dennis. 1977. *A Survey of Coverage of Third World Affairs in Canadian Newspapers and Magazines.* Ottawa: Canadian Council for International Cooperation.

Siegel, Arthur. 1974. "Canadian Newspaper Coverage of the FLQ Crisis: A Study of the Impact of the Press in Politics." Ph.D. diss., McGill University.

———. 1979. "French and English Broadcasting in Canada: A Political Evaluation." *Canadian Journal of Communication* 5 (3): 1–17.

———. 1983. *Politics and the Media in Canada.* Toronto: McGraw-Hill Ryerson.

Sigal, Leon. 1977. "Defining News Organizationally: News Definitions in Practice." In *Women and the News*, ed. E.J. Epstein, W. Laurily and P. Keir. New York: Hastings House.

Sigalman, Lee. 1972–73. "Reporting the News: An Organizational Analysis." *American Journal of Sociology* 79:132–39.

Silverstone, Roger. 1985. *Framing Science: The Making of a BBC Documentary.* London: British Film Institute.

Snider, Paul B. 1967. "Mr. Gates Revisited: A 1966 Version of the 1949 Case Study." *Journalism Quarterly* 44:419–27.

Soderlund, W.C., Walter I. Romanow, E. Donald Briggs and Ronald H. Wagenberg. 1981. "Newspaper Coverage of the 1979 Canadian Federal Election: The Impact of Region, Language, and Chain Ownership." Windsor: University of Windsor.

———. 1984. *Media and Elections in Canada.* Toronto: Holt, Rinehart and Winston of Canada.

Soderlund, Walter, Ronald H. Wagenberg, E. Donald Briggs and Ralph C. Nelson. 1980a. "Regional and Linguistic Agenda-Setting in Canada: A Study of Newspaper Coverage of Issues Affecting Political Integration in 1976." *Canadian Journal of Political Science* 13:347–56.

Soderlund, Walter C., et al. 1980b. "Output and Feedback: Canadian Newspapers and Political Integration." *Journalism Quarterly* 57 (2): 316–21.

Sparkes, Vernone. 1978. "The Flow of News between Canada and the United States." *Journalism Quarterly* 55 (2): 260–78.

———. 1980. "Canada in the American Press and the U.S. in the Canadian Press: A Status Report." *Canadian Journal of Communication* 6 (4): 18–31.

Stanfield, Robert. 1981. "Summing Up." In *Politics and the Media*, ed. Reader's Digest Foundation and Erindale College. Toronto: Reader's Digest.

Stempel, Guido. 1964. "How Newspapers Use the AP Afternoon A-Wire." *Journalism Quarterly* 41:217–29.

Stevens, Geoffrey. 1978. "The Influence and Responsibilities of the Media in the Legislative Process." In *The Legislative Process in Canada: The Need for Reform*, ed. W.A.W. Neilson and J.C. Macpherson. Montreal: Institute for Research on Public Policy.

Stewart, Brian W. 1970. "CBC Television and the Faithful." *Public Opinion Quarterly* 34 (Spring): 92–100.

Stewart, Walter, ed. 1980. *Canadian Newspapers: The Inside Story.* Edmonton: Hurtig.

Taras, David. 1990. *The Newsmakers: The Media's Influence on Canadian Politics.* Scarborough: Nelson Canada.

Tate, Eugene D. 1978. "Canada and U.S. Differences in Similar TV Story Content." *Canadian Journal of Communication* 5 (2): 1–12.

Tremblay, Gaétan. 1984. "Les journaux … illisibles? Les journaux montréalais et la campagne référendaire." *Réseau* 16 (2): 13–16.

———. 1989. "L'Opinion publique: une théorie politique de la représentation sociale." In *Les Savoirs dans les pratiques quotidiennes*, ed. Claire Belisle and Bernard Schiel. Paris: Éditions du Centre national de la recherche scientifique.

Trim, Katharine, Gary Pizante and James Yaraskavitch. 1983. "The Effect of Monopoly on the News: A Before and After Study of Two Canadian One Newspaper Towns." *Canadian Journal of Communication* 9 (3): 33–56.

Tuchman, Gaye. 1971–72. "Objectivity as Strategic Ritual." *American Journal of Sociology* 77:660–70.

———. 1972–73. "Making News by Doing Work: Routinizing the Unexpected." *American Journal of Sociology* 79:538–52.

———. 1978. *Making News.* New York: Free Press.

———. 1983. "Consciousness Industries and the Production of Culture." *Journal of Communications* 31 (Spring): 330–41.

Tunstall, Jeremy. 1971. *Journalists at Work.* London: Constable.

Wagenberg, R.H., and W.C. Soderlund. 1975. "The Influence of Chain Ownership on Editorial Comment in Canada." *Journalism Quarterly* 52 (Spring): 93–98.

———. 1976. "The Effects of Chain Ownership on Editorial Coverage: The Case of the 1974 Canadian Federal Election." *Canadian Journal of Political Science* 9:683–89.

Wagenberg, Ronald H., Walter C. Soderlund, Walter I. Romanow and E. Donald Briggs. 1988. "Campaigns, Images and Polls: Mass Media Coverage of the 1984 Canadian Election." *Canadian Journal of Political Science* 21:117–29.

Weick, K. 1983. "Organizational Communications: Towards a Research Agenda." In *Communication and Organizations,* ed. L. Putnam and M. Pacanowsky. Beverly Hills: Sage Publications.

Whitney, C.D., and L.B. Becker. 1982. "Keeping the Gates for the Gatekeepers." *Journalism Quarterly* 59:60–65.

Wilson, R. Jeremy. 1980–81. "Media Coverage of Canadian Election Campaigns: Horserace Journalism and the Meta-campaign." *Journal of Canadian Studies* 15:56–68.

Winham, G.R., and R.B. Winningham. 1970. "Party Leader Images in the 1968 Federal Election." *Canadian Journal of Political Science* 3:376–99.

Winter, James P. 1979. "The Treatment of State-Owned vs Private Corporations in English Canadian Dailies." *Canadian Journal of Communication* 6 (3): 1–11.

Winter, James P., and C.H. Eyal. 1981. "Agenda Setting for the Civil Rights Issues." *Public Opinion Quarterly* 45 (3): 376–83.

Winter, James P., et al. 1980. "Issue-Specific Agenda-Setting: Inflation, Unemployment and National Unity in Canada, 1977–1978." Paper presented at the International Communication Association, Acapulco.

Winter, James P., Chaim H. Eyal and Ann H. Rogers. 1982. "Issue-Specific Agenda-Setting: The Whole as Less Than the Sum of the Parts." *Canadian Journal of Communication* 8 (2): 1–10.

Worthington, Peter. 1975. "Foreign Affairs: The Irrelevant Beat." In *A Media Mosaic,* ed. W. McDayter. Toronto: Holt, Reinhart and Winston.

Wright, Anthony J. 1979. "Relations entre le parlement et la presse." *Revue de la région canadienne, Association parlementaire du Commonwealth* 2 (3): 55–62.

Zolf, Larry. 1973. *Dance of the Dialectic.* Toronto: James Lewis and Samuel.

2

RELATIONS BETWEEN POLITICAL PARTIES AND THE MEDIA IN QUEBEC ELECTION CAMPAIGNS

Jean Charron

THIS STUDY DISCUSSES the relationship between the media and political parties in Quebec provincial election campaigns since the Quiet Revolution. As a synthesis of research and analysis conducted in Quebec, it has four objectives:

1. to trace the evolution of the climate of relations between parties and the media since the Quiet Revolution, and show how this evolution paralleled the sociopolitical and ideological changes Quebec experienced during this period;
2. to emphasize the contribution Quebec researchers have made in analysing relationships between the media and political parties, particularly (but not exclusively) during election campaigns;
3. to demonstrate the growing sophistication of the political communications techniques and strategies implemented by parties in Quebec election campaigns, and to examine the counter-strategies adopted by the media and journalists to limit the influence of the parties on the production of political news during campaigns; and
4. to assess the content analyses of provincial election campaign coverage by the Quebec media.

It must be noted that there has been no systematic study in Quebec of relations between the media and political parties in election campaigns. This omission may seem surprising, given the importance of elections and the media in a democratic society. It is even more startling in light of the fact that many studies on this subject can be found elsewhere, particularly in English Canada and the United States. The lack of earlier work sets a limit on this synthesis.

Quebec studies on this theme can be grouped in three categories. The first includes studies that deal directly with the issue of party–media relations, particularly in election campaigns (Benjamin 1975, 1976, 1979; O'Neill and Benjamin 1978). In the second category are content analyses of election campaign press coverage (Bourassa and Depatie 1966; Lamothe and Desjardins 1970; Bourgault 1977; Latouche 1977; Lachapelle and Noiseux 1980; Y. Gagnon 1980; Tremblay 1984).[1] The final category includes critical analyses and commentaries by journalists (Lesage 1980, 1990; Martin 1978; Sauvageau 1979).

A review of these studies indicates that there are still gaps in our knowledge of this process that is so fundamental to democratic life. The review also shows that it is necessary to refer to foreign studies to understand the situation in Quebec.

In order to achieve the objectives established above, this study is divided into four sections:

1. The first section outlines a theory of political communications in election campaigns, suggesting that the relationship between political parties and the news media should be approached from a historical perspective.
2. The second section is devoted to the evolution of relations between the news media and the political authorities since the time of Premier Maurice Duplessis.
3. The third section deals with relations between the parties and the media in provincial election campaigns since 1960. This section highlights the role of communicators in election campaigns and shows how the parties have adjusted to the reality of mass communications, especially since the advent of television.
4. The fourth section is devoted to journalistic practices and election campaign coverage by the news media.

A THEORY OF POLITICAL COMMUNICATIONS

The Political Communications System

In election campaigns a communications game develops, involving at least three categories of actors: political parties, the media and the public (whether organized or not). These actors who exchange messages form a system, that is, a set of interdependent elements (Bobrow 1974; Gurevitch and Blumler 1977). Thus the conduct of some influences the conduct of the others. For example, the way the media report an election campaign affects the candidates' conduct and the perceptions and actions of the public. Similarly, the political and strategic choices of candidates and parties affect the conduct of journalists and the media as well as public perceptions. The public, for that matter, is not an inert, passive and undifferentiated mass. It acts within the communications process by sending messages, directly or indirectly, that affect the decisions and actions of both the media and political organizations.

As a result, in order to understand the dynamics of election campaigns, particularly in communications, it is necessary to unravel the intricacies of the relations of influence among the actors and to grasp precisely and accurately how the actors influence each other. Several questions come to mind: How do the media cover election campaigns and how does this coverage affect electors' perceptions and votes? How does it change the strategies of candidates and parties? And how, in turn, do the strategies of candidates and parties affect the work of journalists and the media? How and to what degree can the public influence the media's choices and the orientations of the parties?

Relationships between the members of the system are governed by cultural norms, and by the formal and informal rules of the game, which vary from one political community to another. For example, we know that the attitude of the media to the privacy of candidates and elected officials is much more reserved in Canada than in the United States. We also know that television advertising in election campaigns is often more aggressive in the United States than in Canada.

However, party communications strategies and media coverage in election campaigns vary according to circumstances and the actors' resources. It can be said that election campaigns are contingent realities. The game is not always played the same way. If it were, the result of the election would be known before the campaign had even begun and there would be no reason to hold the campaign at all.

The simultaneously regulated and contingent nature of election campaigns leads us to adopt an evolutionary or historical approach to the phenomenon. To understand what has happened to election campaigns, it is useful, if not necessary, to try to find out what they were like before.

Ambiguity and Contradiction concerning the Role of the Media

The role that the media are supposed to play in the electoral process remains ambiguous. People adopt contradictory views concerning the media's status, levelling criticism from all sides. Some accuse the media of posing as an adversary of the government, while others complain of media complicity with the administration.

As a general rule, Quebec journalists willingly embrace the theory of the social responsibility of the press (L. Gagnon 1981). According to this doctrine, the media must be independent of power; this doctrine dictates a critical attitude that encourages journalists to harbour the greatest distrust toward those in positions of power and their arsenal of persuasion.

This search for independence, which is at the heart of the journalist's credo, effectively induces a tendency toward a critical mind, if not a form of opposition to political figures. But at the same time, the reality of the news industry means that journalists need sources of information in order to carry out their work. Yet political sources are, here as elsewhere, privileged. In fact, the relationship between journalists and political leaders is both conflictual and collaborative (Charron 1990b), the balance changing according to the spirit of the times. Quebec is a good illustration of this pendulum, which, over time, swings from complacency to conflict.

EVOLUTION OF RELATIONS BETWEEN THE MEDIA AND THE GOVERNMENT, 1945–90

The Years before the Quiet Revolution

The Quiet Revolution was a time of abrupt transition in Quebec. Although historians see the coming to power of the Quebec Liberal party (QLP) in 1960 as the beginning of the Quiet Revolution, there is unanimous agreement that the winds of change had begun to blow long before the death of Maurice Duplessis in 1959. The Quiet Revolution of the 1960s is rooted in the reform movements of the postwar period:

> The Quiet Revolution corresponds to a historical phase of adaptation during which Quebec society provided itself with political instruments appropriate to its stage of economic and social development. But this change, before being expressed in concrete political acts, followed a long gestation process. Before being carried out in the 1960s, the reforms had to be viewed as desirable by a majority of the population. It was therefore necessary that their forms first be conceived and formulated, and that their objectives have extensive public circulation. (Desoer 1982, 97)

Although the press was, on the whole, rather conservative while Maurice Duplessis was in power, the media nevertheless played an essential role in propagating new ideas, thereby making a significant contribution to the reform movement that led to the Quiet Revolution.

After 1945, Quebec experienced rapid industrialization, which introduced profound transformations in the realm of ideas. Amid this postwar ferment, the dynamic forces of the time conceived and formulated the projects that were to come into being in the 1960s.

Among these dynamic forces were the "new intellectuals," young people educated in the universities who gathered, for the most part, around the Faculty of Social Sciences at Laval University and the magazine *Cité Libre*. They were involved in a grassroots educational movement to change ways of thinking and create a social consensus on several major political and social objectives.

As Desoer notes, "in preaching the modernization of Quebec society, the new intelligentsia was at the same time working toward its own ascendancy as a social category. It defended a model of society that was summoned to confer on those with economic and social expertise a power and legitimacy they were denied in the ossified society of the Duplessis years" (1982, 99).

It was these new intellectuals who were at the controls of the state and who would begin to enter the pressrooms during the 1960s. A new coalition of press and political leaders was thereby formed.

The mass media were a very important instrument available to the new intellectuals for the accomplishment of their educational and consciousness-raising mission, which at that time continued to be peripheral to political action per se. Indeed, certain publications played a fundamental role in establishing networks of intellectuals and in the struggle against the regime of Maurice Duplessis. Under the direction of such people as Pierre Elliott Trudeau and Gérard Pelletier, *Cité Libre* and its contributors in the academic élite played a leading role in the ferment of ideas at that time. The daily *Le Devoir*, with journalists such as Gérard Filion, André Laurendeau, Gérard Pelletier and Pierre Laporte, and the journal *Vrai*, published by Jacques Hébert, were active in the struggle against *Duplessisme*.

But to reach the masses, the intellectual élite had to turn to the electronic media. Educational radio (Radio-Collège) and especially, from 1952 on, the television network of Radio-Canada were focal points for spreading new ideas. Radio-Canada, a federal institution beyond Duplessis' control, became the preferred medium for free speech and social and political criticism. Young intellectuals who later became leading political figures – Gérard Pelletier, Jean Marchand, René Lévesque, Jeanne and Maurice Sauvé – worked at Radio-Canada.

As Denise Bombardier (1979, 283–86), herself a journalist and television moderator, puts it:

> Television played an exceptional role in Quebec society in the late 1950s. It was a genuine agent of social change, breaking the ideological monopoly of the clergy, and it was also a catalyst of the new nationalism, presenting the Québécois with a coherent image of themselves.
>
> After 1952, everyone considered progressive in Quebec could be found in the Radio-Canada vestibule … This institution of the secular Word was now to be a counterweight to that other, religious and clerical, institution of the Word, the Catholic Church.
>
> That Quebec, led by Maurice Duplessis, who had the bishops eating out of his hand (as he liked to say), was a closed society – protected, some would say – of unilateral discourse. Faith, work, family and homeland were its poles. The intellectuals were, as a whole, fiercely opposed to the old boss and what he represented. The coming of television marked the beginning of open warfare between the premier of Quebec and Radio-Canada, and until his death he declined all invitations to take to the tube.

Duplessis and the Media

By the end of the Second World War, all the newspapers except *Le Devoir* and *L'Action catholique* were subservient to the Liberals. Premier Taschereau had his trusted men at *Le Canada*, *La Presse* and *La Patrie*. His right-hand man, Senator Jacob Nicol, a kind of early press magnate, controlled *La Tribune*, *Le Soleil*, *L'Événement* and *Le Nouvelliste*. Hand-outs from the public treasury and generous printing contracts assured the Liberals of a complacent press.

By relying mainly on radio, the Union nationale (UN) of Maurice Duplessis managed to communicate its message and, ultimately, to take power. Like the trade unionists of the time, Duplessis was one of the first leaders to grasp the effectiveness of radio broadcasting. He also wanted to found a provincial radio network. In 1945, Duplessis, who remembered that Radio-Canada had refused to broadcast his speeches during the election of 1939, put forward a bill to establish Radio-Québec, a provincial radio network. That Radio-Québec never saw the light of day, killed by the federal government to preserve its authority in this area (Bernier 1988, 47ff.).

But Duplessis quickly succeeded in bringing the newspapers to heel, using government printing contracts, which were awarded only to friends of the regime. The Liberal papers gradually abandoned their political allegiance, becoming "sympathetically neutral" (L. Gagnon 1981). Only *Le Canada*, which closed its doors in 1954, remained fiercely

Liberal, to such a degree that Duplessis, who did not take criticism well, barred Edmond Chassé, the newspaper's legislative correspondent, from his news conferences.

Le Devoir, the most influential of the dailies, supported the UN in the 1948 and 1952 elections "as a lesser evil, because [the Union nationale government] was resisting Ottawa's centralizing policy" (Sauriol 1971, 310). But on social issues *Le Devoir* soon became a savage opponent of Duplessis. In 1946, Gérard Filion became the editor of *Le Devoir* and hired André Laurendeau and Gérard Pelletier. These three great person-alities of Quebec journalism then undertook a long struggle against the Duplessis regime. In 1949, the Asbestos Strike, which featured intense police repression, marked the definitive break between *Le Devoir* and the Union nationale government. Duplessis sought to stifle the news-paper, depriving it of printing contracts and even threatening advertisers who dared do business with it (Godin 1981, 85).

The "Corporation de gaz naturel" scandal, which was brought to light by *Le Devoir*, marked the beginning of the end of the Duplessis regime. In June 1958, the newspaper published a series of articles by Pierre Laporte that accused several UN ministers and some UN members of the Legislative Council of lining their pockets from the sale of the Hydro-Québec natural gas system to the Corporation de gaz naturel (the natural gas company). The premier withdrew the right of Laporte, who was *Le Devoir's* legislative correspondent, to attend his news confer-ences. He then had police expel Guy Lamarche, the reporter sent to replace Laporte.[2]

According to journalist Gilles Lesage, this affair "abruptly changed the shape of relations between the government and the legislative press gallery. A few months later, the Gallery incorporated itself, adopted by-laws and decided that from now on all its members would be dealt with on the same footing" (1980, 270).

Duplessis tended to treat journalists like servants assigned to write articles as he dictated them: "Under Mr. Maurice Duplessis, 'It was simple, you had to repeat what he said word for word and not play any dirty tricks on him,' recalled Mr. Henri Dutil, who was a member of the Gallery for more than 25 years. The Friday press conferences were in fact nothing but dictation sessions. Pity whoever took it on himself to modify the boss's wording" (Lesage 1980, 269).

Those who did their work well – and pleased "the boss" – were rewarded in kind or with gifts of hard cash. It must be recalled that in the 1940s and 1950s, journalists' working conditions were such that they were at the mercy of whoever might reward them with a few presents; Michel Roy says that at that time, to support his family, in addition to working 45 to 60 hours a week, for which he would be paid $45 to $60, an experienced journalist would work at home as a translator and editor ... As a reporter, he did not have the heroism to refuse the envelope he was offered, which would contain a five-, ten- or twenty-dollar bill. If he was a regular columnist covering City Hall, the Chamber of Commerce, the university, the Quebec legislature, the political parties, the police or the courts, a few days before Christmas, he would get a larger amount or bottles of liquor in recognition of his faithful services. (Quoted in Godin 1981, 100)

Gérard Pelletier remembers that "a provincial election gave journalists an opportunity to replenish their finances for a year. Because, after each [party] meeting under the Union nationale, when you covered a party meeting, they distributed envelopes to the journalists. And the envelope often contained, for one meeting, more than a whole week's salary"[3] (quoted in Godin 1981, 101).

Journalists who deviated from the path laid down by Duplessis were severely reprimanded; they were threatened and sometimes excluded from news conferences.

With the exception of *Le Devoir* – and the overtly Liberal *Le Canada* – the newspapers hardly ever opposed Maurice Duplessis. But, according to Gérard Pelletier, it was television, which was being besieged by many of the new intellectuals, that shook the press out of its torpor and contributed to the disintegration of the UN regime.

It was to a very large extent television that awakened the press. The emergence of television in 1952 was, in my view, our cultural revolution. Once the public began seeing debates on television every week – it was an extraordinary magnet – the movie houses emptied in Montreal. The theatre almost perished at first. People were staying home! They no longer went out! Associations could no longer meet – no one came. It was a grand-scale social phenomenon. With television, the thaw began sooner than in the newspapers. We began to express opinions, to hold debates, and millions of people were watching. So the newspapers were obliged to follow suit and to express opinions themselves. This was an important factor: we began to express ourselves. (Quoted in Godin 1981, 105)

Contrary to what he had done with radio in the 1940s, Duplessis ignored television. It may be that he feared it.

To sum up, under the Duplessis regime the press remained servile to those in power, except for *Le Devoir*, which in the 1950s conducted a bitter struggle against the premier of the province of Quebec. The intellectuals who challenged the regime used the Radio-Canada television network to spread their messages, particularly in public affairs broadcasts. These programs served as forums to stimulate democratic discussion in a closed society restrained by the political authorities and the Catholic church, and helped awaken the press from its slumber.

Relations between the Media and Political Authorities from 1960 to 1980

In an article published in 1979, Jacques Benjamin argued that, since 1960, the relationship between the media and political authorities in Quebec has followed the general evolution of social relations. From 1960 on, he said, relations between the media and the government went through three distinct phases corresponding to three different social and political contexts.

From 1960 to 1968 – the period corresponding to the Quiet Revolution – Quebec society appeared to be broadly consensual, unified around the goal of modernizing the state, and the relationship between the media and the government was basically cooperative.

From 1968 to 1976, Quebec society was polarized and generally conflictual: relations between the media and political authorities were likewise characterized by conflict.

Since 1976, Quebec society has remained polarized, especially over the national question, but it seems that a sort of ideological dependence has nevertheless been observed between journalists and the Parti québécois (PQ) government. According to Benjamin (1979), the PQ government in 1976 was to some degree "exceptional": journalists and politicians "were part of the same family" (Martin 1978) and they maintained good relations despite the conflict over the constitutional question that was dividing the community.

Before examining each of these periods, we must first qualify Benjamin's (1979) interpretation by pointing out that the issues creating both the consensus and the conflict changed over the years. The great achievement of the 1960s, around which Quebec society unified, was the modernization of the state, which became at the same time the engine of development and the symbol of national identity. Intellectuals, technocrats, political figures and the media all shared a common vision of the work ahead of them. But after 1968, with this work done or well under way, new issues appeared, especially in the social arena.

An extraordinary social ferment affected all Western societies beginning in 1968, leading to the questioning of the very basis of a liberal capitalist society. Quebec did not escape it. At the time, political figures and intellectuals were sharply divided on the new social issues, with which the question of nationalism had become mixed, causing some confusion. Particularly opposed were young intellectuals and unionized workers – groups that had profited greatly from the gains of the Quiet Revolution, were keenly aware of new ideas and were strongly represented in newsrooms. The confrontations between the Liberal government of Robert Bourassa and the unions, popular movements and intellectuals contributed to the deterioration of the social climate.

From the mid-1970s on, the PQ attempted to use progressivist language and a program with social democratic leanings to reconcile neonationalism and the aspirations of competing forces. In 1976, it succeeded in taking advantage of support from progressive groups while completely reorienting issues around the national question. Many journalists – who defined themselves as nationalists and social democrats at the same time – were seduced by the combination proposed by the PQ.

In sum, the fact that the relationship between the press and political authorities was sometimes conflictual, sometimes cooperative, has less to do with the state of social relations than with the changing nature of the social issues at stake in different periods and with the compatibility of government positions with the ideological preferences of journalists.

The Quiet Revolution and the Consensual Society

As we have stated, the 1960–68 period was one of great structural changes, characterized by a substantial social consensus concerning the definition of the major objectives of reforms to be undertaken. It was expressed in the establishment of representative mechanisms with corporatist leanings (Archibald 1983), in which the major intermediary bodies (unions, corporate managers, intellectuals, farmers) participated.

At least in the early 1960s, the media adhered to this consensus in both editorials and reports. There was also a rapprochement between the political and journalistic communities. René Lévesque, the big star of the small screen, became a minister in Jean Lesage's dynamic cabinet, the "équipe du tonnerre." André Laurendeau and Gérard Pelletier, while pursuing their careers as journalists, were frequently consulted by the reform ministers. Paul Sauriol, a reporter with *Le Devoir*, wrote an almost uncritical book about the nationalization of electricity, with a preface by René Lévesque, the Minister of Natural Resources, who was responsible for overseeing the nationalization of electricity companies.

The Liberal defeat of 1966 and the ascent to power of Daniel Johnson's Union nationale made no substantial changes either to social relationships or to relations between the media and the government.

In general, journalists worked to popularize the government's complex projects and undertakings. Opponents of these projects criticized journalists' partiality. One of Benjamin's analyses shows that *Le Devoir*, considered the newspaper of the élite, provided a voice for opponents, preferring those who "criticized the government for not moving fast enough in implementing its reforms" (1979, 68).

The post-Duplessis era has been elsewhere characterized by a formalization of relationships between journalists and the government: "The era of direct relations between the government and the legislative press gallery gave way to the era of increasingly organized, orchestrated, planned and polished relationships. The Friday dictation gave way to proper news conferences mediated by one, then two, then several press attachés or press secretaries. After 10 years of delay, Quebec was following the practice current in the United States since Eisenhower" (Lesage 1980, 270).

Although television played a leading role in awakening Quebec, it had not yet deeply penetrated the political communications process. The newspapers remained the major vehicle through which Liberal politicians got their messages across. In Godin's view (1981), this was "the golden age of information": information was abundant, the press exercised social leadership and newspapers' circulation figures soared.[4]

After 1966, Daniel Johnson's Unionists continued to use the daily newspapers more than television to speak to the Quebec people.

> Under Daniel Johnson's government, the Union nationale politicians and their communications advisers used newspapers more or less the same way, that is, to win over public opinion. Journalists continued to serve as a conveyor belt, thereby playing – unconsciously, no doubt – the government's game. Premier Johnson's media advisers used the headlines in the mass-circulation newspapers – the afternoon dailies in Montreal and Quebec City – more than television to influence public opinion. (Benjamin 1979, 68)

From 1968 to 1976: A Society in Conflict

After 1968, Quebec society tended to polarize substantially on all fronts. The number of labour conflicts increased dramatically and the activity of union militants tended to be more radical. The challenges to the language policy of the Union nationale government of Jean-Jacques Bertrand resulted in some social agitation.

Relations between the government and the media also followed this trend toward polarization. For the first time since 1960, journalists took an adversarial position to the government, systematically questioning its actions and legitimacy (Benjamin 1979, 69).

The consensus that had bound the press and the government together disintegrated as social relations became increasingly conflictual.

According to Benjamin (1979, 75), between 1968 and 1976 the political authorities were no longer perceived to be speaking on behalf of the dynamic forces of society; the unions and the intelligentsia in particular displayed a lively opposition to the regime.

The Quiet Revolution years, says Benjamin (1979), had created nationalist expectations and endowed the government with a new interventionist role. Jean-Jacques Bertrand, elected as leader of the UN and premier in 1968, seems to have had some difficulty grasping this situation, and he alienated many of the most dynamic elements. While society rapidly changed around him, he offered only the image of a traditional leader, not the modern statesman people seemed to want. Many of his decisions were strongly challenged; note, for example, Bill 63 (*An Act to promote the French language in Quebec*).

His successor, Robert Bourassa, presented a contrasting image. But this technocratic image, although popular with a large proportion of the electorate, quickly disintegrated with a succession of crises. Barely five months after his election, the premier was mired in the 1970 October Crisis, which accentuated a climate of hostility between the government and journalists that was to last a long time.

It should be recalled that the Bourassa regime was marked by a long series of important labour conflicts both in the public and parapublic sectors and the major private corporations. The government was forced to resort to special legislation and repressive measures that simply fuelled union solidarity; the commitment of ordinary workers and union members to the struggle against the government increased. Militants, many workers and the unions perceived the government as submissive to the interests of the Canadian urban middle class, the monopolies and the American multinationals. In their view, a change in government and direction was needed.

By this time, journalists, as union members under constant pressure of confrontation in these years, were engaged in long labour conflicts within the media firms. They were not immune to the contemporary union ideology with its radical anticapitalist and antigovernment rhetoric. This trend increased as the young journalists who were filling the newsrooms left the universities where they had been trained according to progressive social theories. These journalists preferred to give voice to those forces that, in all circumstances, opposed the government. It must also be said that Quebec's French-speaking journalists were more militant in their unions and professional organizations than their English-speaking Canadian peers. Clift (1980) explains these differences by pointing out that Quebec society was a sort of French-language enclave. When English-speaking Canadian journalists encountered professional or ideological problems, they could always go and work somewhere else. This was not possible in Quebec; the small size of the French media community did not allow this mobility. The solution for Quebec journalists was therefore to dig in their heels and struggle, getting as much support as they could from their colleagues, their unions and their professional associations. Finally, Clift (ibid., 212) emphasizes that in Quebec, unlike the rest of Canada, class structure is based more on education than on wealth.

In any case, it is clear that ideologically the overall climate favoured a rapprochement between the journalists and the PQ:

> Day after day, editorials in *Le Devoir* (from 1970 to 1973) and news features in most other media harshly criticized the government, whose leader seemed, to them, unprepared for his role in the October Crisis and appeared to owe his election that year to a seductive prefabricated image. Faced with this opposition from the media, the Liberals took the advice of their advertising consultants and communicated directly with the voters without using journalists as go-betweens. (Benjamin 1979, 70)

For Robert Bourassa's Liberal government, governing meant expressing the general will, but in the absence of a social consensus it was impossible to govern effectively. "In short, from 1970 to 1976, the media and the government were adversaries. Journalists refused to legitimate situations fabricated by the government to obtain sympathetic reports. The premier's communications specialists sought to address the electorate directly through 'capsule statements' and attractive slogans, which were not enough to assure the re-election of the Liberals in 1976" (Benjamin 1979, 71).

Relations between the media and the Liberal government were very strained, particularly from 1973 to 1976. Not only was there no ideological common ground between the two groups, but also journalists criticized the government for adopting underhanded communications tactics. This tension is revealed in a documentary on government information prepared by the Fédération professionnelle des journalistes du Québec (1975). It stated: "The Bourassa government has thumbed its nose at the public's right to information, failed to play by the rules with the media, and crossed the threshold of partisan impropriety" (ibid., i). The government was criticized, for example, for using public funds for propaganda. The authors claimed: "Political news in Quebec City is dying, smothered by the partisan propaganda being circulated with the money of every citizen" (ibid., 2). In addition, the journalists criticized the premier for distributing news as if it were a favour: "Like road construction contracts, news distribution depends on the good will of the government and the strategy of the Premier's office, with an eye to rewarding or punishing reporters as their conduct warrants. Carried to an extreme, systems like this end up reserving information for the mandarins and their toadies" (ibid., 4).

The Media and the PQ Government: Journalists in Power? [5]

A new phenomenon occurred with the ascent to power of the PQ; while society remained polarized, a tacit alliance developed between journalists and the government, at least in the early years of the party's regime. The division of Quebec society on the national question cropped up anew in the very heart of the news business. Journalists, who generally supported sovereignty, were not on the same wavelength as media managers, most of whom favoured federalism. Because of this, the managers became increasingly watchful as the referendum date approached.[6]

The PQ star had risen very quickly. In 1970, in its first general election, the party obtained 23.1 percent of the votes. In 1973 it garnered 30.2 percent, and in 1976 it took power with 41.4 percent of the vote.

The PQ was the political vehicle for a new nationalist ideology that had broken with the conservative nationalism of the Maurice Duplessis era. This neonationalism developed primarily among the educated petty bourgeoisie, that is, the very people who had benefited most from the Quiet Revolution. The development of this new nationalist thinking split the intelligentsia into two factions: nationalists primarily inspired by René Lévesque and federalists primarily inspired by Pierre Elliott Trudeau.

The PQ, which was neither a workers' party nor a left-wing ideological party, managed to dissociate Quebec nationalism from its traditional conservative label to create the image of nationalism with social-democratic leanings. With its progressive program, the PQ was able to win the support of the major labour federations. The lack of independent union forces in the political arena and the antagonistic relationship between the unions and Bourassa's Liberal government during the 1970s helped the PQ in this enterprise.

The middle classes, which are composed of intellectuals, artists, teachers, social workers and young executives, constitute the political and electoral base of the PQ. It was these classes that had benefited the most from structural changes of the Quiet Revolution. They were highly educated and had used the educational system as an instrument of social advancement.

Journalists belonged to the class of people who favoured Quebec independence and state intervention. A poll by journalist Pierre Godin

(1979) indicated that a majority of journalists defined themselves as "moderate social-democratic sovereigntists." Four out of five journalists said they had supported the PQ in the 1976 election, and three out of four would have done the same if elections had been held at the time of the poll (spring of 1979).

Moreover, while it was the official opposition in the National Assembly, the PQ was able to attract the sympathy of journalists. First, it had few elected members. Between 1970 and 1973, with a mere handful of MNAs, the PQ managed to hound the Liberal government and win the admiration of the political reporters. Then, from 1973 to 1976, with a caucus that was slightly larger than in the previous period but disproportionate to its popular vote, the PQ managed to stay on excellent terms with the media. Journalists, recognizing the underrepresentation of the opposition forces[7] and operating in an atmosphere that favoured challenge and criticism, used their resources to create a sort of coalition with the PQ in opposition to the Liberal government.

Between 1976 and 1980, journalists' attitudes to the PQ government remained ambiguous. When the PQ was elected, journalists could not hide their enthusiasm. A legislative correspondent, describing during an interview with the author the atmosphere that prevailed in the press gallery at the time, recalled that:

> When the PQ took power and everyone thought it was going to bring about independence, I tell you it was swinging around here. If you tried to keep a bit cool in the face of all that, you were considered a fossil from the age of the dinosaurs, a "liberal," a "*fédéraste*," when in fact you were simply trying to stay cool ... What was happening was that everyone thought the government was heading toward independence, and it might have been said that journalists, too, were bringing about independence.

After a period of good relations whose duration depended on the journalist and the particular media institution, journalists remained in an equivocal position. They continued to be sympathetic to the sovereignty option, and at the same time their professional ideology encouraged them to be critical and keep a healthy distance between themselves and the government, no matter what its allegiance. Another legislative reporter from this period described the malaise in an interview:

> Under the PQ, I think it was the hardest time for journalists. The great majority were PQ followers. The PQ government was made up of people you worked with in opposition. Ideologically, journalists were close to the government. In human and personal terms, too, we were

very close to the six or seven MNAs who had been in the opposition before 1976. I had played cards with them, and with Mr. Lévesque. So it was harder to do our work because, whether we liked it or not, we had problems finding the bad sides of legislation, of government measures. We shared their point of view, so we did not see a lot of negative things.

Finally, some PQ MNAs found it hard to accept that journalists could be anything but unconditional allies. The mutual discomfort has been described by Lysiane Gagnon who was a legislative reporter at the time:

> With the PQ in office, relationships between politicians and the media were even more complicated. First there was an ideological affinity – a great many journalists and PQ members were of the same generation, had been educated in the same places, shared a similar lifestyle and interests ... And on the government side there was a lot of bitterness toward French-speaking journalists who (it was wrongly thought) should have been unconditional allies, but who, once the famous honeymoon was over, were to rediscover their critical faculties. Journalists, for their part, were uneasy because the party in power was pursuing what some viewed as a collective goal over and above partisan politics. Some journalists, therefore, especially the younger ones, found it harder to keep their distance from the PQ ... Especially because they felt provoked to some degree, almost forced to act this way by the rather systematic hostility of the English-language media toward the PQ. (1980, 12)

This uneasiness could only increase as the referendum approached.

Like other governments, the PQ experienced the erosion of power that encourages journalists to criticize government accomplishments. However, journalists did so without reneging on their sympathy for sovereignty arguments. Benjamin refers to this as "sympathetic journalism." These reporters "were no less critical of politicians at any particular point or concerning any particular decision, but they did not adopt an adversarial stance or keep their distance from politicians. This sympathetic approach is similar to the attitude *Le Devoir* journalists took toward the reforms of the Quiet Revolution" (1979, 75).

Journalists, then, formed a sort of coalition with the forces of sovereignty. Federalists did not hesitate to point out that they made strange bedfellows. Some federal government ministers, including Jean Marchand and André Ouellet, made it their business to remind Radio-Canada reporters that the *Broadcasting Act* assigned them the role of promoting Canadian unity.

By contrast, Quebec's English-speaking journalists did not belong to this coalition: "Anglophone journalists did not share in the consensus concerning either the goal of sovereignty association or the role of the media in relation to the government; the anglophone media were more likely to cover events that might interest Quebec's anglophone minority than they were to attempt to explain the concept of sovereignty association to that minority" (Benjamin 1979, 72).

In the press gallery, it was *Globe and Mail* correspondent William Johnson who functioned as a critic, opposed to both the Lévesque government and francophone journalists. The relationship between Premier Lévesque and the English-language media was often strained.

Return of the Liberals and the Depoliticization of Quebec Society

The ideology of postreferendum Quebec was transformed from its very roots, and this transformation strongly influenced the climate of media–government relations. The 1980s were characterized by what has been called a profound "postreferendum slump." After the referendum failed, the nationalist ideal, which had nourished the dynamic forces of the 1960s and 1970s, lost its appeal, becoming unsuited to the new political and constitutional situation and unable – until the failure of the Meech Lake Accord in 1990 – to arouse enthusiasm.

Even more important to the sociopolitical climate, the erosion of nationalist sentiment in Quebec coincided with economic difficulties early in the decade. The lesson in *realpolitik* that followed the 1981–82 recession brought with it a form of general depoliticization that affected all industrialized societies. The emergence of new individualistic values with a neo-liberal tendency resulted in a profound questioning of the ideological concepts on which the political and social effervescence of the 1960s and 1970s had been based.

Journalists, too, became more conservative and individualistic. Some, like Pierre Maisonneuve (1990), think that Quebec journalists have become "bourgeois newsmongers."

Furthermore, structural changes in the media industry, such as the diversification and multiplication of media firms and the resulting fragmentation of the advertising market, threaten the survival of traditional media enterprises and pressure journalists to be prudent and realistic. Some researchers, like François Demers (1989), professor of journalism at Laval University, think that the current situation marks the dawn of a new journalistic ethic (a "good employee's model") that threatens to undermine journalists' critical faculties.

Although journalists continue to play a traditional role in politics as "watchdogs of democracy," they do not question the legitimacy of government. Nor do they pose as adversaries or allies of the political authorities. Journalistic opposition, where it exists, is no longer ideological, but is strictly "professional." Thus, when the Liberal government of Robert Bourassa was faced with problems or crises, such as the ecological disaster at Saint-Basile Le Grand, the language issues arising from Bill 178 (*An Act to amend the charter of the French language*), the 1989 nurses' strike or the Aboriginal crisis in the summer of 1990, it was mildly criticized by some journalists, but its legitimacy was never challenged.

Conclusion

The attitude of the media toward governments and political parties went from one of dependence, characterized by a press that presented partisan opinions, to one of emancipation or achievement of a degree of autonomy. The media, which had become more concerned with information, progressively defined its new position both through periods of collaboration and of conflict with political authorities. These conflictual or cooperative attitudes of journalists reveal the concerns of the media, the spirit of the times and the evolution of the social climate in Quebec from 1945 to the present, as well as the political preferences of Quebec journalists.

In short, this examination of the evolution of media–government relations over more than 40 years shows above all that, beyond the values of impartiality, honesty, independence and critical thought upon which information journalism is supposed to be based, journalists do not live in an ethereal universe, on the fringes of a world whose convulsions they need only observe and describe. They too experience the effects of changes in social relationships. Like everyone else, journalists participate in a society in constant motion, and they report on political and social developments from an outlook that is neither neutral nor foreign to their social position. When analysing specific situations such as election campaigns, it would be wrong to overlook this quite elementary lesson.

In this area, questions are always asked about the relationship between the media and the government. What about relationships between the media and opposition parties? Studies available in Quebec do not provide a great deal of insight into this topic except to show that when the PQ was the official opposition from 1970 to 1976, it enjoyed the support of a great many journalists. But, more generally, we can note that opposition parties are less able than the government to get access to the media. This access is notably related to the degree of support the electorate gives a party; the distribution of popular support among the parties becomes a sort of guide for journalists to the relative importance they should accord to the different political parties. As well, because it holds power, the government is a more credible source.

The next section of this study, which discusses media coverage of election campaigns, shows how the party of the outgoing government generally gets more coverage; this is, however, often a disadvantage in that it is the target of many attacks from the media.

But these matters are not carved in stone. In the 1973 election, the platform of the PQ (the official opposition) received more coverage than the platform of the Quebec Liberal party, which had formed the outgoing government, because sovereignty was the central issue of that election. At other times, the ideological preferences of media managers influenced editorial choices during election campaigns; for example, in the 1976 election, the *Journal de Montréal*, which supported the PQ, covered the PQ platform more fully and favourably than the program of the Quebec Liberals, the party of the outgoing government.

ROLE OF COMMUNICATORS IN ELECTION CAMPAIGNS

Introduction

How have the media and political parties adapted to each other during this period, particularly during election campaigns? What structural changes in party organizations were produced by new political marketing techniques and the importance that media communications have assumed in politics? Although the documentation is incomplete (not all election campaigns have been covered), we can attempt to answer these questions by examining party communications strategies in provincial election campaigns and the roles played by marketing and communications specialists within the parties.

The 1960s

Learning How to Use Television

Television first appeared in Quebec in 1952, and by 1960 most Quebec households had sets. Quebec residents were so fascinated with the small screen that politicians and parties could no longer ignore it. It can be argued that political communications advisers and politicians used the 1960s to learn television techniques, and that television began to dominate election campaigns in the 1970s.

Television demanded specific communications skills that traditional politicians did not have, accustomed as they were to legislative debates and harangues in public. They had to learn new skills and this took time. In the 1960s, therefore, the press remained the means of communication most used by politicians. Television was used only with caution and in exceptional circumstances; for example, for leaders debates.

As political organizations became aware of the importance of television, specialists in this medium came to exert increasing control over election strategies. In the early 1960s, their influence was substantial but limited. The 1960 election was therefore dominated by traditional organizers, joined by advertising consultants. Marketing and communications represented only one aspect of the activities of election organizers. The communicators' sphere of influence was limited to the leader's image and the circulation of programs and policies. It was only in the following decade that this influence would extend to the selection of candidates, the formulation of policies and the definition of election platforms.

Communicators and the Liberals of Jean Lesage

Liberal Premier Jean Lesage was the first Quebec politician to retain the services of a television expert.[8] More at ease in public assemblies than on a television platform, Lesage hired a former Radio-Canada producer, Maurice Leroux, to steer him through the television studios. Leroux taught Premier Lesage to abandon his traditional, rather bombastic oratorical style and adopt a more intimate approach better suited to television. Lesage was also encouraged to display his talent with numbers; in the broadcasts produced by Leroux, *Lesage vous parle*, he advised the Liberal leader to string together some figures on a blackboard to project the image of competence and concern for communicating his knowledge to the electorate.

The precipitous nature of the 1962 election – the central issue was the nationalization of electricity companies – did not allow Leroux to play a very important role in election planning. Although secondary, his role in the 1962 television debate between Jean Lesage and the Union nationale (UN) leader Daniel Johnson was decisive. Not only was this debate a determining factor in the election, but it also marked a turning point in the evolution of election marketing techniques in Quebec. The next section of this study examines this crucial debate in more detail.

In 1964 and 1965, internal divisions developed in Premier Lesage's entourage, and Leroux, who had become director of public relations in the Quebec Liberal party, left one year before this election. Apparently no one was able to replace him, judging from strategic errors the Liberals committed during the 1966 election. The polls indicated that Lesage was clearly less popular than his party and several of his ministers, but the campaign centred on the image of the leader, who seemed to be campaigning alone. In the end, the UN took office, with the assistance of a favourable electoral map.[9]

From 1960 to 1966, under the Lesage government, a balance was struck among the three types of advisers that surround a premier: party advisers, policy developers and communicators. In the years that followed, the communicators were to increase their hold on the decision-making process and ultimately occupy a central position as participants in policy development (O'Neill and Benjamin 1978).

The 1962 Leaders Debate

The 1962 television debate was a revelation to politicians and to all Quebec people. It showed how important it would be to candidates to master the art of looking good on television. According to journalist Gilles Lesage,

> This 1962 television debate marked an abrupt transition: the end of the hegemony, of the unchallenged reign of the press, and the flamboyant début of the magic screen. The representatives of the daily newspapers were no longer the mandatory intermediaries, the only source of information ... [Television] quickly became the preferred medium for politicians, at least for those who knew how to tame it. The concern now was with image, the right profile to present to the camera, the capsule, the off-the-cuff remark and the punch-line. (1980, 272)

Benjamin (1975), who along with advisers and journalists attended the debate at the television studio, has described the hidden side of this memorable debate.

Jean Lesage, skilfully groomed by his communications adviser Maurice Leroux, scored brilliantly over a completely unprepared Daniel Johnson. Leroux had taken lessons from J.L. Reinsch, who advised President John Kennedy in the famous 1960 debates with Richard Nixon. He returned with one big idea and four recommendations. The central idea, revolutionary at the time, was that image counts more than content. The recommendations that followed were simple: make sure your make-up is good; come to the debate well rested; look at the camera and speak only to the voters (never look at your opponent – don't even pronounce his name); and, finally, make sure the lectern and the microphones are at precisely the right height.

As a former producer, Leroux knew television techniques well; he saw to it that the lecterns and microphone stands were placed at the same height – one that was suitable for Lesage but uncomfortable for Johnson, who was slightly shorter. Each candidate had two microphones in front of him: Lesage's were at the same height, but one of Johnson's mikes had been placed a few inches lower than the other so that Johnson, to speak into both, had to stand in an inelegant and uncomfortable position, with one shoulder lower than the other.

Lesage had spent the afternoon relaxing in a hotel close to the television studio, while Johnson, who had spent the day at public meetings, was tired when he arrived at the studio.

> The electorate's first perception, during the first two seconds of the broadcast, was brutal, perhaps even decisive in the minds of the undecided. Mr. Johnson – fat, without makeup, fatigued, nervous, rummaging in his papers. Mr. Lesage – calm, serene, … looking arrogant … Mr. Johnson appeared ill-prepared for television, referring too often to written documents, carrying his notes in a jumble from his desk to the lectern, responding in a defensive tone to Mr. Lesage's attacks and journalists' questions – while forgetting to look at the camera – and failing to make undecided voters believe that they and they alone held his fate in their hands. (Benjamin 1975, 39–40)

Throughout the debate, Johnson was placed on the defensive, and spent his time replying to the arguments and accusations of his opponent rather than advancing his own proposals. Thanks to the advice of Leroux, Lesage had managed to dominate the debate through image: "Sure of himself, superb, Premier Lesage was master of the situation; he dominated it, and his image-makers were ecstatic. The neophyte leader of the UN and the opposition, Mr. Daniel Johnson, was left floundering in the shadows as 'Danny Boy,' a crude hick. He was lamentable" (Lesage 1980, 272).

Communicators and the UN of Daniel Johnson

The 1962 television debate was a lesson for Johnson. He fully realized the importance of the leader's image and how negative his public image was.

Indeed, between 1960 and 1966 Daniel Johnson's public image presented him with some serious problems. He was depicted by the newspapers – which were unfriendly – as a traditional politician, a bit deceitful, given to making demagogic, negative speeches. It was not until 1964 that he found advisers capable of rebuilding his image: Gaby Lalande, president of SOPEQ, an affiliate of the American advertising firm Young and Rubicam; Jean Loiselle, a former Radio-Canada producer; and Paul Gros d'Aillon, manager of the Unionist daily *Montréal-Matin* (O'Neill and Benjamin 1978; Bernier 1988, 73).

They persuaded Johnson to adopt a more direct style and a more genuine tone when speaking to voters. During the 1966 campaign, however, the communicators' role was confined to issues pertaining to the communication of the UN message. Their job was to conceive an advertising campaign that would attack the Liberals' weak point, their leader Jean Lesage, and find some nice packaging for the UN message.

It was only after Johnson's victory that Jean Loiselle's influence on the new premier increased. No longer limited to working only on the leader's image – he was the one who convinced Johnson to wear his glasses all the time to look more serious, and who had Johnson's jacket pockets sewn shut so he couldn't put his hands in them – he began to participate in strategic decisions. It was Loiselle who decided which ministers and MNAs would appear on television. He also played a decisive role in negotiations with the hospital employees in 1966 and in the 1967 teachers' strike, and did it so well that Johnson requested his presence whenever he had to negotiate.

Long manhandled by the media, Johnson relied increasingly on his communicators, who did not hesitate to short-circuit the government's departmental information officers and even ministerial press attachés (Lesage 1980, 273).

His concept of communications and his expertise enabled Loiselle to penetrate the circle of decision makers. He thought of communications as a whole, integrating public relations, information, advertising and marketing. In his view, communicators no longer confine themselves to packaging the message; they participate in defining the message, that is, in developing decisions and policies.

Communicators first appeared in election campaigns in 1960. During the decade that followed, they helped make marketing and communications fundamental aspects of election strategies. The 1960s were the decade of apprenticeship in television. Communications techniques and television did not become dominant until the following decade, however, specifically during the 1970 and 1973 Quebec Liberal party (QLP) campaigns.

The presence of communicators in election strategy teams and premiers' entourages had an impact on the organization and structure of parties. In Benjamin's view (1976), the parties relied less and less on traditional structures, the riding "election fixers." The focus was on selling the election platform within an overall strategy, with less reliance on the local organization. Election platforms also declined in importance, as strategists came to concentrate their efforts on the leader's image.

Communicators also intervened in candidate selection. During the 1966 election, for example, the UN sought out candidates with whom the local electorate would identify, regardless of their ideologies.[10] These different trends were to increase during the 1970s in the struggle between the QLP and the PQ.

We must add that, in the area of government information, the boundaries between politics and administration were not strict. L'Office d'Information et de Publicité du Quebec (OIPQ), created by Lesage and responsible for government information and publicity, actually assumed a degree of executive power. Johnson reformed OIPQ, but kept it under direct executive control. Bernier notes that "the 1966–70 period was the most productive for the development of government information and publicity services, on the one hand, and government executive control over these two functions, on the other" (1988, 77). In fact, under Johnson, the people responsible for government information and publicity (Gaby Lalande, Jean Loiselle, Paul Gros d'Aillon, and Roger Cyr, head of OIPQ) also directed the UN communications strategy! This practice aroused the indignation of journalists and the opposition parties.

The 1970s

The 1970 Election

The 1970 election marked an important stage in Quebec political life. In the first place, it was an election in which political forces realigned (Lemieux et al. 1970); the breakdown in allegiances fractured traditional bipartisanism. After the election of 29 April 1970, four political organizations with appreciable electoral bases were represented in the National Assembly (see table 2.1).

Furthermore, the 1970 campaign, like the one in 1973, marked a high point in the use of American image-making and marketing techniques (Benjamin 1976). Political marketing techniques, which at least the wealthier parties began to use systematically, did not differ from commercial marketing techniques. They were based on three fundamental operations. First, they involved polling, which became more and more precise and sophisticated, to measure voter attitudes and identify the needs, concerns, priorities, preferences and aspirations of the various categories of the electorate. Second, they involved developing a "product" – a campaign concept and a leader's image – that

Table 2.1
Results of the election of 29 April 1970 for the four largest parties

Party	% of votes	Number of seats
Liberal party	45.4	72
Parti québécois	23.1	7
Union nationale	19.6	17
Ralliement créditiste	11.1	12

Source: Directeur général des élections du Québec.

Note: Percentages do not equal 100 due to rounding.

corresponded to the electorate's desires and state of mind, particularly those of undecided voters. Third, they used communication and persuasion techniques to make the electorate aware that the product existed and to persuade them that only this product could meet their needs and aspirations.

Communicators and the UN of Jean-Jacques Bertrand

The UN's communications strategy in 1970 was born of a divided party headed, since Johnson's death, by an ill-advised leader unable to play effectively by the new rules of the political communications game.

After winning the 1966 election, the UN remained divided. Daniel Johnson managed to keep his party together only at the price of substantial ambiguity on the party's constitutional policies. After his death, the leadership struggle between Jean-Guy Cardinal and Jean-Jacques Bertrand further divided the party and tarnished its image.

The government led by Jean-Jacques Bertrand also had to confront serious difficulties: the economic slow-down that followed Expo 67, agitation by students and workers, and the government's inability to respond to the language problem with the 1969 adoption of Bill 63 (*An Act to promote the French language in Quebec*), which allowed freedom to choose one's language of instruction. Unable to control his party, Bertrand could not cope with the problems facing the government.

It was, therefore, a divided and undermined party that went to the voters in 1970, its strength so sapped that for the QLP the opponent to beat was not the outgoing UN government, but a newcomer, the PQ.

Bertrand's image, which was generally positive when he succeeded Johnson, quickly became very negative. Given bad advice on communications, his blunders multiplied. His television appearances were disastrous. Some supporters later claimed that Bertrand was the victim of a conspiracy cooked up by the Johnson-era political advisers and communicators, who had supported Jean-Guy Cardinal in the party leadership race (O'Neill and Benjamin 1978).

In the 1970 campaign, there were too many advisers involved in developing Bertrand's communications strategy. It was poorly coordinated and, above all, designed by people Bertrand did not fully trust, several of whom did not genuinely support the new leader.

Liberal Communicators and the 1970 Election

In contrast to the UN, the Liberals, now led by Robert Bourassa, were endowed with a thoroughly modern communications and marketing machine.

In 1969 the Liberals commissioned a poll from an American firm, Social Research, which indicated that the Quebec people felt a "strong need for confidence." Their major concern was economic recovery, and they thought that only leadership that was both dynamic and conciliatory could help achieve this goal. According to the authors of the survey, the new Liberal leader should have some essential characteristics: he should be "representative of the Quebec people, 'strong' enough to cope with Ottawa and 'able to deal with all aspects of an extremely complex urbanized community'" (Benjamin 1975, 65). The Liberals used this description as a profile to find the person who would succeed Jean Lesage.

Paul Desrochers, an adviser to Lesage who was well versed in U.S. political marketing techniques, was convinced that the young Liberal MNA Robert Bourassa was the leader they were looking for. Once Lesage resigned, Desrochers placed himself at Bourassa's disposal, without waiting to find out who the other leadership candidates would be. He worked so hard and so effectively – always drawing on American techniques, especially those that had put Kennedy at the head of the Democrats – that Bourassa, who was not well known in those days, was elected leader of the Liberal party on the first ballot at the December 1969 convention. After that success, there was no limit to the hopes the Liberals placed in Robert Bourassa and Paul Desrochers.

The next step was to sell this new leader to the voters, which was the purpose of the 1970 election campaign. The campaign theme – the promise of 100 000 jobs – was inspired by the Social Research poll. The QLP had amassed a very handsome election war chest; this money was invested in the purchase of air time and television equipment. The Liberal election campaign in 1970 took place almost exclusively on television, and focused on the image of the new leader.

> The marketing strategy of the Liberal communicators was drawn from J. McGinniss' book *The Selling of the President*, which tells how Richard Nixon was elected President of the United States in 1968 through rigid and constant control of his television appearances, the only appearances he made during the campaign. It went far: from makeup to complete control over all images the viewers would see, the choice of questions that would be put to him and the voters he would meet, etc. In 1970, Mr. Bourassa's election campaign was similarly conducted on television. Sixty percent of the advertising budget was devoted to this medium, and divided three ways: electronic assemblies, television bulletins manufactured by the Liberals (the so-called canned information), and commercials. (Benjamin 1975, 69)

The electronic assemblies were television programs that took the place of the traditional mass meetings and were broadcast by regional television stations as "meetings with the candidate." More than one million viewers watched these broadcasts.

In addition, the Liberals sent out a technical team to film the highlights of Robert Bourassa's day and send selected images to television stations for the news. Radio-Canada did not use them, but private regional stations used them extensively, since they often did not have any other visual materials to illustrate late evening news broadcasts (Benjamin 1975, 70). In short, this was a campaign conducted from the television studio without direct contact with voters.

The QLP's major opponent, the PQ, did not have the same financial resources at that time. It did, however, have a significant number of enthusiastic party members. The PQ therefore turned to public meetings, where it was on familiar ground. These meetings brought together crowds of supporters, and were reported as media events in the newspapers and on television. The meetings also had the advantage of conditioning and stimulating party activists while enabling the PQ to distinguish itself as the party that valued grassroots participation.

The 1973 Election

In 1973 as in 1970, the Liberal party campaign relied on the theme of the separatist threat. The PQ then came up with the idea of countering the Liberal tactic with its own step-by-step policy of not setting the sovereignty process in motion without first holding a referendum. This tactic, aimed at assuaging voters' fears, was ultimately successful in 1976.

The communications plan in the 1973 election was based on that of 1970, and trends observed previously, such as the importance of television, were reinforced.

Benjamin (1975, 167) relates that, as early as July 1973, a leader of the QLP told him that the Liberal campaign would be carried totally in news reports broadcast daily at 10:30 PM on the TVA and Radio-Canada television networks. Also, the campaign would be conducted without the assistance of journalists, whom Liberal communicators saw as political adversaries. The marketing effort would rely on the Liberals' own perception of the electorate, which – the polls indicated – was calling for the pursuit of social peace and a fiscal respite for the middle class.

The Liberals played on the fact that news broadcasters had to give equal time to the major parties. The Liberals could count on one minute per evening. As in 1970, they formed their own television team and each day sent the outlying regional stations images carefully selected and controlled to create a favourable impression of Robert Bourassa.

The following method was adopted: each day Mr. Bourassa would visit only Liberal party committee rooms, he would stop for about 30 minutes only, give a little pep talk conveying a reassuring image, and be loudly applauded since the only spectators would be party members. These would be the only images available; the television stations would have to show them in the evening or be accused of devoting more time to the other parties. Mr. Bourassa repeated the same pep talk in one committee room after another, but the television audience could not see this: they saw only a leader meeting his supporters and receiving their applause. (Benjamin 1975, 172)

Although the QLP offered the television networks nice images to broadcast in their news reports, they did nothing to facilitate the work of print journalists. The candidate travelled by rented airplane and was escorted on the ground by motorcycle police. As well, the Liberal leader continued his tour at such speed that print journalists did not have the time to write and file their dispatches. Thus Bourassa, inaccessible to journalists, was able to conduct his campaign without coming in contact with anyone but the hand-picked faithful.

Also eliminated were uncontrolled walkabouts. The number of times the candidate plunged into a crowd could be counted on the fingers of one hand, Benjamin says (1975). He did so in an unorganized event only once, at Baie Comeau five days before the election, and it was a failure.[11] As Benjamin describes it: "Mr. Bourassa was booed when he attacked PQ followers and some placards labelled him a *vendu* [sellout]; in short, it was a true public meeting with all the attendant risks" (ibid., 172).

As in 1970, the PQ did not have the financial resources to compete with the QLP on their terms. They pursued the strategy they had adopted in 1970, centred on public meetings. The PQ had to count on the press corps and on direct contacts in the community. While Robert Bourassa would visit four or five regions a day, René Lévesque would spend at least 24 hours in each city, meeting the local media and as many people as possible to explain the PQ platform.

During the 1973 campaign the PQ carried off a publicity stunt that backfired: the party released the "Year One Budget" of a sovereign Quebec. The QLP called for a television debate on this issue, and the PQ quickly agreed. The debate was to be between the finance specialists among the candidates of the four parties on the ballot. It was the party's big chance to convince the undecided and allay fears about its plans. But the rules were defined in such a way that Jacques Parizeau, the PQ spokesman, had to defend his budget against three opponents, one of whom (Raymond Garneau of the Liberals) dwelt on substantive issues. At the same time UN and Ralliement créditiste (RC) criticisms dealt with the political consequences and the emotional aspect of the matter. Parizeau made his case by referring to technical data that the average voter did not understand and using learned arguments that only specialists in economic questions could grasp. In short, Parizeau spoke to his debating partners in the studio and forgot that the real public was composed of undecided voters sitting in front of their television screens. "The professorial tone and the arguments on elasticity rates apparently failed to convince either the undecided voter or the Parti québécois activist, neither of whom approved of the élitist and technocratic image Mr. Parizeau and his party presented that night" (Benjamin 1975, 159).

PQ supporters think this debate was the campaign event that caused them the most harm. Parizeau, aware of his failure, even considered tendering his resignation to the party leader.

The Liberal and PQ campaigns may be summed up in one reporter's phrase: "*son et lumière* [a sound and light show] versus human contact." Benjamin employed a different metaphor: "On the one hand, a marketing campaign manufactured by MBAs, on the other hand, an intellectually conceived strategy that the PQ thought stirring" (1975, 174).

The 1973 election was decisive for the small parties. It marked the beginning of the end for the Union nationale led by Gabriel Loubier, which did not elect a single candidate, while the RC, led by Yvon Dupuis, saw its legislative deputation melt from 12 MNAs in 1970 to two in 1973.

It seems clear that these two parties did not have the expertise and financial resources needed to sound out the opinions of the voters or to get a modern election campaign off the ground. They had to rely on their own perceptions in designing their message and on journalists' dispatches to communicate it. And, without the advice of communications experts, the leaders of both parties stumbled from one blunder to another so that media coverage, primarily on television, was generally unfavourable to them.

The UN leader, Gabriel Loubier, was leading a disorganized and moribund party. He kept repeating throughout the campaign that the reporters were miscounting the number of people attending the party meetings, while night after night the television cameras showed viewers the empty halls the leader was addressing.

The RC campaign likewise revealed the weakness of the party's organization, and showed a leader who was unable to control his temper and unskilled in political communications. Yvon Dupuis' negative speeches, which compared the Liberals to socialists, and his sudden mood changes did substantial harm to his image and credibility. He publicly went after the television crews and, as the ultimate blunder, he even expelled the Radio-Canada television crew from one of his meetings.

In short, the UN and RC participation in the communications game was a total failure in the 1973 election. The explanation for this fiasco lies partly in their lack of resources – money and expertise – needed to conduct a modern election campaign in which communications and marketing had become the dominant strategic considerations.

Influence of Communicators under the Bourassa Government

From 1970 on, publicity and marketing consultants occupied a predominant position in Premier Bourassa's entourage. According to O'Neill and Benjamin (1978), Robert Bourassa had a clear vision of what he wanted to do as premier, but he ignored the marketing strategy he needed to succeed. He therefore relied completely on his advisers Paul Desrochers and especially Charles Denis, who were the architects of the 1970 and 1973 victories.

While it was Paul Desrochers who "discovered" Bourassa thanks to the Social Research poll, O'Neill and Benjamin (1978) say it was Charles Denis, his press attaché, who "moulded" him, to the point that his opponents viewed Bourassa as a genuine puppet, the product of his image-makers' talents. Paradoxically, it was Bourassa's anxiety over image that would end up tarnishing that image.

> The thing that struck ... every observer as early as 1970 was the scope (in comparison with the previous decade) of the methods Mr. Bourassa used to project his image and the different nature of his marketing techniques ... Charles Denis acquired the power he had with Mr. Bourassa by providing him with a range of techniques that would get him elected, then re-elected in 1973 with a majority of 102 out of 110 members in the National Assembly. And it was a closed image structure that Mr. Denis first used in the 1970 election campaign, a structure that was controlled in all its details, of a candidate who had changed his hairstyle and would do his entire campaign – this was an innovation – in a television studio. (O'Neill and Benjamin 1978, 169)

Charles Denis' influence was not confined to images and the use of techniques. He held an important decision making role, occupying a higher position than Maurice Leroux in the time of Jean Lesage or Jean Loiselle in the time of Daniel Johnson. According to O'Neill and Benjamin, "up to the end of 1974, the premier did hardly a thing – in the party, the legislature or public – without first consulting his press attaché. In this sense, Mr. Denis exercised a clearly more significant authority than was associated with his duties as the Premier's press attaché" (1978, 170).

With Charles Denis, the QLP governed through polls. The premier always wanted to know what support he had before he acted. Using polls and monitoring the print and electronic media, Charles Denis perfected a sophisticated system of feedback and surveillance of the "collective reflexes" of the Quebec people.

In 1974, the government's popularity went into free fall and Charles Denis lost his influence with the premier, who was then advised by a team of young press and political attachés. But they simply applied the same concepts that Charles Denis had used. They were unable to stem the tide.

Benjamin studied Quebec election campaigns from 1960 to 1973 and concluded:

> An analysis of the five most recent campaigns becomes, in fact, a study of the growing influence of the communications advisers on the decision-making process. The new technology of politics in North America has encouraged party leaders to rely more on image-makers than on regional leaders or party intellectuals in developing the message. As in the United States – but 30 years later – Quebec has come under the influence of partisan communications advisers concurrently with the development of the mass media, particularly television. (1975, 181)

Benjamin notes an example in the Liberal campaigns of 1970 and 1973: "The Liberal party's general staff was ignored in favour of images created in isolation, which showed a self-confident leader who knew how to be likeable; these were the qualities television viewers were looking for. In this case, Liberal communications advisers found manipulation techniques more appropriate than participation techniques" (1975, 182, 184).

The 1976 Election

From 1970 to 1976, Robert Bourassa's government had to confront problems that opened the way for the PQ. As soon as he was installed in office, Bourassa was faced with the October Crisis, an unprecedented emergency for which he was ill prepared. Many observers criticized his inability to stand up to the federal government, which was thought to be seeking to take advantage of the situation to crush the independence movement. The Liberal government also had to cope with serious labour conflicts, in particular with the unions' 1972 Common Front, which ended with the leaders of Quebec's three largest union federations in jail. The wrecking of construction sites at James Bay and strikes in the public sector served to undermine the government's credibility in its relations with workers.

Bourassa also cut himself off from his traditional supporters. The federal Liberals did not approve of his autonomist rhetoric – intended to counter the rise of the PQ – while anglophones criticized the adoption of Bill 22 (*Official Language Act*), which made French the official language of Quebec and limited freedom to choose one's language of instruction. And finally, the government failed to silence persistent rumours of corruption and mismanagement.

So the premier decided on a double-or-nothing gamble; in 1976 he called an early election in the hope of rebuilding his support. The polls told the Liberals that anti-separatists outnumbered people satisfied with the government. So the goal was to win the support of the anti-separatists, as well as the support of those who were satisfied (Bernard 1976, 17). They decided once again to play the "separatist threat" card. This was a strategic error, since the PQ had already sidestepped the problem with its step-by-step policy and its promise to hold a referendum. This meant the PQ could rally dissatisfied voters, even if they were not all supporters of independence.

During the 1976 campaign, the Liberal party adopted an approach similar to the winning strategy of 1970 and 1973 but, as Dupuis notes, "Mr. Bourassa's image concept, as developed in 1970 and 1973, failed to stand up in the political context of 1976" (1986, 131). Marketing techniques and communications strategies were of no avail; the QLP obtained only 33.8 percent of the votes and lost the election.

The PQ also relied on modern political marketing techniques and communications experts. But unlike the Liberals, most of the PQ candidates were themselves able communicators, advised by press attachés from the world of journalism. A number of former journalists ran and were elected, among them Lise Payette, Denise Leblanc-Bantey, Pierre de Bellefeuille, Richard Guay, Jean-Pierre Charbonneau and Gérald Godin.

The best salesperson of the PQ product was René Lévesque himself. He had the attributes of a charismatic leader and projected an image with which Quebec people identified. Political scientist Léon Dion wrote in November 1976, "René Lévesque produces an exceptional synthesis of the major characteristics of a charismatic leader. For 16 years, his greatness has been to intuitively embody a particular national image that is deeply rooted in the history and people of Quebec" (quoted in O'Neill and Benjamin 1978, 237–38).

The PQ leader had no need of advice from communicators; he had been a journalist for 30 years and one of the great television stars of the 1950s. Communications experts would have a small role to play with René Lévesque; his entourage did not contain the kind of image-makers that surrounded Robert Bourassa.

The 1980 Referendum

The 1980 referendum was one of the high points in the history of political communications in Quebec. A mass consultation of popular opinion, the referendum had features that distinguished it from traditional elections. It therefore called for slightly different persuasion and propaganda techniques.

Importance of the Press in the Referendum

Unlike a modern election campaign, the referendum campaign was not a contest of personalities, candidates and party leaders. It counterposed two ideas, two proposals that voters had to understand. Although identification with the leaders of each camp remained a significant element of persuasion, the opponents had to argue in support of their option and explain how it was better than that of the opposition.

That is why television did not play the dominant role in the 1980 referendum campaign that it had in election campaigns. Although television was a factor, it could not be what it was in elections; the main channel for convincing voters. The task was no longer to communicate solely through images – although symbols played a significant role in the referendum campaign – but to appeal to citizens' reason.

Moreover, the strategists of the No Committee (*Comité des Québécois pour le non*) were aware that their leader and spokesman, Claude Ryan, was not very telegenic; therefore, other means of communicating the message would have to be given higher priority. The pro-sovereignty forces, for their part, were accustomed to favouring the press and mass rallies.

Attitude of Journalists during the Referendum

For Quebec journalists, referendum coverage posed a fundamental problem. The election of the PQ had already presented them with an ethical problem. How, in the context of a polarized society, were they to deal fairly and professionally with a government with whose social model they agreed completely? Journalists could take a critical attitude toward the day-to-day management of government affairs. But how should they stand in a crucial and decisive debate on the sovereignty option itself? Would they have to drop the credo of objectivity? On the other hand, would concern for objectivity lead to self-censorship, and ultimately to injustice to the sovereignty option? Would the fear of going too far prevent journalists from going far enough?

The referendum also raised a question about the relationship between journalists, who were sympathetic to the PQ cause, and media managers, who were generally opposed to sovereignty. Who, ultimately, was to determine the policy on coverage and newspaper content? What point of view was going to prevail in the pages of the dailies?

Referendum coverage thus gave rise to a debate within the intellectual and journalistic community. Some journalists and observers sought to ensure that the press, which was important to the referendum, would cover the campaign appropriately, although most newspaper owners opposed the sovereignty proposal (Sauvageau 1979).

Lachapelle and Noiseux write:

> Journalists were torn between their pro-PQ sympathies and their job. This conflict went back to the election of the PQ. Since then, journalists had seldom been so watchful and critical of the government and its legitimacy. Fearing a loss of credibility and accusations that they were government mouthpieces, journalists disciplined themselves with the result that, in the constitutional and referendum debate, the press was quite colourless. As Pierre Godin pointed out, "Quebec journalists feel guilty for harbouring sentiments that are almost too shameful to mention about the allure of the Parti québécois or sovereignty ideas, and in reaction they tend to censor themselves, to sterilize themselves" (Radio-Canada 3 March 1980). The press therefore preferred to sit it out in pseudo-neutrality or pseudo-objectivity, for fear of exhibiting excessive partisanship. This conduct could only satisfy the media owners since it meant that conflicts were avoided, especially over the editorial policy of the daily newspapers. (1980, 139–40)

Strategy of the Comité des Québécois pour le non

While some intellectuals exhorted journalists to take a position – or at least to go beyond the speeches of the political participants and develop a critical approach – the No supporters tried, as Lachapelle and Noiseux point out, to take advantage of the journalists' difficult situation by exerting pressure on them and forcing them to censor themselves:

> The strategy of the No supporters and the federalist forces was now a simple one: let go of the journalists' boat and, if it seemed to touch the opposite bank, brandish the spectre of the relationship between journalists and Yes supporters to get the journalists to shove off from this swampy shore and return to the mainstream of neutrality.
>
> The No supporters who were acquainted with the stifling situation of Quebec journalists did not hesitate to go to war against all the media once the referendum campaign was officially launched. (1980, 142–43)

Claude Ryan, himself a former journalist, called for the establishment of a surveillance committee to guarantee the journalists' objectivity, a suggestion poorly received by some journalists.[12] The Quebec Press Council nevertheless established its own committee, based on the Complaints Committee, to examine complaints related to the referendum campaign.

The pro-sovereignty forces conducted the referendum campaign the same way they fought the 1976 election, certainly placing great emphasis on television reports and bowing to their requirements, but without ignoring the national and regional press. Because of the rather untelegenic character of their spokesman, Claude Ryan, the strategists of the No Committee sought instead to shield him from television cameras. Even in their advertising, they did not use the image of Ryan, who unlike René Lévesque was less popular than his proposals. And since they had some success with public rallies before the referendum campaign began, the members of the No Committee resolved not to emphasize the media directly but rather to use public meetings covered by the media to rally their supporters and get their message across.

> Each assembly organized by the No Committee followed the same scenario, the objective of which was, in part, to complicate the journalists' work. Several speakers would address the crowd, and Claude Ryan would close the discussion. Strangely enough, these meetings were always too long and by the time the leader of the No Committee was introduced, the deadlines for the print and electronic media had often passed. Claude Ryan was quick to protest loudly that the initial weeks of the referendum campaign had been biased in the media. However, it was well known that Mr. Ryan, with his theatrical style, preferred to avoid television cameras because his image did not come across well on the tube. When journalists dared to ask Mr. Ryan and the No strategists to shorten their meetings or move Mr. Ryan's speech so the media could report it, the abrupt reply was "Our campaign is designed for the public and not for the media or the small screen." (*Le Devoir* 9 May 1980) (Lachapelle and Noiseux 1980, 143)

What, in fact, the strategists of the No Committee were apparently seeking was media coverage of their public meetings, especially on television, but without establishing too close a relationship between the federalist option and the image of Claude Ryan.

Federal Participation in the Referendum Campaign
The federal government's participation in the referendum campaign was decisive (Cloutier 1980). In its 1978 *Referendum Act*, the PQ govern-

ment had taken care to establish rules to assure a balance between the sovereignty and federalist forces in the referendum campaign and to establish how much money the two "umbrella committees" would be authorized to spend. Federal intervention shattered this equilibrium.

On the day the referendum campaign began, the federal MPs began a debate on Canadian unity in the House of Commons; it was televised live, and the Quebec media could not help but report it. No one in this debate took the side of the sovereignty option. Moreover, the debate occurred at a time when the National Assembly had suspended its own operations, thus depriving the PQ forces of an equivalent advantage.

Before the campaign, the federal government established major advertising campaigns praising the merits of various government services. During the campaign, the federal government undertook a multi-media advertising offensive on radio and television, in daily and weekly newspapers and on billboards to support the efforts of the No Committee. This federal campaign was directed by a cabinet minister, Jean Chrétien, who also sat on the steering body of the No Committee, "so the federal advertising was not only added to that of the Committee, but was also coordinated at the Committee's highest level" (Cloutier 1980, 80).

The Yes Committee (*Comité des Québécois pour le oui*) filed a complaint with the director general of party financing in Quebec, who was responsible for administering referendum expenditures under the *Referendum Act*. The director general applied to Superior Court for an interim interlocutory injunction prohibiting federal advertising, but the Court held that it was not within its jurisdiction and referred him to the Conseil du referéndum. The latter body ruled several days before the referendum that the application had no legal basis: the federal government was not required to comply with the Quebec *Referendum Act*, because the federal government is not subject to provincial law (Patenaude 1981).

The 1981 Election
Before the 1981 campaign began, the QLP were confident they would win, convinced that the failure of the referendum in May 1980 demonstrated the strength of their election machine. Moreover, the polls favoured them. The PQ, divided over the shelving of the sovereignty option, appeared to be having difficulty emerging from its postreferendum depression. And there was little hope that the Union nationale, which had failed to get organized, could divide the antigovernment vote (Bernard and Descôteaux 1981, 55, 56).

Journalists, too, predicted a Liberal victory. Lévesque grumbled that the press harped on the possibility.

Yet the PQ won. In contrast to what usually happens, the 1981 election was decided during the campaign. According to Bernard and Descôteaux (1981), the PQ victory can be explained by the party's capacity for organization and by the communications and marketing strategies of both leading parties.

As an organization, the PQ was better prepared for the election than the QLP. It had more resources,[13] more members and activists and a more effective organization. Fund-raising is a good example of this: it took the QLP five months to raise $3.3 million, while the PQ was able to raise more than that ($3.4 million) in a single month.

The PQ also had access to marketing and communications techniques that were more modern and effective than those of the QLP.

> The Parti québécois used polls and simulations to identify categories of electors whose support it had not yet won but could – at little cost – and to learn how to reach these voters and influence them positively. Parti québécois representatives openly admitted that the influence of political scientists, sociologists, psychologists and communications specialists, many of whom belonged to the party, had forced the leaders to consider using modern social science methods. Party members who specialized in these methods volunteered to apply them to the election. (Bernard and Descôteaux 1981, 124)

It should be remembered that communications in the 1981 election were atypical. Strikes at Radio-Canada and Radio-Québec forced organizers to turn to the print media. The other large broadcast media enterprises, which did not have the resources of Radio-Canada, were limited to covering the leaders' tours and gave up on the sectoral and regional debates.

The PQ strategy relied, of course, on its leader, René Lévesque, who had a greater sense of image and facility with a punch-line than his opponent, Claude Ryan, then leader of the QLP. In spite of this defeat in the referendum, Lévesque enjoyed more prestige with the electorate than Ryan. The PQ also relied on its show-business sense. The party organized rallies that drew thousands of supporters, attracting media attention and creating a strong positive impression among voters. Even with Lévesque to personify the party's platform and ideas, PQ supporters also wanted to show that their leader was surrounded by a solid ministerial team. Toward the end of the campaign, René Lévesque, confident of victory, became more inconspicuous to avoid committing errors.

In 1976, the PQ had managed to overcome voter reticence on the national question by promising to hold a referendum on sovereignty. The party adopted a similar strategy in 1981; it removed the sovereignty issue by promising not to hold any referendum on this issue during its next term in office. "As in 1976, the PQ leaders were able to remove the national question from their campaign advertising and speeches, despite the feelings of many members. But to do otherwise would no doubt have helped lead the Liberal party to power" (Bernard and Descôteaux 1981, 102).

In contrast to all this was the public image of the Liberal leader. Claude Ryan looked severe and aroused little sympathy. This was why he refused to base his election strategy on his image. Moreover, his traditional views on election campaigning scarcely inclined him to take such matters seriously. The Liberal strategy was instead to increase opportunities for personal encounters between candidates and voters.[14] The Liberals also sought to get their message across through the local and regional media. Early in the campaign, Ryan took a quick tour through Quebec to meet Liberal organizers and the regional media. The national reporters accompanying him were perplexed, since they had little hard news to report (Bernard and Descôteaux 1981, 68).

Although communications and election strategy advisers were plentiful in the PQ camp, Ryan refused to allow himself to be advised by experts from outside the party, preferring to rely on party organizers he trusted. While the PQ made extensive use of modern political marketing techniques and polls, the Liberals preferred the less expensive, but less reliable, technique of spot-checks, and the leader preferred to rely on his own perception of the electorate.

As Bernard and Descôteaux point out, "the [PQ] talent for communications on the one hand and the [Liberals'] lack of communications strategy on the other soon became either significant assets or liabilities when the leaders' deeds and actions were being scrutinized daily and today's faux-pas could be tomorrow's headline" (1981, 67).

The early campaign polls indicated a high rate of satisfaction with the government, and confirmed that Lévesque was the more popular leader. In a few months, the government had managed to reverse an unfavourable public opinion trend established between 1978 and 1980.

The target of numerous attacks since becoming party leader, Ryan had to take the defensive and go to some lengths to rebut allegations against him.

Journalists thought the campaign dull. Even without Radio-Canada, newspaper circulation stagnated, although election campaigns generally increase readership.

As the Liberals became more certain that victory would elude them, they stepped up their criticism of the media, which they accused of favouring the PQ.

PQ television advertising, which presented the star candidates in a "natural" setting, was lively but controlled (Bernard and Descôteaux

1981, 127). Liberal advertising was unexciting. PQ newspaper display ads conveyed positive arguments and dealt with specific items (the 1976 promises that had been realized), while the Liberal messages were vague and negative (the disastrous economic situation, the weakened position within Canada and the disturbing increase in bureaucracy).

Bernard and Descôteaux think the Liberals made two mistakes: they did not emphasize the mass media, and they tried to reach the entire electorate instead of concentrating their efforts on those voters – particularly the undecided – among whom they could hope to make substantial gains at relatively little cost. The result of this strategy was that the media covered only the Liberal leader, whose public image was weak, and this coverage was in situations over which the party had little control. In short, the Liberals lost the election because they tried to go against the trend of modern election campaigns, which are based on mass communications and marketing.

The 1985 Election

During the 1970s, the PQ relied on its leader's image and its broad membership base. The imperatives of government were to change this situation:

> The ascent to power brought about a very clear differentiation between the caucus and the party membership. Outside election campaigns, the former took pride of place, and this tended to cool the members' ardour. The shock of the 1980 referendum defeat and the 1982 repatriation of the Constitution also accentuated demobilization. The recession and the government's 1982 decision to reduce public employees' wages affected a significant portion of the PQ's clientele and cut into its support. Finally, shelving the idea of independence in 1984 produced a genuine split, leading to the departure of members who were the strongest advocates of independence and several leading ministers. René Lévesque's resignation and his replacement by Pierre-Marc Johnson could not overcome the resulting disarray before the 1985 general election. (Linteau et al. 1986, 644)

In 1985, therefore, Pierre-Marc Johnson was leading a divided and disoriented party that now faced a Liberal party that had reorganized around Robert Bourassa. The two parties relied on the same themes: they favoured a less interventionist state and broke from the pattern of the Quiet Revolution that the PQ had resumed in the late 1970s. The policies of both parties concentrated on the same issue: managing slower growth. The voters, tired of the PQ, turned to Bourassa.

In 1985 the weakened and divided PQ had little chance to form another government. As such, the new leader of the party, Pierre-Marc Johnson, opted for a soft, subdued approach in both his speeches and party publicity.

Although there are no thorough analyses of communications strategies employed in the 1985 election, the commentaries that were located for this study indicate nevertheless that the election was not dominated by image-makers. The influence of communicators and other image-makers appears to have been limited to specific communications functions. For example, some journalists noted during the election that "the era of communications specialists, *éminences grises*, image-makers and political fixers, launched by Jean Lesage in 1960, is over" (Deshaies and Germain 1985, 32).

The communicators, publicity and marketing advisers, and pollsters had not disappeared from the electoral landscape, but their duties now seemed essentially technical and designed to enable the candidates and parties to get their messages across. This was something new in comparison with the 1970s.

Communications seemed to have lost, in the eyes of politicians, the magical quality that had made veritable gurus out of advertising specialists. The leaders who contested the 1985 election were seasoned politicians; they had learned to master basic communications techniques (especially on television) and to integrate communications into their strategic decisions. There was no longer a monopoly on such expertise.

Some of the cruder manipulation techniques, such as the distribution of video cassettes to television stations, which the Liberals in particular had used between 1970 and 1976, had been loudly criticized by the media, encouraging parties to be more prudent and reserved.

The candidates' styles had also changed. Robert Bourassa provides an eloquent example. In 1985, his style was quite different from that of 1970. In the 1970s, Bourassa had been strongly influenced and guided by Paul Desrochers, Charles Denis and the like. He learned some lessons from that experience and took advantage of his political exile to prepare in minute detail for his return – he was no longer dependent on anyone. He owed his return to his constant work, between 1980 and 1983, to link the party membership to the electorate. Between the referendum campaign and his return to the Liberal leadership, Bourassa visited every part of Quebec; he made himself available and took advantage of every opportunity to meet voters and solicit their support for his eventual return to active politics. Wherever he spoke, he projected the image of a reflective man matured by experience (Dupuis 1986). He still consulted communication strategists but it was he who made the decisions on both political and strategic issues.

Bourassa no longer cultivated artificial images; he was uneasy with the show-business spectacle that the big American-style presidential campaigns have become – and that the leading federal parties try to imitate, with some success (Cormier 1991) – and he adopted a more natural approach.

On the eve of the 1985 election, journalist Georges-Hébert Germain described Bourassa in the following words:

> During his first term in office, he was accompanied everywhere by his famous hairstylist-dresser, Bernard Marty, who took care of his cowlicks and knotted his tie. He also relied blindly on his advisers, who tried to endow him with firmer, more effective body language. The unfortunate man was scrunched into these images and attitudes, which he thought he had to adopt to improve his performance. Those days are over. Robert Bourassa is still no star of the stage and screen and never will be, but he is now much more natural and more relaxed, sometimes even rumpled and crumpled.
>
> One thing he still does not like is great mass outpourings of emotion. He has no gift for mobilizing crowds, stroking, arousing, caressing the masses, asking people to come into the streets or fill grandstands. Demonstrations like that, compared by some to fascist rituals, neither interest nor affect him, any more than the flag-waving rallies they have in the United States. He has a hard time understanding this passionate, noisy, resolutely populist kind of politics. (1989, 37)

The comments gathered during interviews with members of the press gallery also confirm a change in the attitude Bourassa's team took toward the media. From 1985 to 1989, Liberal government communications were as centralized as they were in the 1970s, but they were more open and frank. Although in the 1970s the press gallery strongly criticized the secretive and manipulative tactics of Charles Denis, the premier's press attaché, the legislative reporters acknowledged the competence and openness of Ronald Poupart, the premier's press attaché and communications director from 1985 to 1989.

The 1989 Election

The 1989 election produced a novel situation. The PQ was not popular enough that it could hope to dislodge the QLP and win the election. The campaign was shaping up as a dull one, the result was so certain. The QLP hoped to drift gently into a second term in office without making any waves. But these expectations were completely frustrated by capricious circumstances. Although the election result was just as expected, the campaign did not unfold as predicted. To some degree, the parties lost the political initiative to a variety of social groups.

During the campaign, a cargo of PCBs was to be shipped from Saint-Basile Le Grand to Liverpool, England, to be burned. British longshoremen refused to unload the toxins, however, and the cargo had to be returned to Canada. The PCBs' Grand Tour provoked a public debate, fed by current events more or less created by several pressure groups, over environmental protection and disposal of toxic wastes.

Also during the campaign, a power struggle broke out between nurses and the government. Negotiations were going nowhere and a series of illegal walk-outs dominated the headlines. Then anglophones, unhappy with the Liberals' Bill 178 (*An Act to amend the charter of the French language*) on the language of signs stepped up their criticism of the government. Finally, there were continuing suspicions that a prominent member of the Liberal party was involved in a conflict of interest. In short, a succession of events, some unforeseeable, others planned, disturbed the parties' carefully laid campaign plans.

Questioned incessantly by reporters about events in the news, Robert Bourassa was obliged to behave as a premier managing a complex tangle of crises, not as a party leader on the campaign trail. As Charron states, "The government's management of these differing crises had more journalistic value than the Liberal party's election message or the planks of the party platform" (1990b, 78).

Some reporters and observers claimed there was no campaign, or that the campaign itself was a dull one. Others, including Bourassa's private secretary, Mario Bertrand, claimed that it was the media that dodged the major issues in the campaign. Some MNAs, including Marc-Yvan Côté, the cabinet minister responsible for the Liberal organization in eastern Quebec, and Réjean Doyon, the member for Louis-Hébert,[15] went so far as to say the PQ enjoyed special treatment from the media.

But reporter Gilles Lesage (1990) argues that it was the voters who imposed their themes and priorities through the intermediary of the media, thereby disrupting the fine strategies devised by the Liberals and the PQ. News events moved fast, from crisis to crisis, and the parties had to adjust. The PQ managed to take advantage of them – taking a position on the issues as they unfolded and criticizing the outgoing government – while Bourassa, imprisoned by his position as premier, was unable to perform his role as party leader.

It was not the media that created, reported and recapitulated the fantastic serial epic of the PCBs, down to the smallest episodes and convulsions, night after night for weeks. The people were the major actors, via the television, in this unlikely odyssey. Did it mean distracting public attention from a campaign that would otherwise have been normal? So be it!

Far from getting in the way of the election debates, the burning issues of the late summer of 1989 fueled these debates with major, if not crucial questions. The government had to render accounts, which is as it should be when the time comes to assess its record. It was not the peaceful stroll to victory that many had predicted. Against all expectations, the government had to go grimly on the defensive, conduct a real campaign and justify itself. Some issues were evaded, some debates neglected. But others took up the slack, a lot of slack, because of the citizens, or rather, thanks to them ... The traditional parties did not dominate the landscape as they had hoped. The issues pursued them and ran them into the ground. The voters and the media were not dragged along by party tactics and strategies as much as they had been in the recent past. (Lesage, 6 April 1990, 9)

Media–party relations in the 1989 election campaign were interesting.[16] This election produced a new situation that could easily occur again. Indeed, while political parties were learning over the years to attract television news coverage during election campaigns by creating spectacular events, other groups were learning to do this too. Parties could therefore find themselves struggling with organized groups to control the agenda in election campaigns. As groups learn to use public communications techniques and strategies, it is possible that they will take advantage of election campaigns to impose their own agendas.

Consequences of the Primacy of Communications and Marketing in Election Campaigns

The importance that marketing and communications techniques have assumed in election campaigns has affected the structure and function of political parties and their concept of the electorate.

An initial observation is that although the use of communications and marketing experts is not in itself enough to carry an election, it is nonetheless a precondition. Accordingly, parties that cannot pay for costly image campaigns are out of the running. The disastrous 1973 campaigns of the UN and the RC illustrate this.

Conceiving election campaigns in marketing rather than information terms also raises a fundamental problem for political action. In effect, marketing and political action establish forces that can work together or be in conflict, depending on the situation. The question is whether the communications strategy should be adapted to the mission, philosophy and program of the party or whether the latter elements should be subordinated to the communications strategy in order to gain victory.

These two contradictory trends have been observed since 1960. Quebec parties have made genuine efforts to democratize their structures and operations, to broaden their base and to give activists a say. But at the same time the electoral preoccupations and imperatives of marketing and communications have meant increasing domination of party hierarchies by technocrats and centralization of decision making in election campaigns around the party leader, which limits the influence of the party rank and file.[17] Election strategies have become more the business of the leader and his immediate advisers than of the membership. In short, communication channels have been created between the membership and the apparatus, but these channels do not seem to be used when election strategy is involved.

Efforts to democratize political parties first began with the Liberal party of Jean Lesage in the early 1960s.

> The parties evolved from loosely structured groups controlled by the leader, the treasurer and a few organizers into much more elaborate organizations with full-time staff and democratic structures that met regularly, and a broad membership base at the local level. The pressure to democratize was undeniable. They sought to create mass parties, recruiting thousands of individual members who would select the delegates and define the broad orientations, help fund the party and provide the foot soldiers in election campaigns. Programs were adopted in policy conventions after grassroots consultation. (Linteau et al. 1986, 635)

Party activities are also shaped by the state, which helps fund the leading parties and lays down clearer rules for the conduct of political and electoral activities. In 1977 the PQ government passed *An Act to govern the financing of political parties* designed to stop secret coffers by prohibiting contributions by companies or organizations and limiting the sums individuals may contribute. As a result, parties had to broaden their base and resort to grassroots financing.

Despite this trend toward party democratization, communicators still exercise increasing control over election campaigns and are working toward the centralization of decision making. Marketing and communications call for a set of techniques and functions that must be coordinated and planned at the level of a party's central organization. As well, these techniques are used in strategic action, which means that they require flexibility in decision making and the management of resources to ensure that the action meets the needs of the moment as much as possible, especially when taking an opponent's manoeuvres into account. The awkward machinery of democratic participation in party organizations is not, therefore, appropriate for this kind of decision making.

Bernier observes the same phenomenon of centralization in Quebec government marketing; he notes that "government marketing is strongly centralized, not only because of the coordination and planning functions inherent in its implementation but also because the government executive wants to apply administrative controls to its marketing" (1988, 168).

Reliance on experts has become more and more necessary as electoral marketing techniques have increased in complexity. This rise of communicators within political parties coincides with the increasing prevalence of television in campaign strategies. Polling has also become common, and the techniques of analysing and interpreting statistical data are more and more complex and sophisticated.

The use of these new communications and feedback techniques encourages party leaders to rely more on communicators and pollsters than on local leaders and members. Local organizers and the rank and file lost their influence on decisions about election strategy to the communicators, whose influence derives from three skills that have become indispensable in contemporary election campaigns: the capacity to interpret poll results to define the product that voters want; the capacity to translate the electorate's state of mind into images, symbols and concepts; and finally, a command of the media, particularly television.

The flair, instinct and experience of local organizers are no longer enough. According to Benjamin: "The membership and traditional politicos have increasingly been ignored in decision making. The political weight of the communications advisers has not been enough to guarantee victory every time in the election battle. But the 'democratic authority of the members' to run their party, the 'power of the people,' has each time yielded more ground to a small group of advisers in the making of the Quebec premier" (1976, 104).

The traditional task of the local organizers, which was to establish an effective electoral machine, is less important now. Campaigns are more national than regional or local. People vote increasingly for the leader, or for the leader's image, and less and less on the merits of local candidates.

In the 1940s and 1950s, local political meetings would draw several hundred people and give rise to lively exchanges between candidates and voters. In the 1960s and 1970s, such meetings drew only a handful of party faithful (Benjamin 1976). From 1970 on, public meetings were taken up again by the PQ; but these were increasingly massive assemblies – such as those held during the referendum campaign – bringing together several thousand people in sports arenas, and party members were bit players in a show staged for the television cameras.[18]

The communicators' influence has also made itself felt in the selection of candidates in constituencies. They look for candidates who have a good personal image, not candidates who can establish a relationship of confidence and participation with the rank and file. Candidates with an effective television presence are considered more likely than others to make an electoral breakthrough. Also sought are candidates who correspond to the overall image that the party hopes to project in the campaign. Thus, the candidates' capacity to be marketed, to merge with the product as defined by the communicators, is an important criterion in their selection.

Judging from the incomplete documentation available, however, communicators appeared to have less influence in the election campaign decision making process during the 1980s than in the 1960s, or, especially, the 1970s. However, if their influence is smaller, it is not because communications imperatives are less onerous, but because the rules of the political communications game seem to be more integrated with standard campaign practices so that the communications specialists have lost their exclusive hold on knowledge of communications techniques. Indeed, candidates are tending to become specialists in communications themselves.[19]

The primacy of communications and marketing in campaigns tends to allocate an increasingly important role to television. Election campaigns look more and more like daily television serials. Television's ascendancy derives essentially from the immense advantages it offers in comparison with the other media: it can reach the most voters, in particular the undecided and the least informed – those who must be convinced or charmed. But television is also the image medium, which means that political parties try to use images to communicate impressions and feelings. They prefer not to convince undecided voters by appealing to intellect.

Benjamin concluded that "television has substantially modified the electoral ground rules. The kind of manipulative efforts we have seen over the last five years appear to run counter to a democratic election process" (1975, 185). Things have hardly changed, except that techniques have become more sophisticated. After the 1988 federal election, journalist André Noël (1989) asked whether democracy could survive television.

These varied trends tend to substantiate an analytical model that defines political action as a communications phenomenon, essentially symbolic, cut off from its material base. In the minds of the strategists – and the journalists – politics can almost be reduced to a game of manipulating perceptions. This model is not only based on a rather cynical view of democratic life, but it also hardly promotes the discussion of ideas.

Whatever the case, we find that to the degree that marketing and communications strategies gain the upper hand and elections become television shows, the media tend to cover election campaigns like major marketing operations, to the detriment of program and policy coverage. What journalists choose to analyse are precisely each leader's image, communications devices and campaign incidents. Journalistic coverage of election campaigns is discussed in the next section.

MEDIA COVERAGE OF ELECTION CAMPAIGNS

Coverage of Provincial Election Campaigns by the Press

Very few studies have been devoted to election campaign coverage in the Quebec media, and no study has been made of provincial election campaign coverage by television networks. For primarily technical reasons (ease of access to sources), the available analyses deal exclusively with the dailies. We were able to identify four analytical reports on provincial elections. All these reports are old, including the report by Bourassa and Depatie (1966) on the 1966 election; the report by Lamothe and Desjardins (1970) on the 1970 election; the report by Latouche (1977) on the 1973 election, and the report by Bernard (1976) on the 1976 election.[20] Although the approach varies from one study to another, general observations may be made.

1. The quantity of daily newspaper coverage – number of articles published or editorial space devoted to the party – is greater for the party of the outgoing government, but the coverage is often more negative. The explanation is simple: the governing party, which must account for its administration, is subject to numerous attacks by its opponents and these attacks are conveyed to voters by the press.

In the 1966 election, the governing QLP received more extensive coverage than their closest rival, the UN, but this coverage was more negative (Bourassa and Depatie 1966). Similarly, in 1970 the governing UN benefited from greater coverage than did the Liberal party, its major rival, but was also the "preferred target of the dailies" (Lamothe and Desjardins 1970, 119), with the exception, obviously, of *Montréal Matin,* which belonged to the UN. In 1976, the governing QLP was given more coverage than the PQ (Bernard 1976).

The 1973 election was an exception to this rule; sovereignty was the central election issue and the daily newspapers gave less space to the governing QLP than they did to the PQ (Latouche 1977); this did not prevent the Liberals from being re-elected with an overwhelming majority.[21]

Some legislative reporters have explained that it is much easier for them to obtain unfavourable information about the government when a change in government is likely. As the government's support declines, journalists have increasing access to negative sources (notably, unhappy public servants), which helps fuel unfavourable press coverage of the government. Internal dissension and repressed frustrations burst into the open and leaks multiply. These negative sources feed the press, which then accelerates the erosion of the government's support. As the level of government support declines, official frustration increases, reinforcing the government's negative attitude toward journalists and accentuating the conflictual aspect of the relationship. Ultimately, the government will no longer have enough support to win the election and will be replaced by a new government (Charron 1990b, 77–80). That is why outgoing governments defeated in elections are strongly critical of the press, which they accuse of engineering their defeat.

2. News reports published in newspapers are not neutral. Daily newspapers favour particular parties, and their preferences become increasingly perceptible as election day approaches (Lamothe and Desjardins 1970).

The analysis of the 1970 election by Lamothe and Desjardins shows that *Montréal Matin*, the UN paper, a vestige of the party press, favoured the UN highly: 91.8 percent of its favourable articles were devoted to the UN, while 70.6 percent of its unfavourable articles were devoted to the QLP. For the Montreal *Gazette*, it was the opposite: 61 percent of favourable articles were on the Liberals while 66.8 percent of the unfavourable articles attacked the UN. *Le Devoir* and *La Presse* avoided this polarization. The *Journal de Montréal*, for its part, favoured the PQ with 49 percent of its favourable articles.

A newspaper's political leanings were also expressed in the discrepancy the authors found between the orientation of the headlines and the articles. The phenomenon was particularly visible in the English-language press, to the detriment of the PQ. In the *Montreal Star*, headlines unfavourable to the PQ outnumbered unfavourable articles two to one. In the Montreal *Gazette*, the discrepancy was five to one. This, the authors say, is "an indication of the division between the reporters – who took no position – and the publishers of these newspapers" (Lamothe and Desjardins 1970, 119).

In some cases, the ideological orientation of a newspaper significantly affected journalistic coverage. In 1976, the *Journal de Montréal*, which openly supported the PQ, devoted more than 82 percent of its column-inches to that party; in other words, the *Journal de Montréal* amply explained the PQ platform to its readers, without doing the same for the other parties (Latouche 1977).

3. It is generally acknowledged that the press is more interested in political polemics and the election race itself ("horse-race journalism") than in party platforms. Although they do not rebut this, content analyses do qualify this statement for the daily press. In fact, they show significant coverage of the platforms.[22] Latouche (1977) found that, in 1973, journalists paid a great deal of attention to economic and social issues, although politicians were emphasizing constitutional issues. Furthermore, the election platforms were mostly covered by the daily papers: "Overall, one finds that, with the exception of agriculture, the themes of election debates as found in the daily newspapers are about the same as those found in the official party programs. The coefficient of correlation between the distribution of themes in the platforms and the distribution in the newspapers remains fairly high, at 0.72" (ibid., 14).

4. Using a complex statistical analysis technique, Latouche (1977) was able to show that the effect of journalistic treatment was to homogenize the themes of election rhetoric; that is, ensure that all parties dealt with the same themes. This homogenization was particularly obvious in the case of the two leading parties running in 1973, the PQ and the QLP: thematic differences evident in the platforms of these parties were blurred in the newspaper reports. The parties were emphasizing different things in their platforms, but in the newspapers they were talking about the same things.

5. However, Latouche's study (1977) shows that, when dealing with the parties' ideological orientations, journalistic treatment tends to distance the parties from each other, that is, to accentuate the ideological differences between them. In other words, by homogenizing themes, newspapers tend more specifically to circumscribe the subject matter for

debate; while they accentuate the differences, they tend to dramatize the debates in order to accentuate conflict.

6. A final observation, in this case derived from the analyses by Gauthier (1982), bears on daily newspaper coverage of opinion polls during election campaigns. Gauthier shows that newspapers do not report all the information needed to assess the quality of polls. Newspaper articles often omit essential information, such as the identities of the sponsor and the polling firm, the time the poll was taken, the population studied, the type of sampling, the response rate, the number of completed questionnaires or interviews, the method of data collection, the wording of questions and the total number of subjects used in calculating percentages. Also, because they misunderstand the nature and limits of opinion polls, journalists often interpret them improperly.

Coverage of the 1980 Referendum

Although newspaper coverage of provincial election campaigns appears to have aroused only moderate interest among researchers, the stance of the press during the referendum campaign, a high point in Quebec's political life, has attracted their full attention. Once again, this analysis has focused exclusively on the daily print media.[23] There are two types of analysis: qualitative – undertaken by Yves Gagnon (1980) and by Lachapelle and Noiseux (1980) – and quantitative – undertaken by Tremblay (1984). These analytical approaches distinguish between the content of both editorials and news articles.

Editorials

When discussing the editorial position of daily newspapers during the 1980 referendum, the case of the Montreal *Gazette*, the only English-language daily in Quebec after the 1979 closing of the *Montreal Star*, must be treated separately. The obvious federalist position of this newspaper was no surprise to anyone. It adopted an editorial style that was "lively, direct, without nuance or subtlety. Editorials are not a place to explain or justify, but a place for commitment and action, contrary to what is done in the French-language press" (Y. Gagnon 1980, 174).

More surprising, and offensive to sovereignty supporters, was that the paper became involved in the political struggle, practising what looked like aggressive "combat" journalism. According to Yves Gagnon, the Montreal *Gazette* was the only paper "to commit itself resolutely to the struggle against the Yes option, using its resources and journalistic skills in an integrated and coordinated way"[24] (1980, 174).

In the French-language dailies, editorial writers were generally hostile to the sovereignty option. *La Presse* expressed its commitment to federalism clearly. The newspaper's position had long been known: it was defined by its director, Roger Lemelin, in 1972 and reiterated in May 1980. The newspaper's management went so far as to refuse to allow one of its editorialists, Guy Cormier, to write an editorial favourable to the Yes option (Lachapelle and Noiseux 1980).

Le Soleil followed a similar course but its involvement was more cautious, as if to avoid offending either camp. *Le Devoir*, which was without an editor at the time, let the members of its editorial board express their preferences and published editorials that favoured both options. Sherbrooke's *La Tribune* came out for the No, but its journalists publicly dissociated themselves from the position expressed by the editor-in-chief. *Le Nouvelliste* in Trois-Rivières, the *Quotidien* in Chicoutimi, and the *Journal de Montréal* and *Journal de Québec* (which do not publish editorials) remained neutral.

Yves Gagnon concluded from his analysis that "while there are pro-federalism editorial positions in the French-language press, there are none that are similarly pro-sovereignty" (1980, 175).

News Articles

The content analyses of news articles on the referendum campaign (Y. Gagnon 1980; Tremblay 1984) show that newspapers covered the referendum as if it were an election campaign. Several dominant features emerge from these analyses.

1. Torn between their political preferences and their mission to supply information, French-speaking journalists seemed anxious to affirm their objectivity through scrupulous respect for balanced views and a noncommittal approach. Yves Gagnon noted a descriptive, careful, sterilized and disembodied journalistic style, as if journalists were trying not to get involved in their stories. He also noted that "the French-language dailies strove to present balanced information on the parties involved. They displayed extreme caution, to avoid the least accusation of intolerance or racism" (Y. Gagnon 1980, 180).

2. News was presented in an essentially factual and decontextualized way, which led Yves Gagnon to state that genuine information remained inaccessible to anyone who did not have an exceptional memory and great capacity for analysis and synthesis.

3. As in election campaigns, stories tended to favour anecdotal and conflictual elements and to personalize the debate. Yves

Gagnon (1980) notes that "the conflictual aspect generally prevailed over substance." Tremblay's analysis shows, for example, that newspapers were more interested in the political sparring over the PQ government's white paper on sovereignty association than in the content of the document (Quebec, Executive Council 1979). The white paper was "more effectively covered in reactions and comments by politicians and social actors than in articles purporting to summarize the contents!" (Tremblay 1984, 15).

4. Newspapers gave greater coverage to incidents in the referendum campaign than to the real issues and principles raised by the campaign. Tremblay (1984) notes, for example, that the historical content of the white paper was ignored; instead, journalists lingered over the chapters dealing with the new agreement and the referendum. In his view, "the media discourse deprived the referendum debate of the historical dimension it needed" (ibid., 15).

   Moreover, although political institutions and processes were relatively well covered, the discussion of political principles tended to be neglected. In this, Tremblay sees a confirmation of the theory that political games (strategies, elections, voting, conventions, etc.) attracted more newspaper attention than did the issues in the referendum campaign.

5. Yves Gagnon (1980) found that most journalists' sources were agents of the economic, political or social establishments. Tremblay (1984) noted that collective noninstitutional entities (nation, people, society, citizens) were less represented in stories than institutional collectives, such as countries, regions, provinces and institutions. He concluded that "the national question, in this kind of discourse, is more the business of the official political institutions than of the people of Quebec" (ibid., 16).

6. Yves Gagnon (1980) found no information generated by journalists themselves; that is, news in which a journalist's initiative is predominant. Here, too, journalists seemed to be trailing their sources.

In short, the conclusions of these content analyses are essentially very similar to the criticisms of observers and political leaders about the election campaign coverage in the news media.

News Media Strategies in Covering Election Campaigns

No researcher has bothered to analyse the strategies and policies adopted by the Quebec media in covering provincial election campaigns.

However, some insight into this subject may be gained from journalists' comments and analysis of the 1984 federal campaign coverage (Cormier 1991).

The evidence shows that parties' communications strategies are increasingly focused on leaders' images as symbols of communities or policies. The effectiveness of these strategies depends on the judicious use of television and tight control over journalists' access to party leaders. This is how political organizers try to control the campaign agenda and prevent journalists from taking the initiative through crafty or unexpected questions. How do journalists react to these strategies?

The logistical elements of media news policies in election campaigns are fairly rudimentary, so journalists are often dependent on party administration. The major media institutions assign a journalist (and a technical crew in the case of television) to cover the campaign of each leader and thereby ensure equal coverage to the major political parties. If necessary, to avoid mind-numbing monotony and make it easier to compare parties, the media rotate journalists assigned to cover leaders' campaign tours.

The journalists following each leader are received and briefed by party organizers, who exercise a significant controlling influence over journalists by taking advantage of the constraints under which they operate and by controlling their access to the party leader. Under these conditions, journalists generally obtain only the information that organizers want to release.

Media organizations that lack the resources (or the will) to defray the costs necessary for a journalist to be assigned to each leader's campaign rely entirely on news agencies. This contributes little to the diversification of information.

The significant costs entailed in covering a leader's campaign mean that the leaders of third parties are often ignored. For example, in the 1984 federal campaign, the biggest private television network in Quebec, TVA, did not assign a single reporter to cover Ed Broadbent's campaign, although Broadbent was not insignificant in Canadian politics. The decision to cover a party leader's campaign tour depends most on the party's popularity with the electorate (Cormier 1991). As Charron notes, "in their assessment of media interest in a news item and the way they treat that item, journalists tend to reflect the level of popular support enjoyed by that particular political source. If a party's support is low, the media publicity it gets will likely be low, sporadic or non-existent, and a further deterioration in its support will sometimes follow" (1990b, 76–77).[25]

During the 1981 election, the major media organizations decided to cover the campaign tour of Union nationale leader Roch Lasalle, despite his low standing, but the party was in such disarray that it was unable even to arrange daily press briefings.[26] The UN did not elect a single member. To the media, this was an unfruitful investment.

The desire for a return on investment can lead the media to produce news even if the information they publish is of little interest or utility to voters. Cormier says: "The concern with getting some return from the technical and financial investment involved in television network coverage of party leaders helps guarantee political organizations a daily spot in the news bulletins, irrespective of the value of the information they produce" (1991, 33).

The obligation to maintain some balance in the coverage of different parties can reinforce this tendency. A close adviser of Premier Bourassa and election organizer for the Liberals says that journalists are the prisoners of political parties during election campaigns:

> In 1985, I went to the Fédération professionnelle des journalistes du Québec and told them what happened on the [leader tour] bus during an election campaign. Some of the reporters hit the ceiling, saying it didn't make any sense. What did I say? That reporters are regimented, that they are controlled, that they are unable to do anything but what they are told. Why? Because, under our democratic rules – which may be right, but the question is to find some flexibility – they have to give us equal time. The media have clearly settled their problem, since for them it's a question of dollars and cents, of nine to five. So they put one reporter with the Parti québécois and another reporter with the Liberal party and tell themselves that each party will get its space. That's it. The media, to ensure that they are making the news as they want it, add all kinds of interviews here and there. But the official news, as a daily item? It's the opposition leader's bus and the premier's bus. And the poor reporters, they are controlled, they are prisoners.
>
> [Question: And you have to give them some news?]
>
> Oh yes, that's our job, we have to find them one story per day. On television, it's two minutes each, with a stopwatch in your hand. That's the CRTC law and it's the election law, they have to comply with it. (Interview with author)

It must be added that the major media (especially Radio-Canada and the leading daily newspapers) also commission specialized journalists to cover specific campaign themes and issues facing the next government. These ventures allow the media to keep a degree of autonomy in election campaign coverage.

Prisoners of the election spectacle, journalists also try to limit the influence of political organizers and frustrate their communications strategies by producing relatively analytical reports and interpreting them from a critical perspective.

But, as Cormier points out:

> The nature of journalistic practices and rituals does not change radically simply because it is applied to an election campaign. Political journalism is characterized by a tendency to dramatize events, to personalize conflicts, to focus attention on the leaders and rivalries of political life. The election exercise does not escape these journalistic shortcomings. In short, during election campaigns reporters seem to be more interested in the personality and style of the candidates than in their policies, and more interested in the election race than in ideas and debates. (1991, 34)

Journalists are often criticized for their poor coverage of substantive issues in election campaigns. These charges are sometimes unfounded, but it is true that journalists find it difficult to deal with complex issues – free trade and the federal Goods and Services Tax are examples of electoral themes that journalists found very difficult to popularize.

To give the public "contextualized" information, journalists decipher and interpret political messages. Most often, however, this means simply situating the leader's most recent statement within the perspective of the election contest.

Journalists rarely bring their critical faculties to bear on the substance of issues. As specialists in politics, journalists covering election campaigns apply an interpretative scale that tends to reduce every issue raised in the campaign to its political and electoral dimension alone; that is, to a level where they can be critical and demonstrate their expertise without jeopardizing their own credibility and impartiality (Cormier 1991; Charron 1990b). So they tend to deal with election issues and programs by emphasizing the political and electoral aspect, without much regard for underlying issues or social controversies.

Journalists also try to frustrate the strategies of political parties by devoting news reports and analyses to these strategies. Increasingly, we see reports on the techniques parties use to persuade voters and on elections as image contests. This practice does not seem to be a genuine threat to political organizers.

Whatever the case, we are struck by the realization that political organizers seem little concerned with strictly journalistic election campaign coverage. What matter are the images coming across on television. Political parties direct their communications efforts at leaders' televised images rather than substantive issues, at the container rather than the contents. In any case, that is what Cormier's 1991 study shows.

Luc Lavoie, a former TVA reporter who is now a communications adviser for the Progressive Conservatives, seems to share this view:

> Between seven and eight million Canadians tune in to the news each night ... By comparison, only a small minority of the population reads the political articles in newspapers. In fact, television is the only thing that counts in an election campaign. It's almost ludicrous, but politicians who don't go along will pay a price. Mulroney thought he was playing an idiot's game. He would have preferred more substantive debates. It's really a sad thing for democracy.
>
> We're prisoners of the tube. Journalists claim they can explain everything in 1 minute and 45 seconds. It's impossible, but we give them what they want: pretty pictures and a few clips. (Quoted by Noël 1989, 64)

Cormier (1991) tells how Bill Fox, the director of communications for the Progressive Conservative party in the 1984 election, shut off the sound on his television set during news reports to measure the effectiveness of the communications strategy. In short, regardless of what reporters say, what counts is to create impressions with television images.

It seems, therefore, that in the struggle for control of the campaign agenda, media coverage strategies are ill-adapted to the strategies used by political parties. Cormier says: "Journalists hold forth at length, analysing the race with the style and expertise of sports commentators, while the parties speak directly to the voter, and with another language, the language of the television image. Their strategies seem to connect on one point only: at the end of the day, no one really cares any more about party programs and substantive issues" (1991, 34, 35).

CONCLUSION

The evolution of relations between the media and political authorities, of electoral strategies and campaign coverage by the media, leads to certain realizations and hypotheses about relations among the actors that form the political communication system: political parties, the media and the public.

Since the end of the 1950s, relationships between the media and political parties in Quebec have formalized. The practices of both journalism and politics have been professionalized in a way, with the establishment of rules and accepted norms, thus contributing to a more honest political communications process.

An opinionated press subordinated to political parties has become an information press claiming independence from parties. Parties, especially when they're in power, no longer pose as lords and masters of information. In his time, Duplessis could bar a journalist suspected of ulterior motives from his news conferences, but it is hard to imagine today's media tolerating such authoritarianism or intimidation – although politicians are not always able to keep their bad moods to themselves and skirmishes do break out. Today, relations are conducted according to formal and informal rules through which journalists and elected officials have found a modus vivendi acceptable to everyone.

In Quebec journalism, influenced by American values, objectivity is a fundamental standard of news. It is a rule of the game, in that it conditions the expectations of parties and candidates, which rely, for example, on the fact that television must give equal time to the leading parties or candidates in the race. Various examples have shown that a media organization suspected of taking sides quickly becomes an open target for candidates.

But the problem of objectivity, taken in the broad sense that journalists use today – honesty, impartiality, balance of viewpoints, etc. – is not peculiar to Quebec journalism. In the 1960s and 1970s, French-speaking Quebec journalists adopted a professional, union-oriented and political commitment that was more radical than that of English-speaking Canadian journalists. It is difficult to fit the media's enthusiasm for the Quiet Revolution and journalists' sympathy at the beginning of the PQ regime into Anglo-Saxon tradition. Perhaps it is because Quebec journalists were operating at the limits of generally accepted practices during this period that the phenomenon of self-censorship appeared at the time of the referendum. Journalists predicted that at that crucial moment, it was the whole normative or ideological system of information journalism that was at risk of foundering if they did not succeed in clearly separating their political preferences from their function as providers of information.

It must be said that Quebec journalists, as a class, are older now and the exercise of their trade has been bureaucratized. The spirit of the times has also changed, so that their social-democratic and sovereigntist ardours have cooled considerably.

Periods of conflict – for example, the end of the Duplessis era, Robert Bourassa's regime in the 1970s or the time of the referendum – have clarified some rules. Political communication will have to be conducted more openly, and the media will be more threatening each time parties or the government show any inclination to control or manipulate information. A government can no longer, for example, politicize at will information about its administrative operations. In any case, it can do it only with prudence and subtlety if it is not to attract thunder and lightning from opposition parties and the media (Bernier 1988).

This formalization does not prevent the actors from breaking the rules whenever they think it profitable to do so. Since the 1960s, for example, it has been common practice during election campaigns for party leaders to debate on television; in 1989, Bourassa did everything he could to avoid a television debate because he had nothing to gain from this kind of confrontation. It mattered little to him that the media complained; the fuss would do him less harm than a bad television performance would have.

In some cases, infractions can be more damaging to the democratic process. For example, the federal government's meddling in publicity during the 1980 referendum campaign was an overt offence against the spirit of Quebec's referendum laws.

The point that must be emphasized above all is that the emergence of political marketing techniques and the importance assumed by communications advisers in political parties also tend to impose new rules and to alter relations between the actors in the political communications system.

We have seen that, increasingly, the electoral messages from political parties during election campaigns as well as the strategies that they launch are the work of communications and political marketing experts. In this, Quebec is but following a general trend in industrial countries. Is this to say that election campaigns have become epic struggles fought only by armies of technicians and communicators?

Indeed, the technicians and other communications and marketing experts are deciding on strategy and are tending, with some success, to decide the conditions of debates. And with television, these debates have become, for many, image battles. The need to deal with television has become a necessity: voters must be able to identify with the leader's television image.

A referendum presents the problem of choosing among ideas, concepts and policies, which heightens the importance of rhetoric and discussion. Consequently, the press also becomes more important, because it can present arguments better than television can. But in an election, the problem is to choose leaders, to summon individuals to government, which heightens the importance of personalities represented by images. The lessened importance of party platforms in modern election campaigns results from both the dominance of television and the use of marketing techniques that encourage parties to concentrate on influencing undecided or uninterested voters. Under these circumstances, if a party sets out to defend a policy or a complex project such as free trade, the federal Goods and Services Tax or sovereignty in an election, it is at a disadvantage if the opposition can counter policies with personalities, ideas with images, and arguments with symbols. For it seems that images are better than arguments for convincing undecided and indifferent voters.

Thus, must we conclude that marketing and communications techniques are the sum and total of every modern election campaign? It should first be pointed out that images and marketing can do nothing to change the deepest convictions of the people; at best, they allow political parties to adapt and take some advantage of them – and that is already plenty. In sum, these methods allow parties to avoid strategic errors. The poor showing of the Union nationale and the Ralliement créditiste in 1973 teaches us that a political party cannot conduct a campaign without the big guns of marketing and communications. Enabling a party to avoid errors, correct use of these techniques can sometimes make the difference between victory and defeat. Hence, the PQ victory of 1981 can be largely explained by the effectiveness with which it used communications techniques. The result of the 1966 election – in which the UN took power with fewer votes than the Liberal party – could have been different if the Liberals had organized their communications better.

Image-makers (as they are called with mild contempt) can certainly improve the image and the performance of a candidate, but they do not actually manufacture the candidate. In the 1970s, Robert Bourassa's overly artificial image finally harmed him. Bourassa's image since 1985 benefits from a much-improved public perception; one can say that this image "works" because it is genuine.

The degree of voter resistance to attempts to influence or manipulate them can no longer be ignored. The admission must be made that research on Quebec elections has not revealed much about voters' ability to resist partisan propaganda during elections, but there are indications that it is not easy to manipulate feelings. First, election propaganda operates in an atmosphere of competition between parties that send out contradictory messages. As well, persuasion efforts are aimed mainly at the undecided, for parties know that it is not easy to influence voters who have made up their minds. Finally, propaganda trumpeted in the media is not the only influence on voters' choices.

Moreover, if marketing techniques do not themselves favour democratic debate, there are other elements in the system that can outweigh them, up to a point. An election campaign can be seen as a battle for control of the political and electoral agenda; the party that succeeds in imposing its preferences is well on the way to carrying off the election. But political parties are not the only participants in this struggle. In the competition to control the electoral agenda, the media act with relative freedom. Latouche's 1977 study shows, for example, how news coverage tends to homogenize the themes of political parties' election discourse, while it accentuates ideological differences. As well, through the efforts of formal and loosely organized groups, the public tends to interfere in the election struggle, forcing parties to involve themselves in issues that they might prefer to ignore. During the most recent federal election campaigns, we saw, for example, women's groups organizing leaders debates on women's concerns, with the result that the federal parties were never able to wriggle out of discussing these issues in their campaign rhetoric. The 1989 Quebec provincial election also gives an example of a campaign in which the political parties lost control of the agenda to the media and to special interest groups. Put another way, pressure groups organize, especially around communications strategies, to forbid political parties a monopoly on defining the themes and issues of election campaigns.

In sum, the media are not mere transmitters to be manipulated by partisan organizations, any more than political parties are manipulation machines. Candidates and political parties that treat voters as an amorphous mass risk eventually regretting their folly. But if the election is to remain significant to democracy (to use the word in its full sense), it must be constantly rethought, especially in its perilous relationships with television and political marketing techniques.

ABBREVIATIONS

c.	chapter
R.S.C.	Revised Statutes of Canada
R.S.Q.	Revised Statutes of Quebec
S.Q.	Statutes of Quebec

NOTES

This study was completed in October 1990.

In this study, quoted material that originated in French has been translated into English.

1. It should be noted here that, although television dominates modern election campaigns, no analysis of television coverage of provincial campaigns is available. The few content analyses of television network election campaign coverage that have been conducted in Quebec have dealt with federal campaigns (Cantin 1974; Cormier 1991).

2. *Le Devoir* responded with a violent attack on Duplessis, an editorial by André Laurendeau on "la théorie du roi nègre [the theory of the Negro king]."

3. Legislative correspondents in Quebec City were given a government bonus of $600 a year, a considerable sum at the time, because, in a way, their work was considered part of the *Journal of Debates*.

4. Between 1945 and 1965, the number of dailies declined, but total circulation rose from 680 000 to more than 1.1 million.

5. "Les journalistes au pouvoir? [Are journalists now in power?]" was the title of the issue of the journal *Le 30*, published by the FPJQ immediately after the PQ victory in 1976.

6. Further on, this study will discuss how content analyses of newspaper coverage of the referendum show that journalists' positions, as revealed in news articles, did not correspond to that of management, as expressed in editorials and in the choice of headlines.

7. In 1970 the PQ, with 23.1 percent of the vote, obtained only 6.5 percent of the seats. In 1973, with 30.2 percent of the vote, it obtained only 5.4 percent of the seats. According to Benjamin, "the weak numerical presence of the Parti québécois in the National Assembly served as a pretext … for a new definition of the role of the media with regard to government members: journalists took the place of the opposition, placing themselves in an adversarial position vis-à-vis the [Liberal] government. They treated all government news releases with distrust and refused to use them as they were, or to give the government 'free air time' in television news broadcasts" (1979, 70).

8. It seems that Lesage was also the first premier to use scientific polling in provincial election campaigns. Under the leadership of Maurice Pinard of McGill University, Le Groupe de recherche sociale conducted polls for the 1960 and 1962 elections.

9. In 1966, the UN won 56 seats with 40.9 percent of the votes, while the QLP, with 47.2 percent, secured only 50 seats. This is explained by the fact that voters in rural ridings, which were less densely populated than urban ridings, generally supported the UN. This allowed the Unionists to win more seats with fewer votes.

10. Furthermore, by this time the Union nationale was a heterogeneous party that seemed to be maintained solely by the presence of Daniel Johnson. Once Johnson died, the internal divisions between the traditionalists and reformers and the federalists and nationalists broke open and weakened the party so much that it never recovered.

11. These techniques – control of the visual context and a lack of direct contact between the leader and reporters (the so-called "scrums") or with "ordinary people" – are now common in American-style election campaigns focused

on television news clips. The Progressive Conservative Party of Canada applied these techniques systematically in the 1984 and 1988 elections (Cormier 1991; Noël 1989).

12. Geoffrey Stevens, an Ottawa correspondent for the *Globe and Mail*, commented the day after Ryan's suggestion: "I also suspect when a politician … starts talking about the need to monitor or control the press, it usually means two things: first, he is in trouble, and secondly, fundamentally, he is not a democrat" (Canada, Canadian Study of Parliament Group 1980, 22).

13. According to data provided by Bernard and Descôteaux (1981, 133–34), the PQ had a membership of about 339 000, including 30 000 active members, while QLP membership was 254 000, of which 20 000 were active members.

14. This strategy yielded good results in the by-elections between 1976 and 1981, leading Bernard and Descôteaux (1981, 140) to say that the Liberal party campaigned in 1981 as if it were fighting 122 by-elections.

15. Côté and Doyon took the floor in the National Assembly to denounce the media's partisan attitude during the election campaign.

16. The FPJQ organized a symposium on media–party relations in the 1989 election campaign. Members of the National Assembly and the Assembly press gallery were invited to present their concept of how journalists should relate to elected members. For a report of this symposium, see Charron (1990a).

17. This is only an overall tendency; there are some significant variations: for example, the PQ, both as a party and as the government, was just as technocratic but much less centralizing in the 1970s than the Liberal party and government of Robert Bourassa in the 1970s and since 1985.

18. A PQ innovation should be noted, however: the party has held many "kitchen meetings" during election campaigns, in which a few voters could discuss issues freely with local candidates.

19. For example, now that they take courses in the art of appearing effectively on television and on how to handle themselves with even the most hardened interviewers, candidates no longer need to be constantly accompanied by television specialists. In Quebec, two specialized companies (Institut Image et Son 2000 and Cominfo) offer this type of media training. Advertising agencies also give training seminars (Crépault 1988).

20. At least two of these studies, Bourassa and Depatie (1966) and Latouche (1977), were commissioned by professional journalists' associations following complaints by political parties during election campaigns.

21. Latouche (1977) indicates that the four daily newspapers he analysed (*La Presse, Le Journal de Montréal, La Tribune,* and the *Montreal Star*) gave as much weight to the PQ as they did to the other three parties combined (Liberals, Ralliement créditiste and UN): 50 percent of the column-inches he inventoried in these newspapers related to the PQ platform.

22. Cantin (1974) observed a similar phenomenon in French-language television during the 1972 federal campaign: despite a clear tendency to personalize politics, more than half of television stories dealt with party platforms and policies.

23. One exception must be noted: Caron et al.'s 1983 study, which analyses television news content during the final days of the 1980 referendum campaign. This analysis focuses only on the formal aspects of the news (number of news items, length of report, style of presentation, etc.) and does not give precise conclusions regarding the role of television at the time of the referendum campaign.

24. What makes the case of the Montreal *Gazette* even more remarkable is that English-language journalists were not then known for "committed" reporting. It must also be said that they had a reputation for a more docile relationship with managing editors, who seemed to exert more control over the daily work of their staff than is the case at French-language newspapers in Quebec (Charron 1990b).

25. This situation is not peculiar to election campaigns. PQ MNAs commented that between 1985 and 1987, when the party suffered a low standing in the polls, the PQ had problems convincing the media that what it had to say was newsworthy. One MNA commented in an interview:

> Between '85 and '87, we [the PQ] were stuck in a hole; if an election had been held at that point, the Parti québécois would have been wiped off the map. During this period, we got a lot less attention from reporters. I had the feeling we were perceived as an insignificant item. What we said didn't get much response, didn't take up much space in the media and went almost unnoticed ... Today, we're still in the opposition, but we have clearly improved our standing in public opinion, we're better established, we have become united again and so we've regained our credibility with the journalists. We think journalists find us more credible. So it's extremely variable, and I think that the basic factor is the credibility of a political formation and its standing in public opinion.

26. In cases like this, the party's organizational deficiency will be the subject of news reports, which can contribute further to the erosion of party support.

REFERENCES

Archibald, Clinton. 1983. *Un Québec corporatiste?* Hull: Éditions Asticou.

Benjamin, Jacques. 1975. *Comment on fabrique un premier ministre québécois: De 1960 à nos jours.* Montreal: Aurore.

———. 1976. "Les partis politiques québécois et le marketing électoral." In *Le processus électoral au Québec: Les élections provinciales de 1970 et 1973,* ed. Daniel Latouche et al. Montreal: Cahiers du Québec/Hurtubise HMH.

————. 1979. "Pouvoir politique et médias au Québec." *Communication Information* 3 (1): 67–77.

Bernard, André. 1976. *Québec: Élections 1976.* Montreal: Hurtubise HMH.

Bernard, André, and Bernard Descôteaux. 1981. *Québec: Élections 81.* Montreal: Hurtubise HMH.

Bernier, Robert. 1988. *Le marketing gouvernemental au Québec: 1929–1985.* Montreal: Gaëtan Morin.

Bobrow, Bavis B. 1974. "Mass Communication and Political System." In *Mass Communication Research, Major Issues and Future Directions,* ed. Phillips Davison and Frederick T.C. Yu. New York: Praeger.

Bombardier, Denise. 1979. "La télévision: moteur et reflet du changement au Québec." In *Dossier-Québec,* ed. Jean Sarragin and Claude Glayman. Paris: Stock.

Bourassa, Guy, and F. Depatie. 1966. "La Presse et les élections du 5 juin." *Cahiers de Cité Libre* (November 1966): 1–32.

Bourgault, Jacques. 1977. "L'attitude des mass-media vis-à-vis du gouvernement québécois." *Études internationales* 8:320–36.

Canada. *Broadcasting Act,* R.S.C. 1985, c. B-9.

Canada. Canadian Study of Parliament Group. 1980. *Seminar on the Press and Parliament: Adversaries or Accomplices?* Proceedings of a seminar held in the Quebec National Assembly, 18–19 April. Ottawa: Queen's Printer.

Cantin, Hélène. 1974. "Analyse d'une campagne électorale aux deux réseaux français de télévision: les émissions de nouvelles." Master's thesis, Laval University.

Charron, Jean. 1990a. "Que disent les élus et les journalistes lorsqu'ils parlent à visage découvert?" *Le 30* 14 (6): 7.

————. 1990b. "La construction de l'actualité politique: Une analyse stratégique des relations entre la presse parlementaire et les autorités politiques." Ph.D. diss., Laval University.

Clift, Dominique. 1980. "Solidarity on a Pedestal." In *Canadian Newspapers: The Inside Story,* ed. Walter Stewart. Edmonton: Hurtig Publishers.

Cloutier, Édouard. 1980. "À deux contre un: les jeux de la campagne référendaire et de la révision constitutionnelle." In *Québec: Un pays incertain. Réflexions sur le Québec post-référendaire.* Montreal: Québec/Amérique.

Cormier, Michel. 1991. "Politique et télévision: le cas du Parti conservateur lors de l'élection fédérale de 1984." In Jean Charron, Jacques Lemieux and Florian Sauvageau, *Les journalistes, les médias et leurs sources.* Montreal: Gaëtan Morin.

Crépault, Michel. 1988. "Êtes-vous télégénique?" *L'Actualité* (January): 47–52.

Demers, François. 1989. "Journalistic Ethics: The Rise of the 'Good Employee's Model': A Threat for Professionalism?" *Canadian Journal of Communication* 14 (2): 15–27.

Deshaies, Guy, and Georges-Hébert Germain. 1985. "Deux solitudes: Ni Bourassa ni Johnson n'ont l'intention de s'encombrer d'une armée d'apôtres: Seulement d'un noyau de fidèles." *L'Actualité* (December): 32, 134.

Desoer, Frank. 1982. "Intelligentsia et médias: De l'éducation populaire au pouvoir." *Politique* No. 2:97–116.

Dupuis, Mimi. 1986. "Étude des techniques de marketing politique illustrées par le cas de l'honorable Robert Bourassa, lors de la campagne au leadership du PLQ en 1983." Master's thesis, Université du Québec à Montréal.

Fédération professionnelle des journalistes du Québec. 1975. *Dossier sur l'information politique à Québec*. Montreal: FPJQ.

Gagnon, Lysiane. 1980. "Comme si la Tribune de la presse était un coin dans un aquarium." *Le 30* 4 (1): 11–13.

———. 1981. "Journalism and Ideologies in Quebec." In *The Journalists' Side*, vol. 2 of the research studies of the Royal Commission on Newspapers. Ottawa: Minister of Supply and Services Canada.

Gagnon, Yves. 1980. "Les quotidiens québécois et le référendum: analyse commentée." *Communication Information* 3 (3): 170–81.

Gauthier, Benoît. 1982. "Les sondages politiques au Québec: leur méthodologie et leur traitement journalistique." Ottawa: University of Ottawa.

Germain, Georges-Hébert. 1989. "Anatomie d'un premier ministre." *L'Actualité* (May): 28–39.

Godin, Pierre. 1979. "Qui vous informe?" *L'Actualité* (May): 31–33ff.

———. 1981. *La lutte pour l'information: Histoire de la presse écrite au Québec*. Montreal: Le Jour.

Gurevitch, Michael, and Jay G. Blumler. 1977. "Linkages between the Mass Media and Politics: A Model for the Analysis of Political Communications Systems." In *Mass Communication and Society*, ed. James Curran, Michael Gurevitch and Janet Woollacott. London: Edward Arnold in association with Open University Press.

Lachapelle, Guy, and Jean Noiseux. 1980. "La presse quotidienne." In *Québec: Un pays incertain. Réflexions sur le Québec post-référendaire*. Montreal: Québec/Amérique.

Lamothe, P., and J. Desjardins. 1970. "Les quotidiens montréalais et l'élection du 29 avril 1970: analyse de contenu." In *Le processus électoral au Québec: Les élections provinciales de 1970 et 1973*, ed. Daniel Latouche et al. Montreal: Cahiers du Québec/Hurtubise HMH.

Latouche, Daniel. 1977. "Le traitement de l'information en période électorale I: le contenu de l'information." *Communication Information* 2 (1): 1–30; "Le traitement de l'information en période électorale II: l'orientation de l'information." *Communication Information* 2 (2): 191–206.

Lemieux, Vincent, Marcel Gilbert and André Blais. 1970. *Une élection de réalignement: L'élection générale du 29 avril 1970 au Québec.* Montreal: Éditions du Jour.

Lesage, Gilles. 1980. "L'information politique à Québec: De Duplessis à Lévesque: les journalistes au pouvoir?" In *Dans les coulisses de l'information: les journalistes,* ed. Florian Sauvageau et al. Montreal: Québec/Amérique.

———. 1990. "Les journalistes face au pouvoir politique." *Le Devoir* (5 April): 7 and (6 April): 9.

Linteau, Paul-André, René Durocher, Jean-Claude Robert and François Ricard. 1986. *Histoire du Québec contemporain, tome II: Le Québec depuis 1930.* Montreal: Boréal.

Maisonneuve, Pierre. 1990. "À la recherche du journaliste 'BS.' " *Le 30* 14 (7): 6–7.

Martin, Louis. 1978. "Le rôle des média dans le processus politique." *Communication Information* 2 (3): 129–36.

Noël, André. 1989. "La démocratie peut-elle survivre à la télévision?" *L'Actualité* (April): 62–68.

O'Neill, Pierre, and Jacques Benjamin. 1978. *Les mandarins du pouvoir: L'exercice du pouvoir au Québec de Jean Lesage à René Lévesque.* Montreal: Québec/Amérique.

Patenaude, Pierre. 1981. "La publicité propagande électorale et référendaire au Québec." *Revue du Barreau* 41 (5): 1045–53.

Quebec. *Charter of the French language, An Act to amend,* S.Q. 1988, c. 54.

———. *Financing of political parties, An Act to govern the,* R.S.Q., c. F-2.

———. *French language in Quebec, An Act to promote,* S.Q. 1969, c. 9.

———. *Official Language Act,* S.Q. 1974, c. 6.

———. *Referendum Act,* R.S.Q., c. 64.1.

Quebec. Executive Council. 1979. *Québec-Canada: A New Deal.* Quebec: Éditeur officiel.

Sauriol, Paul. 1971. "Indifférent aux promesses et aux menaces, *Le Devoir* a toujours servi la liberté en temps de crise." In *Le Québec qui se fait,* ed. Claude Ryan. Montreal: Hurtubise HMH.

Sauvageau, Florian. 1979. "Les média et la campagne référendaire: Rôle exigeant, 'mission impossible.' " *Cahiers de recherche éthique* no. 7 ("Le référendum: Un enjeu collectif"): 57–68.

Tremblay, Gaétan. 1984. "Les journaux ... illisibles? Les journaux montréalais et la campagne référendaire." *Réseau* 16 (2): 13–16.

3

FREE TO BE RESPONSIBLE
The Accountability
of the Print Media

Christopher Dornan

THE CENTRAL ROLE of the news media in Canadian society is now both an acknowledged fact and a consequent cause for concern. As the chief sources of information about and commentary on the political process, the media are charged with documenting the full range of opinion, debate and policy positions in Canadian politics. This is especially true in the coverage of election campaigns, since elections are the crucial moments at which the polity registers its will on the question of how it wishes to be governed. For democracy to function as it should, therefore, it is imperative that the press be fair and unbiased in its coverage – and presumably open to correction if it is not.

There can be little doubt that the print media play an important role in the processes whereby citizens return their elected representatives. When asked to identify factors affecting their voting decisions, 16 percent of Ontario voters in the 1974 federal election mentioned election news in newspapers as very important, and a further 35 percent mentioned it as somewhat important (Fletcher 1981, 80). In fact, the press may wield a greater influence than such figures might suggest, since newspapers are read by politically attentive opinion leaders, and because they influence the agenda of broadcast journalists (ibid., 81). In addition, although editorial endorsements of candidates may no longer be of crucial import in the outcome of federal and provincial elections, in an era of increased voter volatility unfavourable news coverage of a candidate may well contribute to his or her defeat (ibid., 79–80). Certainly, one of the reasons print coverage is of concern to political candidates is that the information presented in newspapers and magazines appears to be the most mediated by journalists, while television, by comparison, because it allows free- and paid-time broadcasts, extended interviews and direct "sound bites," seems more open to control by the parties (Fletcher 1987, 347). It is understandable, therefore, that politicians might welcome some mechanism that would ensure fair and impartial print media coverage of elections and provide avenues of redress in the event of complaints about inadequate or biased reporting.

Yet it is far from clear that at present the press is, indeed, open to correction. Anxieties over press bias, lack of fairness, sensationalism, hurtful or needless invasion of privacy and so on have been expressed by groups as large as political parties and as small as individual candidates and their families. Comber and Mayne's 1986 work *The Newsmongers* is subtitled *How the Media Distort the Political News;* it criticizes the conduct of the fourth estate from a point of view that sympathizes, as Peter Trueman observes in his foreword, not only with "the ordinary Canadians who are at the receiving end of Canadian journalism," but "with the people who are reported on" (ibid., 9). The authors observe that "a favourite journalistic device is to compare politics to a stage play" (ibid., 17) – a metaphor that allows the journalist to assume the mantle of a critic, panning or praising the performances of the various actors on the political stage. Comber and Mayne do not object to this, but, pursuing the metaphor, they argue that the media's "criticism" has begun to usurp the play itself: the press now not only presumes to direct the proceedings, dictating how the actors should comport themselves, but indeed clambers up onto the stage to mount a production of its own. "The actors feel up-staged by all this commotion, but they don't complain. They know that the reviewers are very important to the success of their performances" (ibid., 83). Indeed, since the public is able to follow the play only through the accounts of the journalist-critics, one might well ask: to whom would the actor-politicians complain?

To choose one example among many cited by Comber and Mayne: in 1979 Joe Clark, then leader of the Opposition, embarked on a tour of Japan, India, Greece, Israel and Jordan. During a stopover in Bangkok, Egypt Air neglected to transfer Clark's luggage to a Lufthansa flight. As a result, the baggage was a day late arriving in New Delhi. Comber and Mayne fault the press for seizing upon this minor incident – in which blame could hardly be ascribed legitimately to Clark – so as to engineer an image of the man as a hopeless buffoon, an administrative incompetent, an object of derision (Comber and Mayne 1986, 49–50). In the view of Comber and Mayne, not only was such a portrait unwarranted, but it had more to do with the fact that the journalists on the tour had been inconvenienced by the loss of their luggage, too, than with the capabilities of the Leader of the Opposition. However, the incident illustrates the dilemma facing those who find themselves the objects of unkind press attention: where can one turn for an impartial assessment of whether the press has discharged its duties responsibly?

Doubtless in a free society there will always be friction between the press and politicians. The latter cannot help but resent what they see as the former's control over the agenda of public concern, particularly during elections – those moments at which politicians most desperately desire to appeal directly to the electorate. Compounding the friction is the recognition that there are few means of redress open to those who see themselves as excluded, misrepresented or otherwise wronged in press coverage. Although the principle of "freedom of the press" as enshrined in the *Canadian Charter of Rights and Freedoms* is crucial to liberal democracy, it seems to many that this principle also works to shield the print media from accountability for their conduct. For example, the chapter on regulation of the media during elections in Soderlund et al. (1984) contains no reference to newspapers. Similarly, S.M. Robertson restricts comment on newspapers and election regulation to three sentences, the most important of which states that "there are few limits on what type of reporting may be done by newspapers covering federal or provincial elections" (1983, 92).

In fact, the print media are accountable in various ways. They are governed by legal restrictions such as election legislation, laws of libel and laws pertaining to "hate literature." Nonetheless, there are myriad instances in which recourse to the courts is not an option – one may sue for libel, for example, but not for "bias" – and it is on the areas of accountability not at present covered by legislation that this research study concentrates. In a nutshell, the problem of accountability arises from the fact that there is no higher authority to which individuals who feel they have been maltreated by press coverage can appeal.

Imagine, for example, that one is a candidate contesting a national election in the prime minister's home riding. The editors of the local newspaper decide to deploy their election coverage reporters in such a manner as to concentrate on the party leaders: reporters are assigned to each of the leaders' campaign planes. The result is coverage that may provide excellent and informative accounts of how the campaign is unfolding on the national stage, but unfortunately gives short shrift to the local campaigns of those running against the prime minister in his or her home constituency. As such a candidate, is one not entitled to complain that the newspaper's decision as to how to deploy its resources is unjustly impairing one's chances of winning the election? To whom would one complain? A phone call to senior editors is unlikely to cause the newspaper to reverse its strategic decisions as to how coverage is to be conducted. A letter to the editor hardly undoes the effect of being comparatively ignored in press coverage over the course of a campaign. An appeal to the paper's ombudsman, should such an office exist, might elicit attention to the campaign coverage in the ombudsman's column, but newspaper ombudsmen generally confine themselves to explaining their papers' policies to their readers; they are not empowered to alter such policy. A complaint to the local press council will not receive a ruling until well after the campaign has concluded, and even then the press council has no powers to direct the newspaper to conduct its election coverage differently. In any event, what right should a political candidate have to dictate to a newspaper how it should go about covering election contests?

The issue of accountability of the print media in an election, therefore, is at the core of the role and place of the press in the political process. It raises fundamental questions about the labour of the press and its relation to other social authorities, most notably the state. As a result, the issue of accountability in elections cannot be separated from the question of accountability in general. Accordingly, this study traces how the problem has been framed and discussed in the United States, the United Kingdom and Canada. That it does not arrive at a tidy conclusion or neatly packaged and universally acceptable recommendations is merely emblematic of how thorny and complicated is the issue of accountability for a free press in a free society.

THE PROBLEM OF ACCOUNTABILITY

The problem of the "accountability" of the print media arises from the collision of two mutually incompatible, but nonetheless crucial, tenets of liberal democracy. In that regard, it is an intractable problem. It can be "solved" only by abandoning liberal democratic ideals, or by contravening them. This inquiry into accountability of the press is therefore an investigation of contradiction, incongruity and irresolution. It is an exploration of the tension between, on the one hand, the insistence on liberty of public expression and, on the other, the fiat that no authority, in a democracy, may go unchecked.

That such a tension exists is evident in the marked ambivalence with which the press, prominent and profitable, is greeted in the late-20th-century West. Simultaneously, it is the object of two contradictory discourses, one of congratulation, the other of alarm. In the first instance, the press is a bulwark of democracy; in the second, it is an instrument of its degradation.[1] The celebratory discourse provides the urgency for press freedom; the alarmist raises calls for accountability.

The traditional textbook history of the press perhaps provides the best example of the congratulatory account, told as it is as a protracted but eventually triumphant struggle for the autonomy of the fourth estate from external authority – in effect, precisely to bring into being a fourth estate by securing the "freedom" of the press. It is an account that documents how the printing press made its appearance in western Europe in the context of an authoritarian social order, and that positions the new medium of public address at the heart of a political struggle between an ossified social authority and an emergent rationalist, libertarian order. Indeed, it credits the advent of printing with the eventual overthrow of authoritarian rule and the ascendance of scientific enlightenment, a dynamic and beneficial commerce, and democratic values. In short, the printing press is considered not simply a feature of modernity but one of its principal architectural agents.

It was able to play such a role by virtue of several happy technological features. The first, and most obvious, is that the printing press, a machine for the mass replication of texts, made possible the circulation of ideas and arguments to a vast and dispersed public, and therefore set in motion the circumstances whereby the will of such a public might become a decisive factor on the political stage. In addition, because it was mobile, and because it was relatively easy to conceal, the printing press proved to be notoriously difficult for traditional authorities to control. Although both church and state used the device to entrench doctrines that would support and perpetuate the prevailing order, dissidents of all stripes also used it to challenge the most fundamental of orthodoxies. The result was a new politics that allowed the governed a voice in determining how they were ruled, and simultaneously had at its disposal the means by which this could be accomplished. The printing press made possible a public discourse on human affairs that would provide the foundation for democratic political systems: the recognition that the course of events might be influenced by the simple act of publicly commenting on them. It demonstrated that democracy does not exist merely in a universal franchise exercised periodically at the polls; it requires also the right to contribute to the welter of public argument and opinion on the issues of the day. Without such a right, the franchise alone is empty and illusory. Hence, it is not simply that a democratic society tolerates an unbridled press, but also that a free press makes for a democratic society.

The traditional account of the press lionizes it for its struggle to detach itself from ecclesiastical and state authority, and celebrates a political system founded on the clash of ideas and argument. Clearly, like all liberties in a free society, liberty of expression can never be absolute. Democracy must be protected against those who would engineer its overthrow, and individual reputations must be protected against those who would malign them without due cause. Nonetheless, by historical precedent and philosophical principle, it is a feature of liberal democracy that no political agency should be hierarchically dominant over public expression; no authority (save the courts, in limited instances) should be empowered to police what may or may not see print. It is precisely this freedom from external constraint that ostensibly allows the medium of public discourse to police the conduct of other social institutions and authorities. And given that democracy is therefore anchored in public discourse, any attempt to control or constrain such discourse is to be resisted with the utmost vigour, since control over public debate would amount to control over the political process itself. Accordingly, the congratulatory account hails a free press as essential to a free society, points to liberty of expression as evidence of the superiority of democracy to other social systems, and greets any attempt to limit such freedom, no matter how apparently benignly motivated, as odious and dangerous.

As central to contemporary society as this understanding of the press is, it coexists with a sense of alarm that something has gone seriously amiss with public expression in the late 20th century. In this view, the ideals originally formed in the crucible of democracy have been overtaken, and the principle of freedom of the press is being used for little more than to further the financial and political interests of media proprietors. In brief, a sentiment is growing that the early libertarian rhetoric applied perfectly well when publishing was a relatively low-cost endeavour, when there was relatively open access to the battleground of public opinion, and when this seething and argumentative discourse functioned as a check on traditional sites of authority. However, now that mass communication has become dominated by a small number of huge bureaucratic enterprises devoted to the maximization of profit, the fourth estate is charged with having become a relatively closed social agency, seemingly unanswerable for its conduct, and with having jettisoned its responsibility to function as a forum for meaningful political debate in favour of serving as a tantalizing and titillating compendium of trivia. Far from preserving democracy, the current situation is viewed by many as fundamentally damaging to it. The result has been a widespread and burgeoning call for reform – for a redrafting of the rules by which public communication should be conducted.

Two points should be emphasized about this discourse of alarm. The first is that it is not new. Despite the tendency to think of the present disaffection with the mass media as a post-war phenomenon, it has its roots in the 19th century, as a concomitant of what this disaffection is about, namely the rise of a truly mass commercial press. As early as 1902, the Chancellor of Queen's University, Sir Sandford Fleming, alarmed at the contemporary state of the popular press, announced a $250 prize essay competition on the topic, "How can Canadian universities best benefit the profession of journalism, as a means of moulding and elevating public opinion?" The 13 entries, published in book form the next year, uniformly lamented the fact that the press, unprecedented in its potential as "a popular educator and a moral force" (Queen's Quarterly 1903, 11), was in fact being squandered on the opposite: "It kills time, satisfies the thirst for scandal, and acts as a preventive to thought" (ibid., 152). In turn, each of the essays deplored Canadian journalism's preoccupation with lurid crime, its invasions of privacy (specifically, the privacy of the powerful), the dominance of American news, the unsavoury influence of advertising (on both news content and gullible consumers), the literary bankruptcy of newspaper prose, and the fact that reading matter had become "a 'rivulet of text' amid a wilderness of pictures" (ibid., 131). Indeed, in a strikingly modern passage, W.S. Johnston of Montreal saw the popular papers as part of the degradation of the times, an era characterized by "exaggeration and artificiality" (ibid., 134), and chafed at "the vulgarizing of the news press ... this 'ferment', this 'froth and scum' of the world's news has demoralized our journalism; it threatens our modern culture like some new wave of barbarism ... This is an age ... of gradual decay, of obliteration of the highest ideals, of secularization – the beginning of a period of lapse – the end of a great period of history" (ibid., 126).

The second point is that, as old as the alarmist warnings are, there is little agreement beyond a general consensus that not all is well in the realm of public discourse, on what, precisely, has gone wrong. Some writers, for example, worry that the press, unelected and unanswerable, has acquired a political authority it does not deserve but wields with impunity. Thus Taras observes that "journalists have gone from being relatively powerless to being significant wielders of influence" (1990, vii). The press can make and unmake candidates, starve campaigns of the oxygen of publicity (to borrow Margaret Thatcher's phrase), dwell on gaffes, orchestrate hysteria both favourable and unfavourable. Some insist that this is a power typically exercised in favour of conservative ideologies and the interests of capital, since these are the self-interests of the few individuals who have come to dominate newspaper ownership. Others argue to the contrary that the press is inevitably biased in favour of the political left, since newsworkers themselves are overwhelmingly liberal in their inclinations (see Hackett 1984).[2]

Still others maintain that the problem resides in the press's relative lack of influence in an era dominated by corporate capital and big government. In such a context, the press is said to have become the compliant handservant of interests that are not necessarily those of the public good. Its "irresponsibility" resides in the fact that it is no longer discharging the duties with which it was originally entrusted. If there is a problem of "accountability," it is that the press no longer holds other social actors strictly accountable. Thus, Entman bemoans the fact that "Given the way politics is practised in the late twentieth-century United States, the media become crucial to any theory that government can be made responsive to genuine, independently considered (rather than manipulated) public preferences ... Unfortunately, this burden is too great; the media cannot live up to the demands that modern American democracy imposes on them" (1989, 9). Clarke and Evans, similarly, lament that a lazy and docile press serves to "weaken Congress's public accountability," with the result that "genuine opportunities to 'turn the rascals out' are rare. And the content of press coverage provides a meagre base for fuelling vigorous public debate" (1983, 5).

Still others argue that the difficulty lies, not in the relative powerlessness of the press, but in the logic of the marketplace. The drive for readership and profit, given the example and competition of television, has driven popular journalism to provide sensation and transient gratification, rather than to appeal to reader intellect. It has transformed public discourse into the equivalent of a carnie funhouse. In a clear echo of W.S. Johnston's apocalyptic 1903 warning, the charge is that we, the citizens of late-20th-century North America, are "amusing ourselves to death" (Postman 1985).

These conflicting readings of the status and performance of the press make some sense if considered in light of the manner in which official culture itself has posed the problem. Canada has had two official inquiries into the popular press in the post-war period. Both the Special Senate Committee on Mass Media (Davey Committee) (Canada, Senate 1970) and the Royal Commission on Newspapers (Kent Commission) (Canada, Royal Commission 1981) embarked from the concern that increasing concentration of ownership, a drift toward monopoly newspaper markets, and the rise of multimedia conglomerates together posed a serious threat to the public good. Broadly, the danger came in two forms, one present, the other potential.

The present danger – and, as a charge against the press, doubtless the weaker of the two – was that the open forum of public discourse was being steadily undermined, not by a hostile state, but by commercial imperatives that reduced the number and variety of opinions that saw public light. The potential danger was that "too much power" was being put "in too few hands; and it is power without accountability" (Canada, Royal Commission 1981, 220). The suggestion was not that newspaper proprietors were in fact using their holdings to manipulate public opinion, but that they were in a position potentially to do so, and that this was a possibility that had to be forestalled.

But although grave concerns were raised and stern corrective measures recommended, neither official inquiry prompted much in the way of remedial action. This is not merely because interference in the affairs of the press, particularly anything smacking of government interference, is anathema to liberal democracy. It is also because neither inquiry could show conclusively that its core worries about concentration of ownership merited intervention (Siegel 1983, 146–47). Nor is it clear that such proof is, in fact, possible.

It is important to realize that the defence of corporate journalism against the type of charges laid by Davey and Kent is to be found in the ideal, ideology or practice of objectivity. Although they differ as to when and how the ethos of objectivity emerged as the guiding rationale for modern journalism, both Schudson (1978) and Schiller (1981) see it as a product of a mass, commercial press dependent on advertising revenue. In that regard, it can be argued that the development of the ideology of objectivity was an explicit response to the disappearance of a certain type of journalism (and consequently a certain type of press freedom). As the large-circulation omnibus newspapers squeezed the partisan journals out of existence, freedom of the press shifted from the liberty to agitate for a political platform to the freedom to speak the facts: that is, to provide a neutral and objective record of events. It could hardly have been otherwise. The ethos of objectivity is essential to the creation of newspaper empires. First, a mass press striving for universal circulation risks alienating potential readers only at its peril; accordingly, the partisan press gives way to its objective successor as an effect of market economics. Second, given the reduction in the number of daily newspapers and their concentration in the hands of a few, had these few used the press to promulgate self-interested political lines – in short, to propagandize the population – the newspaper chains would have been dismantled long ago. No free society could risk such centralized and idiosyncratic control of its agencies of public communication: it would be the moral equivalent of allowing private citizens of sufficient means to keep standing armies.

The fact that an objective press is a corporate press does nothing to diminish the right of the fourth estate to autonomy from interference by the state. On the contrary, it buttresses such a right. It is precisely the freedom from external influence that supposedly permits objective coverage, that ensures the ability of the press to speak the truth. An objective journalism is only possible given a press impervious to self-interested pressure. Hence the ethos of objectivity purportedly ensures that reportage is immune from both the blandishments of government and the dictates of proprietors.

According to such a view, mere ownership of the press does not confer the ability to orchestrate public opinion, since one's employees are beholden to, and protected by, professional standards. Similarly, although reporters might well lean toward the political left (or even to the right), their personal convictions properly are smothered by their professional commitments. As to the charge that the range and quality of political debate as presented in the popular press are constricted and shallow, the response is that the press, as objective stenographer of current events, can do no more than record the range and quality of political debate as it is conducted on the social stage. If the former is lacking, it is only because the latter is deficient.

The question of the political power of the press is similarly answered. It is conceded that the fourth estate exercises a certain influence in political affairs, but at the same time there is the insistence that this is largely a neutral power, and one that works only for the public good. While the early, partisan press may have been active in the political sphere in its own right, championing the policies of the publisher (or those of the newspaper's patron party) and ridiculing those of rivals, an "objective" press stands apart from the political sphere, merely documenting events and arguments for the benefit of a heterogeneous readership. It is not itself an actor on the political stage, but simply a paid and necessary witness, the vicarious eyes and ears of its public. Although the newspaper may advocate certain policies and endorse parties or politicians in its editorials, this advocacy is purportedly conducted purely in the interest of what the paper considers to be the public good, not from dogmatic ideological commitments. Thus the fourth estate is in the peculiar position of conceding that it is not without political influence, while nonetheless insisting that such influence is blind, disinterested and non-discretionary: in a word, objective.[3] As Richard S. Salant, then president of CBS news, once told *TV Guide* in a remark much quoted subsequently: "Our reporters do not cover stories from *their* point of view. They are presenting them from *nobody's* point of view" (cited in Epstein 1973, viii). Thus, it is not that the press is a social force unanswerable for its conduct. On the contrary, its work is conducted in the name of the collective, and it is answerable to the collective for the ideals of accuracy and objectivity. Its work merely happens also to be conducted to the financial benefit of proprietors and shareholders.

The results of a January 1991 *Maclean's*/Decima poll would appear to indicate that this view of the press is widely held by Canadians. Less than one-third of respondents said that Canadian journalists do not do their work accurately, and more than half said that journalists are objective in their reporting. Nonetheless, the difficulties with this defence of the cultural labour of the press are legion, and the central tenet of journalistic objectivity has long preoccupied academic commentators. For the present, it should suffice to point to two demurring lines of argument.

The first is the complaint, registered most often and most forcefully by leftist critics of the press, that the ideal of objectivity, far from purging the press of bias, is in fact the most insidious form of bias of all, since it presents as necessary, natural and inevitable a view of social and political affairs that is in actuality highly contingent and politically charged. The ethos of objectivity – what Tuchman (1978) calls the press's principal "strategic ritual" – offers up as *the* version of events what is in reality only *a* version of events, and in so doing both fixes the terms by which the world is to be publicly apprehended and closes off alternative means of interpreting and understanding the same events. In this view, the much-vaunted neutrality of the "objective" press is an illusion, masking its fundamental commitment to (what leftist critics denounce as) an inegalitarian social order (see, for example, Tuchman 1978; Hall 1982; Fishman 1980; Glasgow University Media Group 1976).

The second is a growing awareness that the portrait of the press as detached observer of the passing social scene, standing outside looking in, merely transcribing events in which the press itself plays no part, is a wholly inadequate characterization of the conduct of journalism in the late 20th century. As long ago as 1961, Boorstin in *The Image* pointed to the role that even the prospect of media attention could play in the orchestration of events. More recently, Canadians have had direct and repeated experience of how press attention may work to influence how events unfold – not because journalists consciously work to skew their accounts, but simply because they render accounts. After the summer of 1990, given the collapse of the Meech Lake accord and especially the events at Oka, there can be little doubt that the presence and prominence of society's paid witnesses played a part in determining the eventual course of events. Again, this is not to say that journalists were not objective, or that they deliberately exerted an influence on these events, and it is certainly not to suggest that journalists should have been kept in the dark or muzzled. It is, however, to say that what physicists have known since 1927 as the Heisenberg uncertainty or indeterminacy principle – that it is impossible to observe without influencing the outcome of what one is looking at – is as much a factor in social and political affairs as it is at the level of subatomic particles.

Clearly, even if only in as yet the most tentative manner, this is something that journalism has itself come to recognize: namely, that the press is unavoidably participant in the political processes it documents, and it is in this that its influence resides. There is not first politics and then only subsequently press accounts of political actions; rather, the documentation of and commentary on political affairs by the popular press is part and parcel of the political process.[4]

Thus Taras's 1990 work is subtitled *The Media's Influence on Canadian Politics*, but it is the main title that is more revealing: *The Newsmakers*. The title is a play on words, since "newsmakers" until recently referred to the *sources* of news – politicians, officials, celebrities and so on – but in this instance it refers to the journalists themselves. Coincidentally, 1990 also saw the publication of a volume by Frum, consisting of edited interviews with a series of prominent Canadian journalists. It, too, was titled *The Newsmakers*. And in 1989, CTV ran a series of advertisements in newspapers for its national newscast, featuring a Karsh-like photograph of anchor Lloyd Robertson under the legend "reliable source." Again, the play on words was deliberate: a news "source" once referred to an individual who supplied information to journalists, or whose actions merited coverage; the "source" has now become the journalistic enterprise itself. As well, a *Globe and Mail* promo, displayed on vending stands during the summer of 1991, proclaimed: "Jeffrey Simpson – Commentary that helps shape the nation's political agenda."

These are perhaps trivial examples, but they point to a growing realization that the press can no longer be thought of as merely an inert conduit for the transmission of objective information to the public. Journalists may not wield a discretionary influence on political affairs, but they wield an influence nonetheless that accrues from the mere act of publication – literally, of making things public. The fact that their work has been so little examined in these terms – as opposed to inquiries into whether and in what ways the press is the compliant or unwitting tool of hidden political interests – is doubtless one reason why the issue and problem of the "accountability" of the press remains murky and unresolved.

With this in mind, it is now in order to examine the ways in which the problem of press accountability has been addressed in Anglo-American commissions of inquiry since the Second World War. Although none of these inquiries has arrived at solutions or recommendations satisfactory to all parties concerned, their deliberations nevertheless shed light on the issues at stake and the difficulties they raise.

THE UNITED STATES: THE HUTCHINS COMMISSION AND SOCIAL RESPONSIBILITY

The problem of accountability, and the issues attendant upon it, have prompted a number of official inquiries into the role of the press in the Anglo-American tradition. These have been typically triggered by a concert of incidents which galvanized concern over the press's conduct on the social stage. In the United Kingdom, Canada and Australia these inquiries have been carried out under the aegis of the state in the form of royal commissions, Senate committees or their equivalent. In the United States, however, the most famous and far-reaching of such inquiries was initiated by the *Time* magazine press baron Henry R. Luce, who provided $200 000 to finance its operations.

The fact that this initiative, headed by Robert Hutchins, then president of the University of Chicago, was undertaken at the behest of a media proprietor says much about the difference in tone and circumstance between the American inquiry and British or Canadian royal commissions. Whereas the latter have been motivated by the question of what might be done to correct what are perceived as dysfunctional tendencies on the part of the press, Luce sought a body that would reaffirm the importance and centrality of a free press to the United States, particularly in the face of mounting criticism of American journalism and calls that its excesses and improprieties be reined in. The formation, deliberations, recommendations and outcome of the Commission on Freedom of the Press (COFOP 1947) are expertly documented by Blanchard (1977) and McIntyre (1987), and it is from these accounts that what follows is largely drawn.

Prior to the 1930s, the American newspaper industry had understood and defined the First Amendment to the U.S. Constitution – "Congress shall make no law ... abridging the freedom of speech, or of the press" – in terms of prior restraint over publication. Specifically, the press claimed the right to operate as a business without government interference, a right expressed baldly in an oft-quoted remark attributed to William Peter Hamilton, an editor of the *Wall Street Journal*: "A newspaper is a private enterprise owing nothing whatever to the public, which grants it no franchise. It is therefore affected with no public interest.

It is emphatically the property of the owner, who is selling a manufactured property at his own risk" (Peterson 1956, 73).

Over the course of the 1930s, however, litigation involving newspapers increased, bringing into being an interpretation of the First Amendment that was the product of the courts, not the press. "Freedom of the press was being defined as a right of the people to obtain information necessary for survival in a rapidly changing world, not as a right of publishers to operate without consideration of people's needs" (Blanchard 1977, 4).

At the same time, bills such as wage and hours legislation, which tangentially involved regulating the financial affairs of the press, were working their way through Congress. For example, elements of Franklin D. Roosevelt's *National Industrial Recovery Act* – designed to increase employment, shorten working hours, raise wages and stabilize profits – were greeted by press proprietors as a clear attempt to regulate their affairs. Increasing wages and decreasing hours would diminish newspapers' profitability; limiting child labour might mean replacing newspaper carrier boys with adult employees; required collective bargaining was seen as government intrusion into the newsroom.

Heightening newspaper proprietors' anxieties was the fact that their own conduct was coming increasingly under attack from myriad critics of the press. "Almost with one voice, they labelled the press a representative of established commercial interests and of the upper socioeconomic class, out of step with the general population's wishes for society while reflecting the biases of its owners in its presentation of the news" (Blanchard 1977, 8). The feeling was that the press had used the First Amendment as a convenient shield, subverting its original intention with an undue emphasis on proprietary rights.

It was in this climate that the Hutchins Commission was formed in late 1943, and met for a total of 17 two- or three-day meetings until September 1946. It marked the first attempt in the post-war years to grapple with the problems posed by corporate journalism, its members included some of the most distinguished northeastern American intellectuals of the day,[5] and the proposals it issued in 1947 are germane to any discussion of press accountability.

The Commission members were uniformly committed to freedom of expression and the press. However, they were also convinced that the new circumstances of an uncertain post-war world imposed new responsibilities on a commercial press, and that it was the duty of the Commission to define these. As Commission member Archibald MacLeish reminded his colleagues, "a free society could not permit its press to use freedom to destroy freedom" (McIntyre 1987, 141).

On this much, at least, there was broad consensus within the Commission. But, as McIntyre emphasizes, beyond this most general agreement, there was no easy or obvious commonality of opinion. If Luce had believed that it would be a straightforward matter for a group of first-rate minds to arrive at an unequivocal statement of how freedom of the press could be preserved and exalted, while simultaneously constrained to operate in the public interest, he was to be disappointed.

With the prominent exception of William Hocking (1947), the Commission thought of freedom of expression as a social imperative, but one rooted in individual rights and duties. It was not simply that individuals had a right to have access to the most widespread exchange of ideas and argument, but that the most widespread exchange of ideas and argument depended on the duty of individuals to contribute to public discourse. Thus, and on this Hocking concurred, freedom of the press was held to have a dual nature, including both the right to receive adequate information and the right to express oneself. This is clearly a reversal of the traditional understanding of freedom of the press as a proprietor's right to publish. It places the onus instead on the right of the public to be informed, and saddles publishers with the responsibility to guarantee this right. The "freedom from" government interference that permits unconstrained expression must be conjoined to a "freedom for" individuals to express themselves. The Commission was profoundly disturbed by the fact that a corporate press was prohibiting public access to the means of communication.

The analogy the Commission drew was to mass education. The media, Hocking argued, were similar to private schools in that they were, in effect, "a private taking-over of a public function without full public responsibility" (McIntyre 1987, 144). However, it was entirely unclear as to how the press could be charged with meeting its "full public responsibility" – that is, how a moral duty to serve the common weal could be enforced in practice. In the end, the Commission rejected any suggestion that this moral duty might be legally imposed, holding that "however much the correction of abuse might have to come from external sources, it was still desirable that those external sources should not be government." It looked instead for "remedies that would rely on the moral obligations they had been discussing, not on legal sanctions" (ibid., 146). But behind this call for voluntary acquiescence on the part of the press lay a resignation that assumed the proportions of a threat. As Zechariah Chafee Jr., said, "if it isn't done by voluntary action, sooner or later it is going to be done by law" (ibid., 146).

Although the Commission saw concentration of ownership as damaging to the ideal of an open public forum, it did not accept (with

MacLeish dissenting) that artificially interceding in the media market-place to dismantle chain ownership would produce the type of public discourse it thought necessary for the healthy functioning of a free society. And while the Commission blamed an incessant drive for profit for the media's "trivial, escapist, and repetitious or ludicrously juvenile and trite entertainment" (McIntyre 1987, 147), the Commission did not think it possible or desirable to interfere with the commercial basis of mass communication.

Also problematic for the Commission was the rationality of media audiences. Bluntly, the members had serious doubts about the public's ability to recognize the duties of a citizen of a free society and to discharge these by participating in open debate. The Commission feared that, though its members might conceive of the perfect newspaper, it was an artefact the public would never "live up to."[6] The members resigned themselves to the recognition that, in Hocking's phrase, liberalism "was built on certain over-enthusiastic assumptions" (McIntyre 1987, 148), among them assumptions about the rationality of people.

Nonetheless, the problem remained of how to make a free press accountable for its responsibilities. In searching for a solution, the Commission sifted through a variety of options or models available to it, many borrowed from innovations of the New Deal and the Progressive Era. The Commission considered the notion of trusteeship of the press, and the possibility of federal subsidies to media outlets in areas where the public might be underserviced. Parallels were suggested with endowed universities and with state support of libraries and museums, as well as with responsible consumer pressure groups. The Federal Communications Commission (FCC), the U.S. broadcasting regulatory agency, was at one point considered to be a promising model, especially since many members of the Hutchins Commission thought that the new post-war media would be combinations of the traditional print, film and broadcast media.[7]

Two other regulatory models were taken to be more promising, however: the public utility and the common carrier. Unlike the FCC, a government agency, public utilities and common carriers are businesses, but businesses in areas so essential that they warrant regulation in order to correct the dysfunctional tendencies of a monopoly market. Eventually, the public utility idea was abandoned because it required sharp legal teeth and smacked of direct interference in the profitability of the press. The common carrier notion retained its appeal until quite late in the day, since it involved little more than opening the media of mass communication to partisan advocacy or opinion: "They need not publish every idea, however preposterous, of course; but they should see that 'all ideas deserving a public hearing shall have a public hearing'. The public as well as the editors and owners should decide what ideas deserve a public hearing" (Peterson 1956, 101). Ultimately, however, the common carrier notion, too, foundered on the fact that it would require, in some measure, legal enforcement.

The eventual solution was not, in fact, a solution but a compromise that "came by default or as a consequence of the commission's lack of faith in any other source of control" (McIntyre 1987, 151). It was the suggestion that citizens' participation in the communication process might be effected by the creation of a citizens' agency or agencies that would monitor press performance and function as the only means whereby the press might be brought to account. It had been an idea present from the start of the Commission's discussions, but one on which the members were reluctant to focus, perhaps because it was in fact an old idea: the first press council had been created in Sweden in 1916 (Desbarats 1990, 160).

Nonetheless, the proposal for a citizens' agency was the best the Hutchins Commission could do. Untainted by government or industry influence, "it was the only workable external mechanism they could agree on to protect the unenforceable right of freedom of the press" (McIntyre 1987, 152). In effect, what the Commission proposed was the permanent creation of a body such as itself, a hand-picked élite group that would hector the press into living up to its responsibilities on behalf of the less-enlightened masses.

The lack of unanimity among the members of the Commission is evident in the fact that the eventual main report went through nine revisions by three authors. (There were a number of ancillary volumes and research reports.) Most members were convinced that, since the report called for voluntary cooperation on the part of the press, any indictment of the media should be softened and qualified by a sensitivity to the intricacies newspaper work involved and indeed by praise, lest the document anger and alienate the journalists who would receive it. Others argued that moral indignation was not only necessary, but lay at the heart of the call for reform. In the final instance, the report was written tersely and simply (or so the Commission members believed) so as to be accessible to the press and public, and it shied away from both radical recommendations and radical rhetoric.

This was not enough to ensure an enthusiastic reception by the press itself. Although some journals received the document as a constructive, bracing tonic that delivered a well-deserved critique, in many quarters it was faulted for the absence of distinguished journalists as Commission members and authors, and denounced vituperatively as slipshod, woolly-minded and obscure, and a dangerous invitation to government censorship (Blanchard 1977, 29–48). There is still some confusion over the reaction of its patron, Luce. He may well have accepted its general conclusions; he may also have railed at the report's "appalling lack of even high school logic" (Schmuhl 1984, 40).

As Blanchard (1977) emphasizes, however, the report ultimately served as an indication of the increasing attention paid by the fourth estate to its own responsibilities – and the increasingly perceived need for such attention – and opened up the press's activities to serious, on-going criticism. By no means was the report an anomalous document, out of step with shifting opinion on the question of press conduct. On the contrary, the newspaper industry itself had already begun to take steps in line with the recommendations tabled by the Commission. In February 1946, the American Press Institute was founded. The Society of Nieman Fellows of Harvard published the first issue of *Nieman Reports*, the United States' first journalism review, twelve months later. The television series "CBS Views the Press" came on the air in New York City in June 1947. The following month the National Council of Editorial Writers was formed. A book of press criticism by Nieman Fellows, *Your Newspaper*, appeared in 1948. *Editor and Publisher* sponsored a panel discussion devoted to the self-improvement of newspapers in 1949. Later that year, the American Society of Newspaper Editors set up a committee to examine the need for self-criticism by newspapers, which by 1950 became a permanent body (Blanchard 1977, 48–50).

Indeed, the enduring legacy of the Hutchins Commission, at least in the United States, was not its suggestion of a citizens' monitoring agency. The concept of a press council has never been enthusiastically embraced in the U.S. Although a National News Council was established in 1973, it failed to secure the support or cooperation of the major papers even in New York City, where it was headquartered, and it voted to dissolve itself on 22 March 1984 (see Brogan 1985). Rather, the legacy of the Commission was that its broad recommendations crystallized relatively quickly into a call for what Peterson would later characterize as "social responsibility of the press" – in effect, the demand that journalists, editors and publishers comport themselves with the best interest of the public foremost in their minds. This demand echoed the arguments of the Queen's University essayists who held, 44 years before the Hutchins Commission report, that the deficiencies of the popular press might be remedied if only newsworkers were "inspired by the ideals cherished in the university" rather than those of "the counting room" (Queen's Quarterly 1903, 109).

Similarly, the Hutchins Commission encouraged journalism to assume a professional spirit, along the lines of that maintained by medicine or law. The Commission did not mean by this that journalism should license its practitioners, but rather that newsworkers should recognize that they had obligations beyond those of mere career advancement and circulation gains. As the final report put it, "there are some things which a truly professional man will not do for money" (COFOP 1947, 92).

This is an interesting response to an interesting dilemma. In a sense, the call for social responsibility can be read as an objection to the populist tendencies of what is manifestly and necessarily a popular medium. The excesses, outrages and irresponsibility of the press are traced to the fact that it is a commercial enterprise driven to make its profit by pandering to popular taste; it is the compulsion to maximize readership that ostensibly sullies the practice of journalism. The solution holds that the excesses of the press can be corrected if only the men and women of the press would behave as gentlemen and gentlewomen. They should mimic the professional comportment of doctors and lawyers (a suggestion that intriguingly supposes that in the United States medicine and law are not driven by the pursuit of personal gain). Thus, although the problem with the press is located at the institutional level – in the fact that it is an agency governed by the dictates of market economics – the solution is to be found at the level of the conduct of individual journalists. Although the members of the Hutchins Commission began by discussing the notion of "accountability," in the end this had been transformed into the concept of "responsibility." The shift is not insignificant, for while the former suggests a responsibility imposed from the outside (a policing function), the latter is accountability imposed from the inside (implying a conscience).

There can be little doubt that the notion of social responsibility – that the press has obligations to its readership and to society that override the simple pursuit of profit – conjoined to the practice of objectivity in reporting, has become the de facto operational ethos of American (and, indeed, Canadian) journalism. As recently as 1986, Merrill was able to reiterate that, since responsibility could be imposed neither by government nor by a professional body (the first would fly in the face of the First Amendment, while the second entails licensing), the only form of responsibility congruent with "our ideology, our constitution, our tradition, and our concern for a pluralistic society" is that which "is pluralistically defined or determined by the individual journalists themselves" (Merrill 1986, 49). This depends on a moral consciousness such that newspaper workers "will voluntarily act more responsibly in accordance with their own ethical principles" (ibid., 53). The advantage of such a system of responsibility, presumably, is that the existence of a conscience implies that journalists and newspapers are vulnerable to shame in instances where the code of conduct (albeit unwritten) has been violated. It is via shame, or its prospect, that transgressions of responsible coverage might be forestalled or redressed.

This description of the state of affairs with regard to the American press leaves important considerations unresolved. The first has to do with the fact that the Hutchins Commission conceived of "accountability" primarily in terms of citizen access to the realm of public discourse. It did not grapple directly with the question of what avenues of recourse are, or should be, open to those who have not been libelled by the press, but who nonetheless judge themselves to have been wronged by unfair press coverage. The second concerns what happens in a society with a mass commercial press when that press displays little conscience and therefore is impervious to shame. Both of these issues have been squarely addressed in Britain, which has lately been much more vigorous than either the United States or Canada in pressing for mechanisms that would hold the press accountable. Accordingly, it is to the British experience that we now turn.

THE BRITISH EXPERIENCE: TOWARD THE RIGHT OF REPLY

As similar as the American and British news media are, there are also marked differences in their tone and content, the economic foundation of their operations, their relations to their respective states and the political climate within which they work. It should suffice here to point to two of the most prominent of these differences.

The first difference has to do with the ambiguous status of the state in British debate over media regulation and press accountability. While in the U.S., even advocates of press reform view the intrusion of the state into matters of public expression as unacceptable, in Britain this is not necessarily the case. True, each of the three royal commissions on the press (United Kingdom, Parliament 1949; 1962; 1976 and 1977) since the end of the Second World War has refused to entertain the possibility of state regulation of the fourth estate, casting such an option as a threat to freedom of expression. True, measures such as the government's ban on broadcasting interviews with Sinn Fein and 10 other Northern Irish republican or loyalist organizations have generated heated controversy. At the same time, however, state involvement in mass communication via broadcasting is generally seen as a benign intervention, a necessary corrective to the inevitable tendencies of an unbridled market and a means by which the public good may take precedence over private gain. This provides advocates of press reform with an extant model of arm's-length regulation that might be applied to newspapers.

The second difference has to do with the nature and conduct of the press itself. The United States and Canada have developed a press that is predominantly parochial. Although there are national newspapers (*USA Today*, the *Globe and Mail*) and magazines (*Time, Newsweek, Maclean's*), most North American print journalism takes the form of omnibus newspapers that serve and cover their city of origin, but (with occasional exceptions such as the *New York Times*) are little read outside local environs. Britain, by contrast, has a local press (the so-called regional or provincial papers), but the most prominent journals are nationally distributed from London: the *Times*, the *Independent*, the *Daily Telegraph*, the *Mirror*, the *Sun*, etc.[8] This gives the British papers enormous readerships by North American standards, especially the populist tabloids, which may have circulations measured in multiples of millions.

Indeed, it is not only the national character of the British press that distinguishes it from the North American, but along with it, precisely the prominence of the tabloids. North America has its tabloids too, but (again, with certain exceptions in New York City) they are of an altogether different order from those that thrive in Britain. The large-circulation North American tabloids are typically weeklies (the *National Enquirer*, the *National Examiner*, the *Globe*, the *Weekly World News*, etc.) that eschew coverage of political affairs in favour of celebrity gossip, oddball human interest stories, tales of the supernatural and credulity-stretching weight-loss programs. They may spread false rumours about the romantic liaisons of soap opera stars, but they pose little political threat to elected officials or government agencies. And while the headlines of the daily tabs, such as those of the Canadian *Sun* newspapers, may be bolder and larger than those of the broadsheets, and while their contents may be skewed toward news of crime and opinionated commentary, generally the daily North American tabloids are bound by much the same ethos of social responsibility as their more sober competitors. The most popular British tabloids, by contrast, have heretofore flouted such an ethos – or, at least, the notion that excess and sensation must be curbed by a sense of gentility and fair play. At times, it appears that the British tabloids are driven by a deliberate impulse to offend polite sensibilities. No headline is too arresting, no photograph too shocking, no story too sensational, no revelation too intimate.

The result is that British authorities have recently been much more vigorous than their North American counterparts in advocating means to bring the press to heel. While it is also true that many in Britain believe the press is at present *too* accountable to government – the 1911 *Official Secrets Act* in particular is viewed as a pernicious shield that protects government from press scrutiny – the most prominent initiatives of late have been aimed at holding the press to account for exploitative, intrusive and unwarranted coverage. On 1 January 1991, the British Press Council was disbanded and replaced by the Press Complaints Commission (PCC), a voluntary self-regulatory body like its predecessor, but one with a more focused mandate. The PCC has been given 18 months to demonstrate that press self-regulation can work. If not, the threat is that it will become a statutory body, with the legal authority to impose its decisions and levy fines.

As in the United States, the debate over press accountability in Britain began in earnest almost immediately after the Second World War. The first Royal Commission on the Press reported in 1949 and the second in 1962. Both of these inquiries held that, in the phrase of the 1949 Commission, "free enterprise is a prerequisite of a free press" (Curran and Seaton 1988, 247), argued that unrestricted freedom to publish produces a diverse and representative press, and attached great importance to the role of competition in rendering the press accountable: if errors or distortions saw public light, surely it would be to the profit of rival papers to set the record straight. At the same time, however, both Commissions worried that the trend of the marketplace was toward a reduction in competition and an increase in concentration of ownership, thus directly undermining the neutral guarantor of accountability. Hence, each in its turn advocated antimonopoly policies. The first recommended that the Monopolies Commission monitor changes in press ownership, but this had no effect on the changes in the British press system that occurred between 1949 and 1962. The second recommended the creation of a Press Amalgamations Court, a version of which came into being in 1965. It required large press groups to secure the permission of the Secretary of State to purchase additional newspapers. Again, its effectiveness was minimal, since not one of the 50 acquisitions by major press groups between 1965 and 1977 was disallowed (ibid., 253–54).

Like the Hutchins Commission, the 1949 Royal Commission also recommended the creation of a "General Council of the Press." This body was originally conceived of as well financed, widely respected and devoted to the investigation of complaints about press conduct, the recruitment and education of journalists, and the promotion of research into the press. A press council was founded in 1953, but it proved to be a pale imitation of what had been called for. Dependent on the press barons for financial support, it "functioned during its first ten years as little more than a public relations agency for the newspaper industry" (Curran and Seaton 1988, 255), and the reforms that followed the 1962 Commission were limited.

By the time the third Royal Commission was formed in 1977, the exercise of proprietorial power, once seen as a guarantee of diversity in the press, was viewed as a threat to diversity. Three men now controlled two-thirds of all newspaper sales in Britain. Commission members began to speak of the need to "protect editors and journalists from owners" (Curran and Seaton 1988, 249). At the same time, however, the Commission was ambivalent about how the situation might be rectified. It wanted a public service orientation to the British press, similar to that of British broadcasting, but was opposed to the framework of public regulation on which such an orientation is founded. It wanted a more balanced, responsible journalism – one untainted by inflammatory impulses – but was also committed to the tradition of partisanship and outspoken comment upheld by the free market tradition of the press (ibid., 258). It saw the problem as one rooted in the economics of newspaper publishing, but rejected economic intervention as a remedy on grounds that it was either impractical or politically unacceptable. The best it could do was to argue that press antimonopoly legislation should be greatly strengthened, a suggestion that was once again ignored.

The Commission reserved much of its stinging criticism for the Press Council, which it "excoriated ... for its lack of independence, its failure to enforce clear standards, and its general ineffectiveness" (Curran and Seaton 1988, 255). Commission members outlined 12 recommendations for its complete overhaul, including a charter of good journalistic practice to be policed by a reformed Press Council on a voluntary basis for a trial period. Of these recommendations, however, the Press Council rejected nine, including the suggestion for codified rules of conduct.

But while most of the recommendations of the 1977 Commission went ignored in the short term, they laid the groundwork for more recent attempts at reform, most having to do with the operation of the Press Council. By 1980, the National Union of Journalists had withdrawn from the body as a signal of its lack of confidence, and over the course of the 1980s criticism mounted that the council was ineffectual in upholding and enforcing standards of responsibility in British print journalism (see, for example, G. Robertson 1983). The impetus for current attempts at reform, however, came directly from the lobby group Campaign for Press and Broadcasting Freedom (CPBF), set up by the print unions in 1979. It was the CPBF that spearheaded the drive for a guaranteed right of reply, which would allow "victims" of press coverage the right to put their case in the very publications that had besmirched them. Since politicians were prominent among the targets of the tabloid press, the initiative, not surprisingly, found considerable parliamentary support. Opinion varied on what this right of reply should consist of, with some MPs holding that it should be restricted to the correction of demonstrable errors of fact, and others arguing that it should permit the correction of "distortions" in the widest possible sense. In the late 1980s, a number of private member's bills introduced in the Commons would have made some form of reply a legal right, and these received broad all-party support.

In 1989, two such bills, one introduced by a Conservative MP and the other by a Labour MP, were blocked only because the government promised yet another body of inquiry, the Calcutt Committee on Privacy and Related Matters, which delivered its report in June 1990, after nine months of investigation (United Kingdom, Parliament 1990). Both the industry and the Press Council had been making efforts to reform themselves; in April 1989, for example, the *Sun* appointed an ombudsman, an idea it had imported from North America, and within a year, there were 18 such "readers' representatives" working for British newspapers. On Calcutt's recommendation, however, the council was dissolved and replaced with the Press Complaints Commission.

Many in the press had feared that Calcutt would urge wide-ranging new laws on privacy and right of reply.[9] In fact, the Committee rejected such legislation, although it recommended that three new criminal offences be created for England and Wales, outlawing entering private property to obtain personal information for publication, placing eavesdropping devices on private property and photographing or recording individuals on private property for the purposes of publication. It recommended as well that the law preventing the identification of victims of crime such as rape be extended to cover the victims of other sexual assaults, and that the courts have the power to prevent identification of anyone alleged to have been assaulted. The government has indicated its willingness to pass such legislation.

However, it was Calcutt's recommendations for the creation of a Press Complaints Commission (PCC), which came into being in January 1991, that were most significant. Unlike the Press Council, which ruled on complaints about press conduct and agitated for freedom of the press, the PCC is to concentrate only on the former, on the grounds that adjudicating on complaints and defending press freedom are distinct functions that are not easily reconciled. Because the PCC is a voluntary, non-statutory body, it wields no powers to discipline editors and journalists or to impose fines on offending publications. Its function instead is to adjudicate on claims of unjust or unfair treatment by newspapers and claims of unwarranted infringement of privacy. It can recommend that papers publish an apology in cases where it rules in favour of the complainant, thus giving a form of right of reply, and it can also specify the placement of such an apology in the paper. In addition, it operates a "hot-line" service open to anyone being pursued against his or her wishes by journalists and photographers, which could result in prior restraint of publication. Its main tasks, however, are to conciliate between the press and aggrieved parties, to ensure "fast-track" corrections of factual errors (within days rather than months of the initial complaint), and where necessary to initiate inquiries into press conduct.[10]

Toward these ends, the PCC has drawn up a code of practice to which journalists are expected to adhere. Although the code merely sets out the most obvious ground rules for responsible conduct,[11] it is noteworthy that it was drafted by a working party of 11 editors chaired by the editor of the *News of the World,* in the past one of the main journalistic offenders. Indeed, the PCC distinguishes itself from its predecessor by virtue of the cooperation it has secured from the newspaper industry, including the aggressive tabloids. As opposed to the Press Council's annual budget of £600 000 per annum, the PCC has been promised a budget of £1.5 million, and a majority of its 16 members are editors or former editors. Lay members include such figures as Sir Richard Francis, director general of the British Council and a former BBC managing director, and Dame Mary Donaldson, a former lord mayor of London.

This cooperation on the part of the press, and especially on the part of the tabloid press, has been won by virtue of the threat that hangs over the PCC. When the government accepted the Calcutt Committee's recommendations, it accepted with the proviso that if self-regulation did not work this time, legislation would surely follow. The home secretary, David Waddington, told the Commons that the PCC was "positively the last chance" for voluntary self-regulation, adding, "that is not an idle threat." Press compliance was no doubt hastened by the fact that MPs overwhelmingly supported the report, and those who did not generally withheld their approval on the grounds that Calcutt did not go far enough.

Accordingly, the performance of the press and the PCC is to be reviewed after 18 months of the Commission's operation. The government has threatened that if even one maverick publication fails to abide by the Commission's rulings, the body will be replaced by a statutory tribunal headed by a judge and empowered to levy fines on offending publications.

Although the British example is instructive, it is doubtful that many of these initiatives could be practicably applied in Canada, at least not at this juncture. This is not just because a number of the British measures are likely to be seen in Canada as a dangerous encroachment on press liberty, but rather because the circumstances that have prompted the British actions simply do not exist in Canada. Bluntly, Canadian journalism has not been tarred by the sort of allegations directed at the British tabloids. That is to say, it is not decried as licentious, sensation mongering, intrusive and vulgar. The British measures have been invoked to combat a type of excess (or a style of journalism, depending on one's perspective) of which Canadian journalism has heretofore been innocent.

Nor do the British measures really offer a satisfactory resolution of the tension between the need to preserve liberty of the press and the desire to hold the press accountable for its actions. It is true that, thus far, the regulation of the U.K. press is voluntary, but this voluntarism has been secured only in the face of the forceful threat of statutory compliance. And when volitional self-regulation is born of compulsion, it is merely mandatory regulation, one step removed.

CANADA: THE LEGACY OF THE KENT COMMISSION

The last major inquiry into the state and conduct of the Canadian newspaper industry was the Royal Commission on Newspapers, the Kent Commission, which published its findings and recommendations in 1981. A great deal has been written about this Commission, and it is not necessary here to reiterate in detail what it argued and what came of its recommendations. However, the Kent Commission's deliberations and the reception of its suggestions give an indication of what is and is not politically or practically feasible in Canada in the area of press reform.

Although the Kent Commission did not tackle the problem of press accountability per se, this issue nonetheless featured in the inquiry's investigations. In essence, the Commission embarked from the same concern that motivated the Hutchins Commission in the United States and the three British royal commissions on the press. Prompted by the simultaneous closings of the Ottawa *Journal* and the Winnipeg *Tribune* on 27 August 1980, the Commission was founded on the proposition that the economics of newspaper publishing was undermining the principles by which the press ought to operate in a liberal democracy. Accordingly, the Commission understood its work as an attempt to salvage the classical role of the press: to preserve variety of expression in the face of an iron economic logic that appeared to lead inevitably to increased concentration of ownership, fewer newspaper titles and press ownership by conglomerate interests. Insofar as the problem of accountability was considered, the solution was again thought to lie in a return to robust competition: a competitive press would keep itself accountable.

It was obvious to the members of the Commission that to correct the situation there would have to be intervention to compensate for the economic tendencies of the newspaper-publishing market. The difficulty was that the only institution with the hierarchical authority to redraft the rules of commerce is the state, while under liberal democracy state interference in the affairs of the press historically has been proscribed. Thus the dilemma faced by the Commission was the same one that opened this report: to preserve the press as an agency for the expression of the widest possible variety of public and political opinion, it seemed necessary to contravene one of the most cherished principles of liberal democracy, namely the independence of the press from regulation by the state.

The rationale the Kent Commission invoked to justify such action was as follows: First, like the Hutchins Commission, it defined liberty of the press as a right that properly resided with the public, not with newspaper proprietors. Indeed, the first sentences of the first chapter of the Commission's report read: "Freedom of the press is not a property right of owners. It is a right of the people" (Canada, Royal Commission 1981, 1). Second, it split the editorial performance of the press from the economics of its ownership. It proposed that the state should have no right or opportunity to involve itself in editorial matters; it should have no say in the press's coverage of social and political events. But it should have the right to regulate ownership in the best public interest. The rules the Commission proposed to govern press ownership, it argued, entailed no external, direct control of a paper's content. It would have had to concede, however, that these measures entailed an indirect influence on newspaper content, since it proposed the ownership strictures precisely so as to enhance the variety of information and opinion available to the Canadian public.

Like the 1977 British royal commission, therefore, the Kent Commission sought to "protect editors and journalists from owners." Among its many recommendations was a call for the insulation of editorial operations from interference by chain and conglomerate superiors. Publishers whose assets exceeded the value of the newspaper itself would be required to appoint an "editor-in-chief" under a contract that would specify the publisher's commitment to the editorial operation. The editor-in-chief would publish an annual report in his or her newspaper evaluating the performance of the paper against the standards set out in the publisher's contract.

In addition, each newspaper that was not classified as "individually owned" would be required to appoint an Editorial Advisory Committee with seven members: two representing the publisher, two elected by the paper's journalists and three drawn from the local community. The Editorial Advisory Committee would receive the annual report of the editor-in-chief, and would itself report annually to a national Press Rights Panel.

The Press Rights Panel, composed of three members, was to be appointed by the federal Cabinet,[12] and report to Parliament through the minister of justice. Although its broad functions were conceived as predominantly geared to monitoring matters of ownership, it would also, by virtue of receiving the annual reports of the various editorial advisory committees, report on newspaper performance in the country, and could therefore have delivered a type of annual performance audit of the nation's press.

Had these recommendations been put into effect, Canada might have had mechanisms in place to allay fears about press accountability, since both the committees and the national Panel would have functioned as watchdogs of newspaper conduct. In the event of a truly egregious transgression of the unwritten code of social responsibility, these bodies would presumably have been well placed and had the moral authority to sound a public alarm. The work of the press could have been held to account by shaming its conscience.

It was the press itself, however, that reacted with alarm to such suggestions. On 19 and 20 August 1981, the nation's dailies made it clear that they would not go willingly into any future of the Kent Commission's design. Indeed, they would fight the implementation of the report with all the powers at their disposal – which is, ironically, to say that they would shout it down using their considerable influence as agencies of public address. The *Globe and Mail* characterized the report as "a veritable idiot's delight of interference in the ownership and operation of the nation's press." Under the heading "Big Brother for the papers," the *Winnipeg Free Press* judged that in the Press Rights Panel the Commission had crafted "a monster ... a powerful government bureaucracy ... [with] immense arbitrary powers." The Edmonton *Journal* held that if the recommendations were implemented "then democracy ... is looking on its own decay." The Vancouver *Province* argued that "no government in its right mind would fashion the suit of shackles the commission suggests," while a more colourful commentary by Jamie Lamb in the *Vancouver Sun* described the report as "rambling, subjective ... out of touch with reality," and dubbed it "Tom's Turkey, alias Kent's Cud." An editorial in the same paper called it "Draconian" and referred to "the leg irons of government control." The *Toronto Star* was the least incensed of the major metropolitan dailies, agreeing that alternative viewpoints should have access to the media, but otherwise the paper disagreed with the report's proposals.

The reaction of the press to the Kent Commission, and the fact that in the end nothing concrete came of the recommendations, provides a salutary lesson in what Canada will tolerate – or, rather, will not tolerate – in the way of press regulation. Parties hoping for a newspaper court of appeal, a higher formal authority to which the aggrieved may have recourse, are going to be disappointed. But this is not to say that the Kent Commission did not have an effect. An unkind reading of the Commission would hold that it was merely a sop to public concern over a newspaper industry that could act with such seemingly cold and sinister collusion as to close two newspapers on the same day, and then insist that it was mere coincidence. The commissioners would wag their fingers at the press barons, rattle the sabres of their recommendations and then, like old soldiers, fade away. But such a reading is too harsh, not to say paranoid. Just as the Hutchins Commission report was not written in a vacuum, and had its effect despite rejection by the press, the Kent Commission served to focus critical attention on the conduct of Canadian newspapers, and in so doing caused a change in the climate in which they operated. It is no accident that the first Canadian press councils – Windsor (1971), Ontario (1972), Alberta (1973) and Quebec (1973) – appeared during or immediately after the Davey Committee inquiry into the mass media, which was critical of press performance. It is no accident that the appearance of other press councils – in the Maritimes, Manitoba and British Columbia – was delayed until the 1980s, after the Kent Commission.

Indeed, in lieu of any formal regulatory agency, and apart from the letter to the editor or the angry phone call, press councils and ombudsmen (the British broadsheets prefer the gender-neutral term "readers' representative") are the only two avenues of redress for the injured or the outraged. Desbarats (1990) ably charts the history and operations of both press councils and ombudsmen in Canada, and Pritchard (1991) offers a detailed account of the structure and workings of the Quebec Press Council. It should suffice here to make a few simple observations.

The first is that both press councils and readers' representatives are welcome developments, particularly inasmuch as they provide a genuine assurance that the newspaper's actions do not go unscrutinized. In the long run, as well, they constitute checks and balances such that, in the event of a crisis of irresponsibility – say, an unscrupulous publisher actually using a newspaper as an unabashed instrument of propaganda – the hue and cry can be raised. Nevertheless, both press councils and ombudsmen have their limitations.

The work of the readers' representative is valuable and often necessary, but its nature is such that efforts are expended ruling on matters specific rather than strategic or structural. Most of the ombudsman's time and column inches are typically taken up with adjudicating on whether this story should have appeared in a family newspaper, whether that photograph was in bad taste, whether this headline was offensive or misleading, and so on. Also, as an internal staff appointee, the ombudsman finds it difficult to become highly critical of the performance of the newspaper without becoming a pariah. As a result, ombudsmen are often dismissed by the more critically minded as mere apologists for the paper, as the newsroom's public relations arm. This is unfair to the individuals who hold such positions and who are serious about their office. But it is true that ombudsmen do not "go after" incompetent or morally bankrupt reporters or editors in the way in which reporters "go after" incompetent or morally bankrupt public officials, nor are they in a position to express scepticism about the very rules by which the newsroom operates.

One of the limitations of the press council is that, because it is a body of sober reflection, its rulings are often quite distanced from the coverage that gave offence. The British Press Council, a complaint-adjudicating body, was itself the object of the complaint that its rulings were often delayed by between eight and 12 months (G. Robertson 1983, 39). This tends to diminish its effectiveness as an agency of accountability, precisely by eroding the sense of gratification a complainant might feel at a favourable ruling.

Some of the most trenchant observations on the status of the press council have been made by Clift (1981), not coincidentally in the form of a research report for the Kent Commission. He notes that the appointment of ombudsmen and the creation of press councils did not flow from purely high-minded motives. They also have their commercial aspects: "Apart from a desire to cultivate the loyalty of the readers, the intention was to preserve the homogeneity of the mass of readers and consumers by creating new lines of solidarity between the daily press and its audience. In this way, the unity and the cohesiveness of the advertising market could be defended against fragmentation along class lines" (ibid., 138–39). At the same time, press councils are advantageous to journalists themselves: "Press councils constitute a valuable line of defence for journalists, both unionized and part of management, against the commercial requirements which are persistently undermining professional values" (ibid., 140). In short, they are protection for "editors and journalists from owners," the party whips, not of accountability but of responsibility.

Nonetheless, press council jurisprudence addresses itself primarily to individual rights, and it is only via occasional statements of principle that group or collective rights are recognized (Clift 1981, 151). Clift points out that Canadian press councils have all adopted a procedure based not on a code of ethics applicable to all situations, but on an assessment of each complaint as it arises. Reflecting the difficulties of actually drafting a meaningful and universal code of ethics, the current system involves "recourse to a still undefined custom" (ibid., 150). This is a procedure better adapted to the needs of self-regulation and makes it easier for individuals to seek redress, but seriously inhibits any group seeking to challenge established values or claiming access to the platforms of public address. In 1976, the Ontario Press Council received almost 100 letters complaining about diffuse but inherent sexism in news and advertising. The Council replied that "it could best deal with this issue by following its normal practice of considering specific complaints about specific stories or specific advertisements." Still, it seemed that this was a case in which it might be more effective to formulate general guidelines than require readers to launch innumerable individual complaints about specific articles. Consequently, the Council formed a committee to look at the question in general. Clift observes that in doing so the Council indirectly cast doubt on its own policy of proceeding only on individual complaints prompted by a sense of personal wrong (ibid., 154).

This points to a further limitation of the press council as an agency of accountability. Generally, the press council is a body that adjudicates on whether the press has played by the rules. It is not therefore in a position to entertain seriously charges that the rules themselves are suspect. As a consequence, groups considered "marginal" or "fringe" are likely to get short shrift when complaining that they are excluded from the main diet of news coverage. Complaints that turn on the assertion that the very ideals of objectivity and social responsibility work to restrict the range of debate are likely to be frustrated. It is not that the members of the council dismiss such arguments out of hand – yesterday's fringe, after all, is tomorrow's mainstream: witness the rise of concern over the environment – but that the press council, as a body, is structurally ill suited as a forum for the debate of such issues.

In addition, both ombudsman and press council are constrained in the amplitude they can accord their rulings. To a party injured by press coverage, the wound is glaring: the newspaper has announced a hurtful distortion for all to read, and only an equally public – or indeed more prominent – retraction will undo the damage. Even if the press council finds in the complainant's favour, the decision cannot help but be more muted than the original wrong. Newspaper accounts of press council decisions are invariably run as inside-page stories (no striking headlines, illustrations or layout) and rendered in the most scrupulously deadpan manner, with not an iota of the narrative artifice that injured parties always detect in the stories that give offence in the first place.

Indeed, to add irony to injury, even press councils are not immune to distorted coverage on the part of the press. The Ontario Press Council (OPC), for example, does not oblige its member papers to run council rulings with a prominence equal to the original offending item. Until 1989, the OPC required merely that newspapers "publish all conclusions of the Council involving their newspapers, and wherever practical all other reports and conclusions of the Council" (article II, section B of the OPC constitution). Prompted by the fact that some papers "on occasion had not published a fair account of adjudications on complaints" (OPC 1989, 86), the council amended the relevant section to require that newspapers "publish a fair and comprehensive report, including the text of the adjudication" and threatened to issue press releases identifying newspapers that persistently failed to do so.

Finally, there is the lingering scepticism over whose interests, exactly, press councils serve. Can a toothless watchdog serve any policing function whatsoever, or do such bodies provide the mere illusion of accountability? Alternatively, do press councils represent the intrusion of the state into the affairs of a formerly free press? That is, are press councils delegated agencies whose distance from the state simply masks what is in fact an extension of the state's grasp?

Writing about the Australian Press Council (APC), a body remarkably similar to its equivalents in Canada, O'Malley (1987) considers precisely these questions. O'Malley's conclusion is that the APC is neither a covert operative of an interventionist state nor a tool of capitalism for the deflection and absorption of criticism. Rather, it is a body founded upon inconsistency, incongruity and contradiction, and as such it necessarily reflects these contradictions. Like all press councils, it was created to resolve the essential tension at the heart of the problem of press accountability. Since this tension cannot be resolved, the APC is condemned to its contradictory status. Quoting Michael Ignatieff, O'Malley argues that it is typical of an array of institutions "which fail their constituencies and which limp along because no alternative can be found or because conflict over alternatives is too great to be mediated into compromise" (ibid., 105). This is remarkably similar in tone to Pritchard's conclusions with regard to the Quebec Press Council: it is an imperfect body whose influence on the quality of journalism in the province is difficult to determine (1991, 89). Nonetheless, at present it is the best solution available to a persistent and otherwise insoluble problem.

CONCLUSION

In lieu of a formal press watchdog, a regulatory agency charged with policing press performance, the best way to keep the press accountable is precisely the manner in which the press, in turn, keeps government accountable: namely, to hold its actions up to public attention. As recognition grows that the press is a player on the political stage, a participant in how events unfold and not merely a stenographer, it is important that the press itself become an object of public scrutiny and commentary. If the storyteller is a factor in how the story turns out, the actions of the storyteller should themselves command attention. Certainly, it would be to the benefit of the population at large to have some acquaintance with the methods and priorities of the press, the organizational and other constraints under which it functions and its political play as an agency of public record. As Shapiro notes, "the general public knows next to nothing about the complex, often arbitrary, mechanisms by which truth is processed into news copy, and about how the day-to-day decisions are made that will largely dictate not only what readers will and will not know about the present state of the nation and the world but what the future holds for people who become the objects of press attention" (1989, 27).

Journalists themselves have been notoriously resistant to press attention to the press. They find it incestuous. (See Desbarats 1990, 104–107 for a litany of examples of journalists' discomfort with becoming the object of others' critical attention.) While former Chicago *Tribune* correspondent George Seldes held that "serious, searching, and regular criticism of the press is the ultimate safeguard of its freedom" (Blanchard 1977, 42), he was also aware that "nothing is sacred to the American press but itself" (ibid., 8). Nonetheless, a mature and responsible press is one capable of subjecting its own labours to the same type of public appraisal as it brings to bear on other areas of social affairs. As Robert Hutchins remarked in 1947, to a convention of journalism teachers: "Though the press regards itself as competent to criticize everybody, it also holds that nobody is competent to criticize it. Since the press will not criticize itself, it must remain uncriticized. And uncriticized power is a menace to a democratic society" (ibid., 49).

Happily, there are signs that the press is coming to attract at least a measure of critical scrutiny. The Canadian Association of Journalists (CAJ) holds an annual convention at which media workers not only discuss but also appraise the performance of their craft. The CAJ also publishes a quarterly periodical, the *Bulletin*, that casts a critical eye on the conduct of Canadian journalism. Until recently, CBC Newsworld devoted half an hour per week to the affairs of journalism in its program

"MediaWatch," as did CBC radio with "Media File." The Carleton University School of Journalism publishes *Content* magazine, a periodical review of Canadian journalism, six times a year, and the Ryerson School of Journalism publishes the thoughtful and handsomely produced *Ryerson Review of Journalism* twice a year. The Graduate School of Journalism at the University of Western Ontario has been active in sponsoring conferences and symposia on journalistic conduct, as well as publishing an annual volume of essays on aspects of press performance. Other schools of journalism and departments of communication at various Canadian universities have similarly functioned as sites for the examination of the labours of the press (witness the proliferation of symposia on the media's conduct in covering the Persian Gulf war in the aftermath of Operation Desert Storm). As well, a number of media-monitoring groups have sprung up, among them the feminist collective MediaWatch and British Columbia's Fraser Institute, whose evaluations of news coverage are designed to keep the press honest and accountable for its work.[13] Also, increasing attention is being paid to the role of the press on the social stage in "op-ed" commentary.

Many of these sites and outlets for press criticism in Canada are as yet underdeveloped, particularly when compared with those of other nations. *Content* magazine, for example, has a meagre advertising income and is understaffed and underresourced.[14] It is not the *Columbia Journalism Review*. CBC Newsworld's "MediaWatch" similarly was a low-budget enterprise limited mostly to studio interviews. In comparison, "Hard News," a production of Britain's Channel 4, was a documentary-style program that did to journalists what journalists did to others: for example, the program "doorstepped" the editor of the *Sun*, that is, camped out on his doorstep, dogging his every movement – a journalistic technique favoured by aggressive tabloids such as the *Sun*. While journalistic attention to journalism may still be tentative in Canada it is a welcome development and one that should be encouraged.

At the very least, existing programs and publications offer opportunities to dissect and debate instances of controversial journalistic coverage. For example, both the CBC "National" story that senior Liberal party officials were seriously considering dumping leader John Turner in the midst of the 1988 general election, and the CBC "Journal"'s hidden-microphone coverage of the 1989 New Democratic Party convention were the subject of much subsequent commentary and argument in the media. The role of the press in the course of events at Oka, Quebec, in the summer of 1990 was scrutinized as carefully and debated as hotly as the actions of the Mohawk and the authorities themselves. Media coverage of the 1988 general election was the subject of a post-mortem hosted by Queen's University and broadcast on CBC Newsworld. It is to be hoped that this sort of ex post facto dissection becomes a regular feature of Canadian elections.

Welcome as such developments are, they are likely to do little in the short run to allay the misgivings political candidates may harbour about being at the mercy of an unaccountable press. Accordingly, there may well still be calls for some sort of press-monitoring agency. The British experience provides an example of how such an agency might work: a special Elections Press Council could be established for the duration of an election campaign to rule swiftly on complaints about unfair press attention. As with more conventional press councils, its decisions would be published by participating newspapers. Such a flying-squad adjudicating body is likely to be expensive, and voters would have to be convinced that such expense is warranted. It would also have to secure the cooperation of the press itself. In the absence of some triggering incident – in which due electoral process was undermined by an irresponsible press – such cooperation is not likely to be forthcoming. The press would doubtless see such an agency as simply a mechanism by which politicians would attempt to wrest control of the agenda of coverage. Had such a body existed during the 1988 general election, for example, a party such as the New Democratic Party might have used it to complain that newspapers were damaging its chances of electoral success by focusing inordinately on the single issue of free trade. Therefore, many in the press would greet any suggestion for an Election Press Council as an open invitation to infringe on editorial liberty. Accordingly, it is likely to be resisted with all the vigour with which the press denounced the recommendations of the Kent Commission.

Thus this study comes to an untidy conclusion. The problem of accountability persists because the press is answerable to no higher authority. But the press cannot be so answerable without compromising its essential freedom. This may be an uncomfortable fact, but it is also a fact of democracy.

NOTES

1. This is perhaps most visible in the manner in which journalists are represented in popular culture. It is not at all uncommon for journalists to be depicted in popular fiction, films and television drama as heroic and stalwart defenders of the public interest, exposing corruption in the face of intimidation, taking up the cause of the oppressed, and in general righting wrongs. At the same time, it is not uncommon for journalists to feature as morally bankrupt scoundrels, preying on human frailty and pursuing sensation with little regard for the cost to their victims. For every Clark Kent

there is a Peter Fallow (*Bonfire of the Vanities*); for every Lou Grant there is a Walter Burns (*The Front Page, His Girl Friday*).

2. Interestingly, a January 1991 *Maclean's*/Decima poll reported that 19 percent of respondents said they detected a left-wing bias to the news media, exactly the same percentage as those who detected a right-wing bias.

3. The press is not alone in giving an ambiguous account of its own status on the social stage. Advertising, too, is subject to complaints that it wields a manipulative power over the public, by creating consumer needs and demands where none would otherwise exist. Although the advertising industry is presumably one founded on the effectiveness of its product, the industry is in the odd position of protecting itself against the persistent criticism that it is manipulative by arguing against its own efficacy. Industry wisdom holds that one cannot artificially create a market for a product through sheer advertising, and that while advertising may accelerate the growth of new markets, it probably has little to do with the eventual size of the market for a product (see Leiss et al. 1990, 36–39).

4. This is perhaps clearer if one thinks of an example such as the financial market. The notion that the market performs autonomously of the public documentation of its affairs is flatly untenable. It is not that financial transactions are conducted and the press merely records these transactions after the fact. On the contrary, the market exists only insofar as information about its performance circulates publicly. One might go so far as to say that the market *is* information about itself in action. Certainly, the doings of the market and the work of financial journalists are indissoluble: the press is part of the overall phenomenon of the market. Similarly, in the case of fashion, the fashion system operates on the basis of the fact that what is and is not fashionable is talked about and publicly recognized. The notion that there might be some style of dress that is fashionable but no one knows to be fashionable – say, plaid lobster bibs – is an impossibility.

5. Commission members included: from the University of Chicago, Charles Merriam, professor emeritus of political science, and Robert Redfield, dean of the Division of Social Sciences; from Harvard, Zechariah Chafee, Jr., professor of law, William Hocking, professor emeritus of philosophy, and Arthur Schlesinger, Sr., professor of history; other academics included John M. Clark, professor of economics at Columbia, John Dickinson, professor of law at the University of Pennsylvania, George Schuster, president of Hunter College, and Reinhold Niebuhr, professor of ethics and philosophy of religion at Union Theological Seminary; from government came Harold Lasswell, director of war communications research at the Library of Congress, and the poet Archibald MacLeish, Librarian of Congress and then briefly assistant secretary of state; from the private sector came Beardsley Ruml, formerly dean of the Division of Social Sciences at the University of Chicago, but then treasurer and subsequently chairman of the board of the R.H. Macy Company. Foreign advisers included

John Grierson, head of the Canadian National Film Board, Kurt Riezler, professor of philosophy at the New School for Social Research, Hu Shih, former Chinese ambassador to the United States, and Jacques Maritain, visiting professor of philosophy at both Columbia and Princeton. No working journalists were appointed to the Commission, because of a fear that their presence might restrict its independence, although prominent media representatives were invited to offer testimony as witnesses.

6. Again, this was a sentiment that had been expressed as early as 1903 by the Queen's University essayists. Fred Hamilton of the Toronto *News* recognized that a paper of the most admirable traits would simply perish in the marketplace; even if financial subsidy guaranteed its survival, it would be ignored by the mass of readers and would be valueless, therefore, as an instrument of public edification (Queen's Quarterly 1903, 195).

7. This was not an untoward expectation, as subsequent developments have attested, and the question as to why broadcasting is regulated while the print media are not is likely to be raised again and again. If one holds that print escapes government regulation only by virtue of a historical and technological coincidence, it is legitimate to ask whether newspaper companies are entitled to such special privilege once they begin to deliver their product over fax lines and electronic mail networks.

8. As always, there are exceptions. "National" papers such as the *Times* or the *Independent* are little read in Scotland, for example, where the situation is more akin to that in Canada. Residents of Edinburgh may read the *Scotsman*, while Glasgow's largest daily is the *Glasgow Herald*.

9. While the notion of a mandatory right of reply has prima facie appeal, it presents a host of difficulties. Should such a right be restricted to correcting misstatements of fact? Should it apply to responses to "distortions" in the widest possible sense? Or should it extend to anyone who feels maligned by press coverage for whatever reason? Given that different people in different situations have widely diverging perceptions of what is true, accurate, fair, balanced, responsible, warranted, etc., who shall decide in what instances and on what grounds a "right of reply" can be invoked? It is therefore difficult to imagine a statutory right of reply without an accompanying judicial or quasi-judicial mechanism capable of ruling in such matters. As the *Independent* observed, this "would require the full panoply of the courts to ascertain fact – evidence on oath, cross-examination, legal representation and discovery of documents" (lead editorial, 22 June 1990, 18). Not only would this be cumbersome and expensive, but just as in cases of libel, the ruling might follow months after the initial event. A right of reply is presumably hollow if it is not a right of immediate reply. Also, just as libel laws at present tend to favour those with the means to pursue lengthy court actions, such a judicially mediated right of reply might become predominantly an instrument of the rich and the powerful for the protection of their own interests. Finally, once statutory controls are in

place they can be toughened in the future. There is the danger that they might be used by government as a cudgel to cow the press. Who, more than government, is the object of sustained criticism in the pages of the press? What government would be able to resist continually invoking the "right of reply" so as to "set the record straight"?

10. The hot-line service and "fast-track" adjudications and corrections are ideas borrowed from the Press Council's attempts to reform itself.

11. For example, main points include: that newspapers should take care not to publish inaccurate, misleading or distorted material; that inaccuracies should be promptly corrected; that apologies should be published where appropriate; that fair opportunities for reply should be offered where reasonably called for; that newspapers should clearly distinguish between factual reporting, comment and conjecture; that intrusion into individuals' privacy is justified only when in the public interest; that journalists should not obtain material by misrepresentation or harassment, except in the public interest; in cases involving personal grief, inquiries should be carried out with sympathy and discretion; that relatives or friends of individuals accused or convicted of crimes should not be identified unless the information is germane to the story; victims of sexual assault should generally not be identified; and that the press should avoid prejudicial reference to a person's race, colour, religion, sex, sexual orientation, or physical or mental handicap, and omit reference to such traits unless directly relevant to the story.

The difficulty with drafting a journalistic code of conduct is that it either stalls at the most general level, iterating a canon of Boy Scout slogans, or it dissolves into newsroom minutiae. Attempts at detail tend to founder on myriad shifting decisions. Once newsroom staff have been ordered not to accept gratuities, is it necessary to insist that the books given to reviewers be paid for by the newspaper? What about the boxloads of books publishing companies send to the books editor every year without charge in the hope that they will be reviewed? Paying for these titles would likely cripple the books section's budget. And what about the free albums sent to the music critic? The free food at the political rally? At what point does honour give way to financial expediency?

12. Just as the Hutchins Commission's proposed citizens' monitoring committee was essentially a permanent version of the Hutchins Commission itself, the proposal for a national Press Rights Panel may be read as a call to install a permanent body on the order of the Royal Commission. The Press Rights Panel was to have a chairman and two other members who would be appointed by the federal Cabinet. The Royal Commission comprised a chairman (Tom Kent) and two commissioners (Borden Spears and Laurent Picard) appointed by the federal Cabinet.

13. Many view the pronouncements of such groups with scepticism, if not outright suspicion, on grounds that their evaluations of press performance are "politically motivated." (The Fraser Institute, for example, has been charged

with rendering criticism of the press that merely expresses a right-wing bias, although the Institute hotly denies this, insisting that its evaluations are staunchly objective.) Politically motivated or not, however, such media-monitoring groups at least open up the conduct of the press to debate. In any event, in a liberal democracy, what is wrong with criticism of the press rendered from a political perspective?

14. This is unlikely to change in the near future. While some publications – such as those devoted to travel, or to home computing, for example – thrive on an available advertising constituency, there is as yet no obvious advertising constituency for a magazine devoted to media criticism.

BIBLIOGRAPHY

Blanchard, M.A. 1977. "The Hutchins Commission, the Press and the Responsibility Concept." *Journalism Monographs* 49:1–59.

Boorstin, D. 1961. *The Image: A Guide to Pseudo-events in America.* New York: Harper and Row.

Brenner, D.L., and W.L. Rivers, eds. 1982. *Free but Regulated: Conflicting Traditions in Media Law.* Ames: Iowa State University Press.

Brogan, P. 1985. *Spiked: The Short Life and Death of the National News Council.* New York: Priority Press.

Canada. Royal Commission on Newspapers. 1981. *Report.* Ottawa: Minister of Supply and Services Canada.

Canada. Senate. Special Committee on Mass Media. 1970. *Report.* Ottawa: Queen's Printer.

Clarke, P., and S.H. Evans. 1983. *Covering Campaigns: Journalism in Congressional Elections.* Stanford: Stanford University Press.

Clift, D. 1981. "Press Councils and Ombudsmen." In *The Journalists.* Vol. 2 of the research studies of the Royal Commission on Newspapers. Ottawa: Minister of Supply and Services Canada.

Comber, M.A., and R.S. Mayne. 1986. *The Newsmongers: How the Media Distort the Political News.* Toronto: McClelland and Stewart.

Commission on Freedom of the Press (COFOP). 1947. *A Free and Responsible Press.* Chicago: University of Chicago Press.

Curran, J., ed. 1978. *The British Press: A Manifesto.* London: Macmillan.

Curran, J., and J. Seaton. 1988. *Power without Responsibility: The Press and Broadcasting in Britain.* 3d ed. London: Routledge.

Desbarats, P. 1990. "Accountability." In *Guide to Canadian News Media.* Toronto: Harcourt Brace Jovanovich.

Edelman, M. 1988. *Constructing the Political Spectacle.* Chicago: University of Chicago Press.

Elliott, D., ed. 1986. *Responsible Journalism*. Beverly Hills: Sage Publications.

Entman, R.M. 1989. *Democracy without Citizens: Media and the Decay of American Politics*. Oxford: Oxford University Press.

Epstein, Edward Jay. 1973. *News from Nowhere: Television and the News*. New York: Vintage Books.

Fishman, M. 1980. *Manufacturing the News*. Austin: University of Texas Press.

Fletcher, F. 1981. "The Special Case of Elections." In *The Newspaper and Public Affairs*. Vol. 7 of the research studies of the Royal Commission on Newspapers. Ottawa: Minister of Supply and Services Canada.

———. 1987. "Mass Media and Parliamentary Elections in Canada." *Legislative Studies Quarterly* 12:341–72.

Fletcher, F., and B. Everett. 1989. "An Unusual Campaign." *Content* (Jan./Feb.): 8–10.

Frizzell, A., J. Pammett and A. Westell. 1989. *The Canadian General Election of 1988*. Ottawa: Carleton University Press.

Frum, L., ed. 1990. *The Newsmakers: Behind the Cameras with Canada's Top TV Journalists*. Toronto: Key Porter.

Glasgow University Media Group. 1976. *Bad News*. London: Routledge and Kegan Paul.

Globe and Mail. 1981. "The National Globe." 19 August.

Hackett, R.A. 1984. "Decline of a Paradigm? Bias and Objectivity in News Studies." *Critical Studies in Mass Communication* 1:229–59.

Hall, S. 1982. "The Rediscovery of 'Ideology': Return of the Repressed in Media Studies." In *Culture, Society and the Media*, ed. M. Gurevitch, T. Bennett, J. Curran and J. Woollacott. London: Methuen.

Hocking, W.E. 1947. *Freedom of the Press: A Framework of Principle*. Chicago: University of Chicago Press.

Lamb, Jamie. 1981. "Biases Show in Tom's Turkey." *Vancouver Sun*, 19 August.

Leiss, W., S. Kline and S. Jhally. 1990. *Social Communication in Advertising: Persons, Products and Images of Well-being*. 2d ed. Scarborough: Nelson Canada.

McIntyre, J.S. 1987. "Repositioning a Landmark: The Hutchins Commission and Freedom of the Press." *Critical Studies in Mass Communication* 4 (2): 136–60.

Merrill, J.C. 1986. "Three Theories of Press Responsibility and the Advantages of Pluralistic Individualism." In *Responsible Journalism*, ed. D. Elliott. Beverly Hills: Sage Publications.

Montreal *Gazette*. 1981. "Kent Muffles Message." 20 August.

Neil, J. 1991. "British Press 'on Probation.'" *Content* (March/April): 25–26.

O'Malley, P. 1987. "Regulating Contradictions: The Australian Press Council and the 'Dispersal of Social Control'." *Law and Society Review* 21 (1): 83–108.

Ontario Press Council. 1989. *17th Annual Report.* Toronto: OPC.

Peterson, T. 1956. "The Social Responsibility Theory." In *Four Theories of the Press*, ed. F.S. Siebert, T. Peterson and W. Schramm. Chicago: University of Illinois.

Postman, N. 1985. *Amusing Ourselves to Death: Public Discourse in the Age of Show Business.* New York: Penguin.

Pritchard, D. 1991. "The Role of Press Councils in a System of Media Accountability: The Case of Quebec." *Canadian Journal of Communication* 16 (1): 73–93.

Queen's Quarterly, ed. 1903. *How Can Canadian Universities Best Benefit the Profession of Journalism as a Means of Moulding and Elevating Public Opinion?* Toronto: Copp Clark.

Rivers, W.L., and W. Schramm. 1969. *Responsibility in Mass Communication.* 2d ed. New York: Harper and Row.

Robertson, G. 1983. *People Against the Press: An Enquiry into the Press Council.* London: Quartet Books.

Robertson, S.M. 1983. *Media Law Handbook.* Vancouver: International Self-Counsel Press.

Roth, R. 1990. "Muffled Voices." *Content* (July/August): 21–22.

Schiller, D. 1981. *Objectivity and the News: The Public and the Rise of Commercial Journalism.* Philadelphia: University of Pennsylvania Press.

Schmuhl, R., ed. 1984. *The Responsibilities of Journalism.* Notre Dame: University of Notre Dame Press.

Schudson, M. 1978. *Discovering the News: A Social History of American Newspapers.* New York: Basic Books.

Seymour-Ure, C. 1974. *The Political Impact of Mass Media.* Beverly Hills: Sage Publications.

Shapiro, I. 1989. "No Comment." *Saturday Night* (March): 27–29.

Siegel, A. 1983. *Politics and the Media in Canada.* Toronto: McGraw-Hill Ryerson.

Soderlund, W.C., W.I. Romanow, E.D. Briggs and R.H. Wagenburg. 1984. *Mass Media and Elections in Canada.* Toronto: Holt, Rinehart and Winston.

Strentz, H., K. Starck, D.L. Anderson and L. Chiglione. 1974. "The Critical

Factor: Criticisms of the News Media in Journalism Education."
Journalism Monographs 32:1–40.

Taras, D. 1990. *The Newsmakers: The Media's Influence on Canadian Politics.*
Scarborough: Nelson Canada.

Toronto Star. 1981. "Kent's Wrong Remedies." 20 August.

Tuchman, G. 1978. *Making News: A Study in the Construction of Reality.*
New York: Free Press.

United Kingdom. Parliament. 1949. *Royal Commission on the Press 1947–49
Report.* Cmd. 7700.

———. 1962. *Royal Commission on the Press 1961–62 Report.* Cmnd. 1811.

———. 1976. *Royal Commission on the Press Interim Report.* Cmnd. 6553.

———. 1977. *Royal Commission on the Press 1974–77 Final Report.* Cmnd.
6810 and 6810–1–6.

———. 1990. *Report of the Committee on Privacy and Related Matters.* Cm. 1102.

Vancouver Sun. 1981. "Freedom at Stake." 19 August.

Vermeer, J.P., ed. 1987. *Campaigns in the News: Mass Media and Congressional
Elections.* New York: Greenwood Press.

Winnipeg Free Press. 1981. "Big Brother for the Papers"; "Papers State Views."
19 August.

4

SMALLER VOICES
Minor Parties,
Campaign Communication
and the News Media

Robert A. Hackett
with the assistance of James Mackintosh,
David Robinson and Arlene Shwetz

To WHAT EXTENT are competing political parties able to state their case and appeal to potential supporters through the mass media? The ways in which parties are covered or accorded access through press and broadcasting formats – from news reports to paid advertising to free-time political broadcasts – influence the stability, flexibility and perceived fairness of the entire electoral system. More directly, news coverage and media access influence the relative ability of each party to set the agenda of an election campaign to its own advantage. For major parties seeking to attract support from an electorate whose attachment to particular parties is decreasing while its reliance on mass media for political information is increasing (Clarke et al. 1984; Blumler and Gurevitch 1982), setting the agenda can mean the difference between electoral victory or defeat.

Yet media access is also important for emerging and minor parties which have no foreseeable hope of forming a government. To be sure, the emergence of new parties is influenced by many factors in addition to media coverage, such as the existing electoral and party systems, the leadership and organization of a new party, and its ability to articulate and aggregate important social interests. Moreover, media coverage on its own is unlikely to catapult a minor party into an electoral contender if no potential political constituency exists for it. Still, it seems reasonable to presume that by fostering or inhibiting voter awareness of new or currently small parties, media attention can influence their electoral fortunes. The "flip side" of the agenda-setting role of mass media is the "spiral of silence" effect originally proposed by Elizabeth Noelle-Neumann: the media's continued denigration or exclusion of certain political options tends to discourage individuals from publicly expressing or even privately supporting such options (Fejes 1984, 224–25). What is at stake for minor parties is not political power, but their very existence as meaningful political players.

Indeed, media treatment of minor parties may well be one of the most contentious aspects of electoral reform. Minor parties themselves have expressed considerable dissatisfaction with their treatment by the mass media, as attested for example by their presentations to a 1987 hearing of the Canadian Radio-television and Telecommunications Commission (CRTC), by current litigation involving minor parties and broadcasting organizations, and by some of their briefs to this Royal Commission. Nor is it an issue that is likely to fade away, for several long-standing reasons – the dependence of political parties on mass media for reaching potential supporters, the government's responsibility for broadcasting policy, and the inevitable "fuzziness" and subjectivity of criteria for determining what constitutes appropriate or equitable treatment of parties. The issue is rendered more acute by the recent emergence of new and formerly minor parties (Reform, Bloc québécois) as significant political players at the federal level, a trend underscored by the surprising strength of minor parties in the 1990 Ontario provincial election.

This study considers the media's performance in covering minor-parties during election campaigns and some policy implications. First, it presents a content analysis of news coverage of minor parties in selected media during the 1988 federal campaign. Second, it summarizes interviews with minor-party representatives on their interaction with, and perspectives on, the media. In parallel fashion, the third section presents the perspectives of some working journalists. Fourth, it presents an overview of the policies and practices of other selected liberal democracies on campaign communication and minor parties. Finally, it suggests a general policy approach to campaign communication, especially as it affects minor-party access to the media.

MINOR PARTIES IN CAMPAIGN NEWS: A CONTENT ANALYSIS

The content analysis examines the treatment by mass media (particularly television and the daily press) during the 1988 federal election campaign of "minor" parties (officially registered parties other than the Progressive Conservatives, Liberals and NDP). In the 1988 federal campaign, there were nine minor parties, none of which (at the time the election was called) had parliamentary representation. These minor parties included three right-wing parties with a base in western Canada – the Reform Party, Christian Heritage party (CHP), and Confederation of Regions Western Party (COR). Other registered minor parties were the environmentalist Green Party, the Communist party, the satirical Rhinoceros Party, the philosophically individualist Libertarian party, the remnants of the national Social Credit party and the uncategorizable Commonwealth party (adherents of the right-wing American iconoclast Lyndon LaRouche). In addition, several candidates ran as independents or as representatives of small non-registered parties in 1988; they were combined into a single "other/independent" category for the content analysis.

Although none of the minor parties elected any members of Parliament in 1988, candidates from these parties were able to attract important chunks of the vote in some ridings. The Reform Party showed particular strength in the West (15 percent of the vote in Alberta and 5 percent in British Columbia), and since 1988, opinion polls and victories in a federal by-election and Alberta's election in connection with a Senate vacancy have demonstrated that the Reform Party is now a serious electoral contender. Although well behind the Reform Party, the CHP garnered about 1 percent of the popular vote in both British Columbia and Alberta, placing it well ahead of most other minor parties.

The purpose of the content analysis was to provide data to assess both the validity of minor parties' expressed concerns about access to the media, and the effectiveness of regulation intended to ensure that parties have equitable media access during election campaigns. The focus of the content analysis was on the frequency and themes of news media treatment of minor parties. It was felt that equitable treatment concerned not only the amount of air time or newspaper space accorded to minor parties, but also the type of attention they receive.

Because of the limits of time and resources, the content analysis sample and coding protocol was designed to emphasize the following comparisons:

- *Major parties v. minor parties*   How much coverage do minor parties receive compared with the major parties? Do minor parties receive the same type of coverage, or do different news values apply (e.g., trivialization)?
- *Newspapers v. television*   Are there any substantial differences in treatment of minor parties between newspapers, as a non-regulated medium, and the regulated broadcasting media? Such

a comparison has important implications for the effectiveness of existing policy instruments intended to promote equitable treatment of registered parties in the broadcasting media.

- *Local media v. regional and national media* Do local media provide relatively greater opportunity for minor parties and their candidates to reach voters within individual constituencies?
- *Different minor parties* Does coverage appear to vary according to each party's ideological position, evident public support, or other variables?

The Sample

Originally it was hoped that existing studies and datasets could be drawn on to help address the above questions. In the event, however, it became apparent that existing published studies virtually ignore minor parties. The Carleton Election Study of 1988 (Frizzell et al. 1989) does at least code the presence of minor parties in news items, but the data were not designed to address many of the above questions. Datasets from analyses conducted by other researchers or organizations proved to be inaccessible even when they existed, due in part to current litigation pitting the Green Party against some broadcasting organizations. Archival videotapes of network news and current affairs, the raw material for coding, proved not to be readily available. The lack of archival resources is even more evident in the case of local television, community cable and radio.

Accordingly, the sampling strategy was shaped by these practical constraints. Transcripts obtained from the National Media Archive (affiliated with the Fraser Institute in Vancouver) were used to content-analyse CTV's "National News," and CBC's "National" and "Journal." Two limitations to these data must be noted. First, some dates during the 1988 campaign period were missing from the television transcript data, mainly between mid-October and the start of November. Second, the reliance on typed transcripts obviously precludes the analysis of the visual dimension of television news. Although these limitations are regrettable, the available printed transcripts proved to be adequate for the specific purposes of this study.

The sample, totalling 525 items, comprised the following:

- All election-related items (including letters to the editor and opinion pieces as well as news reports) in the *Globe and Mail*, the *Vancouver Sun*, CTV's "National News," and CBC's "National" and "Journal" for a seven-day "constructed-week" sample during the 1988 election campaign. The campaign began on 1 October and ended on election day, 21 November. The sample of dates selected began on Sunday 2 October and comprised every eighth day until election day so that each day of the week was represented, viz., Monday 10 October, Tuesday 18 October, Wednesday 26 October, Thursday 3 November, Friday 11 November and Saturday 18 November. For dates when the relevant medium did not publish (e.g., the *Globe and Mail* and *Vancouver Sun* did not publish on Sundays) or when transcripts or back copies were unavailable, the following day was used wherever possible.[1] In cases when more than one edition of a newspaper was available for a given date, the first or morning edition was used in preference over later editions.

- All significant items (news reports, features, editorials) on any of the minor parties in the *Globe and Mail, Vancouver Sun, Winnipeg Free Press*, Montreal *Gazette*, CTV's "National News" and CBC's "National" and "Journal" that were published or broadcast during the 1988 campaign. For the television material, the transcripts were scanned, and any item mentioning one or more minor parties was coded. The relevant newspaper articles were identified using the topic headings for each of the registered minor parties in the *Canadian News Index*, which catalogues stories on an ongoing basis from several major Canadian daily newspapers. The use of the *Canadian News Index* imposed another important qualification on the sample, since the Index does not list all articles mentioning minor parties; rather, it catalogues articles that it considers significant and which focused on one or more minor parties.

- All available election- and party-related items during the 1988 campaign in a selection of community newspapers circulated in the four Vancouver and Edmonton-area ridings chosen for particular attention. These ridings comprise Vancouver East, Vancouver South, Edmonton Southeast and Wetaskiwin (a rural riding south of Edmonton). They were selected on the basis of logistical convenience, the existence of one or more community papers within their boundaries, and the fact that the candidates in these four ridings taken together represented the full spectrum of registered minor parties, with the exception of Social Credit which ran only a handful of candidates nationally in 1988. Some of the minor parties fared relatively well in the selected ridings.[2]

From the above-mentioned four ridings, the following community newspapers were included in the content analysis sample: *Vancouver*

Echo and *East Ender* from Vancouver East; *South Vancouver Revue* from Vancouver South; *Edmonton Examiner* from Edmonton Southeast; and eight published in different parts of the sprawling Wetaskiwin riding: *Leduc Representative, Ponoka News & Advertiser, Ponoka Herald, Community Voice* (Calmar), *Wetaskiwin Times Advertiser, Devon Dispatch, Rimbey Record* and *Lacombe Globe.* As local media, the community papers were hypothesized to be more receptive to local campaigns and to minor-party candidates running locally than were the television networks and big city dailies. Community cable television and local radio talk shows are other potential avenues of media access for local and minor-party candidates, but the content of these media during the 1988 campaign has generally not been preserved or archived.

The media sample was constituted to combine economy with the ability to address the questions posed above, albeit in a necessarily exploratory and provisional way. The coding of all newspaper items focusing on minor parties or television items mentioning them, combined with the constructed-week sample of all election coverage in the daily newspapers and television, enables a comparison between coverage of major and minor parties. The television–newspaper comparison is facilitated by the inclusion of the *Globe and Mail* as the newspaper that most closely approximates the national newscasts and CBC's "Journal" in their national scope and their journalistic standing within their respective media. If these represent national media, the *Vancouver Sun* constitutes a regional newspaper with a large circulation and influence in British Columbia, well beyond its Vancouver-area base. By contrast, the community weeklies have a much more local orientation; their newsgathering and distribution areas are often confined within a single electoral riding, making possible a much more intimate relation with local campaigns. Finally, since minor parties appear in the news relatively infrequently, the coding of all items involving minor parties in these media was necessary to compare the coverage of different minor parties.

The newspaper sample included news reports, editorials, columns, features, letters to the editor and even photographs. The television sample included news reports on the national newscasts and segments between changes of format (e.g., the start and end of an interview) or between commercial breaks on CBC's "Journal." For both television and newspapers, these items or segments constituted the basic units of analysis.

Although resources did not permit the systematic and quantitative analysis of newsmagazines, the 1988 campaign coverage of *Alberta Report* and *Maclean's* was reviewed impressionistically. Each of these periodicals has a substantial readership. *Maclean's* can be considered a major English-language national news medium, and *Alberta Report* (along with its sister edition *Western Report,* now *B.C. Report*) has a strong market base in British Columbia and Alberta, where the selected ridings were located. Some respondents suggested that *Alberta Report* provided an important platform for the Reform Party, perhaps to the relative detriment of other minor parties. It seemed advisable to consider the evidence for such claims.

Political advertising was not coded, since for this study, the relevant question regarding political advertising is the extent to which the parties were accorded access to free and paid air time and newspaper space – and whether these parties had the financial and other resources needed to take full advantage of such media opportunities. For logistical and methodological reasons, such a question was considered to be better addressed through interviews than through content analysis.

The Coding Protocol

Space constraints preclude reproducing the coding protocol and code book, but the kind of information recorded for each relevant item can be summarized.[3]

The first group of variables identifies characteristics of the item itself: its date of broadcast or publication, the medium or program within which it appeared, its position within the newscast or newspaper relative to other items (lead item, inside page, front page of a section, etc.), its relative size, and its format (in the case of newspapers, whether the article consisted of text only or included graphics; on television, whether the item was a field report presented by a correspondent or simply a script read by the newscaster).

Another group of variables begins to consider some of the more substantive characteristics of the item's content:

- *Presentational genre*   Was it a column, editorial, analytical feature, letter to the editor or a news report?
- *Level of campaign*   Does the item focus on a local riding campaign, on the provincial or regional level, on the national campaign (e.g., the leader tours or nationwide polls), or on relevant international events (such as statements by Canadian politicians travelling abroad or comments on Canadian election issues by foreign media or governments)?
- *Origin of the item*   Was it internally generated by columnists, reporters, editorialists, freelancers or others from within this news organization, or did it derive from an external news organization (most typically, a syndicated column or a news service)?

- *The main focus of the item*   On what political issue(s) did this item focus – the Free Trade Agreement, leadership, the environment, the Constitution, the televised leaders debates and so on? Did the item particularly focus on any one of the political parties contesting the election?

The remaining variables concerned 10 aspects of the presentation of each of the three major and nine minor registered parties. In each item, and for each party plus the "other" category, the following 10 dimensions were coded. (Bear in mind that in most items, the majority of parties were not mentioned at all; consequently, the analysis was less complex than it may seem.) Unless otherwise noted, a theme was coded as present whether it was expressed by the journalist narrating the article or by people quoted within it.

1. Was each party's position on issues mentioned or explained?
2. Was each party mentioned in connection with polls, strategy or other "horse-race" aspects of the campaign?
3. Was the leader or other representative of each party the subject of a personality profile within the news item? Were the traits or background of individuals associated with each party emphasized in the item?
4. Within each item, was there a substantive response to each party's policies or campaign by another political party? (This variable helps to indicate whether each party was treated as a serious electoral contender or as a serious initiator of new ideas that deserve to be debated.)
5. Were the qualities of each party's leader, or the capacity of the party itself to lead the country, a subject of comment or debate?
6. Were any positive themes (strength, seriousness, attributes such as integrity, competence or popular support) or phrases ("jubilant crowd") mentioned in connection with each party?
7. Was each party trivialized in any way – its electoral chances dismissed, its policies or campaign treated as a humorous or quirky human interest story? Were dismissive terms ("political oddity," "fringe party") applied to each party or its candidates?
8. Apart from trivialization, was each party associated with any other negative terms or themes – for example, incompetence, patronage, conflict of interest, a "bad day" on the campaign trail, shortage of funds, insincerity, electoral opportunism or party disunity?

9. What was the highest degree of "access" accorded to each party in this item? In ascending order, these degrees of access could include the following: the party was not mentioned; the party was mentioned by name, but none of its actions or statements were reported; the actions of a party or its representatives (e.g., the leader's itinerary) were mentioned but not its statements; a party's statements were paraphrased; a party's statements were directly quoted (in the press) or presented in the form of an interview clip or "sound bite" (on television). There was also a code for the unusual situation in which a party representative's off-the-record statements were recorded and broadcast by television news; since such a "leak" is unintended by the party and since it could have potentially embarrassing results (as was the case with two of the leadership candidates at the 1989 federal NDP leadership convention), this kind of coverage was considered to be a low form of access.

10. When each party was quoted, interviewed or paraphrased, what kind of person spoke on behalf of the party – its leader, a candidate in some particular riding, a strategist or official, a member or activist, or an ordinary voter who happened to support the party?

By coding the above dimensions, we can move beyond simply noting the relative frequency with which minor parties are covered in the news media, which other research on the 1988 campaign found to be quite low (Roth 1990a, 1990b). We can, in addition, note the kind of coverage that minor parties received. Were they treated as serious or frivolous political forces? Were their policies explained or debated? Were they permitted to speak for themselves, or were they simply spoken about? And how do the minor parties compare with the major parties in these respects? It appears that no previously published Canadian research has addressed such questions.

Findings

The most salient findings of the content analysis are presented in the 10 tables included with this report. The discussion that follows elaborates on those tables, suggests some of their implications, and incidentally introduces some data not presented in tabular form. It considers respectively the relative frequency and prominence of the coverage of the different parties, the topics and themes associated with each party, the campaign level at which parties are mentioned, and the extent to which parties are quoted and who speaks for them. Throughout, it emphasizes comparisons between coverage of the major and the minor parties, and between coverage in the different types of media included in the sample – network television, daily newspapers and community newspapers.

It must be emphasized that the small size of the sample and the constraints noted in the preceding section render the findings exploratory and provisional. They are nevertheless pertinent.

Frequency of Mention

The relative frequency with which parties are mentioned in news items is displayed in table 4.1, and the proportion of items that focus on each

Table 4.1
Proportion of all items containing mentions of each party, by medium
(percentages)

Party	A (N = 525)	B (N = 246)	C (N = 35)	D (N = 34)	E (N = 83)	F (N = 94)	G (N = 242)
Progressive Conservative	77.5	88.2	91.4	79.4	89.2	89.4	69.0
Liberal	63.8	81.3	80.0	73.5	78.3	87.3	49.2
NDP	58.6	69.5	68.6	61.8	67.5	72.3	50.4
Reform Party	17.7	4.9	5.7	2.9	2.4	7.4	27.7
Green Party	5.7	3.3	2.9	—	2.4	5.3	4.5
Rhinoceros Party	4.0	2.4	2.9	—	1.2	4.3	4.1
Libertarian	3.6	2.4	2.9	—	2.4	3.2	2.5
Christian Heritage party	10.3	2.0	—	—	2.4	3.2	17.8
Communist party	4.2	1.6	—	—	2.4	2.1	4.1
Confederation of Regions	10.3	1.2	—	—	2.4	1.1	19.0
Commonwealth	2.3	0.8	—	—	2.4	—	2.1
Social Credit	1.1	0.4	—	—	1.2	—	1.2
Independent/ non-registered party	8.8	3.7	2.9	—	4.8	4.3	14.9

Notes: Column headings are as follows:
A = all items, whole sample
B = all items from the constructed-week sample for the major media (CBC, CTV, *Globe and Mail*, *Vancouver Sun*)
C = constructed-week sample, CBC (the "National," "Journal" and "Sunday Report")
D = constructed-week sample, CTV ("National News")
E = constructed-week sample, *Globe and Mail*
F = constructed-week sample, *Vancouver Sun*
G = whole sample, community newspapers

Percentages are not cumulative, since more than one party can be mentioned in the given item.

particular party, i.e., the party is a principal political actor as distinct from being merely mentioned as shown in table 4.2. Of initial interest is column B in table 4.1, which represents the constructed-week sample for the major daily media – the two television networks, CBC and CTV, and the two daily papers, the *Globe and Mail* and the *Vancouver Sun*. This sample is roughly representative of these news organizations' campaign coverage. The contrast between major and minor parties is quite clear. Each of the three major parties (Conservative, Liberal, NDP) was mentioned in at least 69.5 percent of campaign-related news items. No single minor party was mentioned in as many as 5 percent of items.

As columns C, D, E and F attest, the pattern of coverage is remarkably similar in the major media. The rank order for the three major parties is the same in each news outlet. In three of those media (CBC, CTV, the *Vancouver Sun*), the largest minor party, the Reform Party, is in fourth place, albeit well behind the three major parties. The most substantial difference between these large daily media seems to be the greater variety of minor parties referred to in the newspapers as compared with television, indicative of more comprehensive and detailed election coverage in the press.

By contrast, the community newspapers offer more frequent coverage of minor parties, and the contrast between major and minor parties is less sharp than it is in the big-city dailies and the networks (table 4.1, column G). The Reform Party, CHP and COR tower above the other minor parties. As can be gleaned from data not presented in the tables, this finding is largely an artefact of the high degree of attention accorded to these three parties (or at least their candidates) by the eight community newspapers in Wetaskiwin, where Reform, CHP and COR all fielded candidates, but the other minor parties did not. Although the data are hardly definitive, there seems to be little evidence of partisan bias in the amount of community weekly coverage accorded to the different parties. Rather, there is a strong local orientation, favouring candidates in ridings within the newspaper's distribution area. The sample of community weekly coverage includes 111 community paper items that mention minor parties, yielding a total of exactly 200 mentions of minor parties. (Two or more references to a given party within a given item were counted as only one mention.) Of these 200 mentions, only 26 were of parties not fielding candidates in each newspaper's own riding. (Interestingly, 8 of those 26 non-local mentions were of the Rhinoceros Party, indicative perhaps of its human interest newsworthiness!)

Aggregates of the results for the three major and the three minor parties, and for all television, daily and community newspaper items are shown in table 4.2. The table confirms the dominance of the major parties in frequency of coverage but also the relative accessibility of community papers to minor parties. Almost half (45.8 percent) of election items in the community paper sample mentioned at least one minor party. It should be noted that this table inflates the relative frequency of minor-party mentions for television and dailies, since the totals for these media include not only the constructed-week sample, but also those items specifically selected from the *Canadian News Index* and television transcripts for their focus on minor parties. However, the table shows that even with these "minor-party" items included, TV (2.6 percent) and dailies (6.8 percent) are less likely than are community papers (13.2 percent) to devote items exclusively to minor parties. All three types of media were similar, however, in that minor parties were usually mentioned in items that also referred to major parties.

Even more interesting, television news and current affairs have a smaller proportion of items (14.1 percent) mentioning minor parties than do the daily papers (20 percent). In addition to the constructed-week sample, *all* television items that simply mentioned minor parties were added to the sample, whereas only newspaper articles that "headlined" a minor party were added. Thus methodological bias cannot account for the greater frequency of minor parties in daily newspapers than on television news; quite the contrary. To be sure, the sample is very small, and caution must be exercised in extrapolating the results. Nevertheless, the results are consistent with the hypothesis that broadcasters' formal mandate to provide balanced and equitable coverage has not led television news to be more accessible to minor parties than are daily newspapers.

Table 4.2
Media type by mention of major and minor parties (whole sample)
(percentages)

Parties mentioned	All items (N = 525)	TV (N = 78)	Dailies (N = 205)	Community papers (N = 242)
No party mentioned	1.3	—	0.5	2.5
Major parties, no minor	67.6	85.9	79.5	51.7
Minor parties, no major	9.1	2.6	6.8	13.2
Both major and minor parties	21.9	11.5	13.2	32.6
Total	99.9	100.0	100.0	100.0

Note: Percentages may not total 100 due to rounding.
Significance = .0000.

The frequency with which different parties are mentioned in news items is one indication of their relative prominence in the news agenda. An alternative measure is to identify the party or parties that are the focal point or the principal political actor(s) in each item. Apart from further indicating which parties received the most sustained or in-depth coverage, this measure has the advantage of enabling a comparison with data from the Carleton University Media-Election Project 1988 (Frizzell et al. 1989).

Table 4.3
Proportion of all items that focus on each party, by medium
(percentages)

Party	A (N = 525)	B (N = 246)	C (N = 242)
Several major parties	25.1	40.7	12.0
Several parties, including minor	12.0	4.9	18.6
Progressive Conservative	20.2	20.7	21.9
Liberal	13.3	19.9	8.3
NDP	9.0	10.2	9.1
Reform Party	5.0	1.2	5.8
Green Party	2.1	—	2.5
Rhinoceros Party	0.8	—	1.7
Libertarian	1.0	0.4	0.8
Christian Heritage party	2.9	0.4	4.1
Communist party	1.1	—	0.4
Confederation of Regions	3.8	0.4	7.0
Commonwealth	0.2	—	0.4
Social Credit	—	—	—
Independent/non-registered party	2.3	—	5.0
No party	1.3	1.2	1.7
Total	100.1	100.1	100.1

Notes: Column headings are as follows:
A = all items, whole sample
B = all items from the constructed-week sample for the major media (CBC, CTV, *Globe and Mail*, *Vancouver Sun*)
C = whole sample, community newspapers

Percentages may not total 100 due to rounding.

The principal party for each item in the entire sample is displayed in table 4.3, column A. The relative prominence of minor parties in the mainstream media is greatly exaggerated, since the sample includes community weeklies as well as items included specifically for their mention of minor parties. However, the differential frequency of the various minor parties is shown in column A. Again, Reform (followed by COR) led the pack of minor parties, and the minuscule Commonwealth party and the remnants of Social Credit were the focus of almost no news items.

Based on the constructed-week sample for television and daily papers, the gates of the major media were largely closed to the minor parties, as shown in column B of table 4.3. Minor parties were the focus of just 2.4 percent of items; they shared the spotlight with the major parties in a further 4.9 percent.

These findings are quite similar to those of the Carleton University study of 1988 campaign coverage. It found that of all CBC campaign news items, 24.2 percent, 21.4 percent and 18.6 percent focused on the Conservatives, Liberals and NDP respectively, and 13.9 percent included all three major parties. On CTV, the comparable figures were 22.7 percent, 23.8 percent and 18.2 percent, with 9.5 percent emphasizing all three major parties. Minor parties were the principal actors of only 1.9 percent of CBC and 2.8 percent of CTV items (and 4.7 percent on Global television) (Roth 1990b). Similarly, the present study shows the Conservatives to be the focus of 20.7 percent of TV daily items, Liberals 19.9 percent, NDP 10.2 percent, and two or three of the major parties 40.7 percent. (By comparison with the Carleton study, this study identifies far more multi-party items and far fewer non-party or non-applicable items; the discrepancy is probably due to different coding rules.)

Parenthetically, data not displayed in the tables show that 60 percent of TV network items, but only 40 percent of daily newspaper items, focused on just one of the three major parties. Conversely, more daily newspaper items than TV items included several of the major parties. Such a contrast probably reflects the greater dependence of network TV campaign coverage on the three major party leader tours, which yielded stories with a single-party focus.

That community papers were more accessible for minor parties than were the large media is confirmed in table 4.3, column C. Community papers had proportionately far fewer items emphasizing the major parties to the exclusion of the minor parties, and they had less coverage of the Liberals in particular, perhaps due to that party's relative weakness in British Columbia and Alberta. Conversely, the community papers gave more attention to almost every minor party, especially COR, Reform and CHP as well as to independent candidates.

It is possible that minor parties could be "compensated" for relatively infrequent coverage by the greater "play" given to items in which they are principal actors. Accordingly, as described in table 4.4, an index based on the placement, format and length of each item was devised

Table 4.4
Average prominence score for items focusing on each party (whole sample)

Focus	N	Mean
Several parties, including one or more minor	62	3.81
Several major parties	128	3.69
Christian Heritage party	15	3.67
Libertarian	5	3.60
NDP	47	3.60
Rhinoceros Party	4	3.50
Reform Party	26	3.46
Progressive Conservative	106	3.42
Liberal	70	3.41
Independent/non-registered party	12	3.17
Confederation of Regions	20	3.00
No specific party	2	3.00
Commonwealth	1	3.00
Communist party	6	2.83
Green Party	11	2.82
Social Credit	—	—
Total/mean for all items	515	3.51

Notes: Between-group significance: .6479.

The "prominence" of each item is a score from 2 to 8 calculated by adding scores based on each of three criteria: the item's position within the program or newspaper, its format and its relative size. Point values were awarded as follows:

Points	Prominence
0	newspaper item on inside pages; TV items in 4th- to 2nd-last position
1	newspaper item on front page of inside section; TV item in 3rd position
2	newspaper item on front page, non-lead story; TV item in 2nd or last position
3	newspaper item on front page, lead newspaper story; TV item in 1st position
1	TV item, news anchor script only; newspaper photo or graphic without accompanying story *or* story without accompanying photo or graphic
2	TV item narrated by a reporter; newspaper article with photo or graphic
1	small item
2	medium-sized item
3	large item

(A code book detailing definitions of the variables and their values is available from the author.)

to measure its relative prominence.[4] Minor-party items were in fact not more prominent than average as shown in table 4.4. Only CHP and Libertarian items were somewhat above average; the remaining minor parties' items were less prominent than average. Items mentioning several parties, including at least one minor party, were on average the most prominent – which probably reflects the inclusion of a greater range of political actors in longer news items. In any case, the between-group differences are not statistically significant.

Themes of Coverage

Whether minor parties receive equitable news coverage is not simply a question of the amount of coverage; it is also a question of content. It is possible that even though minor parties receive a certain amount of coverage, they are regarded and treated differently as news actors. For example, it can be hypothesized that because very small parties are not taken seriously as political actors, they may be disproportionately treated as human-interest oddities when they do appear in the news.

Table 4.5 displays the main topic or theme of all sampled items, cross-tabulated with the party that is the principal actor in each item. There are some interesting apparent examples of successful agenda-setting by major and minor parties alike in the table. For example, the Conservatives had a higher proportion of items on the centre-piece of their platform – free trade – than did any other party; the Liberals, who staked their campaign on opposition to free trade, were next. More pertinently, several minor parties seemed to attract some (albeit limited) coverage on issues of particular concern to them. Nearly half of the items in which the Green Party was the principal political actor were on environmental issues; a further 27 percent of Green Party items concerned the televised leaders debates, about which the Green Party strongly protested its own exclusion. Similarly, 25 percent of COR's items were on constitutional and related issues, and 13 percent of the CHP's handful of items concerned abortion. These examples could be interpreted positively as cases of modestly successful agenda-setting by minor parties. But they can also be seen negatively, as the effects of media stereotyping minor parties as "single issue" advocates; minor-party policies on issues other than their perceived primary preoccupation appear to be relatively less newsworthy.

In that light, it is significant that whereas the three major parties were principal actors in items on a broad range of issues, the minor parties were virtually shut out of coverage of most issues as shown in table 4.5. In particular, only a tiny proportion of items focusing on free trade included minor parties as principal actors. Given that the Carleton study shows that free trade was the focus of 58 percent of all major media coverage of issues (Frizzell et al. 1989, 86), and given the importance of this issue to the election's outcome, this exclusion is significant. Minor parties were similarly absent in items discussing the results of polls, thus presumably restricting the extent to which voters could identify minor parties as meaningful political options. Conversely, minor parties were most likely to appear in items about campaigns in individual ridings (such as all-candidates meetings) or in party profiles – items that supply general background on some particular party. This latter finding is not surprising; newsworkers could safely assume that their audiences were relatively unfamiliar with new and minor parties. To the extent that such parties were considered newsworthy at all, a profile item would be a reasonable way to present them to readers. Interestingly, the Reform Party received more such profiles than any other minor party, indicative both of its newness and its increasing newsworthiness as an electoral contender.

The themes that are mentioned directly in connection with each party (as distinct from the overall topic of each item) are shown in table 4.6. The percentages in this table represent the proportion of those items (from the entire sample) mentioning each party in which a given theme is associated with that party. For instance, 54.5 percent of those items mentioning the Conservatives describe some aspect of the party's position on one or more substantive issues.

Somewhat surprisingly perhaps, minor parties do not appear to have a substantially lower proportion of references to party positions on issues, compared with major parties (table 4.6, column PSN). To be sure, whether they apply to minor or to major parties, perusal of the original news reports indicates that these references are often quite brief and rarely constitute detailed explanations of party programs.

Not surprisingly, minor parties are much less likely to be mentioned in connection with "horse-race" themes (polls, campaign strategies) compared with major parties (table 4.6, column HOR). This finding likely indicates the media perception of minor parties as electoral noncontenders and the general absence of minor parties in the reporting of poll results. The one exception is the Reform Party, whose popularity was perceptibly on the rise in western Canada. In 18.1 percent of items mentioning the Reform Party, the party is connected with "horse-race" themes, placing it between the major parties and the other minor parties.

The relative weakness of the minor parties as perceived electoral contenders is also suggested by the relatively few reported responses to or criticisms of minor parties from their electoral rivals

Table 4.5
Main theme of items focusing on each party (whole sample)
(percentages)

Theme	PC (106)	Lib (70)	NDP (47)	Ref (26)	Grn (11)	COR (20)	Com (6)	Cwl (1)	Rhi (5)	Ltn (4)	CHP (15)	Ind (12)	A (132)	B (63)	C (5)
Free trade	32	24	21	—	—	—	—	—	—	20	—	—	20	5	80
Local race	22	20	32	38	—	45	33	100	25	20	60	75	12	67	—
Party profile	3	3	13	54	18	25	50	—	50	60	27	8	2	2	—
TV debates	—	9	—	—	27	—	—	—	—	—	—	—	11	3	—
Polls	4	1	4	—	—	—	—	—	—	—	—	—	16	3	—
Campaign strategy	5	9	2	—	—	—	—	—	—	—	—	—	13	2	20
Constitution, national unity, federal-provincial relations	2	—	—	4	—	25	—	—	—	—	—	8	2	2	—
Regional development, welfare, unemployment	—	3	2	—	—	—	—	—	—	—	—	1	—	—	—
Leadership	1	4	2	—	—	—	—	—	—	—	—	—	2	2	—
Environment	—	1	4	—	45	—	17	—	—	—	—	8	2	2	—
Deficit/interest rates	4	3	—	—	—	—	—	—	—	—	—	—	1	2	—

Table 4.5 (cont'd)
(percentages)

Theme	Party N	PC (106)	Lib (70)	NDP (47)	Ref (26)	Grn (11)	COR (20)	Com (6)	Cwl (1)	Rhi (5)	Ltn (4)	CHP (15)	Ind (12)	A (132)	B (63)	C (5)
Native issues		—	—	2	—	—	—	—	—	—	—	—	—	1	—	—
Abortion		5	—	—	—	—	—	—	—	—	—	13	—	3	—	—
Women's issues, childcare		1	4	—	—	—	—	—	—	—	—	—	—	2	2	—
Taxes		3	3	2	—	—	—	—	—	—	—	—	—	1	—	—
Electoral reform		2	1	—	—	—	—	—	—	—	—	—	—	—	—	—
Defence		2	—	—	—	9	—	—	—	—	—	—	—	2	—	—
Other		16	14	15	4	—	5	—	—	25	—	—	—	12	11	—
Total		102	99	99	100	99	100	100	100	100	100	100	99	103	103	100

Notes: Column headings are as follows:

PC = Progressive Conservative
Lib = Liberal
NDP = New Democratic Party
Ref = Reform Party

Grn = Green Party
COR = Confederation of Regions
Com = Communist party
Cwl = Commonwealth

Rhi = Rhinoceros Party
Ltn = Libertarian
CHP = Christian Heritage party
Ind = Independent

A = several major parties
B = several parties, including minor
C = no specific party

N = 523.
Significance = .0000.

Percentages may not total 100 due to rounding.

Table 4.6
Themes mentioned for each party as a proportion of all items (whole sample) mentioning each party
(percentages)

Party	PSN	HOR	PER	RES	LDR	POS	TRI	NEG	N
Progressive Conservative	54.5	24.0	6.9	32.7	6.2	46.0	1.0	66.1	407
Liberal	47.5	24.6	6.5	21.7	10.1	39.7	2.7	59.2	335
NDP	45.8	27.3	5.5	21.7	4.5	47.0	2.9	54.8	307
Reform Party	48.4	18.1	11.7	17.0	7.4	45.7	6.5	28.3	93
Green Party	41.4	3.4	17.2	—	—	46.4	35.7	21.4	30
Confederation of Regions	48.1	1.9	16.7	3.7	7.4	38.5	9.6	19.6	54
Communist party	47.6	—	38.1	47.6	4.8	38.1	28.6	33.3	22
Commonwealth	11.1	10.0	10.0	—	—	10.0	30.0	20.0	12
Rhinoceros Party	22.7	—	4.8	—	4.8	23.8	35.0	19.0	21
Libertarian	47.1	—	17.6	5.9	—	36.8	38.9	21.1	19
Social Credit	—	—	16.7	16.7	16.7	—	20.0	20.0	6
Christian Heritage party	51.9	3.8	11.3	5.7	7.4	36.0	8.0	20.0	54
Other	45.8	2.1	26.0	2.1	—	27.3	11.4	17.8	46

Notes: The themes referred to in the column headings are as follows:
PSN = position on issues
HOR = horse-race
PER = personality focus
RES = response from other parties
LDR = leadership
POS = positive themes
TRI = trivialization
NEG = other negative themes

The *N*s on which the percentages for each cell are based may fluctuate slightly due to random miscodes or missing values.

Percentages are not cumulative since more than one theme about a given party may appear in each item.

(table 4.6, column RES). References to the major parties are generally more likely to be bracketed by comment or criticism. Again, the Reform Party stands between the major parties and the other minor parties. The high proportion of responses to the Communist party is an anomaly, apparently the result of anti–Communist party statements reported in some community weeklies.

The personalities and backgrounds of party candidates and leaders constituted a more frequent theme in minor-party coverage, by contrast with coverage of major parties (table 4.6, column PER). This finding may indicate the relative importance of "human interest" as a criterion of newsworthiness applied to minor parties.

Compared with major parties, minor parties in general were somewhat less likely to be associated with positive themes (table 4.6, column POS) and considerably less likely to be covered negatively (table 4.6, column NEG). This finding is consistent with the Carleton study, which found that 90.3 percent of items in which "other parties" were the principal actor were neutral, compared with an average of only 66.9 percent of major party items. Conversely, 5.6 percent of minor-party items, and 5.9 percent of major-party items, were favourable; 27.2 percent of major-party items, and only 4.1 percent of minor-party items, were unfavourable (Frizzell et al. 1989, 89). This finding probably reflects the relative disinclination to subject to critical scrutiny parties that are seen as having little or no chance to form a government. This explanation would be consistent with the relative lack of unfavourable coverage of the perennial third party, the NDP, in federal campaigns (Soderlund et al. 1984, 67–71).

However, minor parties are far more likely to receive trivializing or dismissive coverage – for example, labels such as "fringe" or "oddity," or statements that denigrate their electoral chances (table 4.6, column TRI). Once again, the Reform Party stands between the major parties and the other minor parties in this regard. Although the total numbers are very small, it is interesting that both the Green and the Libertarian parties received proportionately as much trivializing coverage as the self-consciously satirical Rhinoceros Party.

Campaigns and Media: National and Local Levels
It is possible that the relatively infrequent coverage of minor parties in the national and metropolitan media (network television, big-city daily papers) is related to the orientation of those media toward institutions that are provincial or national in scope, and routinely able to produce potentially newsworthy information. Major parties have the resources to mount national tours for their leaders, operate national and regional offices with full-time staff and hire media consultants and communications directors.

By contrast, for the minor parties, more of the burden of conducting a campaign appears to fall on the shoulders of local candidates. Consequently, it can be hypothesized that the minor parties are likely to be relatively more dependent on local media for as much coverage as they are able to attract. These local media could include community cable TV, as well as the community papers, which Fletcher (1981, 10) describes as a fourth layer in Canada's news system, behind national media, regional media, and small-city dailies and stations. Such community weeklies are "a supplement to other news sources ... filling the gap in local coverage left by the 'metropolitanization' of many dailies."

Although the data in tables 4.7 and 4.8 are not definitive – they would require more detailed analysis, as well as additional information – they tend to support the above interpretation. As table 4.7 suggests, compared with the major parties, a higher proportion of the references to minor parties occur in items that focus on local races rather than the national campaign. (Interestingly, the Rhinos receive a higher

Table 4.7
Level of campaign by party mention (whole sample)

Party	N	Percentage					Significance at 0.01?
		International	National	Provincial/ regional	Local	Total	
Progressive Conservative	407	0.5	61.4	4.9	33.2	100.0	Yes
Liberal	334	0.6	59.9	5.4	34.1	100.0	Yes
NDP	306	0.7	56.5	5.2	37.6	100.0	No
Reform Party	92	—	27.2	4.3	68.5	100.0	Yes
Green Party	30	—	33.3	10.0	56.7	100.0	No
Confederation of Regions	54	—	27.8	3.7	68.5	100.0	Yes
Communist party	22	—	22.7	9.1	68.2	100.0	No
Commonwealth	12	—	41.7	8.3	50.0	100.0	No
Rhinoceros Party	20	—	50.0	—	50.0	100.0	Yes
Libertarian	19	—	47.4	5.3	47.4	100.1	No
Social Credit	6	—	66.7	—	33.3	100.0	No
Christian Heritage party	53	—	24.5	1.9	73.6	100.0	Yes
Other	45	—	13.3	—	86.7	100.0	Yes
All parties (average)	524	0.4	55.0	5.0	39.7	100.1	—

Notes: The table breaks down the items mentioning each party into the percentage that focused on the international, national, provincial/regional and local levels of the election campaign.

Percentages may not total 100 due to rounding.

proportion of national-level coverage than most other minor parties, suggesting the newsworthiness of their antics beyond the context of local campaigns.)

Cross-tabulating the three types of media with the level of campaign coverage shows that network television had the highest proportion of items (82.1 percent) focusing on the national level of the campaign. That finding is consistent with, and can be partly explained by, the very strong emphasis in television campaign coverage on the leaders of the three national parties. According to the 1988 Carleton Election Study, 62.8 percent of CBC-TV items, and 54.4 percent of CTV items, focused on the party leaders. Television also had more provincial-level coverage, indicative of its practice of offering province-by-province or region-by-region summaries of the campaign.

The dailies likewise had a high proportion of national-level coverage (74.1 percent), but also a higher proportion of local coverage (17.6 percent) than did television (9 percent) – no doubt due to the hybrid nature of metropolitan dailies. With their regional or national distributions combined with a strong readership base in a single urban centre, the dailies disseminate international, national, provincial and metropolitan news.

By contrast, community papers emphasized mostly local campaigns (68.5 percent). Combined with the higher dependence of minor parties on such local campaigns for media coverage (table 4.7), this finding helps explain the relatively high frequency of minor parties in the community papers noted in table 4.2.

Table 4.8
Media type by level of campaign (whole sample)
(percentages)

Level of campaign	TV (N = 78)	Dailies (N = 205)	Community papers (N = 241)
International	—	1.0	—
National	82.1	74.1	29.9
Provincial/regional	9.0	7.3	1.7
Local	9.0	17.6	68.5
Total	100.1	100.0	100.1

Note: Percentages may not total 100 due to rounding.
Significance = .0000.

Party Spokespeople: Who Gets On?

Another dimension of the media treatment of different parties concerns the extent to which they are afforded the opportunity to present their own case in their own words. It can be very revealing to distinguish between "sources" and "actors" in the news, between groups who "appear in the news as speaking 'subjects,' and those who appear as 'objects' whose actions are deemed newsworthy ... but whose statements, rationales, or viewpoints are not" (Hackett 1985, 264). Hackett also states: "Sources appear in the news by virtue of their provision of information or viewpoints which are considered to be credible, authoritative, legitimate and/or relevant. Actors, by contrast, are deployed in journalistic narrative because their actions are newsworthy – often they constitute a threat or a spectacle, or they suffer horrendously, or they engage in public disruption – rather than through their ability to make authoritative pronouncements; actors are spoken about more than they are permitted to speak for themselves" (1991, 205).

Criminals and terrorists are often mentioned in the news, for example, but, understandably, they are rarely permitted to argue their own case. It is possible that some minor parties may be perceived as "extremist" or as lacking a credible program; consequently, they may be quoted or interviewed in the news even less frequently than they are mentioned.

As table 4.9 indicates, however, such is not the case. Minor parties may be mentioned less frequently than are major parties, but when they do appear, minor parties (i.e., their representatives) are as likely to be quoted or interviewed as their major-party counterparts. That is the case for all three types of media – network television, dailies and community papers. (Indeed, as a proportion of references in commu-

Table 4.9
Proportion of items mentioning each party, in which a representative of that party is quoted or interviewed
(percentages)

Party	All items (N = 525)	TV (N = 78)	Dailies (N = 205)	Community papers (N = 242)
Progressive Conservative	44.0	60.6	57.5	23.4
Liberal	41.8	54.4	50.3	24.4
NDP	40.1	54.9	47.0	27.9
Minor parties (average)	44.7	54.8	55.1	38.8

Note: The Ns on which the percentages are based are actually different for each cell. Only items in which a given party was mentioned are used as the basis for calculating percentages, which are thus not cumulative.

nity papers, minor parties are more likely to be quoted than are major parties.) The explanation for such apparent equivalence of treatment may be that each major party is often spoken about in campaign coverage without being quoted. An item on the NDP leader's day on the campaign trail may well include criticism of the Tory government's policies, for example, without any statements from the Conservative camp, whose views would be reported in a separate item.

It is noteworthy that compared with the large media, community papers are less likely to quote any of the parties. A perusal of the community papers' election items suggests one explanation of this finding: many such items consist merely of photos with captions, or brief "fillers" that offer little more than the names and perhaps a brief background of the local candidates. This tendency suggests the possibility, to be explored in the next two sections, that many community papers may not be terribly serious about covering federal elections. To speculate, some community papers may shy away from political events, from campaigns that are seen as lacking immediate local interest and relevance, or indeed from journalism itself. Such publications may lack the resources or the will to initiate news coverage, focusing instead on producing an efficient advertising vehicle. If that is the case, there are significant implications for minor parties that disproportionately depend on the community papers for news coverage: such papers could not then really be seen as a counterweight to the more influential media as an avenue for the expression of minor-party views.

The types of people who are quoted or interviewed on behalf of each party are shown in table 4.10. The results for the minor parties are aggregated.

As the table indicates, somewhat surprisingly, the national leaders of minor parties are as likely to speak on behalf of their organizations as are their major party counterparts. The data do confirm, however, the relatively high dependence of minor parties on their local candidates as media spokespeople and, conversely, the relative shortage of professional consultants or officials as minor-party spokespeople. Still more noticeable is the virtual absence of rank-and-file party members or ordinary voters speaking in support of minor parties.

A Note on Newsmagazine Coverage of the 1988 Campaign
How did newsmagazine coverage of minor parties during the 1988 campaign compare with the patterns discussed above? Although it was not quantitatively content-analysed, political news in the seven weekly issues of *Maclean's* and *Alberta Report* published during the campaign was carefully reviewed.

Table 4.10

Type of party spokesperson by party, in TV and daily newspaper items in which each party is quoted or interviewed
(percentages)

Party	N	Type of spokesperson						Total
		L	C	S,O	M	V	2+	
Progressive Conservative	151	35.1	27.8	17.2	6.6	5.3	7.9	99.9
Liberal	127	42.5	16.5	15.7	10.2	3.9	11.0	99.8
NDP	102	42.2	26.5	16.7	4.9	2.9	6.9	100.1
All minor parties (average)	62	43.5	35.5	9.7	1.6	—	9.7	100.0

Notes: Column headings are as follows:
L = leader
C = candidate
S,O = strategist or official
M = member
V = voter supporting this party
2+ = two or more types of spokespeople in this item.

Percentages are based on the number of TV and daily newspaper items (from all sample dates) in which representatives or supporters of each party are interviewed, quoted or paraphrased.

Percentages may not total 100 due to rounding.

Maclean's appeared to follow the lead of the other major media, paying scant heed to minor parties. Only a single three-column article under the byline of John Howse (7 November 1988) focused on them, devoting a paragraph or two to each of the nine minor parties. The article's title was revealing of the interpretive frame: "Outside Looking In: The Fringe Parties Join in the Race to November." The label "fringe party" was applied to Reform as well as the other eight minor parties, although the article conceded that Reform had mounted "the most effective campaign." The article concluded as follows: "*Like the other fringe candidates,* few, if any, Rhinos will come close to winning a seat on Nov. 21. But their parties will continue to exist – as long as there are Canadians who feel strongly that *their particular interests* are not being served by *the country's mainstream politicians*" [emphasis added].

A clearer example of the marginalization of the new and minor parties would be difficult to imagine. Other campaign news in *Maclean's* focused on the free trade issue or on one or several of the major parties.

Campaign coverage in *Alberta Report* was strikingly different from the other major media considered here. The newsmagazine evidently regards itself as reflecting both the interests and concerns of western Canada, and offsetting what it perceives as the central Canadian biases of the dominant national media. At the same time, *Alberta Report* apparently seeks to weld the sentiment of western political alienation to a right-wing discourse on moral and economic issues; news judgement and interpretation seemed to be influenced by editorial positions in favour of free trade and against abortion, for example. Ideological as well as geographical proximity to western protest parties appears to have influenced *Alberta Report*'s coverage of the 1988 campaign. Of 35 campaign articles, at least five gave prominent attention to the Reform Party. The headlines suggest that Reform was treated respectfully, even supportively, as a serious political alternative to the Progressive Conservatives:

- "The Other Election Issue: Senate Reform Is Vital to the West, and Its Last Hope Is the Reform Party" (31 October 1988).
- "Manning Hangs Tough: The RPC Leader Ousts a Candidate Considered Extremist" (7 November 1988).
- "The Clark–Manning Road Show: The Reform Party Leader Closes the Gap on the Former PM" (14 November 1988).
- "A Race Without a Frontrunner: [A] Weak PC Candidate Is in a Close Race in Strathcona" (14 November 1988).
- "Tackling the Tory Corner: A Reformer Threatens a PC Stronghold" (21 November 1988).

Interestingly, no *Alberta Report* articles focused on the NDP, even though that party finished second in the federal popular vote in Alberta in both 1984 and 1988. The Liberals, who finished fourth behind Reform in Alberta's popular vote in 1988, were headlined in only one or two articles, mainly critical: "Turner Leads the Promise Parade: Campaign Largesse Would Add Billions to Ottawa's Debt" (21 November 1988). The Progressive Conservatives, the dominant federal party in Alberta since 1958, received the lion's share of coverage, some supportive, some critical. Apart from Reform, other minor parties received little attention. One item (21 November 1988) concerned a challenge to Liberal leader John Turner in his Vancouver Quadra riding from a Rhino candidate with the same name. Another (14 November 1988), concerning the abortion issue, gave the CHP some positive attention.

Summary of the Content Analysis Findings

Following is a summary of the main findings of the content analysis. Given the small size of the sample, their provisional nature must be emphasized. Most of the results, however, are consistent with other research on news content, news production and Canadian election coverage.

- In the national and regional media examined (network television and daily papers), minor parties received much less coverage than did major parties in the 1988 campaign.
- Community newspapers gave the minor parties relatively much more attention, especially those parties fielding candidates within each newspaper's respective distribution area.
- Television network news did not offer more coverage to minor parties than did daily newspapers.
- Some minor parties were able to attract some coverage on their own chosen issues, but, generally, minor parties were restricted to a relatively narrow range of issues, and were most likely to appear in party profiles or reports of local races.
- Minor- and major-party positions on issues were reported with proportionately similar frequency. Minor parties were generally less likely than major parties to be linked to the electoral "horse race," to criticism from other parties, or to positive or negative themes in general. However, they were more likely to receive personality oriented and trivializing themes.
- News coverage of the Reform Party stood in several respects between that of the major parties and the other minor parties. Compared with other minor parties, it received more coverage, was more likely to be associated with the electoral "horse-race" and with critical response from other parties, and was less likely to be trivialized. But in each of these respects, coverage of Reform still did not compare with news of the three major parties.
- Minor parties were more likely to get news attention in local rather than national levels of the campaign. Community newspapers offered relatively much more coverage of local campaigns than did the large media, which probably helps to account for the higher degree of access accorded to minor parties in community papers.
- There were some very provisional indications that the Rhinoceros Party was more newsworthy than most other minor parties outside the local races.
- Minor parties were not disproportionately treated as mere "actors" rather than as "sources" in 1988 campaign coverage.
- The low proportion of quotes in community weekly coverage implies that this medium did not offer in-depth coverage of the federal campaign.
- Minor-party spokespeople were more likely to consist of local candidates, and less likely to include officials, members and voters, compared with major parties.

CAMPAIGNS AND THE MEDIA:
PERCEPTIONS OF MINOR-PARTY REPRESENTATIVES

Although content analysis can reveal patterns of media treatment, an assessment of media treatment of minor parties must consider also the forces underlying the manifest content of news. These forces include the communication practices of minor parties, their interaction with the media, and the journalistic routines, policies and judgements shaping media coverage of parties. Accordingly, interviews were conducted with media practitioners and with representatives of minor parties. The 18 minor-party respondents included the leaders of the CHP and COR, as well as several candidates, particularly in the four Vancouver and Edmonton-area ridings chosen as a focus for analysis. Eight of the nine registered minor parties were represented in interviews, excluding only Social Credit which contested just nine ridings.

Interview data share the methodological biases of some other obtrusive methods. The selection of respondents is shaped (and perhaps skewed) not only by research considerations, but by their availability and willingness to participate. Selective perception and selective reporting, as well as the frailty of human memory, also shape the results; indeed, two years after the event, respondents were often able to speak only in general terms of their experiences and recollections of the 1988 federal campaign. Nevertheless, there is no substitute for the views of the "players" themselves, and they added important insights regarding interaction between minor parties and media that would not otherwise be available. The validity of their perceptions can sometimes be checked by comparing them with the content analysis findings reported above. Moreover, the perceptions of minor-party candidates and other players are important in themselves, since the legitimacy and fairness of the electoral process is in considerable measure a question of how it is perceived.

The interviews revolved around several pertinent themes: perceptions of news media coverage of minor parties and of imperatives or factors shaping that coverage; the media relations strategies and resources of minor parties, including the use of free broadcast time and paid advertising; comparisons between different media and different parties; and potential regulations or reforms to achieve more equitable media treatment. Given the differing circumstances of each respondent and of each interview situation, however, the schedule of questions was not standardized.

The interviews with minor-party representatives are summarized in this section, and those with media practitioners in the next.

Minor-Party Views of the Importance of Media Coverage

Most minor-party representatives agree that access to the media is important, if not essential, to their political prospects. The main exception appears to be candidates from the Reform Party, which is perhaps not surprising given the party's initial rise to prominence without a great deal of media attention. Reform's director of communications, Ron Wood, argues that his party would have achieved comparable support without media coverage, since in his view the party has been listening to people at a grassroots level and recruiting members at rallies. Likewise, Don Evans, Reform's candidate in Vancouver South in 1988, argues that "further media coverage" would not likely have increased his vote total.

Most other respondents, however, feel differently. Robert M. Roth, in personal correspondence to the principal investigator, attributes greater influence to the media: "Having participated as a candidate in four municipal and one provincial election [for the NDP], I am convinced that mass media images are becoming more significant than 'grassroots' activities such as the traditional volunteer canvassing of ridings. That is not to say such grassroots activities are not important; rather they are becoming less important."

Likewise, Dr. Harry Garfinkle, Green Party candidate in Edmonton Southeast, feels that a small party needs media access "simply to break out of talking to the people you've already got within the ranks." He adds that the Green Party's goals are not necessarily "political," in that "building public consciousness" of the need for an ecologically considerate economy is a greater priority. However, the Green Party's concern to change social attitudes rather than simply to win seats in no way diminishes the importance of media coverage: "We need an opportunity to explain and show the connection between environmental and economic matters."

David Reimer of the CHP argues that the influence of television coverage of candidates and national leaders could be "overwhelming," especially in tightly contested campaigns.

From quite different points on the political spectrum, candidates Naomi Rankin (Communist) and Bill Tomlinson (Libertarian) share the perception that mass media are essential for a small party with few resources. Tomlinson also makes an important distinction between advertising and news coverage, and argues that the latter is especially crucial to a minor party: "The only way we can get our message out to the people is through the media. In common with the other smaller parties we don't have big budgets and we can't spend the money on advertising because we don't have it, so the only way is through news media. If we have no coverage, then as far as the readers or the viewers are concerned we might as well not exist."

Media Relations: Minor-Party Strategies and Resources

Notwithstanding the perceived importance of media coverage, most minor-party candidates report that because of limited resources, they had little or no infrastructure to deal with the media. As to whether their own efforts made any difference to the quantity and quality of the coverage they received, minor-party representatives are divided. Some feel that media were responsive to their efforts; others, that media were not interested, regardless of how forthcoming they were.

Libertarian candidate and organizer, Bill Tomlinson, indicates that his campaign had no paid help, just volunteers, and had no personnel assigned to public relations. The Libertarians could not afford to supply newspapers with press releases except "maybe one or two" to local papers. Media and public relations would be a top priority were more funds available.

In the experience of Oran Johnson, COR candidate in Edmonton Southeast, media coverage has been minimal and of little assistance to his party. But he implies that minor parties nevertheless hold their fate in their own hands, to some extent: "If you're a fringe party, a party that doesn't have a million dollars ... You'd have to start early. I would say a year ahead of time. And simply start making your rounds, getting people together for small meetings ... and educating them on your policies."

David Reimer, CHP candidate in Wetaskiwin, claims that he took an aggressive stance to the media, realizing that "the only way we were to make any progress was if we got our fair share of the coverage." Initially he contacted all the media himself, and as time went on he claims they contacted him, even some from outside his riding. As the CHP was "a relatively new party with no infrastructure" to handle media relations, the onus fell on him as local candidate and on his campaign manager to respond. Reimer had an extensive network of more than 100 volunteers, which he felt was very important to his campaign, but he would still have liked to supplement door-to-door canvassing with a campaign manager who would have time to set up media interviews. He also attended a CHP candidate training session in Burlington, Ontario, which he feels provided useful tips for those candidates who had already been nominated.

Doug Main, Reform candidate in Edmonton–Strathcona, drew on his extensive experience in broadcasting and handled the media relations himself. He did not have a media relations person, or any centralized party "machinery" to assist. Main argues that the coverage he received was not only earned (through the Reform Party's credibility), but also had to be struggled for: "I had to fight for credibility, we had to push and insist when we were not invited; when some of the forums were split into two camps, big parties and little parties, we had to fight to be with the New Democrats, the Liberals and the Conservatives. We had to fight to be on the platform with them as a major party and I had to say: 'Listen, we're running candidates in every constituency across western Canada and we have thousands of members' ... This proves that we are not a fringe party."

Other Reform candidates, and a few from other parties, echo the theme of pulling themselves up by their own electoral bootstraps, and being "aggressive with the media." On the other hand, CHP leader Ed Van Woudenberg claims to have been quite proactive in generating press releases on a regular basis, but to little avail. In the national media at least, CHP was "lost in the shuffle" of a campaign that focused on free trade: "We had our campaign office in ... Burlington. We had a media contact and we also had personnel trained in journalism. We sent regular press releases, we had a fax, we were accessible and we forwarded all our material to the media at regular times ... They were picking them up but they were not printing them."

To garner media attention – with some success as our content analysis suggests – the Rhinoceros Party used quite a different approach – jokes and buffoonery. But behind the antics are some serious messages. Marcel Kotowich, Rhino Party candidate in Edmonton–Strathcona, notes that although he had more fun than most candidates, there was a method in his madness: "I talked to more people, I said a lot of silly things but if you look behind the initial foolishness of the statement ... You're able to say things that are very valid but as long as you make them sound stupid, sound ridiculous ... you get the coverage."

Douglas Dunn, Green Party candidate, would agree that such tactics attract media attention. He describes attracting national news attention by chaining himself to an aircraft carrier in English Bay during a provincial election. But he asks whether it is "necessary for a person with a legitimate registered federal party with legitimate concerns ... to have to basically do silly stunts to get coverage which he should be entitled to, to put [a] message out?"

Dunn argues that even the Green Party's most effective media tool, letters to the editor, has its limits, since the perspectives and issues raised are not necessarily pursued elsewhere in the paper.

Minor-Party Perceptions of Their Own Media Coverage
Generally, minor-party candidates report in interviews their satisfaction with coverage in local community newspapers, as well as some

coverage by local cable stations through all-candidates forums, and some access to radio in formats such as open-line talk shows. Thus, Bill Tomlinson, Libertarian candidate in Capilano–Howe Sound, reports receiving some air time on the local community cable station, as well as coverage in "little local newspapers," coverage that he considered reasonably respectful and unbiased. Similarly, Jim Henderson (Reform candidate in Wetaskiwin) perceives that "by and large local newspapers are good; they are close to their customers so they don't get too far out in any direction." The Communist standard-bearer in Vancouver South reports coverage in the University of British Columbia campus newspaper, local community newspapers and Vancouver Co-op community radio. His counterpart in Edmonton East likewise noted some "fairly decent articles" in the *Edmonton Examiner* community paper, and the local cable station covered election forums in which all candidates were invited to participate. Ed Van Woudenberg, CHP leader and candidate in Fraser Valley West, has "no complaints about local media, none whatsoever"; local papers provided "fair and objective coverage" and the local cable station gave "equal time to all candidates and we were treated equally, no problems." Other candidates have similar perceptions of local media.

By contrast, many minor-party respondents report being denied coverage by the major dailies with the exception of short pieces in formats such as an election supplement, or brief "filler" pieces that treat the minor parties as a "novelty" or a "joke." Generally, they feel that they have been denied access to the major broadcast media such as CBC and CTV. Although allowance must be made for selective perception, such observations are broadly corroborated by the content analysis of 1988 election coverage. Thus, COR party leader Elmer Knutson asserts that he received no national media coverage except for a two-hour interview with CBC television that yielded just 90 seconds of actual air time. The COR candidate in Wetaskiwin likewise perceives a near total absence of national media coverage, especially by contrast with Reform and the three major parties. (Such a perception is broadly corroborated by content analysis; see tables 4.1 and 4.3.) Candidates from the Libertarian, CHP, Green and Communist parties similarly note a pattern of exclusion from national and major metropolitan media (daily newspapers and network affiliates). Naomi Rankin, Communist candidate in Edmonton East, rates the major media coverage of her campaign as "between nonexistent and minuscule," with the exception of the *Edmonton Journal*'s election supplement in which each candidate in each riding was given 200 words to state his or her position. As for the broadcast media, she reports one interview with CBC television, but "the slant on that was what it's like to be an also-ran." In the view of the CHP's Van Woudenberg, the Vancouver dailies and the national media "shut us out. They just didn't give us the time of day." He notes, though, that CBC television did provide some good coverage of the CHP's national tour: "They gave all small parties the same kind [of spot], and CBC spent approximately three or four hours on the road with us, and they covered part of my campaign and did a fairly in-depth interview. We were treated cordially and I have no problem."

Green Party candidate Douglas Dunn calls the coverage of his campaign, apart from that in community papers, "pathetic." He accuses the major media of having "no desire in the election process to act as a vehicle of balanced distribution of information." By contrast, the Edmonton–Strathcona Rhino candidate expresses satisfaction with the newsworthiness of his party's satirical approach to politics. His coverage was "filler," the lighter side of the election. He received more media attention than some of the other minor parties because "I was a novelty, and that's strictly why they came around to talk to us."

As might be expected from the results of the content analysis, Reform Party representatives were less likely to feel excluded by the media. Doug Main, a Reform candidate in 1988 and later an Alberta cabinet minister, reports receiving extensive coverage in the initial stages of his campaign, albeit partly due to his own high public profile as a television personality. Robert Slavick reports that his experiences in Saanich–Gulf Islands varied with different media. He received "absolutely nothing" from television, with a rather significant exception – a local television report on his door-knocking campaign. A personal connection resulted in a guest spot on a radio open-line show, and other invitations followed. With the exception of one columnist, Slavick felt ignored by the daily *Victoria Times-Colonist*, but he rates his coverage in some of the community newspapers quite highly. In his view, it was comparable to, even better than, that of the three major parties and was more extensive than that of the other minor parties.

How did minor-party respondents rate the quality or objectivity of their news coverage, as distinct from its sheer quantity? Perhaps reflecting the relative lack of negative (or critical?) attention paid to minor parties revealed in table 4.6, there were relatively few complaints of overt, hostile bias. On the whole, coverage was "very fair and gave us a lot of good exposure," says Reform's Doug Main. Acknowledging that his party received less coverage than the three major parties, Don Evans (Reform candidate in Vancouver South) is not sure that Reform could have expected equivalent treatment during its first campaign, when the party was still perceived as "a total non-contender before the election," and in a riding where the Conservative incumbent was speaker of the house. The Wetaskiwin CHP candidate claims to have "no complaints about the fairness and objectivity of the coverage," although allowing that this was partly because of his own assertiveness in offering his personal opinions and party's positions to the press. Even one Communist candidate perceives his party's coverage as "fairly professional and objective" compared with the days of the Cold War.

Still, some minor-party respondents have major reservations about the media's objectivity. COR leader Knutson alleges that the media dismiss him as a "kook" or "radical." Reform's Doug Main sees some exceptions to generally fair coverage. Toward the end of the campaign, with the growing salience of the free trade issue, the Reform Party was unable to convey that it too favoured free trade, and thus possibly lost free trade supporters to the Conservatives. (The media's apparent tendency to define minor parties as single-issue advocates was noted in the content analysis.) The item that most rankles Main, though, was a poll taken by the *Edmonton Journal* shortly before the election that greatly underestimated his support relative to the actual result on election night. Main believes that the story demoralized campaign workers, stopped the inflow of funds, and caused a slippage of voter support to the Conservatives.

Although regarding the coverage as becoming more "objective," Ron Wood, communications director for the Reform Party, claims that when Reform was a new party, the media reacted with cynicism and labelled it as "a bunch of radical westerners ... They're all extreme right-wingers, they're eccentrics, they're radicals, probably separatists." In 1988 the media, especially in "the east ... probably dismissed [Reform] as a western protest party, another populist movement." Mr. Wood also detects a tendency toward "cynical" and "subjective" coverage of Reform in Albertan dailies, compared with weekly newspapers and radio stations.

Minor-Party Candidates' Perceptions of Media Coverage of Their Political Rivals

Notwithstanding the generally benign perceptions of the fairness if not the quantity of their own party's news coverage, some respondents perceived an undue weighting toward the three major parties. Such an orientation bothers the Libertarians' Bill Tomlinson: "When you switch on the 'National,' for instance, and you find that the big news of the night, the headline item, is Brian Mulroney and John Turner stepping out of an airplane in some town or other, you begin to worry where the priorities are. It's just nuts ... when you have about eight other parties, all of them with something to say, and they are totally ignored. It really makes you wonder why the media spend the time they do with the three major parties."

A CHP candidate likewise reports receiving very little media attention compared with the major party candidates in his riding, and the Green Party's Dr. Harry Garfinkle detects discrimination in coverage of local races: "In terms of panels, local meetings, a number of places only invited the top three. The CBC panel and one other called us all, but there were three places where I showed up and I could only raise a protest from the floor."

The COR candidate in Wetaskiwin argues quite plausibly that major party candidates have the inherent advantage of riding on the "coat-tails" of nationally recognized, media-accessed leaders: "When you hear in the local riding that [a candidate] is running for the Conservative party, all at once everyone knows that he is going to be running for Mulroney's party. You hear that the local candidate Hayward Dow is running for the COR party and that leaves a lot of people wondering: Well, who's the leader of the party? We've never seen it in the *Edmonton Journal*, we've never seen it in the *Sun* and we don't see it on CBC ... Who is the leader? Is he an independent, is it an organization? Better coverage would have done better for the whole [COR] party."

Some minor-party respondents in Alberta, where the Progressive Conservatives have long dominated, expressed a certain degree of resentment at the ability of Conservative incumbents to win media attention – and re-election – without investing much apparent effort in the local race. As Gilsdorf (1981, 64) notes with respect to the national level, a major party can count on the journalistic conventions of balance to accord it coverage even when it chooses to run a low-profile campaign. There is evidence from both Alberta ridings examined in this study, though, that such inactivity can attract negative media comment. In the words of one of his minor-party rivals, the Wetaskiwin PC candidate "started to show up" at all-candidates forums "due to the pressure of a public outcry."

To the extent that any minor party was perceived by its rivals to have benefited from undue media attention, the Reform Party was most likely to be identified. The content analysis showed that indeed Reform was beginning to emerge in the media from the minor-party pack. CHP's David Reimer opines that the Reform Party, "being a provincial phenomenon (in 1988), because of the candidate for the Reform Party being a former cabinet minister of the Social Credit under Ernest Manning and now his son Preston Manning being the leader of the

Reform Party, got a little more ink, not because of the aggressive style or what he had to offer, just because of the fact that the Reform Party was getting major opposition ink."

Another CHP candidate agreed: "The Reform Party was starting from scratch like we were and the coverage was definitely biased," singling out the newsmagazine *Alberta Report* as having actively promoted Reform. The review of newsmagazine coverage in the previous section indicates that such a perception may not be without foundation.

However, Ron Wood, the Reform Party's communications director, argues that Reform had earned the status of fourth party through its standing in the polls and therefore deserved more attention than parties that between them "probably only have one or three percent." He concedes that the media are "a little bit Gallup-driven," but sympathizes with the media's contention that there is a limit to how much coverage they can give all of the parties: "It becomes a judgemental thing."

In the interviews, there was some discussion of the coverage of the Rhinoceros Party, revealing a perception that it also received more media attention than some of the other minor parties. An impressionistic reading of 1988 election coverage by the *Edmonton Examiner*, a community paper, suggests that the Rhinos received much more coverage than, for example, the Green Party. The relative newsworthiness of the Rhinos is modestly supported by the content analysis; as table 4.7 suggests, the Rhinos were more likely to receive coverage outside the context of local campaigns than were most other minor parties. Some minor-party respondents do not begrudge the media attention accorded to the Rhinos, on the grounds that the Rhinos are bright people who have achieved "credibility of a different sort," who are making "a very legitimate statement about Canadians," and who "consistently get a higher than expected fringe vote." By contrast, other candidates regard Rhino coverage as a reflection of possible media irresponsibility and a search for sensationalism. Says a CHP candidate: "When the CBC would make humorous remarks about statements that the Rhinoceros Party made but they would not give us equal time as a minor party, that bothers me."

Minor-Party Perceptions of Factors Underlying Media Coverage

Asked to identify influences on the media's coverage of political parties, respondents tended to focus on three presumed factors: party credibility, media favouritism, and the media's personality and leadership orientation.

Most frequently mentioned was each party's own credibility. It is significant that many minor-party respondents were willing to concede that coverage was shaped, at least in part, by their own party's leadership, policies and evident popular support. CHP leader Ed Van Woudenberg regards media scepticism toward new parties as "a logical reaction" and concedes that as a new party, "we must earn our stripes." Doug Main, Reform candidate in 1988, claims that coverage and exposure follow credibility, not the other way around. The Reform Party started out as just another "fringe wacko party" from the West: "But the leader was strong, the candidates were strong. It all made sense. Nobody said anything outrageous and people said, 'Oh well, they are not a fringe party, they do make sense.'"

Media spokespeople could well argue that they lack the time or money to cover all the parties in detail, and, accordingly, they focus on the parties that they feel their audiences want to be informed about and ignore those that will in any event attract few votes. Mr. Main, himself a former newscaster, has some sympathy for this kind of argument: "Let's make sure that you earn your place on the evening news. And you do that by working hard for several years to develop a credible party."

However, some minor-party respondents perceive a second, more sinister kind of influence on election news. One COR candidate sees a link between advertising revenue and favouritism toward the major parties: "Of course the papers know where their bread and butter comes from, and in elections they reap their rewards from the particularly large parties because of advertisements and so on, and they certainly don't from us." Discussing barriers to the amount of coverage some minor parties receive, a CHP candidate also perceives a systemic bias. "The system begs the question, do we have democracy?" he argues. Minor parties are not given the coverage they deserve because of "power and the dollar. Who owns the media? Who owns the papers? What is patronage? Then you realize we're on a very greasy pole based on spinoffs." Several other candidates who do not criticize the media so sweepingly nevertheless perceive partisan bias influencing the amount or type of coverage accorded to each party and the type of questions put to candidates.

Dr. Harry Garfinkle (Green Party) identifies a third kind of handicap for a policy-oriented party in the current electoral environment. He argues that elections have become personality contests and that the Green Party's lack of a recognized leader costs it coverage: "We're still going on the basis that the better argument is what we're relying on. This, I think, is the failure of the media, that they don't provide that kind of outlet."

The point may well be valid. To be sure, the content analysis shows that the party leader was more likely than anybody else to be the Green Party's spokesperson when the party was occasionally quoted on network television or in daily newspapers (six of eight items in the sample).

However, it is probable that the Green Party was able to attract such (minimal) coverage on the basis of its stand on issues – the environment, the TV debates – rather than its possession of "media-genic" leadership.

Minor Parties and Advertising

On the whole, neither free broadcasting time nor paid advertising appeared to figure prominently in minor parties' 1988 campaigns at the local level or, insofar as was determined, at the national level. For instance, according to party leader Ed Van Woudenberg, CHP had one two-minute free-time spot in English and one in French, as well as an ad in the *Globe and Mail* that ran across the country and cost the party a lot of money relative to its budget. But that was all CHP could afford. And Van Woudenberg points to an important limitation of the brief free-time broadcasting slots currently offered to minor parties: "How much can you say in two minutes? ... You can say we love Canada, we love our nation, we love our people and we will give you a fair, honest government – and your time is up."

Without a large advertising budget or very much free broadcasting time, minor parties may well be especially dependent on news coverage; yet in the 1988 election, the specific concerns of parties like CHP were buried in the news agenda, due in part to the polarization of the free trade issue.

J.G. Jackman of the Commonwealth party speculates that his party may have had some free and paid time "back East," but in the West the party could not afford paid advertising. Even with regard to free-time ads, Jackman makes a telling point: they are not as "free" as they might seem, since "you still have to have the money to produce the ads. My campaign [budget] was under a hundred dollars."

Reform Party candidate Don Evans likewise notes that his campaign did not purchase any ads because of a very limited budget. However, he did have a flyer inserted into the local newspapers in lieu of advertising.

"It all comes down to the people with the money basically telling the people who don't have the money how to vote through these very cleverly scripted and crafted news ads," according to Marcel Kotowich of the Rhinos. And free-time political broadcasts such as *The Nation's Business*, which Kotowich notes aired in Alberta at 11:50 AM – hardly prime time – are mainly available to the major parties. He suggests "throwing it open to everyone" at least once during the election campaign, giving each candidate 10 minutes in every major medium to state what he or she stands for.

Minor-Party Comments on Media-Election Reforms

Many of the minor parties see the roots of perceived electoral unfairness not in the media as such, but in the existing electoral system. Some of them, as outlined in briefs to this Royal Commission and comments from respondents to this study, advocate some version of proportional representation or reforms to party financing to remove perceived bias in favour of the dominant parties.

At the same time, minor-party respondents do have specific grievances and suggestions regarding their access to the media. Many of them expressed discontent about the amount of news coverage, the allocation of free and paid broadcasting time, and participation in candidates and leaders debates. Many of the respondents feel that minor parties need and deserve more and better access to the media, but they are divided on whether access could or should be enforced through government regulation.

Respondents from "progressive" parties generally favour a regulatory approach to electoral fairness. Thus, Reginald Walters, Communist candidate in Vancouver South, cites a promise by a television producer to supplement a forum involving the three major parties with a second program for six minor parties. The promise was not kept, and the candidate argues that equal treatment of all parties in such matters "has to be enforced in legislation." His colleague, Naomi Rankin, would recommend "more stringent spending limits ... that would tend to equalize opportunity between the parties that have a lot of money and those that don't."

Marcel Kotowich (Rhino) notes that although there is a very fine line between promoting pluralist debate and giving extremist positions undue access to the public forum, coverage should ideally be fair and equal to everyone running for office. He favours combining funding restrictions with subsidized media access, so that each candidate would be accorded "at least a minimum amount of time to stand up and say what [he or she] would like to say." To define fair and equal access may be more problematic for the print media than for broadcasting, but he sees a solution in the form of subsidized election inserts: "Why don't we take all the deposit money, the $200 per person that comes in and use that to fund these programs where everybody gets a chance. During the election campaign, one election insert in the newspapers, every newspaper distributed everywhere, in every corner of Canada."

Green Party candidate Douglas Dunn regards as a priority reform of election financing to end discrimination in favour of candidates receiving more than 15 percent of the vote. But he also argues for fairer allocation of media time by a process less subject to manipulation by the parties in power: "The buzz word should be equality and balance, not the rule of the largest dollar or those with the biggest current political clout because, through history, those who come to power aren't necessarily the best ones in power."

Similarly, Dr. Harry Garfinkle of the Green Party recommends that the press as well as broadcasters should offer opportunities, distributed throughout the campaign to every party that meets specified criteria, to present a message. He proposes a graduated system of time allotments based on criteria such as the number of candidates fielded, and concedes that major parties would receive larger allocations. Garfinkle also proposes federal subsidies for small parties "that have not yet become major players but which have shown that they are serious enough, they have been running candidates. The criteria have to be worked out. There has to be some kind of recognition that the democratic process requires a facilitation of the role of small parties rather than [having them] completely ignored." At the other end of the political spectrum, some candidates from "free enterprise" parties argue for a laissez-faire approach to campaign communication. For example, the Reform Party's communications director does not think that an all-party leaders debate should be made mandatory: "Because it is a media event, it should not be regulated by the electoral commission or anybody else. It's a media-driven thing and it's their invention, their initiative. If they want us, fine; if not, fine. We can live with it."

The Libertarians' Bill Tomlinson favours privatizing the CBC, and although he would like to see more coverage of his party, he opposes legislation to force privately owned media to provide it.

Likewise, Don Evans of the Reform Party maintains, "as far as the media is concerned, the less regulation the better." Doug Main argues that in a "free market system," it is "not fair" to force broadcasters "to expose equally all the political parties" and thereby jeopardize their return on investment. Main offers a classic "consumer sovereignty" argument against regulating election coverage, leaving the audience alone to determine whether broadcasters are providing fair and adequate news coverage: "If they don't, if their news coverage is biased or slanted or they don't cover what is the essence of the campaign, then they will lose their audience and they will lose sponsors and they will lose dollars and they will be at the mercy of [those whom] they should be at the mercy of, their audience."

One respondent from COR also puts forward a free enterprise argument. In regard to equal opportunity, he sees regulation as fitting uneasily with his philosophy: "I think it's up to the small party to simply convince enough people that [its] policies are right." He cites the rise of Social Credit in Alberta. "They just came like termites out of the woodwork in 1935 and the media didn't know anything about it. I maintain that's the only way it's ever going to happen again." (It must be noted, however, that such a view overlooks the very significant role played by radio – notably broadcasts by the party's charismatic leader, William "Bible Bill" Aberhart – in the rise of Social Credit in the 1930s.)

Some implications of a market-driven approach to campaign communication are discussed below, in the sections on policy options. The point here, though, is that notwithstanding the "free enterprise" arguments summarized above, there is substantial support, even among parties on the "right," for a positive financial or regulatory role for the state to enhance electoral fairness. Thus, Elmer Knutson complains that even though he leads a political party (COR), the "news people" do not consider him sufficiently important "to even print what I say." Accordingly, "if we have freedom of speech and if we have freedom of thought, then there has to be a way found somehow to subsidize the small parties so they can buy advertising because how can you bring new thought out if you can't get published?" He suggests that the process of registering new parties be made tougher and that parties meeting the necessary criteria for registration then be treated as equivalent to small opposition parties.

Another COR candidate argues that the media, whether print or electronic, should give all candidates equal time. The CBC should be regulated, and private stations "strongly urged," to do so.

Notwithstanding his general opposition to media regulation, Reform's Don Evans agrees that there should be a spending limit that "itself limits how much [media] time you can have," since "you don't want a rich party being able to go in there ... running television advertising that nobody else can meet." He regards the current disparities between the three main parties and the others on free and paid air time as too great. Even the Libertarians' Tomlinson would require CBC, so long as it remains in the public sector, to "devote equal time to whoever is involved."

Ed Van Woudenberg, CHP leader, favours regulating the media to some degree, "especially when we see the media in the hands of a few huge corporations." In his view, both free time and the opportunity to purchase paid time should be offered equally to all parties. Even though paid time would actually only be purchased by those who could afford it, "we have no difficulty with that." An election commission should ensure that the media do not "show favour to just one party or group of people." Programs like the CBC's "Journal" should offer an in-depth interview with each party. Citing his party's brief to this Royal

Commission, Van Woudenberg argues that the Canadian electorate has the right to sufficient information as a basis for choice: "We feel that for the sake of democracy, in getting the message out, it should not only be a matter of who can afford it. It should be a matter of what we want to present to the Canadian people as an option."

JOURNALISTS' PERSPECTIVES ON MINOR PARTIES AND THE MEDIA

How does minor party–media interaction look from the other side of the fence? To address this question, 12 interviews were conducted with news media practitioners, primarily newspaper editors in the four selected ridings. Other research on journalistic practices undertaken for this Royal Commission, as well as previously published studies (Fletcher 1981, 79–101; Gilsdorf 1981; Soderlund et al. 1984; Taras 1990) have examined national and major media coverage of federal campaigns. This study did not attempt to duplicate that research but concentrated on the two aspects most relevant to it: journalists' perceptions of minor parties and the role of community newspapers in campaign communication. This medium is particularly important for minor parties, as the content analysis suggests, yet it has been largely neglected by researchers. Community cable TV is another potential avenue of access for minor parties; although some community cable practitioners were unfortunately not available, a senior representative of Rogers Cable kindly consented to an interview. The managing editors of the two Edmonton dailies were also interviewed, to compare their perceptions of and approaches to campaign coverage with those of their community weekly counterparts.

Journalists' Views of Minor-Party Coverage in the 1988 Campaign

Representatives of both major dailies and community newspapers tend to agree that minor parties were not allocated the same amount or frequency of coverage as their major counterparts. However, if the coverage of minor parties was not equal, journalists nevertheless feel that it was fair. Understandably, media personnel deny any overt bias against minor parties; rather, they tend to argue that certain structural and organizational constraints in the news production process affect the quality and quantity of minor-party coverage.

Respondents from the major dailies cite "newsworthiness" as a factor working against minor parties. This finding is consistent with earlier data showing that most editors "did not use equal space as a basis for ensuring balanced coverage of campaigns," insisting that "newsworthiness was the only criterion of coverage" (Fletcher 1981, 82). But as previous media research has suggested, the criteria of newsworthiness are difficult for practising journalists to specify (Hall 1973, 181). Such criteria are embedded in the occupational ideology and everyday routines of news production, and journalists refer to "gut feelings" and "common sense." However, several of the respondents did at least imply that one of the criteria for judging what constitutes a "newsworthy" story is its potential to interest or attract the public, or the medium's audience. Following this logic, news organizations are often reluctant to devote equal coverage to minor parties because of their relative lack of electoral support. Media coverage, it was suggested, simply reflects an existing "reality" of Canadian politics in which minor parties play a relatively insignificant role. Relying for guidance largely on polls and attendance at election rallies, newspaper journalists judge which political parties merit primary attention. From this viewpoint, most minor parties are not deemed to be legitimately newsworthy. Media practitioners generally did not concede the possibility, intimated by some of the minor-party respondents, that mass media play an active role in sustaining the hegemony of the major parties and in inhibiting the emergence of new and minor parties.

Respondents at both community and daily papers do admit that they tend to provide more coverage to parties like the Rhinos (and in the case of the Wetaskiwin riding, the non-registered Western Independence Party) because they provide humour in an otherwise serious campaign. In such cases, minor parties are deemed to be newsworthy for their human interest or entertainment value, rather than for their political relevance or significance.

The media respondents also generally feel that minor parties must themselves take more of the responsibility for getting their message to the public. One respondent, a staff reporter with the *West Ender/East Ender* Vancouver community paper, claims that like their major party rivals, "minor candidates mostly weren't too difficult to get. They wanted the publicity ... that's probably one reason why they were so quick to reach me." However, other respondents at both daily and community newspapers suggest that minor parties are not sufficiently adept in public relations skills during election campaigns. Minor parties must be more aggressive in directly seeking out media coverage of their campaigns because it is not the mandate of the press to "track down" the candidates. Thus, an executive for Rogers Cable in Vancouver explains that each candidate was sent a registered letter notifying him or her of all-candidates forums that would be covered by the community channel. The onus was on each candidate to take advantage of the opportunity. Subsequent pleas for "special time" from candidates who missed the original event were rejected on the grounds that such treatment would constitute favouritism and result in counter-demands from other candidates.

Given the time constraints of daily media and the limited news-gathering resources of community newspapers and community cable television, such an approach would not appear to be unreasonable. To varying degrees, media organizations appear to be more willing to accord some access to minor parties, but only if the latter take the initiative.

However, as the interviews with minor parties suggest, there may be a chicken-and-egg problem with such apparent access. Because of resource limitations, it seems likely that many minor parties would be unable to generate the aggressive media campaigns that the major parties can stage. Thus, the barriers separating minor parties from substantial news coverage include more than a lack of direct access to media time and space. Perhaps as important, given the practices of media election coverage, minor parties lack access to "media experts" – strategists skilled in public and media relations. Both the content analysis (table 4.10) and the interviews with minor-party respondents suggest the shortage of expertise and professional staff available to smaller parties. Furthermore, there is no guarantee that even if minor parties did approach the media more proactively that more coverage would result, since – especially in the major media – they would still have to clear the hurdle of "newsworthiness." Indeed, the minor-party interviews suggest that there is no clear relationship between minor-party proactivity and news coverage, especially in network television and the daily press.

Other factors limiting minor-party access to the media include the economic and organizational pressures that all media claim to face. The community papers tend to operate with a skeletal journalistic staff and thus lack the personnel or resources to follow all the candidates running in local ridings. Accordingly, they tend to concentrate on major-party candidates who have a well-organized campaign itinerary.

Major dailies argue that equal space for all political parties would require not only additional resources and organizational skills that are not currently available, but also a complete restructuring of format. During elections, daily newspaper journalists see it as their mandate to cover other news events as well as elections. To cover all parties thoroughly and thoughtfully while maintaining regular newsgathering services would, they suggest, be impossible. They argue that the dailies do not ignore minor parties, but within the pressures to serve the interests of a broad public, they cannot reallocate resources from non-election news reporting to cover minor-party campaigns.

The Distinct Role of Community Media

For the most part, the community newspapers see their journalistic mandate as limited to providing information that is not covered by the major dailies to their readership. The focus of their coverage is on community events and local personalities and issues, including a major emphasis on municipal politics. Consequently, federal election coverage is not a major priority for most of the community papers since, they argue, the dailies can provide a far better service. The focal topics of election coverage are local candidates and events and local angles on issues, aspects of the campaign not covered substantially by the major dailies. Moreover, since community papers typically publish weekly or semi-weekly, election news quickly becomes dated. It is for such reasons, claim the respondents, that community papers limit their election coverage to formats such as candidate profiles, reports of local election forums, and written submissions from candidates. The review of community papers for the content analysis suggests impressionistically that election news coverage was limited in scope, with relatively little "hard news" of leader tours, campaign promises and the like. Nor was analytical or critical background very much evident in community papers.

Such inter-media differences in approach were suggested by the content analysis. The relative infrequency of quotations in community newspaper coverage was already noted (table 4.9). Results not presented in the tables show that a full 13 percent of community paper election coverage consisted of direct interviews or statements submitted by candidates, a format that does not appear in the sample of dailies at all. By contrast, dailies were much more likely to offer columns or analytical pieces (16.6 percent) than were community papers (6.2 percent).

Respondents from community papers feel that the dailies can afford to include much more content in each edition. On the other hand, because the urban dailies are attempting to cover the election campaign over a geographical area that includes various ridings, they cannot hope to provide equal coverage of all candidates in all constituencies. The community papers thus see their role as "filling in the gaps" left by the major dailies.

Similar points could be made about community cable television. The community channel, in Vancouver at least, puts much greater emphasis on municipal than on federal politics. According to David Liddell, programming vice-president at Rogers Cable, community cable is not compelled by regulation to cover federal politics; nevertheless, the cable channel did cover selected all-candidates forums, which were rebroadcast at different points in the schedule. Within such a context, all candidates, including those from minor parties, had equal opportunity for access.

Given such considerations, it is not surprising that minor-party coverage is much more evident, quantitatively, at the local level than it is in the major metropolitan or national media. One could also argue, however, that such coverage falls qualitatively far short of that offered in the major media.

Questions of Balance and Bias in Election Coverage

From the interviews, it appears that community papers are more reluctant than are the dailies to make editorial endorsements of parties. Such a finding perhaps parallels the apparently greater tendency of smaller, more than larger, daily newspapers to avoid federal election endorsements, noted by Fletcher (1981, 86). This practice, in many respects, appears to derive from the limited advertising market for community papers: endorsing a particular candidate could potentially cost a paper much-needed advertising revenue and alienate readers, increasing the potential for new competition to emerge. Accordingly, providing coverage that is perceived to be balanced and fair to all parties and local candidates is economically important to community papers.

However, such "balanced" reporting tends to apply mainly to the three major parties. Respondents from the community papers indicate that they try to cover all the candidates in an equal manner, in some cases giving minor parties more coverage than they "deserve" in relation to their electoral support. Again, there is a parallel with smaller dailies, which are more likely than the larger dailies to employ such "tape measure objectivity" (Fletcher 1981, 82). However, as the content analysis confirms (table 4.1), even community newspapers tend to focus more attention on the major parties. The community newspaper respondents agree that minor-party candidates merit some space, and this is provided primarily through coverage of local all-candidates forums and the opportunity for candidates to submit written statements. In other reportage, though, if forced to choose between running an item on the local Tory candidate, for example, and one on a minor party, the Tory will be preferred since he or she is considered more important. The only apparent potential advantage that some minor-party candidates may enjoy in the community press is local residency. Since community papers consider local issues and personalities part of their journalistic mandate, candidates from the local community are likely to receive more local media attention than candidates "parachuted" in from outside the riding – or indeed, candidates who live in a town in another part of the riding, in the case of a sprawling rural district such as Wetaskiwin.

Surprisingly, two respondents from a rural Alberta community paper make a point that echoes the suspicion voiced above by a minor-party candidate: political advertising may well play a role in determining which candidates receive more coverage in their newspaper, even if this is not a conscious decision. Although all other papers denied that this bias exists in election coverage, one respondent insisted that parties that buy advertising space and in effect help to pay the staff's salary may well receive more favourable coverage: "From a purely journalistic sense, it's wrong. But unfortunately you have to make a dollar too, to stay in business; so you have to compromise your values sometimes."

It may well be that small-town weeklies are rather less independent of individual advertisers than are urban dailies. For their part, the dailies argue that they do not face this problem because of their greater internal division of labour: news editors are separated from the advertising department and are thus "screened" from any advertising pressures. Perhaps for this reason, dailies appear to be more likely editorially to endorse a particular candidate or party. However, respondents from dailies stress that such editorial judgements are kept stringently separate from news reportage. Although critics and media scholars (Hall 1973) often detect values embedded in the most seemingly objective news, media practitioners themselves (including respondents in this study) often assert that news is intended simply to "reflect" the "real world," by contrast with editorials and columns which seek to interpret and assess that world. Consequently, in their view, minor parties need not fear any negative bias in news coverage resulting from editorial endorsement of a major party.

Can Media Reform Improve the Fairness of Coverage?
Some Journalists' Views

Not surprisingly, respondents from both the community and daily press are united in their opposition to the regulation of news content. Such a move, they argue, would severely infringe freedom of the press as guaranteed under the *Canadian Charter of Rights and Freedoms*. In their view, judgements of newsworthiness cannot be legislated, and any government interference in this direction would likely lead toward state agenda-setting. Apparently accepting the logic of the market system and commercialism in the media, respondents from both dailies and weeklies suggest that if minor parties are dissatisfied with the amount of coverage they receive, they are welcome to buy advertising space. The two daily newspaper editors interviewed both argued that regulating the amount of space allocated to political parties would undermine their mandate of providing the public with a balanced and truthful account of news. A requirement of more coverage of minor parties, they argue, would produce an "unrealistic" picture of who the legitimate contenders are.

Just as they did when the Royal Commission on Newspapers released its recommendations in 1981, newspaper spokespeople offer the notion of self-regulation as an alternative to government involvement. They assert that there is an unwritten journalistic code, which they suggest could be strengthened for future election coverage, that demands that journalists provide fair representation of all newsworthy political parties, regardless of the journalists' biases or preferences. Accordingly, decisions on what is reported, and how, remain safely in the hands of people who understand "the public interest." In essence, the newspaper respondents support the status quo.

Some community weekly newspaper spokespeople, however, would favour or at least accept some form of limitation on the allocation of advertising in the press. It was suggested that major parties, armed with bountiful resources, can quickly grab the available advertising space early in the election and effectively shut out the less well-heeled parties or candidates (a surprising claim, given that, unlike broadcasting, newspapers can increase the amount of advertising space available in a given edition).

By contrast, the daily editors suggested that, rather than limit political advertising, the government could increase subsidies to "legitimate" minor parties (those that have established roots or are growing at a reasonable rate) so that these parties could buy more advertising space in larger circulation media. Since it would increase the pool of potential advertising revenue, such an approach would seem to be in the self-interest of commercial media organizations.

Some minor-party respondents, fearing that polls discourage potential voting support, proposed restrictions or a ban on the reporting of polls during election campaigns. Newspaper respondents reject such proposals as unrealistic and a potential threat to the public's right to be informed.

While recognizing their own responsibilities, all our media respondents also argued that minor parties themselves could deal more appropriately or aggressively with the media. They suggested that at the local level, candidates must make themselves known to the press. Respondents from the community press feel that the opportunity for equal representation exists but that minor parties do not always take advantage of the available avenues of access, such as biographical profiles, written or photo submissions, and letters to the editor. The community papers themselves feel that they do not have the time or resources to chase after all the candidates, and thus they must focus much of their election coverage on those who appear to be the main contenders. For their part, daily newspaper editors suggest that if minor parties consistently provided them with proper notice of campaign events, then the press would be better able to plan coverage. They reiterated the point that minor parties need to make themselves "newsworthy" to deserve media coverage. It can be argued, however, that although such a position is not without merit, it overlooks the possibility of a "spiral of silence" effect: continued exclusion from the media may make it more difficult for a party to achieve a degree of success that would render it more newsworthy.

POLITICAL PARTIES AND CAMPAIGN COMMUNICATION: A COMPARATIVE POLICY OVERVIEW

The preceding sections have presented evidence that minor parties may not be equitably served by the current system of campaign communication. The barriers facing minor parties include the constraints and imperatives of news production, as well as the limited resources of minor parties themselves. But the ability of minor parties to communicate to voters is also greatly influenced by state policies and practices with respect to the allocation of broadcasting time, the format of leaders debates, public funding and other kinds of subsidies for the communication activities of parties, and the criteria used to define political parties and their eligibility for such subsidies. This section presents an overview of some relevant policies on these matters in other liberal democracies, notably the United States, Britain, the Federal Republic of Germany and the Scandinavian countries.

Some political systems are relatively "petrified," restricting minor-party access to the political process. Such "petrification" refers to the lack of innovation or change in a party system, and it has two dimensions: the reinforcement of large parties over small ones and of established parties over new ones (Nassmacher 1989, 248). Different liberal-democratic political systems display differing degrees of petrification. In Canada, laws and regulations in areas such as broadcasting, public funding and the rules for registering parties arguably discriminate against minor parties in favour of the major parties. Moreover, the electoral system itself plays a crucial role: it is relatively difficult for small parties to elect candidates in the single-member constituency systems of Canada, the United States and Britain. By contrast, the Scandinavian countries of Norway, Sweden and Denmark are characterized by multi-party systems and a history of governing coalitions. Along with Germany, they have variants of a proportional representation system. As Nassmacher (ibid., 262) notes, "The 'petrification' of party systems in Austria, Italy, Sweden and West Germany has neither kept the governing party in power nor excluded new parties from successfully competing for parliamentary representation."

Nevertheless, it is important to note that in all cases studied, the bulk of public subsidies are paid to the established parties, including the main opposition party, and reforms of campaign financing have generally been designed and enacted by the major party participants. In Canada, Great Britain, the Federal Republic of Germany, and Sweden, the major beneficiaries have been incumbents and major-party interests, although in some countries, particularly West Germany and Denmark, there is a more accommodating regulatory atmosphere for minor parties. As Paltiel (1979, 19) points out, "adapted as these schemes are to existing party systems, constitutional, electoral, and parliamentary arrangements, it is evident that the control mechanisms in each case will be heavily influenced by the incumbents and the other major actors on the respective party scenes." Alexander (1989c, 20) argues that ideally laws regarding public funding must apply equally to all participants. But the consequences of government policy do not always equally affect all parties and candidates: "The party or parties in power may regulate to their advantage, or may write laws that tend to squeeze out minor emerging parties."

Although regulation of campaign financing and communication may well favour established or larger parties, a laissez-faire approach by no means better ensures a more level playing field for minor parties. The U.S. experience is instructive. Attempts to limit campaign expenditures have proved unsuccessful in the United States, and the courts have declared them unconstitutional. This has created gross financial inequalities between the various parties and candidates and has served to solidify the advantages of incumbency. For example, in their perusal of various countries, Goldenberg and Traugott (1987a, 454) argue that the greater the free-market approach to the purchase and placement of political advertisements, the greater the imbalance between opposing candidates. Some European countries, such as Austria, Italy, Sweden and West Germany, make even less effort than do Canada and the United States to regulate party financing: "Whereas Canada and the United States have deliberately introduced spending and/or contribution limits as well as public agencies to enforce specific regulations of political finance, European countries have taken a more or less *laissez-faire* stand towards the control of party finance: there are neither spending nor contribution limits, there is incidental disclosure of large donors only, there are no independent controlling agencies and practically no sanctions" (Nassmacher 1989, 251).

However, as we shall see, the European countries considered in this report have at least somewhat offset the potential interparty inequalities resulting from a free-market approach by offering various forms of public subsidies, including media access, to the contending parties.

The Concept of Fairness: Equal or Equitable?

The principles of equity have a long history in political broadcasting in Canada. The policy of "equitable, varied and comprehensive" political programming began in Canada in the late 1920s, when the first Canadian Royal Commission on Radio Broadcasting, popularly known as the Aird Commission, stated: "While we are of the opinion that broadcasting of political matters should not be banned, nevertheless, we consider that it should be very carefully restricted under arrangements mutually agreed upon by all parties concerned" (Canada, Royal Commission 1929, 11).

However, the concept of "equitable" political broadcasting runs into several difficulties in practice. One is the question of what constitutes an equitable degree of access for the various parties, including smaller ones. Another is the question of enforcement, of how to ensure that broadcasters in practice provide equitable political programming. The Green Party believed that broadcasters during the 1988 federal election discriminated against it as a smaller party and that the Canadian Radio-television and Telecommunications Commission (CRTC) failed to take remedial action. Consequently, the party has initiated court action against several networks. Such resort to litigation highlights the difficulties of defining and enforcing equity in political broadcasting.

The CRTC in its Public Notice 1987-209 claims that "throughout the history of broadcasting in Canada, licensees, as part of their services to the public, have been required to cover elections and allocate election campaign time 'equitably' to all political parties and rival candidates." CRTC Circular No. 334, 1987 notes that the thrust of section 8 of the Television Regulation 1987 is "that time shall be allocated to rival candidates and parties on an equitable basis." The CRTC expects that some parties and candidates will receive more coverage than others, in that "equitable" does not mean "equal." However, minor parties should reasonably be expected to receive some coverage. In Circular No. 334, the Commission writes, "But generally, all candidates and parties are entitled to some coverage which will give them the opportunity to expose their ideas to the public."

"Equitable," as a notion, however, has potentially different interpretations. Some minor parties claim that "equitable" means "equal" and that in the implementation of these principles they should be afforded equal time in the allocation of free time on the broadcast media. The broadcasters, however, are generally happy with the CRTC's directive in its Circular No. 334 that states, "The determination of what is equitable coverage is left, in the first instance, to the licensee." The CBC, in its response to CRTC Public Notice 1987-209, argues: "Rules must be loose enough to ensure balance without inhibiting the free flow of information and the application of journalistic principles," principles which are outlined in the CBC's manual on journalistic policy.

In Canada, the *Canada Elections Act* permits the parties to nominate by consensus a broadcasting arbitrator, who is appointed by the chief electoral officer. The arbitrator is required to establish the allocation of paid political broadcasting time for use in the next federal election by consultation with the registered parties. If the parties cannot reach a satisfactory agreement, the arbitrator is empowered to make binding allocations. Since 1985, the broadcasting arbitrator has held meetings at which various registered parties have been represented from time to time for the purpose of consultation as envisaged by, in particular, sections 308 and 314 of the Act. During the course of these meetings, the broadcasters and the major and minor parties have never unanimously agreed on the allocation of broadcast time. Since 1981, the courts have been asked to force broadcasters to open the airwaves further to minor parties during election campaigns. In almost every instance, the result has been either a refusal to proceed with the case or a verdict in favour of the broadcasters.

Britain has likewise grappled with the problem of fairness in political broadcasting. The right of access for minor parties has been accepted in principle, although arguably, the actual practices have been rather restrictive. Since the inception of broadcasting in Britain, this issue, particularly the allocation of air time to parties, has been examined by a series of committees that the government has periodically established to review broadcasting policy.

British campaign broadcasting pivots on negotiated arrangements between the major parties and the broadcasters. Legal challenges to these arrangements have not been successful. The first such challenge was *Grieve v. Douglas-Home* (1965), in which a Communist Party candidate claimed that the party political broadcasts violated section 63 of the *Representation of the People Act 1949*. Grieve argued "that the BBC and ITA had incurred expenses in presenting the candidate to the electors without the consent of the candidate or his agent, and without making any return of these expenses as required by s. 63(2)" (Ewing 1987, 88).

The challenge failed, and in 1969, Parliament foreclosed the possibility of any similar challenges in the future. Of lasting importance, according to Ewing, were remarks made by Lord Kilbrandon, which seemed to prevent any further challenge on another ground based on BBC's Royal Charter, "by which the Corporation is under a duty to provide broadcasting services as a means of dissemination of information, education and entertainment." But BBC's Charter seems to leave little scope for such a challenge. With regard to the allocation of time, Lord Kilbrandon commented: "The machinery of consultation and of apportionment of time seems to me to be conclusive of good faith. For the rest, their discretion must, I think, on the evidence inevitably involve the exclusion from the air of some of the participants in a general election and may involve the exclusion of minor parties" (Ewing 1987, 114).

In contrast with the BBC, political programming by British commercial broadcasters is governed directly by statute rather than by a corporate charter. "The Independent Broadcasting Authority [IBA] Act 1981 requires broadcasters to preserve due impartiality as respects matters of political or industrial controversy or relating to current public policy. It also requires the IBA to ensure that programmes maintain a general high standard, and a proper balance and a wide range in their subject-matter" (Ewing 1987, 114). However, it appears that in the cases of both the BBC and the IBA, the "voluntary arrangements" between parties and broadcasters are effectively beyond legal remedy in the event of a dispute. Indeed, neither the BBC nor the IBA is required by statute to permit the political parties to have access to their facilities. Nor are the procedures whereby time is allocated to the different parties governed by statute. In practice, though, both broadcasting organizations do make time available to political parties. Such time is provided free of charge, with the broadcaster bearing the cost.

As with Lord Kilbrandon's statements on minor-party access to the BBC, Lord Ross precluded the possibility of successful challenges to independent broadcasters' political programming on the grounds of balance: "I accept that when arranging party political broadcasts in connection with a general election, all possible political viewpoints cannot be covered, and, for example, some participants in a general election and some minor parties may be excluded" (Ewing 1987, 115). Thus, the Scottish courts endorsed the arrangements for political broadcasts outlined in the 1981 Act and in particular "the exclusion of small parties from the process."

In Britain, the principles of equity are vague and imprecise. They offer ample scope for interpretation but little concrete guidance. In practice there is little concern for the equity principle or for encouraging innovation in the representational system. Jane Jenson (1991) notes in her study for this Commission: "The assumption which underpins the arrangements for public support of the parties in the UK is that the state has little responsibility for fostering a healthy climate of democratic pluralism."

The British experience raises again the question of what constitutes equitable treatment. In the simplest two-party system, equality of treatment between government and opposition will generally be an appropriate test. However, in more complex cases, involving a greater number of parties, the broadcasters have not always thought equality of treatment appropriate. As Boyle (1986, 573) points out:

> Thus in party political and election broadcasts, although the Conservative and Labour parties have generally had equal coverage, the share of the smaller political parties has depended instead on their proportion of votes or seats, and none of the parties receives anything like equal treatment in news and current affairs programmes, where a quite different basis of treatment seems to apply. When two small Northern Ireland parties complained in court that the BBC had not given them equal time with the larger parties in election broadcasts, the court upheld the BBC's practice and agreed that the BBC had a discretion in achieving balance and impartiality which did not require it to give equal treatment to all parties regardless of electoral support or the number of candidates.

In Sweden, which has a long-standing multi-party system, there is no specific government law or regulation that requires the Swedish Broadcasting Corporation to maintain absolute balance regarding the five parties, but there is a general mandate to be fair. As Mickelson (1972, 139) points out: "No effort is made to count minutes and seconds of coverage for one party or the other, but an endeavour is made and enforced by executives to maintain at least a rough balance. There is no system of enforcing such a balance, but the management assumes that the parties tape and record all broadcasts during the campaign ... By so doing they are able to keep accurate records and grounds for protest, should protests be in order."

More than any other country surveyed here, Denmark goes furthest toward interpreting equitable access as equal access. This interpretation has been upheld by the courts and put into practice through public subsidies and free broadcast time. For those who argue that "equitable" means "equal," Denmark could serve as an exemplar. Siune (1987, 412) argues that: "The Danish case of equal time for all parties, independent of whether they are new or old, what proportion of seats they hold in parliament, or what proportion of the vote they won at previous elections, emphasizes the equality dimension underlying the rule of equal access. Other systems based on access more favorable for those already represented in parliament emphasize the stability of the established system, making it more difficult for new parties to reach the electorate. Compared to the rest of Europe, the Scandinavian principle of 'equal access' shows respect for representative democracy as an ideal political system." Such a system makes particularly acute the question of what political entities deserve equal time in the media. How are political parties to be defined? What sort of subsidies do they receive? Policies on these matters directly influence the ability of minor parties to acquire the legitimacy and resources needed to communicate with voters through the mass media.

Public Subsidies and the Definition of Political Parties

To qualify for funding subsidies, as contained in the *Canada Elections Act* and various provincial statutes, as well as access to free and paid time in the broadcast media, a political entity must be registered. In a "free and democratic" society, the question becomes how to facilitate a group with a legitimate political agenda to become a registered political party and, at the same time, prevent the electoral system from being overwhelmed by a crescendo of competing voices from "beyond the fringe." To what extent do qualifications for public subsidies promote fairness and innovation in the political system? To what extent do they act as exclusionary barriers to new and small parties?

Central to any enforcement machinery is the definition of political parties. These are bodies that would be obliged to disclose or limit their expenditures, and that would have a right to public funds or air time. And it is on the basis of registration that free and paid broadcast time is allocated. It is thus crucial to discern whether this threshold for access to subsidies is flexible enough to allow "equitable, variable and comprehensive" political broadcasting and to make it possible for all political parties to participate in the political process. Does the threshold favour incumbents and major parties, or does it encourage the emergence of minor parties?

In Canada, registered political parties must meet applicable qualifications as outlined in the *Canada Elections Act*, and in various provincial statutes. The Act requires that a political party be registered to aid the enforcement and administration of the Act, as well as to benefit potentially from its financial provisions. There is a close relationship between registration and the regulation of party finances: "The Election Expenses Act 1974, which introduced a comprehensive framework of law for party funding generally, requires each party to register with the Chief Electoral Officer and each registered party to appoint an agent. Party agents are in turn required to transmit annually to the Chief Electoral Officer an audited statement of receipts and expenses" (Ewing 1987, 179).

Care must be taken to ensure that the registration process and criteria do not unduly limit the right to compete in elections. Ewing (1987, 190–91) warns that registration could become a device to control or to exclude minority parties or groups of people holding unpopular views. He writes: "Whatever its effect in practice, registration is arguably wrong in principle because although it may begin in a benign fashion, it could easily become malignant, with the state imposing conditions on registration and thereby on the right to compete at elections." Ewing regards the provincial registration threshold in Ontario, and possibly in Quebec, as too high. However, he concedes that registration at the federal level, based on the requirement that a party nominate 50 candidates in a general election, appears to work well, without any untoward effect on the democratic process. It is worth noting, however, that this requirement means that a new party cannot register, and hence become eligible to receive tax-deductible donations and subsidies, until it contests a general election.

Indeed, Canadian law regarding not only registration, but also public subsidies of political parties, concentrates on the formal campaign period. Paltiel (1989, 73) argues that "pre-writ spending goes largely unnoticed and uncontrolled, and the advantages of incumbency are barely compensated; essential elements of the electoral process are thus neglected." In Canada, the election expense legislation favours the major and established parties and inhibits the introduction of new parties or the expansion of small ones. "Whereas Ontario and Alberta provide for a method of registration during the inter-election period through a public petition signed by several thousand electors, federal law appears to opt for less rather than greater public participation, except through the established parties" (ibid., 57–58).

In addition to the registration threshold, there is some debate over whether the financial subsidies potentially available to registered parties are equitable. Some critics, ranging from the Green Party's Greg Vezina to Ontario provincial Progressive Conservative leader Mike Harris, argue that the system of tax credits for individual donations to political parties discourages participation by lower-income social groups who receive no tax benefits from their donations. Others, however, argue that tax credits work better than public subsidies in linking parties with individual citizens (Nassmacher 1989, 262).

More germane to the concerns of this study, however, is the impact of the tax credit and subsidy system on minor parties. Paltiel (1989, 71) concludes that, in sum, "the system of tax credits and ex post reimbursements tends to favour incumbents and the registered parliamentary parties and their candidates. The thresholds for eligibility are so high as to make it difficult for candidates of new formations to cross the qualifying barrier."

Minor-party candidates must win at least 15 percent of the vote in their riding to qualify for a 50 percent reimbursement of their election expenses. This threshold is quite high compared with some other countries studied. In many cases, it means that local campaigns are actually more expensive for minor parties than for established ones. Smaller parties must spend at least 10 percent of the maximum they are allowed to spend as a party to qualify for the 22.5 percent federal subsidy for party expenses, although there is no minimum vote required. As Paltiel (1989, 71) points out, "The reimbursement to registered parties also favors the registered parties with large budgets since it is payable only to those parties which have spent at least 10 percent of the permitted limits."

The Canadian system of subsidies thus arguably discriminates against minor parties that lack the financial resources to mount a campaign of the scale necessary to benefit from the reimbursement provisions of the legislation. However, "the tax credit systems for political donations adopted in most parts of Canada do appear to give substantial assistance to those parties and candidates prepared to organize efficacious fund-raising efforts at the grass roots [level]" (Paltiel 1989, 71–72).

In the United States, grassroots activity has a long history as part of election campaigns. But reforms of election finance in the 1970s that imposed spending limits on candidates, coupled with the high cost of television advertising, have led to an emphasis on centralized campaign strategies and tactics at the expense of decentralized, local campaigning. Alexander (1989a, 117) argues: "The relatively low expenditure limits [contained in the *Federal Elections Campaign Act of 1971*] have encouraged candidates to favour mass media advertising, which is more cost-effective and less time-consuming than grass-roots campaigning but may not be as informative."

It is clear that public subsidies provide considerable support for party activity in most countries studied. However, the purpose and recipients of party subsidies vary among political systems. One difference is of particular relevance to new and minor parties in a regionalized federal polity such as Canada. Some systems (such as that in Italy) subsidize national party organizations only; others, most notably Sweden, subsidize all levels of party organization, local as well as national. Nassmacher (1989, 262) criticizes the national-level subsidies as fostering centralization of power and bureaucratization of parties rather than local grassroots activity, and this is certainly no small concern. However, it can be argued that for new and minor parties in Canada, an equally pressing problem is the shortage of resources at national headquarters; such parties need paid staff, specialized expertise, access to metropolitan and national media, and the ability to mount leader tours if they are to become perceived as electoral contenders.

One matter of potential concern to some minor parties is the legal definition of a political party. Some of the Canadian federal and provincial election statutes define parties by their purpose of nominating and supporting candidates for election to Parliament. But there is a concern in some quarters that this definition is not comprehensive enough. For example, in Britain there are political parties (such as socialist parties to the left of Labour) that do not nominate parliamentary candidates or might strongly argue that although they do field candidates, that is not their "prime purpose" (Ewing 1987, 189). Indeed, one of the Green Party candidates interviewed for this study made a similar point about his party.

In every country studied, small and new parties must meet certain legal and regulatory qualifications to obtain recognition as a political party and access to public funding and free broadcast time. The threshold of access varies among countries, and it does seem to influence the electoral viability of new and minor parties and the system's degree of receptivity to them. (Low thresholds and systemic tolerance, of course, do not guarantee electoral success for minor parties. Thus, in the view of Siune (1987, 400): "Danes are receptive to the formation of new parties, yet most new parties receive relatively few votes on election day. Danes seem not to have committed themselves to vote for the parties they find serious enough to recommend for a place on the ballot.")

Scandinavian countries have relatively low thresholds, a factor that helps to sustain multi-party systems. In Denmark, for instance, a party can become accepted by the Ministry of Internal Affairs as "participating in the election" if it collects signatures amounting to 1/175 of the valid votes cast in the previous election (Siune 1987, 400). In Sweden, it is likewise accepted that an exclusive focus on parliamentary representation as a measure of party support would be too narrow. Therefore there are subsidies for parties that gain the support of 2.5 percent of the electorate. Even lower thresholds apply in some other European countries – 2 percent in Italy, 1 percent in Austria, and 0.5 percent in Germany (Nassmacher 1989, 248).

West Germany was the first European country to adopt a system of direct state subsidies to political parties. Actually, the German system of public financing was originally instituted to make opportunity less equal – to discourage fringe parties and inhibit the kind of political environment that allowed the Nazis to come to power (Alexander 1989c, 17). However, the original threshold of 2.5 percent was lowered to 0.5 percent at the insistence of the Federal Constitutional Court in 1968, which found the former threshold excessive.

Nevertheless, the greatest beneficiaries of public subsidies in West Germany, as in other countries, have been the major parties. The Social Democrats and Christian Democrats have benefited from the financial provisions of the election finance legislation. But public subsidies have also been essential for the Free Democrats and the Greens, the two smaller parties that have enjoyed parliamentary representation in recent years. Indeed, Nassmacher (1989, 248) regards the Greens as an example of "party building by public subsidies." Such support for smaller parties through public subsidies has apparent advantages for the flexibility of the party system. Jenson (1991) argues that the German party system adapted relatively smoothly and quickly to the emergence of new issues like feminism, ecology, and the new styles of politics – due in part to "the monetary support mandated by the larger parties to their competitors – under pressure from the Court to be sure."

In Sweden, state subsidies have been paid since 1966 to every political party with any significant support from the voters, as manifested in the general elections. Subsidies take two forms, "party subsidies" (general support for the party's activities) and "secretariat subsidies" (specifically for each party's parliamentary support staff). A party is eligible for a general subsidy if it has gained at least one seat in Parliament or 2.5 percent of the votes throughout the whole country in either of the last two elections. To qualify for secretariat subsidies, a party is required either to have won a seat in Parliament in the last election or to have received at least 4 percent of the votes in the whole country at either of the last two elections. Siune argues that the threshold value of 4 percent in Sweden militates against the representation of new parties in Parliament, compared with Denmark's threshold of just 2 percent. In greater contrast, "Finland and Norway have no such threshold values. The difference in the success of new parties must also be highly related to their access to broadcasting" (Siune 1987, 397).

In Norway, the government monopoly of broadcasting renders especially important the requirement of fairness and balance in the treatment of political parties, especially during election campaign periods. However, according to Siune (1987, 401), to receive such "equal treatment," a party must meet three criteria: "It must have been represented in the Norwegian Stortinget in one of the last two election periods, have run candidates in a majority of the districts, and have a current national organization. One exception is that a minor party which is part of a coalition forming the government or a clear alternative to the government can participate with more than one representative in the final broadcast debate. But taking all this into consideration, the principle is that equal time is given to all the parties to allow them to participate in the broadcast debate."

Free Broadcast Time and the Partisan Press

The U.S. system of campaign funding and communication places a great deal of emphasis on television exposure, especially paid advertising. The mandated allocation of free broadcast time does not appear to be typical of the U.S. electoral process, and indeed the very idea seems to be controversial.

The Watergate scandal brought about reform of the laws regulating election campaign finances in the 1970s. Public funding, contribution limits, expenditure limits and disclosure requirements were intended to minimize opportunities for undue financial influence on office-holders and to make the election process more open and competitive. "Public matching funds have had the effect of helping to establish candidates, such as Jimmy Carter, George Bush, Gary Hart, John Anderson and Jesse Jackson, who lacked early access to traditional sources of contributions" (Alexander 1989b, 4).

But the laws also altered traditional campaign strategies and tactics. Alexander (1989a, 99) reports that advertising costs increased by 56 percent between 1980 and 1984, a rate far exceeding inflation. Candidates must rely on television to reach large numbers of voters, and they devote a substantial portion of funds to television advertising. As Alexander (ibid.) points out, "The Hart campaign, for example, spent more than $5.6 million on television time and production costs."

Other strategies involve attempting to gain media attention at no direct cost to their campaigns. Again, Alexander points out: "Jesse Jackson, whose campaign raised less than one-fourth the amount raised by the Mondale campaign, was particularly successful in attracting coverage by television and radio networks and stations. Said Jackson: 'If you make the news at 6, you don't have to buy commercials at 7:01'" (Alexander 1989a, 100). However, we have seen that during the 1988 Canadian federal campaign, news coverage in the major media did not provide a publicity alternative to paid advertising for most minor parties in Canada.

It was hoped at the time of its passage that the spending limitations in the United States imposed by the *Federal Election Campaign Act*

of 1971 and interpreted by Federal Communications Commission guidelines would result in a sizable reduction of money spent by candidates
on broadcasting and other media. Since 1971, however, interpretations
by the U.S. Supreme Court have held that independent individual and corporate campaign expenditures (all of which gravitate toward broadcast
advertising) could not be restrained. The Court has upheld public disclosure and funding of presidential campaigns, but it has overruled limitations on candidate expenditures and ceilings on independent spending
by individuals and groups. The Supreme Court ruled in *Buckley v. Valeo*
that expenditure limits can be applied only as a condition of acceptance
of public funding by a candidate and political party. As Alexander
(1989c, 19) points out, "In all other circumstances the Court found spending limits to be unconstitutional, and this also applies to amounts candidates can spend of their personal funds in their own campaigns." Thus,
the Court has permitted evasions of the spending and contribution limits that reformers imposed on campaign election financing.

Combined with the relative lack of restrictions on funding in the
United States, the substantial cost of network television advertising places
minor parties and independent candidates at a substantial disadvantage
compared with incumbents, the major parties, and candidates with
wealthy supporters. As Goldenberg and Traugott (1987a, 454) argue in
their comparative study of the United States, Britain, West Germany and
Scandinavia, "The greater the free market approach to purchasing and
placement of political advertisements, the greater imbalance of media
attention to opposing candidates."

Canadians often quite understandably use the U.S. political system
as a benchmark for comparison with their own. But it should be noted
that the U.S. system, in which electoral success virtually necessitates
spending large amounts of money on television advertising, is relatively distinct in the Western world. Some liberal democracies have followed a policy of simply not permitting paid broadcast advertising.
Boyer (1983, 443) argues that the difficulty of acquiring access to political broadcasting without substantial financial resources confirms U.S.
politics as "a rich man's game." He writes: "The American practice is
unusual, since other countries, such as Britain, Germany, Italy, Sweden
and Japan, have two principal threads running through their laws
respecting political broadcasting in elections. First, time for candidate
presentations is provided to the candidate without charge; the burden
is assumed either by the network in question or by the government
through subsidy. Second, program production is a responsibility of the
candidates or parties and, except for special debates or discussion features, not of the distributing network."

The Canadian practice of free-time political broadcasting is paralleled most closely perhaps by that of Britain. In discussing the principles by which air time is allocated to the parties, it is necessary to distinguish between party political broadcasts and party election broadcasts. Discussions between the BBC and the main political parties in 1947 led to the creation of a party political broadcasting committee and established the main principles governing this form of broadcast: they would be allocated on a yearly basis after discussion between the parties and the BBC, and the opposition could choose the subjects for its own broadcasts.

Currently, party political broadcasts comprise a series of radio and television broadcasts made every year. As Mickelson (1972, 134) points out, this is different from the U.S. system "which provides no formal opportunity for this sort of political outlet during the off-campaign period." The total amount of time is agreed on by the Committee on Party Political Broadcasting made up of representatives from the major parties (Alliance, Conservative and Labour parties, together with representatives of the BBC and the IBA). Neither the BBC nor the IBA is obliged to carry party political broadcasts, but they have in practice always done so, and the Annan Committee's 1977 report on the future of broadcasting endorsed this approach. Although, as noted below, much depends on negotiations between the broadcasters and parties, the Annan Committee did identify one allocation formula: "In the first two years after a general election, a party qualifies for one ten-minute broadcast for every 2 million votes polled in its favour. Any party with a remainder of votes exceeding 1 million is entitled to an extra ten-minute broadcast. After the first two years from the date of the election, the arrangements are varied, with the allocation being based partly on the votes cast at the general election and partly on the votes cast at any intervening by-elections" (Ewing 1987, 110).

Not surprisingly, these measures do not satisfy those minor parties that remain excluded. For example: "In representations to the most recent Committee on Broadcasting the Socialist Party of Great Britain argued that it should be permitted to make party political broadcasts, and the Communist Party of Great Britain contended that all national parties should be members of the Committee on Party Political Broadcasting. But these claims fell on deaf ears. For unlike earlier Committees on Broadcasting, Annan gave no serious consideration in its report to the problem of minority representation" (Ewing 1987, 112–13).

The Annan Committee's main criticism of party political broadcasts in 1977, besides the perception that they constituted very dull television, was that the rules governing the allocation of broadcasting time were little known or understood. As Boyle points out, little has changed since the Annan Committee's report. Although certain broad principles can be discerned, these allocations of broadcasting time seem not to be the product of any exact formula, but owe a great deal to the bargaining in the Party Political Broadcasting Committee. Boyle claims there is evidence that the influence of the BBC and IBA, acting as impartial brokers, helped secure broadcast time for the Scottish and Welsh nationalist parties and for the Social Democratic Party. However, he cautions that: "Even this does no more than ensure the fairer operation of the parliamentary model on which impartiality and balance in political broadcasting have been fashioned. It makes no allowance for parties which have no electoral following of significance or political groups with no wish to seek election. Such groups fall wholly outside the present system" (Boyle 1986, 578).

Party election broadcasts are arranged when an election is called. The party political broadcasts are suspended, and the committee meets to arrange the allocation of time. As Ewing (1987, 110–11) points out, these broadcasts "are not confined to the established parties, in the sense that all parties qualify for broadcasting time if they have 50 or more candidates in the field on nomination day." Thus, minor parties have been allowed a national election broadcast, even if they have no parliamentary representation, so long as they can field 50 candidates. Such allocation on the basis of candidates has allowed, at various elections, the Communist Party, the National Front, the Workers' Revolutionary Party and the Ecology Party to be given one broadcast of half the normal duration: "This usually represents 1/10 of the maximum allocation of time for contesting about 1/12 of the seats, regardless of the level of previous electoral support" (Boyle 1986, 579).

For the broadcasters, the British system of allocating partisan air time has the advantage of reducing their vulnerability to criticism and controversy, since established parties are involved in the decision-making process. As Boyle (1986, 578) points out, "This is satisfactory so long as the existing parties agree among themselves and are responsive to new political forces, but if they are not, then the final responsibility for a fair allocation of broadcasting continues to rest with the BBC and IBA."

Public broadcasting corporations in Austria, Sweden, West Germany and Italy also provide free radio and television time for campaigns. In West Germany, the provision of free radio and television time is based on performance in past elections but also recognizes the need to allocate time to new or previously unsuccessful parties (Jenson 1991). During election periods, the parties receive "a modest amount of free advertising as a public service (there is no paid political advertising)" (Dalton 1989, 149). Parties supply the advertisements themselves; broadcasting stations are not allowed to assist parties in their production. In addition, election broadcasting includes extensive air time for interviews with party representatives and debates among party leaders.

In Austria, interestingly, not only parties but also important interest groups are allocated free radio time even during off-campaign periods (Nassmacher 1989, 240).

As already noted, Scandinavian political systems are characterized by a multi-party structure. Siune (1987, 411) maintains that the heavy use of broadcasting in Scandinavian countries, coupled with the principle of equal access and equal time has made it easier than in most European countries to establish and keep new and small parties alive. The guiding principle of Danish broadcasting in particular has been equal access for all parties participating in an election. Thus, "new parties in Denmark have a greater chance to set the agenda for a national or local election, since they get news coverage on top of access to programs structured around the principle of equal access" (ibid., 411–12).

During the 1980s, Scandinavian countries experimented with local radio and television, and political parties make use of these media. Scandinavian local broadcasting has apparently not been without controversy, both because of its financial arrangements (which combine public and private funds) and its appropriate role in politics. Local stations provide an additional outlet for political broadcasts, including those from minor parties, but they are not uniformly and equally available to all parties. This is for reasons both of political affiliation and cost:

> In Sweden approximately 15% of the local radio stations ... are politically attached. In Denmark none of the local radio stations is directly linked to a party, but some stations – radio as well as television – are in the hands of the labour organizations with a very clear attachment to the Social Democratic party. The bourgeois parties are only indirectly attached to the experiments with local radio and television, but have contact indirectly via the bourgeois press ... In Denmark, Norway, and Sweden, one can usually gain access to some of the local stations if one pays. Some political parties have been able to do so, and many more have been interested but were economically disadvantaged. In most of the Danish cases, access was free, with only a very few stations asking for payment. (Siune 1987, 402)

High thresholds for access to public subsidies or free broadcasting time are not the only potential barrier facing minor parties in their efforts to communicate with voters. There may also be real or perceived pro-government bias in the news coverage of state-owned media, as well as ideological criteria for participation in the political process. Dalton (1989, 149) maintains that examples of outright government influence are rare in West German public broadcasting; effort is made to ensure autonomy for broadcasters. However, the potential for abuse still exists. Although representatives of "legitimate" non-governmental groups – such as legal political parties – have free access to the public media, views considered "subversive" by controlling authorities may not be aired.

A more important factor influencing the ability of political parties to reach voters is the nature of the press system. In contrast with the press in the United States and Canada, many newspapers in West Germany and Scandinavia are explicitly partisan. Most newspapers in Denmark, for example, belong either to the Agrarian Liberals or to the Conservatives. The partisan press is still active in Norway and Sweden as well. Even as newspapers become less explicit about partisan attachments and declare themselves independent of partisan control, the coverage of political parties in the Scandinavian press continues to lack balance and to reflect previous party affiliations: "In principle, [newspapers] are open to communication from all political parties; in reality, the coverage of political parties in news stories, articles, and columns within a given newspaper is still somewhat unbalanced in favour of its former party affiliation. New parties as well as small old parties often lack press coverage, especially in Denmark; but journalistic norms and especially an emphasis on selling newspapers counterbalance this tendency" (Siune 1987, 400).

Still, given its many active political parties, Denmark today has a very unbalanced press structure (Siune 1987, 400).

In Britain, the press today is more strongly partisan, and more uniformly supportive of the Conservatives, than in the past. And in West Germany, where few political parties own newspapers or magazines, the press nonetheless has easily identifiable partisan leanings. The vast majority of West German newspapers are conservative, particularly with regard to economic issues, and openly reflect their partisan nature. "Many of them lean more or less openly toward a specific political party or at least a political ideology (such as free enterprise or the social responsibility of the state)" (Schoenbach 1987, 377).

Other Kinds of Subsidies

In addition to the allocation of free broadcast time, other kinds of subsidies influence the relative capacity of competing parties to communicate with voters. These include press subsidies in some European countries, as well as direct subsidies to the parties themselves.

The Scandinavian principle of politically affiliated newspapers traditionally gave the existing parties rather good coverage of their activities. In Norway and Sweden, the partisan press has been kept alive primarily by government economic support introduced in the 1960s. This support was specifically intended to maintain the political variety of papers, under the assumption that a balanced press structure is needed to keep democracy working (Siune 1987, 399). At the same time, however, it could be argued that such subsidies militate against new parties (as well as old parties without supportive newspapers) and thus constitute an element of "petrification" in the party system.

In Denmark, the number of newspapers had already declined too far by the time the issue of state support was introduced. As Siune (1987, 399–400) maintains, "The arguments for economic support presented by the Social Democrats, whose press had almost died out, failed to persuade other Danish parties of the benefits that Norway and Sweden had realized from press support; many of the bourgeois parties already had a rather well-established and functioning press."

After some debate and delay, press subsidies were introduced in Sweden in the 1960s. The rationale for this kind of aid was as follows: "The daily press contributes towards efforts at strengthening and deepening Swedish democracy by supplying information and comment on social affairs, scrutinizing the activities of influential [sic] and facilitating communications within and between political, trade union and other voluntary groups. It is in order to safeguard this participation and strengthen the diversity of the daily press that the State subsi[dizes] undertakings publishing daily newspapers" (K.E. Gustafsson, cited in Ewing 1987, 159).

The effect of press subsidies has been to arrest the decline of the socialist newspapers, rather than to increase their strength. The bulk of the press supports the more conservative parties; only about one-fifth of papers support the Social Democrats.

As for parties themselves, all parties in Sweden now receive a substantial proportion of their income from the state. Cash subsidies are paid at both the national and local level. Such subsidies do not eliminate financial inequality between the competing parties (especially in the absence of spending limits), and some of the smaller parties perceive the wide variation in the annual budgets of the different parties as contributing to lack of equality of opportunity in the political arena (Ewing 1987, 166). However, state subsidies "have been widely perceived in Sweden as having been an outstanding success." As Ewing (ibid., 165) points out: "The Swedes have managed to avoid the problems which in Britain it is claimed would arise from state funding.

There is no evidence of any state interference in the activities of the parties; there is no evidence that subsidies have led to falling membership; and funding at [the] local level has ensured that the central parties are not reinforced at the expense of the local organisations."

Televised Leaders Debates

Televised debates among the leaders of political parties constitute another potential means for parties to communicate with voters during election campaigns.

There is no evidence of legislative requirements in other countries that require broadcasters to air leaders debates. Rather, debates seem to be encouraged informally, with their organization typically being left to the broadcasters and the political parties.

Mickelson (1972, 265), canvassing arrangements for leaders debates in various countries, expressed appreciation for the model widespread in western Europe and Japan: "programs in which representatives of all parties appear simultaneously on a single stage to discuss issues and answer questions or simply state points of view." In each of these cases the format roughly follows that employed by the 1960 Kennedy–Nixon debates, rather than a formal debate routine. Japan appears to have made special efforts to accommodate the smaller parties with parliamentary representation: "In the December 1969 election the Japanese Broadcasting Corporation, NHK, scheduled six separate fifty-minute confrontation programs on six consecutive days leading up to the election. The parties were paired off in six separate combinations. The two parties which had gained the most votes in the previous election, the Liberal Democrats and the Socialist Party, each were assigned three appearances; and the other three, the Democratic Socialists, Komeito, and the Communist Party, were each given two" (ibid., 210).

Debates involving all parties are regular features of Swedish political campaigns. As Mickelson (1972, 209) points out: "The procedure there is to conduct three debates during the campaign. There are six contestants in each one each representing the leadership of the five parties and a second representing the party in power. The reason for this concession to the party in power is that it is felt that the four opposition leaders will be attacking the government, and the government, thus, deserves a bit of extra time to protect itself."

Finland and Italy also have multi-party and proportional representation systems. There, too, leaders debates are regular features on television. To be sure, the attempt to accommodate a large number of parties can lead to rather cumbersome formats, as the Finnish experience suggests: "The procedure adopted by the Finnish Broadcasting Company is to permit each of the seven parties to assign two of its personnel – so the Finnish confrontation includes a total of fourteen persons. In the 1966 Finnish election both the Prime Minister and the Minister of Foreign Affairs participated for the party in power, and four party chairmen represented minority parties. The program took up a good part of the evening, running from 7:40 PM until 11:55, with an hour and twenty minutes intermission between 9:15 and 10:35" (Mickelson 1972, 209).

Debates in Italy are also complicated, but the Italians have been able to handle a situation that at first sight seems to pose an untenable problem for broadcasters: "In Italy eight parties qualify to participate in inter-party discussions. The Italians solved the problem by scheduling two debates of four parties each. By carefully drawing a line down through a theoretical political centre, it is possible to balance each program: two parties from left of the centre and two from the right" (Mickelson 1972, 209–10).

Although these specific arrangements may not be applicable in Canada, they do demonstrate that other liberal democracies are committed to providing significant access to the public forum for more than the two or three dominant parties.

MANDATED ACCESS: SUGGESTIONS FOR A POLICY APPROACH TO CAMPAIGN COMMUNICATION

Having reviewed patterns of news coverage of minor parties, minor party and media interaction as perceived by the participants, and policy arrangements in other liberal democracies, this study concludes with a consideration of some policy options. It does not attempt to offer detailed recommendations; rather, it suggests some policy approaches emerging from the research.

Minor Parties and Campaign Communication: The Need for Fair and Balanced Reform

The following discussion takes as a starting point the need to find a delicate balance in electoral reform. On the one hand, the electoral and campaign communication systems need to be perceived as fair and legitimate. Equitable treatment of the contenders, including minor parties, is an important component of perceived legitimacy. Moreover, minor parties can help maintain the flexibility and capacity for innovation in the political system: they can represent interests excluded from the major parties' coalition-building strategies, introduce issues and policy proposals that major parties are unwilling to address, and perhaps help to stimulate voter interest in elections and satisfaction with the political system. It can further be argued that the media, as vital institutions of political communication, should offer voters information about the full range of available political choices, including new and minor parties.

On the other hand, major parties have democratic legitimacy derived from their demonstrable capacity to attract voter support. A proliferation of small parties combined with a lowered threshold for parliamentary representation could reduce the prospects for majority government and workable national coalitions, and accord "extremist" positions greater and possibly disproportionate influence. If the media paid excessive attention to parties that have little chance of electing candidates, let alone forming a government, their limited resources for covering campaigns and analysing political issues would be further stretched, and voters could experience "information overload," reducing their ability to weigh the relative merits of those parties with a reasonable chance of forming the government.

Although this latter set of considerations must be granted due weight, the assumption might sensibly be made that registered political parties deserve a reasonable opportunity during an election campaign to state their case to the electorate as a whole through the mass media, which are a primary source of political information for most voters. Conversely, the assumption might also be made that the mass media should subject those parties and their policies and leadership to at least some measure of critical scrutiny. No doubt, parties themselves can influence the extent to which they are seen as credible by the media and the electorate. No doubt also, most minor parties would remain unattractive to voters no matter how much publicity they received. But surely registered parties ought to be afforded sufficient and equitable access, and to be treated with some degree of seriousness as electoral options.

To what extent do the news media make available to voters adequate information about the full range of political options? Of course, empirical research alone cannot answer this question, since any answer depends on normative assumptions about what constitutes adequate information and which political options are legitimate and credible. But the content analysis and interviews for this study suggest that there is at least some cause for concern about news coverage of registered minor parties.

To be sure, minor parties are not entirely excluded from the media, particularly the locally oriented community press. Even the large metropolitan and national media accord small parties coverage insofar as they are perceived to be newsworthy and credible. There is not much evidence of a partisan-motivated, systematic policy of exclusion. And minor-party respondents themselves express general satisfaction with the quantity and fairness of news coverage in community media.

On the other hand, some of the minor parties expressed frustration, sometimes bitterly, with their perceived lack of access to the metropolitan and national media. The content analysis indicates not only the relative infrequency of minor-party coverage in major media, but also suggests that on several qualitative dimensions, minor parties are not treated as serious political actors. As for the community press and television, the interviews show that these media lack the perceived mandate and the resources for in-depth and sustained coverage of federal election campaigns, and the content analysis indicates that community papers may fall short on quality-relevant dimensions. The very satisfaction that minor parties express with the community press may indicate its lack of substantive and critical coverage. In any event, it is a few national media organizations, not the community media, that set the agenda of political news in Canada (Taras 1990, 86–91), and, arguably, that shape voters' perceptions of parties. For their part, few minor parties can bypass the news media's gatekeepers by mounting extensive advertising campaigns; they lack the funds and expertise.

Such considerations suggest a positive role for the state in promoting fair electoral communication.

Media as Businesses and Political Institutions

The responsibilities of the state with regard to the role of mass media in campaign communication pose a fundamental philosophical problem. On the one hand, the logic and ideology of the economic market-place, as well as the traditional liberal concept of freedom of the press, reinforced by trends in North American judicial interpretation of freedom of the press, encourage a view of media corporations as private businesses. In this view, decisions about editorial and programming content are the prerogative of media owners and managers. Such decisions are formally constrained by laws (such as those applying to defamation, contempt of court or the revelation of state secrets) intended to protect competing individual rights, as well as the functioning of essential institutions (the integrity of the justice system, and the security of the state against insurrection or invasion). In this view, ownership decisions about media content are also informally constrained by the discipline of the market-place, which ensures the realization of consumer sovereignty: through their reading, viewing and purchasing decisions, media consumers (audiences) influence media content (Seiden 1974, 5). Such is the classic "libertarian" theory of freedom of the press, which has historically been associated with the print media. However, as some of the briefs to this Commission have suggested, broadcasters also sometimes argue that a similar definition of freedom of the press should apply to their own industry.

On the other hand, mass media, press and broadcasting alike, unavoidably perform political functions in contemporary liberal democracies. Indeed, some observers argue that for several reasons, mass media cannot be regarded simply as the private preserve of corporate owners; rather, media ought to accept (or be required to accept) certain social responsibilities, such as projecting "the diverse views and opinions of society's different groups to each other" and providing "a general forum of comment and opinion" (Black 1982, 29). The reasons for mandating social responsibility to the media include their role as a primary source of political information for much of the electorate, their oligopolistic nature, the usually high costs of entry to mass media industries and the imperfections of the media market-place: if the logic of the political market-place is one person, one vote, the logic of the commercial media accords disproportionate power to media owners, advertisers and the affluent consumers whom advertisers most want to reach. It has been argued that, historically, the pressures of commercialization have acted as a kind of informal censorship, militating against the survival of media which, however popular, do not satisfy the imperatives of marketing commodities (Curran 1977).

In the case of broadcasting, there has been a further reason, a technological one, for mandating social responsibility: the scarcity of broadcasting frequencies has led the state in most liberal democracies to adopt public-interest criteria in awarding broadcasting licences. Thus, in Canada, broadcasters have a legal mandate to offer balanced and diverse views on public issues.

By contrast, newspapers are a non-regulated medium, arguably imbued for historical reasons with an even stronger commitment to a definition of freedom of the press as independence from government. Print journalists and executives sometimes accept that newspapers have a public trust or social responsibility, but they are very suspicious of any external efforts to oversee their performance. Yet a strong case can be made that the press as much as broadcasting should be regarded for some purposes as a public resource, not just a private business. If broadcasting has historically been characterized by technological scarcity, newspapers are increasingly characterized by economic scarcity. Newspapers remain vital media of political communication, yet economic pressures have virtually eliminated competition between daily newspapers in most Canadian cities. With respect to competition law, Cody-Rice (1981, 143–44) notes that the newspaper has been characterized, for the purpose of legislation, "as an object of trade or commerce rather than as a component in the communications industry with special interests which must be protected." In her view, this situation is a cause for regret: "To exclude newspapers from policies which govern the rest of the communications industry is anomalous, as their function is akin to that of television or radio. They provide a variety of information on a large number of subjects on a frequent and regular basis. In effect, they broadcast on paper. To isolate this one segment of the communications industry and group it, for the purpose of legal control, with lamps, matches, and other objects of commerce, cannot help but court an unjust, if not dangerous, result."

The policy suggestions with which this study concludes are based on the assumption that freedom of the press ought not to be interpreted as simply a property right of media owners. There is, again, a need to find a balance. On the one hand, media practitioners are quite legitimately concerned to avoid both an unwieldy or costly regulatory regime and restraints on their editorial independence (especially from government). Moreover, judicial interpretations of the constitutional guarantee of freedom of the press must be taken into account. On the other hand, the performance of mass media unavoidably influences the adequacy of voters' information about their choices and the fairness of electoral competition among political parties. There is a particular need to address the communication problems and the lack of media access faced most acutely by new and smaller parties.

Some Suggestions for Electoral Policy

Interviews with journalists and minor-party representatives, as well as the comparative review of policy in other countries, suggest that a completely market-driven approach to campaign communication would result in substantial inequalities in the ability of competing parties to communicate with voters, to the particular detriment of new and smaller parties. The advantages of wealth and incumbency in the U.S. political system are especially instructive. It is appropriate for the state to take some responsibility for ensuring a healthy degree of pluralism in the party system.

As a primary mechanism for increasing the fairness of campaign communication, the state could mandate that each party contesting a federal election should be accorded a minimum level of access to the mass media. The principle of mandated access should apply to major mass media; notwithstanding tendencies toward market fragmentation and channel abundance, a handful of media organizations are likely to remain a dominant source of political information for most voters for some time to come.

As our comparative policy review confirms, free-time political broadcasting is a well-established means of mandating such access. In Canada, the amount of aggregate free time made available to the various political parties for direct messages to voters could be expanded by maintaining the granting of free time on CBC networks, as well as by extending the practice to major private broadcasters (either through CRTC regulation, or as a requirement under the *Canada Elections Act*) and to specialized broadcasting services, such as the parliamentary channel.

Moreover, within the available blocks of free broadcast time, a substantially greater proportion should be allocated to the smaller registered parties. The rationale is that since large and established parties already enjoy overwhelming advantages through incumbency, funding, news coverage, and the permitted allocation of resources to use paid advertising on television, free time ought to be used to offset these advantages at least partially. The Scandinavian countries provide ample precedent for a more egalitarian approach to free-time allocation.

It must be recognized, however, that free-time political broadcasting as currently constituted has important limitations as a solution to minor-party communication with voters. It arguably lacks the status and credibility of news and current-affairs programming, in which minor parties are frequently invisible. Another problem is the small size of its audiences, especially when the broadcasts are outside prime time. The format of many party messages – a monologue delivered by a "talking head" – does not add to their audience appeal. Experimentation with more dialogic and even adversarial formats, such as a debate among several parties simultaneously, or question-and-answer sessions with journalists, might make such broadcasts more appealing and informative. Another problem is that the production costs of "free-time" broadcasts can constitute a real drain on minor parties' resources; perhaps free-time allocations could include subsidies for production costs.

A further problem for minor parties is that free-time broadcasts are concentrated in election campaigns to the relative exclusion of the interelection period. Such timing, compounded by the brevity of most free-time spots, further handicaps most small parties, given the relative lack of voter awareness of their very existence at the start of a campaign. Canada might consider extending the British practice of interelection party political broadcasts, adopting allocation criteria that are not based exclusively on parliamentary representation and support at the previous election. The allocation criteria should allow for air time to minor and new parties that have met the registration requirements.

Although an examination of televised party leaders debates was somewhat beyond the scope of the present study, they might usefully be approached as an aspect of mandated access and free-time broadcasting, rather than as a journalistic undertaking. Such an approach could have advantages for news organizations: by being distanced from decision making on the format of, and participation in, leaders debates, news organizations could both reduce their vulnerability to external criticism and feel freer to cover the debates as political events. In this approach, relevant networks could be required to make available an appropriate time-slot for a leaders debate during a given campaign; the responsibility for actually arranging its format and deciding its participants could be assigned to the broadcasting arbitrator, in consultation with the broadcasters and all registered parties. As for who should be represented in such debates, some other liberal democracies (for example, Italy, Japan, Finland) have found ways to include many parties. It may well be decided in the Canadian case that the full inclusion of leaders of parties with minimal voter support would be too unwieldy, as well as counter-productive to voter assessment of the relative merits of the leaders and parties with potential to form the next government. At the same time, it would be detrimental to the perceived fairness of the electoral process to exclude smaller registered parties altogether from leaders debates. It is to be hoped that a format can be found that achieves the required balance – for example, a series of debates each involving different parties, or, more likely, the opportunity for minor-party leaders to make brief televised statements in response to the major-party leaders debate.

Given the gaps in press coverage of minor parties previously discussed, a case could be made that the principle of mandated access should be extended to the print media, at least in a limited way, and at least to newspapers over a certain size and frequency of publication. To be sure, newspapers are a non-regulated medium, with a status quite different from broadcasting. However, newspapers have historically received benefits from tax expenditures (subsidized postal rates, exemption from the federal sales tax until 1991) and from other federal policies (for example, a provision in the *Income Tax Act* that encourages advertising revenue in Canadian-owned publications) (Canada, Royal Commission 1981, 53–57). Newspapers might reasonably be required to offer an equal amount of free space to all candidates running in their respective coverage areas during a campaign, for example, in the form of an election supplement. Such a requirement would formalize and generalize a practice that some newspapers already follow. They might also be required to ensure that the contending candidates or parties have equal opportunity to purchase advertising during a campaign, a concern raised by at least one media respondent. Such a requirement would be particularly justifiable for general-interest newspapers (especially those with a monopoly in their respective markets) as distinct from special-interest periodicals.

There is, however, no question of attempting to regulate editorial policy or news coverage directly, in either print or broadcasting. That kind of approach would encounter enormous legal obstacles, particularly with respect to the press, as well as practical problems of enforcement in both media. It would create problems worse than those it sought to resolve. However, it would not be inappropriate for journalists and news organizations themselves to recognize the relative lack of coverage of minor parties as an ethical problem to be addressed from within. Such coverage is important to facilitate parties' communication with voters, as well as voters' critical assessment of parties that, however small, could affect the electoral outcome in some ridings and regions of the country. The provision of free time or other forms of mandated access is not a substitute for thorough, balanced and analytical news coverage of domestic politics. There would likely be widespread support for stronger and clearer codes of ethics for media coverage of elections.

Should mandated media access and other kinds of public subsidies be accorded to parties as organizations or to candidates (including those without party affiliation) at the local level? Although a strong case can be made for the mediating and representational role of parties in a political system such as Canada's, this question involves philosophical choices and is one to be addressed within the broader context of general electoral reform. From the viewpoint of media access, however, it seems reasonable to propose that parties be mandated equitable access to national and regional media; access to relevant local media, such as community television, would be accorded to individual candidates.

Following the example of Sweden and some other European countries, Canada could well supplement mandated media access with more direct public subsidies for the activities and organization of registered parties. Such an approach can be philosophically justified as a positive role for the state in promoting pluralism and reducing the relative influence of money in determining the competitive ability of parties to mobilize for elections. Direct subsidies would have the further advantage of increasing the communications options available to smaller parties, and they would perhaps reduce the pressure on broadcasters to provide free time. Indeed, a judicious combination of spending ceilings (particularly for paid advertising), direct subsidies and mandated media access could lead to a substantially more level playing field for all political parties.

Whether such an approach would unduly expose the electoral system to a cacophony of competing fringe voices depends greatly on the chosen thresholds, the criteria used to determine eligibility for subsidies and media access. A strong case can be made for introducing a graduated system that is capable of distinguishing between those parties that were collectively categorized as "minor" during the 1988 election. For example, parties scoring higher in terms of specified criteria would acquire greater access to mandated media time. Such an approach seemed to command broad support among minor-party respondents, and it makes a good deal of sense. Indeed, some minor parties are prepared to accept higher thresholds for party registration if it would mean more (perceived) equitable and respectful treatment at election time. It became apparent during this research that all minor parties are not equal: some have greater degrees of popular support or greater commitment to coherent political goals than do others.

Of course, threshold criteria in a liberal democracy cannot be based on an evaluation of political goals. Rather, a combination of more "objective" criteria is relevant – not only the number of candidates fielded or votes received in an election, but also the compilation of voters' signatures, evidence of support and membership in different provinces, and organizational continuity over time. The latter kind of criteria would enable a new party to become registered between elections. At the same time, the threshold should not be so low as to encourage the formation of frivolous parties seeking mainly to obtain access to subsidies, tax credits or media time. Here, as elsewhere, an appropriate balance must be found.

ABBREVIATIONS

c.	chapter
Pub. L.	Public Law (U.S.)
R.S.C.	Revised Statutes of Canada
S.C.	Session Cases
U.S.	United States Supreme Court Reports

NOTES

This study was completed in May 1991.

The principal investigator would like to thank the following associates and assistants: James Mackintosh for reviewing and summarizing much of the policy literature and interview data; David Robinson for co-designing the content analysis, carrying out much of the coding, and summarizing some of the interview data; Arlene Shwetz for conducting most of the interviews; Tanya Bahrisch and Karen Stuart for content analysis coding; and Eva Kral, Lianne McLarty, Pilar Riano, Judy Schlachter and Margo Vandaelle for their painstaking transcription of the interviews. David Taras (Communications, University of Calgary) and Allan Tupper (Political Science, University of Alberta) provided some valuable insights. Anthony Sayers kindly made available from his own research for this Royal Commission an interview with Ethan Minowitz, staff reporter for the Vancouver *Westender/Eastender*. Ronald Roth, journalist and associate business manager, *Content: About Canadian Journalism*, shared his data on media coverage of smaller parties and provided valuable advice. The administration of the research funds by Simon Fraser University made this project possible, and the administrative assistance of Pam Parford was, as usual, deft and invaluable.

1. According to this principle, the actual sample dates for each medium were as follows: CBC's "National" and "Journal" (2, 9, 18, 27 October; 3, 11, 19 November); CTV's "National News" (3, 6, 20, 27 October; 4, 12, 19 November); *Globe and Mail* (1, 10, 18, 26 October; 3, 11, 19 November); *Vancouver Sun* (1, 11, 18, 26 October; 3, 10, 19 November).

2. The candidates and results in these ridings were respectively as follows:

   Vancouver East, of 39 663 votes cast: Margaret Mitchell (NDP), 20 108; Raymond Leung (Liberal), 11 692; Paul Nielsen (PC), 6 248; Robert Light (Green), 401; Heinz Holzschuher (Libertarian), 278; Ruff Tuff Duff Duff Scott (Rhino), 277; Kim Zander (Communist), 180; Cheryl Stephens Soroko (no stated affiliation or unregistered party), 88 (spoiled ballots, 391).

   Vancouver South, of 50 573 votes cast: John Fraser (PC), 21 222; Woody MacLaren (Liberal), 14 468; Martin Toren (NDP), 11 939; Don Evans (Reform), 1 052; John Clarke (Libertarian), 946; Douglas Dunn (Green), 327; Brian Salmi (Rhino), 123; Barbara Waldern (no stated affiliation or unregistered party), 74; Reginald Walter (Communist), 54 (spoiled ballots, 318).

   Edmonton Southeast, of 48 579 votes cast: David Kilgour (PC), 23 597; Chris Peirce (Liberal), 10 104; Harbans Dhillon (NDP), 9 161; Wes McLeod (Reform), 5 192; Harry Garfinkle (Green), 184; Oran Johnson (COR), 102; Dorothy Bohdan (Commonwealth), 76; Peggy Morton (no stated affiliation or unregistered party), 66 (spoiled ballots, 97).

   Wetaskiwin, of 40 085 votes cast: Willie Littlechild (PC), 20 090; Jim Henderson (Reform), 7 418; Terry Atkinson (NDP), 5 741; Roy Barrett (Liberal), 3 351; David Reimer (CHP), 3 087; Hayward Dow (COR), 223; Mike Hermansen (no stated affiliation or unregistered party), 113 (spoiled ballots, 62).

   Source: Canada, Elections Canada 1988.

3. An inter-coder reliability test of three randomly selected items by two coders yielded 85.6 percent agreement. Since "absent" variables were excluded from the calculation of inter-coder agreement, this result can be considered quite acceptable for this kind of coding.

4. The index is adapted from one kindly supplied to the principal investigator by Andrew M. Osler in 1980, and employed in Hackett (1983).

INTERVIEWS

Party Respondents

Caplan, Gerald, New Democratic Party (NDP).

Dow, Hayward, Confederation of Regions Western Party (COR) candidate, Wetaskiwin.

Dunn, Douglas, Green Party candidate, Vancouver South.

Evans, Don, Reform Party candidate, Vancouver South.

Garfinkle, Dr. Harry, Green Party candidate, Edmonton Southeast.

Henderson, Jim, Reform Party candidate, Wetaskiwin.

Jackman, J.G., Commonwealth party candidate, Vancouver Quadra.

Johnson, Oran, COR candidate, Edmonton Southeast.

Johnston, Ron, director of communications, British Columbia, NDP.

Knutson, Elmer, leader, COR.

Kotowich, Marcel, Rhinoceros Party candidate, Edmonton–Strathcona.

Main, Doug, Reform Party candidate, Edmonton–Strathcona, and now a cabinet minister in the Alberta government.

O'Grady, Terry, director of communications, Federal NDP.

Rankin, Naomi, Communist party candidate, Edmonton East.

Reimer, David J., Christian Heritage party (CHP) candidate, Wetaskiwin.

Slavick, Robert, Reform Party candidate, Saanich–Gulf Islands.

Tomlinson, Bill, Libertarian candidate, Capilano–Howe Sound, and now a party organizer.

Van Woudenberg, Ed, CHP national leader, and candidate in Fraser Valley West.

Walters, Reginald, Communist party candidate, Vancouver South.

Wood, Ron, Reform Party, director of communications.

Representatives of the three major parties were sought for their views, but only officials of the NDP proved to be available. An interview was also done with a candidate for the CHP who wished not to be identified.

Media Respondents

Brown, George, editor, *Wetaskiwin Times Advertiser*.

Carr, Kimberley, news editor, *Devon Dispatch*.

Davis, Murdoch, managing editor, *Edmonton Journal.*

Johnston, Hugh, publisher, *Devon Dispatch.*

Liddell, David, vice-president programming, Western Canada region, Rogers Cable TV, Burnaby.

McDonald, Randy, managing editor, *Edmonton Sun.*

Raglin, Rod, publisher and editor, *South Vancouver Revue.*

Rainone, Mike, editor, *Ponoka Herald.*

Roberts, John, editor, *Rimbey Record.*

Shore, Randy, managing editor, *Vancouver Echo.*

Tougas, Maurice, editor, *Edmonton Examiner.*

Treleavan, Allan, publisher, *Lacombe Globe.*

We gratefully acknowledge the assistance of all our respondents.

REFERENCES

Alexander, H.E. 1989a. "American Presidential Elections since Public Funding, 1976–84." In *Comparative Political Finance in the 1980s,* ed. H.E. Alexander. Cambridge: Cambridge University Press.

———. 1989b. "Introduction." In *Comparative Political Finance in the 1980s,* ed. H.E. Alexander. Cambridge: Cambridge University Press.

———. 1989c. "Money and Politics: Rethinking a Conceptual Framework." In *Comparative Political Finance in the 1980s,* ed. H.E. Alexander. Cambridge: Cambridge University Press.

Black, Edwin R. 1982. *Politics and the News: The Political Functions of Mass Media.* Toronto: Butterworths.

Blumler, Jay G., and Michael Gurevitch. 1982. "The Political Effects of Mass Communication." In *Culture, Society and the Media,* ed. M. Gurevitch, T. Bennett, J. Curran and J. Woollacott. London: Methuen.

Boyer, J. Patrick. 1983. *Money and Message: The Law Governing Election Financing, Advertising, Broadcasting and Campaigning in Canada.* Toronto: Butterworths.

Boyle, Alan E. 1986. "Political Broadcasting, Fairness and Administrative Law." *Public Law:* 562–96.

Buckley v. Valeo 424 U.S. 1 (1976).

Canada. *Canada Elections Act,* R.S.C. 1985, c. E-2.

———. *Canadian Charter of Rights and Freedoms,* Part 1 of the *Constitution Act, 1982,* being Schedule B of the *Canada Act 1982* (U.K.), c. 11.

Canada. Elections Canada. 1988. *Report of the Chief Electoral Officer, Thirty-Fourth General Election.* Ottawa: Minister of Supply and Services Canada.

Canada. Royal Commission on Radio Broadcasting. 1929. *Report*. Ottawa: King's Printer.

Canada. Royal Commission on Newspapers. 1981. *Report*. Ottawa: Minister of Supply and Services Canada.

Canadian Radio-television and Telecommunications Commission. 1987a. "Election Campaign Broadcasting." Public Notice CRTC 1987-209. Ottawa: CRTC.

———. 1987b. "Political Broadcasting – Complaints re: Free Time and Editorial Time Allocations." Circular No. 334. Ottawa: CRTC.

Clarke, Harold D., Jane Jenson, Lawrence LeDuc and Jon H. Pammett. 1984. *Absent Mandate: The Politics of Discontent in Canada*. Toronto: Gage.

Cody-Rice, Edith. 1981. "The Treatment of the Term 'To the Detriment or Against the Interest of the Public.'" In W. Tarnopolsky, C. Wright, G.-A. Beaudoin and E. Cody-Rice, *Newspapers and the Law*. Vol. 3 of the research publications of the Royal Commission on Newspapers. Ottawa: Minister of Supply and Services Canada.

Curran, James. 1977. "Capitalism and Control of the Press, 1800–1975." In *Mass Communication and Society*, ed. J. Curran, M. Gurevitch and J. Woollacott. London: Edward Arnold.

Dalton, Russell J. 1989. *Politics in West Germany*. Glenview: Scott, Foresman.

Ewing, Keith. 1987. *The Funding of Political Parties in Britain*. Cambridge: Cambridge University Press.

Fejes, Fred. 1984. "Critical Mass Communications Research and Media Effects: The Problem of the Disappearing Audience." *Media, Culture and Society* 6 (3): 219–32.

Fletcher, Frederick J. 1981. *The Newspaper and Public Affairs*. Vol. 7 of the research publications of the Royal Commission on Newspapers. Ottawa: Minister of Supply and Services Canada.

Frizzell, Alan, Jon H. Pammett and Anthony Westell. 1989. *The Canadian General Election of 1988*. Ottawa: Carleton University Press.

Gilsdorf, William O. 1981. "Getting the Message Across: Media Strategies and Political Campaigns." In *Communication Studies in Canada/Études canadiennes en communication*, ed. Liora Salter. Toronto: Butterworths.

Goldenberg, Edie N., and Michael W. Traugott. 1987a. "Mass Media and Legislative Contests: Opportunities for Comparative Study." *Legislative Studies Quarterly* 12 (3): 445–56.

———. 1987b. "Mass Media in U.S. Congressional Elections." *Legislative Studies Quarterly* 12 (3): 317–39.

Grieve v. Douglas-Home, [1965] S.C. 313 (Scotland).

Hackett, Robert A. 1983. "The Depiction of Labour and Business on National Television News." *Canadian Journal of Communication* 10 (1): 5–50.

———. 1985. "A Hierarchy of Access: Aspects of Source Bias in Canadian TV News." *Journalism Quarterly* 62 (2): 256–65, 277.

———. 1991. *News and Dissent: The Press and the Politics of Peace in Canada.* Norwood: Ablex.

Hall, Stuart. 1973. "The Determinations of News Photographs." In *The Manufacture of News: Social Problems, Deviance and the Mass Media,* ed. Stanley Cohen and Jock Young. London: Constable.

Howse, John. 1988. "Outside Looking In: The Fringe Parties Join in the Race to November." *Maclean's,* 7 November.

Jenson, Jane. 1991. "Innovation and Equity: The Impact of Public Funding." In *Comparative Issues in Party and Election Finance,* ed. F. Leslie Seidle. Vol. 4 of the research studies of the Royal Commission on Electoral Reform and Party Financing. Ottawa and Toronto: RCERPF/Dundurn.

Mickelson, Sig. 1972. *The Electric Mirror: Politics in the Age of Television.* New York: Dodd, Mead.

Nassmacher, K.-H. 1989. "Structure and Impact of Public Subsidies to Political Parties in Europe: The Examples of Austria, Italy, Sweden and West Germany." In *Comparative Political Finance in the 1980s,* ed. H.E. Alexander. Cambridge: Cambridge University Press.

Paltiel, K.Z. 1979. "The Impact of Election Expenses Legislation in Canada, Western Europe, and Israel." In *Political Finance,* ed. H.E. Alexander. Beverly Hills: Sage Publications.

———. 1989. "Canadian Election Expense Legislation, 1963–85: A Critical Appraisal or Was the Effort Worth It?" In *Comparative Political Finance in the 1980s,* ed. H.E. Alexander. Cambridge: Cambridge University Press.

Roth, Robert M. 1990a. "Dancing around the Totem: The Ideological Role of the Leaders' Debates in the Canadian Electoral Process." M.J. thesis. Carleton University, School of Journalism.

———. 1990b. "Muffled Voices." *Content* (July/August): 21–22.

Schoenbach, Klaus. 1987. "The Role of Mass Media in West German Election Campaigns." *Legislative Studies Quarterly* 12 (3): 373–94.

Seiden, Martin H. 1974. *Who Controls the Mass Media?* New York: Basic Books.

Siune, Karen. 1987. "The Political Role of Mass Media in Scandinavia." *Legislative Studies Quarterly* 12 (3): 395–414.

Soderlund, Walter C., Walter I. Romanow, E. Donald Briggs and Ronald H. Wagenberg. 1984. *Media and Elections in Canada.* Toronto: Holt, Rinehart and Winston.

Taras, David. 1990. *The Newsmakers: The Media's Influence on Canadian Politics.* Scarborough: Nelson Canada.

United States. *Federal Election Campaign Act of 1971*, Pub. L. 92-225, Feb. 7, 1972.

United Kingdom. *Representation of the People Act, 1949*, 12, 13 and 14 Geo. VI, c. 68.

5

MASS MEDIA AND THE REPRODUCTION OF MARGINALIZATION

Eileen Saunders

THE ESTABLISHMENT OF the Royal Commission on Electoral Reform and Party Financing reflects a belief in the importance of the electoral process in maintaining a strong and viable democracy. The work of the Commission is designed to assess the current health of the Canadian electoral system and, where necessary, to make recommendations for appropriate reforms to the process by which we select our government and our leaders.

A key component of the work is an attempt to come to grips with the role played by the mass media in both the conduct of political campaigns and the more general process of fostering the flow of information necessary to nourish and sustain high levels of public debate over political issues.

The goal of this study is to contribute to the work of the Commission by focusing on the role played by the mass media during the general election of 1988 in facilitating the participation of particular minority groups in the wider political process. The study will focus specifically on the situation of two distinct groups: ethnic minorities and persons with disabilities. The key issues of concern are whether the media are contributing to the development of an adequate level of public information and education about the situation and concerns of these groups (as opposed to a reliance on stereotypes and inaccurate information) and whether these groups are fully included in the public debates that characterize the electoral process (as opposed to suffering from a degree of relative exclusion).

In studying ethnic minorities and persons with disabilities within the same research study, we do not wish to suggest one can merely collapse those issues that uniquely define the situation of these groups in Canadian society. Rather, we are seeking to investigate the extent to which certain underrepresented social groups may be alienated from the political process and to establish whether this is a consequence, at least in part, of their possible alienation from the media campaign. What these groups share is, for the purposes of this investigation, more important than what distinguishes them. Their common link is their marginal location in the sociopolitical structures of Canada. This frames their status as minority groups: the politics of exclusion have kept both groups from the mainstream of Canadian society; both have been victimized by traditional prejudices and stereotypes that define them as "different"; both are overrepresented among the poorest groups in our society; and both have been promised full social and economic integration by successive Canadian governments. What is interesting, then, is to examine the situation of two very different minorities that are nevertheless both defined by their marginalization.

There are an estimated 3.2 million Canadians with disabilities, representing 13 percent of the population (Canada, Secretary of State 1990, 1), and approximately 30 percent of Canadians belong to an ethnic group. (There are various definitions of ethnicity in circulation, although the most commonly accepted is that which defines ethnic individuals as non-British, non-French, non-native immigrants and their descendants; see Stasiulis and Abu-Laban 1990, 595). Surprisingly, there is not a great deal of literature on the role of either group in Canadian political/electoral processes.

Any attempt to understand the relative access of minority groups to participation in the wider political process must focus on the interrelated issues of image and access. The issue of image focuses on the information about ethnic minorities or persons with disabilities provided to consumers of media images. The focus at this level is on the images of particular minority groups offered both to the general public and to minority group members. The concern is with the general process of socialization and with the specific question of the production or transformation of social positions within the political process. The issue of access focuses on the ability of ethnic minorities and persons with disabilities to place issues of concern on the public agenda. The focus at this level is on the ability of these groups to gain access to the media and, perhaps more important, to participate actively in the production of mass media images.

Thus, the question of image raises a number of concerns regarding minority groups as a topic of media coverage, while the question of access turns our attention to minority groups as participants in the production of information.

The focus of this study is on the media coverage of ethnic minorities and persons with disabilities during the 1988 federal general election. The study will be divided into four sections. The first section will review two related sets of literature: theoretical work on newsmaking processes and analyses of media representations of persons with disabilities and of those in ethnic communities. It will deal specifically with the issue of how the organization and routinization of news practices privileges certain voices and particular images. The argument in this section will be that the news frame necessarily narrows one's view of the electoral landscape and of the participants and interests within it. This theoretical discussion will provide the backdrop for the descriptive analysis of the coverage of ethnic minorities and persons with disabilities during the 1988 federal general election.

The second section will describe the methodological approach used in conducting this study. The study deals with print media. More specifically, the approach used involves a content analysis of the coverage of issues and events related to ethnic minorities or persons with disabilities in the English-language daily press during the 1988 federal election campaign. These data are supplemented by interviews with a sample of representatives of groups for/of persons with disabilities and of ethnocultural organizations.

The third section will describe the data and discuss the findings of this study. The main argument will be that the news coverage of these groups is relatively scarce, of low priority, and marked by the absence of direct participation in the newsmaking process. Thematically, the coverage of these groups has been dominated by a restricted number of issues. This has the impact of limiting the public's knowledge and awareness of the concerns of these groups and therefore limiting these groups' potential to use the electoral process to advance their issues and concerns.

The final section will discuss the conclusions of this study and present a series of recommendations aimed at improving both the representation of these groups in the media and the access of these same groups to the media production process.

NEWS AND MARGINAL VOICES: THE NARROWING FRAME

The first major consideration in our examination of the media coverage of ethnic minorities and persons with disabilities during election campaigns is the extent to which the nature of newsgathering and news-processing routines predetermines our frameworks for understanding ethnic and disability issues and groups. For this reason it is necessary to examine the scholarly literature on news production as well as some key case studies on the general news coverage of the two designated groups.

Newsmaking: The Nature of News

The news is a practical organizational accomplishment, the result of a complex set of social relations. The structural conditions of news production will vary from organization to organization, but common to each is a certain bureaucratic logic.

One element of this pattern, of key significance here, manifests itself in an array of institutional definitions known as news values. Through news values, journalists are able to determine precisely which of the myriad of occurrences in the social world will be constructed as a newsworthy event on any given day of the week. News values help to orient or cue the journalist to particular occurrences; they are the "unstated and unstatable criteria of *the significant*" (Hall 1981, 148). Researchers, while perhaps in disagreement over the particular salience of any one criterion, can nevertheless point to a fairly consistent set of factors in play. Drawing on an extensive literature (see, for example, Ericson et al. 1987; Galtung and Ruge 1965; Gans 1979; Hall et al. 1978; Hartley 1982; Tuchman 1978; van Dijk 1988a), we see that the following are representative of the key news values:

- conflict (balanced journalism dictates that each story has two sides);
- relevance (events should be seen to impinge, however indirectly, on the news audience's daily activities);
- timeliness (the timespan taken by the event should be easily handled in the light of institutional constraints and pressures);
- simplification (events are preferably unambiguous: the diversity of potential interpretations should be kept to a minimum);
- personalization (the emphasis on human actors is preferred to sustained descriptions of faceless structures, forces or institutions);
- consonance (the predictability of an event lends it to the routinized dictates of newsgathering);
- unexpectedness (an event that is out of the ordinary or novel has a higher chance of being caught in the news net);
- continuity (events should allow for a sense of where they fit in; continuous events allow for prescheduling);

- composition (a mixture of different types of events must be processed on any given day; events are thus chosen in relation to fluctuations in the news hole to be filled);
- reference to élites (a hierarchy can be discerned, whether in terms of nations or persons, which prioritizes those actors seen to affect readers' lives at the expense of others, who are relegated to infrequent newsworthy status);
- cultural specificity (if all events are culturally specific, those that conform to the maps of meaning, or in an ethnocentric sense are shared by the journalist and the news audience, have a greater likelihood of being selected); and
- negativity (bad news is favoured over good news, because the former usually conforms to a higher number of the above factors).

The above list should not be read as an attempt to reduce the role of news values in journalism to questions of distortion, manipulation or bias. Rather, we need to understand how assumptions about preferred news values are enmeshed in the social organization of newswork and how the dictates of organizational and professional work routines have significant implications for the types of news stories that are told and the types of voices that are permitted to tell them.

To understand the impact of institutional imperatives on the preferred news values and news frames, analysts have tried to grapple with the actual skills and methods used by journalists as they go about their daily routines. The beginning point in such analyses is usually to ask how an occurrence becomes an event in the eyes of the journalist (see, for example, Molotch and Lester 1974). Journalists need to bring to the task of event detection a series of framing procedures capable of imposing order and coherence on the social world. Consequently, researchers have attempted to illustrate how these frames work to include particular topics and particular voices and to exclude others. It is important to note that these framing procedures are, as Todd Gitlin suggests, "negotiated among sources, editors and reporters; how they will emerge in practice is not preordained" (1980, 274). Rather, as Tuchman argues, they constitute a news net that is cast upon the social world as a means of catching or identifying relevant news events; a net, she argues, that is "intended for big fish" (1978, 21). Tuchman demonstrates how the news net is anchored in a manner that has geographical, bureaucratic and topical determinations embedded within it and how journalists develop classifications or typifications of eventsas-news that enable the journalist to routinize the unexpected.

Fishman's work (1980) extends Tuchman's analysis by an investigation of the procedures through which information sources are centralized and the consequences of this centralization for excluding some occurrences and voices from consideration by the news net. As Ericson et al. note, "journalists face the bounds of powerful sources who mobilize strategically to variously avoid and make news" (1987, 364).

The very basis upon which the journalist is able to detect events, according to Fishman, rests on a commonsensical understanding that society is bureaucratically structured (1980, 51). It is this perspective that provides the reporter with a "map of relevant knowers" for newsworthy topics. Whether it is the fire department for a local fire or the police for a dramatic homicide, "whatever the happening, there are officials and authorities in a structured position to know" (ibid.).

The issue of competence and reliability in sources is of critical concern to the journalist: exactly who qualifies as a satisfactory knower or observer? Fishman argues that officials and bureaucrats are ascribed competence through their position in the official hierarchies; "they have a social warrant, they are entitled or authorized, to know certain things" (1980, 93). Moreover, as Tuchman notes, "the higher the status of sources and the greater the scope of their position, the higher the status of the reporters" (1978, 69). The end result is a "hierarchy of credibility" (Becker 1967) among sources. Hall et al. attempt to document how notions like competence and credibility can, in turn, "give rise to the practice of ensuring that media statements are, wherever possible, grounded in 'objective' and 'authoritative' statements from 'accredited sources' " (1978, 58).

The practical conflation of intense time pressures, together with the professional demands of balance and objectivity, produces a "systematically structured *over-accessing* to the media of those in powerful and privileged institutional positions" (Hall et al. 1978, 58). Hall et al. conclude that "the result of this structured preference given in the media to the opinions of the powerful is that these 'spokes[persons]' become what we will call the *primary definers* of topics" (ibid.).

A recurrent theme, then, in the literature on the social relations of news production is the unequal distribution of the power to communicate. Arguably the most important point about the relationship defined above between the news media and the hierarchy of institutional definers is that it permits the most powerful of the latter to set the framework for debate. This is accomplished through setting the "initial definition or *primary interpretation* of the topic in question. This interpretation then 'commands the field' in all subsequent treatment" (Hall et al. 1978, 58). This is not to suggest that other interpretations do not enter the debate; rather, they must begin with the issues as they have been pre-established.

How then, one must ask, can those who speak from marginalized social locations establish their voice in the news and their status as authoritative, newsworthy subjects? How have the various agendas of marginalized groups and their institutions been made to cater to the dictates of news production? What are the prerequisites to be met before a voice "deserves" inclusion in the media debate? We turn now to a brief discussion of the manner in which our two designated groups, ethnic minorities and persons with disabilities, have traditionally entered the news frame.

Patterns of Coverage

There is a fair amount of research on the representation of different minority groups, especially visible minorities, in the mass media. The major focus of that research has been on media stereotyping and the underrepresentation of these groups in a range of different genres, including prime time entertainment, advertising and news accounts (for selected examples of this research, see Canadian Multiculturalism Council 1988; Deverell 1986; Driedger 1989; Gartner and Joe 1987; Granzberg 1983; Singer 1983; and Sutherland 1981). The patterns of coverage are clearly documented:

- Minorities are underrepresented in the media.
- When present, minorities are represented in a limited range of roles, and those are usually characterized by their marginal status.
- Minorities are represented as being different, whether in terms of basic personality characteristics or general aptitude for particular social roles.
- Alternative or oppositional definitions of their situation, emanating from minority groups themselves, receive little play in the media.

The 1988 Report of the House of Commons Standing Committee on the Status of Disabled Persons, chaired by Conservative MP Patrick Boyer, documented the extent of exclusion from news processes of persons with disabilities (Canada, House of Commons 1988). Because of the paucity of research studies focusing specifically on the media treatment of disabled persons in comparison to other marginalized minority groups, the research studies commissioned by the Standing Committee provide valuable evidence on the nature of exclusion. The studies note, among other things, the absence of media coverage (fewer than one item per issue in the newspapers examined), the presence of twice as many negative images as positive ones, the use of demeaning and pejorative language (e.g., retarded, handicapped, afflicted, wheelchair-bound), the dominance of a charity perspective, the invisibility of disabled persons who speak on their own behalf, and the failure of media to address policy or advocacy issues. A recent study of the U.S. press treatment of disability issues speaks to this latter issue. It describes an "incident in which a reporter at a political action convention chose to write from a traditional, debilitating 'frame' rather than focus on the issues of discrimination, civil rights, and political organizing that were the meat of the conference" (Biklen 1987, 79). Bogdan et al. describe the link often made in the press and in popular culture between disabilities and negative themes of violence/crime/evil: "The image of the handi-capped as dangerous dominates cultural media and, ironically, goes almost unnoticed and unchecked, except by people who have disabili-ties and who are constantly bombarded by these insults" (1982, 35).

Finally, researchers such as Longmore have documented the "lan-guage of disability," which essentializes individuals with disabilities to the extent that "they are perceived exclusively in terms of their dis-abilities" (1985, 419).

The case studies of media representation of ethnic minorities in both Canadian and other national contexts point to the fact that defi-nitions/news about these groups are usually framed by the dominant white institutions of society and that representatives of these groups have much less access to the news production processes. According to van Dijk, for example, in the majority of western European countries, where visible minorities represent about 5 percent of the population, news about these groups usually stands at between 1 and 2 percent of total news and editorial space in the press (1988a, 156). Research also shows that the press pass on value-laden stereotypes of these groups that, among other things, serve to reproduce their marginality. Indra, for example, argues in her analysis of the Vancouver press that "South Asians were only one of several groups whose ritual degradation by the press legitimated the ethnic stratification of Vancouver" (1979, 186). Other research documents the exclusion of ethnic groups from partic-ipant roles in the news; in a recent report prepared for the Secretary of State, it was found that only 3 percent of all broadcasters or reporters on English-language newscasts were members of an ethnic or racial group (Generations Research 1988, iii). In studies conducted by Erin Research for the Canadian Radio-television and Telecommunications Commission (CRTC), it was found that visible minorities accounted for 10 percent of on-air appearances by staff in news and current affairs,

5 percent of those interviewed on English television news in 1988 (Erin Research 1990, 14). The figures for French television news and current affairs demonstrated that visible minorities accounted for less than one-half of one percent of on-air staff appearances and 5 percent of interviewees (ibid., 36). Finally, analyses such as the now classic study of the coverage of race in the British press by Hartman and Husband have argued that "much of the bias in race related news would seem to stem from the habitualized 'news sense' which is integral to [journalists'] professionalism" (1974, 209).

Thus, there is general agreement in the research that the dominant tendency is to subordinate and marginalize minority groups in media representations and in media access. The question, for our purposes, is the extent to which these patterns hold true for our two groups in the context of Canadian election coverage. Before turning to a description of the parameters of this specific study, we must first consider the specificity of election news coverage in terms of its own framing devices.

Election News

Research on the interplay between media and elections reveals particular features of election news coverage of relevance to this study (see Fletcher 1987; Frizzell et al. 1989; Paletz and Entman 1981; Soderlund et al. 1984; and Taras 1990). It is important to note that within the restraints of journalistic discursive practices discussed earlier, there are specific features of news coverage characteristic of election campaign coverage worthy of attention. Fletcher, for example, notes four normative practices that have appeared in news coverage in recent years: proportional coverage of the major parties; more direct attention on party leaders' performances; more coverage of party strategies and strategists; and less willingness to accept off-the-record briefings (1987, 352). The consequences of these conventions, particularly the first three, are significant in that political campaigns increasingly conform to the imperatives of media (most notably television) production.

Data in Fletcher's research confirm that the volume of news coverage of the parties roughly reflects their standing in the House of Commons before the election. Not only does this favour the three main parties over minor parties; it also creates problems for the third party wishing to carve out a more visible share of the coverage. This is coupled with giving increasing attention to the leaders and the parties, and less to substantive issues. As Fletcher notes, between the 1974 and 1980 elections, issues garnered increasing coverage, but this was no longer the case by the 1984 election (1987, 352–53). The effect on the campaign has also been noted: increasingly, campaign strategists for the parties have downplayed the policy issues and local candidates, and focused instead on the leaders. The result, as noted by Taras, is that "it has made leadership into an all-consuming issue and, to some degree, 'presidentializes' the Canadian political system" (1990, 166). This pattern of coverage was combined with a predominantly single-issue focus in the 1988 election on free trade. As noted by Frizzell et al., 58 percent of all election news stories in the daily press dealt with free trade issues (1989, 86).

Finally, media analysts have noted the tendency of media, particularly television, to allow the parties to set the agenda of issues. As noted by Soderlund et al. in their research, "our data tend to characterize the electronic media as holding the fiddle for the politicians to play, rather than attempting to call the tune" (1984, 72). This dominance of a national campaign has several consequences, but for the purposes of our study, the most significant is the narrowing of the public agenda for debate. The nationalization of issues, controlled by party strategists, has meant the exclusion of other issues and experts from the media frame. As noted by Fletcher, "those in the media who provide opportunities for other actors to force their issues onto the public agenda thus make a valuable contribution to the campaign process" (1987, 363). To what extent this is accomplished for the marginalized communities of ethnic and disabled individuals is the focus of our concern in the following sections.

METHODOLOGY

Data for this study have been gathered through a content analysis of press coverage of election news with relevance to ethnic minorities and persons with disabilities during the 1988 election period (i.e., between 1 June 1988 and 15 January 1989). The timeframe was chosen to pick up news items regarding the candidate-selection process, the actual campaign, election day (21 November) and the post-election period. The analysis is designed with two broad questions in mind: how much news coverage was there during the 1988 federal election concerning ethnic and disabled minority groups, and what were the features of that coverage? The focus of the study is the English-language daily press. One must recognize the limitations this places on our ability to generalize from the findings. We have not, for example, considered the role of the ethnic press as an information resource during elections, although there is an interesting body of literature emerging on more general questions of this press (see, for example, Lam 1980; Miller 1985; Zybala 1982). There is not much research available on questions concerning the use of ethnic media during election campaigns or the nature of these media's coverage. There are studies, however, that indicate a declining usage of the ethnic media over time; in other words, its main function seems to be at the stage of immigrant adaptation (see Black and Leithner 1987). In addition, we need to examine the role of the French-language press in this area. Finally, there is room for more research on questions regarding television and radio coverage, research that could perhaps compare the access of our designated groups to print as opposed to broadcast media.

The Sample

The newspapers for examination were chosen on the basis of both circulation figures and coverage of regional markets to produce a sample that was both regionally balanced and included the leading papers in each market. Seven papers were chosen: the Halifax *Chronicle-Herald*, the Montreal *Gazette*, the *Ottawa Citizen*, the *Toronto Star*, the *Globe and Mail* (national edition), the *Calgary Herald*, and the *Vancouver Sun*. The sample of news items was constructed through the use of two on-line data bank services, Infomart (for the Montreal *Gazette*, *Ottawa Citizen*, *Toronto Star* and *Vancouver Sun*) and INFO GLOBE (for the *Globe and Mail*). The Halifax *Chronicle-Herald* is not catalogued by either service, and the *Calgary Herald* did not come on-line with Infomart until late in 1988. For these papers, we used the Canadian News Index (CNI) to select relevant news items.

To focus our analysis only on the coverage of these groups as it was relevant to the federal election, we had to choose carefully the access codes to the on-line data banks. Through several trials using different access codes, it was determined that combining "election" with different terms commonly used to refer to members of the designated groups (disabled, handicapped, minorities, etc.) yielded the news items sought. After the papers had been electronically scanned for the entire timeframe and a pool of news items generated, it then became a matter of reading through each news item to ensure its basis for inclusion in the sample. Many items, for example, were eliminated from coding because they concerned school board or civic elections. Then again, items not relevant to the study were picked up; for example, several stories from the sports sections of papers concerned the Blue Jays placing one of their players on the disabled list – a standard phrase in baseball! Similar codes were used when examining the CNI for the two papers not accessible electronically.

It is perhaps worth noting here that the on-line services, while useful and certainly efficient in reducing search time, did not prove entirely reliable in flagging all relevant news items. Some news items uncovered through the CNI search clearly should have appeared in the on-line database, but did not. As a consequence, the research strategy was expanded to use the CNI as a backup means of sample construction. We therefore went though the CNI for all papers (with the exception of the *Ottawa Citizen*, which is not indexed) to ensure as representative a sample as possible.

Coding

The total number of news items that had any bearing on election news and persons with disabilities or members of ethnic groups amounted to 90 for persons with disabilities and 201 for members of ethnic groups. To be included in the initial sample, an item had to make explicit reference to the federal election and to one of the designated groups (this included individual members and organizations as well as issues of direct concern to these groups). These items were then divided into two categories in a preliminary coding: those that were single-reference and those that could be considered as having some topical focus on the groups in question. We thought it important to distinguish between news accounts that could be said to be about ethnic groups/ethnicity or persons with disabilities/disability issues (although the degree of attention can vary widely) and those in which there is a barely noticeable mention of these groups. The instructions to the coders were quite explicit on this point; an item had to have at least one paragraph referring to the designated group, a group member or issue, even though the rest of the news item may concern something else, to be included in the topical-focus category (see van Dijk 1988a, 162, for elaboration on these coding criteria). Single-reference items are those where the designated group, group member or issue is mentioned in passing, often as one in a series of references to different social groupings. We then separated these two categories and were left with 38 topical-focus items and 52 single-reference items relevant to persons with disabilities and 143 topical-focus items and 58 single-reference items relevant to ethnic minorities.

The news items identified as having a topical focus were analysed on separate coding sheets that included a mix of standard, preformulated information categories (source, type of news account, section placement, etc.) and open-ended information categories (e.g., names of particular organizations cited in the account). The full coding sheet is attached in the appendix. Coders were given an orientation session, and pre-tests of a sub-sample of stories were done to identify any problem areas and establish inter-coder reliability.

The news items identified as single-reference items were not coded. Rather, we merely sought to establish the frequency of these items relative to those with some topical focus.

Interviews

To supplement the information derived from the analysis of actual coverage, we contacted a small sample of representatives and spokespersons from organizations for/of persons with disabilities and ethnic (including visible) minorities. The objective underlying these interviews was not to conduct a full-scale canvass of these two communities; rather, we sought to contact key players who could provide their perspectives on the question of media access during the 1988 election. Those interviewed are listed in the "Interviews" section. We certainly do not want to suggest that the views of those contacted exhaust the range of possible interventions; other organizations who were not contacted may offer different views. Nevertheless, one can argue that there is a striking consensus on key issues of access and representation among those interviewed. In the interviews with organization representatives, four areas were identified: the central election issues for their particular organization, their views on the media coverage of these issues, the nature of their contact with the news media during the election, and their recommendations for improving media practices.

ANALYSIS OF FINDINGS

In this section, the data from this study are presented and discussed within the parameters of the theoretical issues raised earlier. The discussion is organized in terms of two general areas of analysis: the presentation of news and the frames of news. Following van Dijk, we define the presentation of news to mean "the structure of occurrence and visual properties that influence its chances of perception and attention" (1988a, 163). Included here are factors such as frequency, length, type of account, placement in the paper and size of headlines. The frames of news address the question of the nature of content and include factors such as primary and secondary news focus, types of sources, and event categories.

A word of caution is necessary at this point regarding the small number of news items in the sample, particularly in the case of news concerning persons with disabilities. With only 38 sample items about persons with disabilities, percentage distributions must be considered with caution. That does not mean we cannot speak of certain patterns in the coverage; indeed, the small sample is itself an indication of marginal news status. We do, however, need to remain sensitive to the limitations of this analysis.

The Presentation of News

The first, and perhaps most striking, feature of the nature of news about ethnic groups and persons with disabilities during the 1988 federal election is its relative invisibility. The total sample of items, including single-reference accounts, was 201 for ethnic groups and 90 for disabled groups. However, the number that made more than a passing reference to these groups was considerably smaller. Approximately 29 percent of the total number of ethnic-group items (58 of 201 items) and 58 percent of the disabled group items (52 of 90 items) were coded as single-reference accounts. The evidence demonstrates that persons with disabilities are more likely than members of ethnic groups to enter the news frame in this marginal manner. It is perhaps interesting to note that the papers differ considerably on this dimension. The *Globe and Mail*, for example, tended to have a low proportion of single-reference items; only 12 percent of their news items about either group were classified in the single-reference category. In the *Ottawa Citizen*, on the other hand, the majority of items for both groups (58 percent) were in the single-reference category.

In table 5.1, the distribution of election news items with a topical focus on these designated groups is given for five of the newspapers in the sample and compared to the distribution of all news items regarding the federal election in those papers. As is demonstrated in this table, news about ethnic groups accounts for only 2.2 percent of total election coverage, while news about persons with disabilities accounts for a mere 0.6 percent. The tendency to focus on the party leaders over other groups or substantive issues has already been suggested as a common feature of election news, and these figures confirm and provide some evidence

Table 5.1
Frequency of coverage

	Number of mentions		
Newspaper	All items[a]	Ethnic groups	Persons with disabilities
Vancouver Sun	792	14	7
Globe and Mail	1 798	34	7
Toronto Star	1 367	46	6
Ottawa Citizen	1 417	14	8
Montreal *Gazette*	706	28	7
Total	6 080	136 (2.2%)	35 (0.6%)

[a]The total sample of election items was drawn from INFO GLOBE and Infomart and therefore does not include the numbers for the *Calgary Herald* or Halifax *Chronicle-Herald*.

of the extent of exclusion of other voices. Given the distribution of these groups in Canada (30 and 13 percent respectively), the data point to a clear and pronounced underrepresentation of their views and interests in the daily press during election campaigns.

The frequency of coverage for all newspapers in our sample is presented in table 5.2. The *Toronto Star* had the highest coverage of ethnic groups, constituting about a third of all news items in this category, while the Halifax *Chronicle-Herald* had only one item in the sample. That the *Toronto Star* had the highest proportion is not surprising, given that in the greater Toronto area there is a high concentration of various ethnic and visible minorities and that several key ridings there were the focus of a new ethnic political activism (Stasiulis and Abu-Laban 1990; *Toronto Life* 1988). The lower percentage in the *Globe and Mail* (24.5), it should be noted, may have been partially influenced by the fact that INFO GLOBE uses its national edition for constructing the on-line database.

News about persons with disabilities, although scarce for all papers in the sample, was highest in the *Ottawa Citizen*, with over 20 percent of the sample items, and lowest in the Halifax *Chronicle-Herald*, which again had only one news item; the *Calgary Herald* had two items.

The majority of the items in the sample were standard news reports and news briefs (57 percent of the items about ethnic groups and 68 per-

Table 5.2
Distribution of coverage by newspaper

	Focus of item			
	Ethnic groups		Persons with disabilities	
Newspaper	*N*	%	*N*	%
Vancouver Sun	14	9.8	7	18.4
Calgary Herald	5	3.5	2	5.3
Globe and Mail	35	24.5	7	18.4
Toronto Star	46	32.2	6	15.8
Ottawa Citizen	14	9.8	8	21.1
Montreal Gazette	28	19.6	7	18.4
Halifax *Chronicle-Herald*	1	0.7	1	2.6
Total[a]	143	100.1	38	100.0

[a]Because of rounding, percentages do not always total 100.

cent about persons with disabilities), while very few editorial or opinion columns were devoted to either group (14 to the former and 5 to the latter). The figures for other categories such as features and backgrounders were quite small and fairly evenly distributed. The implication here is that in the majority of cases, election news regarding these groups enters the news frame through a specific event orientation rather than through a sustained analysis of issues. It is interesting to note that there was only one photograph in our sample of items about ethnic groups and none in the items regarding persons with disabilities.

For both groups, the primary producers of the news were staff reporters on the papers (59 percent of news items about ethnic groups and 45 percent of news items regarding persons with disabilities). There was a heavier reliance on CP wire services for news items regarding persons with disabilities than was the case for ethnic groups (34 compared to 13 percent), and items designated as special assignments were rare (about 5 percent for both groups). The latter finding has interesting implications in that this category is often a route for special interest groups to get their views into the media and may indicate how successful the public relations of organized lobby groups are in practice.

As is shown in table 5.3, the majority of election news regarding both groups tends toward short items, although it is certainly more striking for news regarding the disabled. Almost 80 percent of those items fall under 600 words, and there are none over 1 200 words long. Of news items about ethnic groups, 52.5 percent were under 600 words, while 13.3 percent were articles of over 1 200 words.

Table 5.3
Length of news item

	Focus of item			
	Ethnic groups		Persons with disabilities	
Number of words	N	%	N	%
1–300	27	18.9	17	44.7
301–600	48	33.6	13	34.2
601–900	37	25.9	6	15.8
901–1 200	12	8.4	2	5.3
Over 1 200	19	13.3	0	0.0

The distribution of news items by headline size, as measured by column width, is shown in table 5.4. There is evidence to argue that items about ethnic groups are more likely to have larger headlines (five or more columns in width) than those concerning persons with disabilities, though both groups tend toward small (one or two columns) and medium-length headlines (three or four columns).

The location of news items in a newspaper has long been a standard means of measuring the prominence of different types of news. In table 5.5, the evidence shows that news about ethnic groups or persons with disabilities is seldom front-page news. A full 89.4 percent of the news

Table 5.4
Headline width

	Focus of item				
	Ethnic groups			Persons with disabilities	
Headline width (columns)	N	%		N	%
1 or 2	26	18.2		9	23.7
3 or 4	86	60.1		25	65.8
5 or more	31	21.7		4	10.5
Total	143	100.0		38	100.0

Table 5.5
Location of news items

	Focus of item				
	Ethnic groups			Persons with disabilities	
Page/section	N	%		N	%
Page 1/first section	12	8.4		6	15.8
Other page/first section	91	63.6		16	42.1
Front page/inner section	3	2.1		3	7.9
Other page/inner section	37	25.8		13	34.2
Total[a]	143	99.9		38	100.0

[a]Because of rounding, percentages do not always total 100.

about ethnic groups and 76.3 percent of the news about persons with disabilities appeared on inner pages of the papers, whether in the first section or other sections.

News Frames

A variety of factors were examined to uncover the nature of election news about ethnic groups and persons with disabilities. One was the extent to which direct reference was made to general election issues. In other words, we sought to measure the presence or absence of a larger news frame, one that links minority or marginal group interests to a discussion of campaign or electoral issues. We began with a list of all election issues appearing in the press, as coded by Frizzell et al. in their analysis of the 1988 election (1989, 85–89). This was modified to include immigration issues as a separate category and to collapse other categories where no items were tabulated during coding (peace/defence issues, environmental issues and women's issues). As table 5.6 demonstrates quite clearly, news items about people with disabilities seldom mention any broad election issues and, instead, are focused more narrowly on issues related specifically to persons with disabilities. Other than five news items linking the news frame of persons with disabilities to broader social issues in the election campaign, there were no

Table 5.6
References to election issues

| | Focus of item | | | | |
| | Ethnic groups | | | Persons with disabilities | |
Election issue	N	%		N	%
Social issues	43	30.1		5	13.2
Immigration	11	7.7		—	—
Free trade	6	4.2		—	—
National unity	2	1.4		—	—
Economy/unemployment	1	0.7		—	—
Other	18	12.6		—	—
None cited	62	43.4		33	86.8
Total[a]	143	100.1		38	100.0

[a]Because of rounding, percentages do not always total 100.

other references to election issues. This effectively indicates the inability of persons with disabilities to link their political concerns to the larger public debates about a range of election issues. So, for example, real concerns that persons with disabilities had (as will be discussed later) regarding the impact of the Free Trade Agreement on the provision of various social services to their community were not part of the media coverage of free trade matters.

A high percentage of the news items dealing with ethnic groups also made no reference to election issues (43.4 percent), although they were four times more likely to do so than news about persons with disabilities. Ethnic news items that did refer to election issues did so most often for social issues (30.1 percent of the items) and least often for issues regarding the economy or unemployment (only one news item). A very small percentage made reference to free trade (4.2 percent) and immigration (7.7 percent), while the rest cited a range of other issues (for example, tax reform, defence matters and patronage appointments).

Following from our review of the theoretical issues, we now consider the question of voices in the news. We need to ask whether some voices are given greater access and are more frequently used as sources of information and opinion than others in the area of election coverage. To investigate the types of sources who appear in these news items, we analysed the sample for the relative frequency of appearance of two broad categories: federal political actors and organizations for/of persons with disabilities and minorities.

The presence of federal political actors was examined to determine the extent to which they were used as sources in these news items and whether particular parties were more visible than others. In tables 5.7 through 5.9, the frequency of appearance of the three main political parties (in the sense of a direct reference to one of the parties), the party leaders, party/campaign officials and political candidates is demonstrated. The references to other parties were too few to justify inclusion in the analysis. Based on our earlier discussion of election news conventions, one would expect to find more attention to party leaders and the parties than to the marginalized groups and more coverage of the Liberals and Progressive Conservatives than of the NDP. Therefore, it is interesting to note in table 5.7 that election news items concerning persons with disabilities are less likely to have federal parties cited in the item than election news concerning ethnic groups. There is not a strong political presence for the former, and what little there is leans more toward the Progressive Conservatives. Some might also argue that the low visibility of the Liberal party in news about persons with disabilities is surprising, given that social policy concerns have generally

Table 5.7
Frequency of appearance of political parties

	Focus of item			
	Ethnic groups		Persons with disabilities	
Party	N	%	N	%
Progressive Conservative	69	48.3	10	26.3
Liberal	58	40.6	7	18.4
NDP	33	23.1	7	18.4

been associated with Liberal platforms. Perhaps equally surprising is the higher visibility of the PCs in ethnic news items, given that the Liberal party has traditionally been well supported in ethnic communities and that Toronto was the site of several hotly contested Liberal nomination battles in which ethnic candidates figured prominently. The NDP receives little press in either category, confirming a pattern of proportional news coverage and indicating its low priority as a news source.

The number of news items in which party leaders were directly quoted or paraphrased is indicated in table 5.8. The total absence of party leaders in news about persons with disabilities is quite striking, since it reverses the usual convention of targeting the leader as the focus in election news and is perhaps indicative of the low priority persons with disabilities have in party campaign strategies. There is slightly more visibility of the three leaders in items concerning ethnic groups, and again the PCs are more visible than the Liberals, with the NDP trailing a distant third.

Similar patterns are evident, and indeed accentuated, in table 5.9. This time measuring direct references to any party officials, we again find the invisibility of all three parties in news items about persons with disabilities (with the exception of two stories citing PC party officials). In news items concerning ethnic groups, PC officials were twice as likely to be used as a source as Liberal officials (35 to 18.2 percent), and the NDP barely appears (three news items). Again the Progressive Conservatives received more press coverage in this domain than the other two parties combined. Whether this speaks to a stronger grass-roots organization in ethnic communities or a better press relations strategy that effectively routinized their contact as a source cannot, unfortunately, be determined from this analysis.

The final measurement for the visibility of federal political actors as news sources, the appearance of political candidates, is shown in table 5.10. Of items concerning persons with disabilities, a small number include references to party candidates, with the PCs only minimally in the lead. It is interesting that half of these stories referring to candidates concerned Patrick Boyer's riding (Boyer, a Conservative incumbent, is the former chair of the Standing Committee on the Status of Disabled Persons). In news items concerning ethnic groups, Liberal candidates appear as sources more often than either other party, a finding that runs counter to the pattern noted above. This is due, no doubt, to the press coverage of the Toronto-area ridings, where Liberal nomination meetings and election battles were framed in terms of the ethnic factor, a point to which we will return later. In any case, Liberal

Table 5.8
Frequency of appearance of political leaders

| | Focus of item | | | |
| | Ethnic groups | | Persons with disabilities | |
Party leader	N	%	N	%
Progressive Conservative	34	23.8	—	—
Liberal	22	15.4	—	—
NDP	11	7.7	—	—

Table 5.9
Frequency of appearance of party officials

| | Focus of item | | | |
| | Ethnic groups | | Persons with disabilities | |
Party officials	N	%	N	%
Progressive Conservative	50	35.0	2	5.3
Liberal	26	18.2	—	—
NDP	3	2.1	—	—

Table 5.10
Frequency of appearance of political candidates

	Focus of item			
	Ethnic groups		Persons with disabilities	
Candidates	N	%	N	%
Progressive Conservative	35	24.5	8	21.1
Liberal	54	37.8	7	18.4
NDP	31	21.7	5	13.2

candidates are quoted in over one-third of these news items, while PC candidates appear in one-quarter.

The relative use of groups from within the communities of ethnic persons and people with disabilities as sources of information is an important area of consideration. In the content analysis, news items were examined for the frequency of appearance of both spokespersons for organizations of ethnic groups and persons with disabilities and individuals from within these communities (i.e., whose appearance is not framed as being on behalf of any particular organization). The analysis revealed that organizations and individuals from our designated groups, and ethnic groups in particular, are seldom used as news sources. As shown in table 5.11, in 58 percent of all the items about ethnic issues, no ethnic organizations are cited; in 83 percent of these items, no individuals from ethnic groups are cited. The higher visibility of organizational voices confirms what was suggested in the theoretical discussion as a news orientation toward bureaucratic sources. This is framed within the context of both the status of the (bureaucratic) source on a hierarchy of sources and the fact that journalistic election practices favour attention to the parties over other groups. Thus, when we compare the figures in table 5.11 to those discussed in table 5.7 for political parties, for example, we see that the Progressive Conservative party has a higher probability of appearance as a source on ethnic issues than any ethnic organization.

It is interesting to note from table 5.11 that organizations representing persons with disabilities and individuals with disabilities themselves are more likely to be cited in election news items relevant to their concerns than is the case for ethnic organizations and individuals. They also outnumber appearances by all categories of federal political actors, as shown in tables 5.7 through 5.10. This could be interpreted as evidence

Table 5.11
Frequency of appearance of ethnic actors and actors with disabilities

	Focus of item			
	Ethnic groups		Persons with disabilities	
Source of citation	N	%	N	%
Group/organization	60	42.0	25	65.8
No group/organization	83	58.0	13	34.2
Total[a]	143	100.0	38	100.0
Individual cited	24	16.8	12	31.6
No individual cited	119	83.2	26	68.4
Total	143	100.0	38	100.0

of a higher organizational profile for this particular community, although more analysis would be required on this point. Persons with disabilities are cited in only slightly less than one-third of all relevant news items, again giving weight to the argument that news is oriented toward organizational and official voices.

Table 5.12 is a list of the most frequently cited organizations working on behalf of ethnic persons and people with disabilities, indicating the percentage of total mentions each organization received. It is evident that there is no clear, central voice speaking for either community; rather, a wide range of different organizations is reflected here. Nevertheless, two organizations appear slightly more visible for ethnic groups: the Japanese-Canadian Citizens Association (with 11.6 percent of all organizational mentions) and the Canadian Ethnocultural Council (with 16 percent of mentions). The former can be explained by the fact that the announcement of the compensation package for Japanese-Canadians, just before the call of the election, was one of the key news issues among the ethnic items in the sample (as discussed in the next section of the analysis). The only organization among persons with disabilities that appears slightly more visible as a source is the Canadian Disability Rights Council, which received 8.9 percent of all mentions for organizations for/of ethnic persons or people with disabilities.

As was noted in the theoretical discussion of issues in news analysis, it is important to distinguish those sources who enter the news as primary definers from voices that enter in a more subordinate role. This distinction was examined in the sample of news items by attempting to distinguish among three different roles groups could play: originating roles (their actions, information or views framed the news peg or were central to the news lead), reacting roles (they were called on to offer comment, elaboration, etc., to issue[s] already established in the lead), or incidental roles (the reference was minor, marginal to the main narrative, and the groups were not quoted directly in the item). The objec-

Table 5.12
Designated group organizations as a percentage of mentions

Group organization	Mentions
Canadian Ethnocultural Council	16.0
Japanese-Canadian Citizens Association	11.6
Canadian Disability Rights Council	8.9
Canadian Race Relations Foundation	6.2
Ukrainian Canadian Committee	5.3
Canadian Jewish Congress	3.5
Canadian Association for Community Living	2.6
Canadian Coordinating Council on Deafness	2.6
Immigrants' Association of Canada	2.6
B.C. Association for Community Living	1.7
Canadian Institute for Minority Rights	1.7
Canadian Paraplegic Association	1.7
Ethnic Press Association of Quebec	1.7
Ottawa and District Association for the Mentally Retarded	1.7
World Sikh Organization	1.7
Black Coalition for Equal Rights	0.8
Canadian Multicultural Council	0.8
Disabled People for Affirmative Action	0.8
REACH (Resource, Educational and Advocacy Centre for the Handicapped)	0.8
Other	26.8
Total[a]	99.5

[a]$N = 112$; because of rounding, percentages do not total 100.

tive was to determine which of the three roles was the most significant for each of our groups; therefore, a group or individual was not coded as playing more than one role in any one news item. Nevertheless, different groups could play the same role; for example, multiple actors might be called on to comment on an issue.

The results of this analysis for news items regarding ethnic persons and people with disabilities are presented in tables 5.13 and 5.14, which compare the source roles played by the federal political actors (including party, leader, party officials and political candidates) to the source roles played by actors from the designated groups (including organizations and individuals from both designated communities). Given our earlier discussion of journalistic conventions in election news and the tendency of the media to adopt election issues as they are established by the parties, there was an expectation that the parties would be the primary definers in the majority of news items. From table 5.13, we see that the Conservatives and Liberals play a significantly more central role as primary definers of ethnic news frames than ethnic groups themselves. The PCs and Liberals were originators of the items in 36 percent and 34 percent of the cases. Ethnic actors, on the other hand, were originators in only 23 percent of the news items. There are no significant differences in their roles as reactors to the news, except that the NDP is seldom called on for comment in this area. We also find that ethnic groups are far more likely to appear as incidental sources than any of the political actors. In 43 percent of all the ethnic news items, the primary role played by ethnic groups and individuals was of this marginal, voiceless character.

News items about persons with disabilities, however, yield somewhat different findings. Individuals with disabilities and organizations

Table 5.13
Distribution of source roles, ethnic items

	Role					
	Originator		Reactor		Incidental	
Source	N	%	N	%	N	%
Progressive Conservative	52	36.4	32	22.4	26	18.2
Liberal	49	34.3	34	23.8	20	14.0
NDP	16	11.2	17	11.9	16	11.2
Ethnic group	33	23.1	40	28.0	62	43.4

Table 5.14
Distribution of source roles, disability items

	Role					
	Originator		Reactor		Incidental	
Source	N	%	N	%	N	%
Progressive Conservative	6	15.8	4	10.5	6	15.8
Liberal	4	10.5	3	7.9	5	13.2
NDP	4	10.5	3	7.9	5	13.2
Persons with disabilities	16	42.1	8	21.8	14	36.8

for them are more likely to play a central role in the news item than political actors (table 5.14), and they play the role of originator to a far greater degree than ethnic groups. Individuals and organizations from the community of persons with disabilities were originators of the news in 42 percent of all the relevant news items. This is not surprising, given the very low profile of federal political actors in this news frame. It should also be noted that the primary role played by the disabled was characterized as incidental to the news in 36.8 percent of all items.

Analysis of the news items containing references to any other organizations and individuals, outside the categories of federal political actors and designated group members, revealed few significant patterns. References to other organizations, agencies or institutions were noted in only 28 (or 20 percent) of the news items about ethnic groups and in 18 (or 47 percent) of the news items regarding persons with disabilities. There is no clear pattern to the organizations cited, and the main role played appears to be that of reactors to the issues (in 20 percent of items about ethnic groups and 34 percent of items regarding people with disabilities).

The final area examined in the content analysis concerned the question of news focus. Here we attempted to determine the primary news event or news issue for every item in the sample. (In the original coding, there was also an attempt to discern secondary news focus, but this did not prove a particularly clear coding category and is not included in the analysis.) Coded in an open-ended format, items were then grouped by key themes (tables 5.15 and 5.16). In the list of primary news events and issues for items about ethnic groups, 10 themes are identified. The primary news focus ranged across a variety of issues, although certain clusters were more visible than others. The three cat-

Table 5.15
Distribution of primary news events/issues, ethnic items

	Item	
Event/issue	N	%
Ethnic candidates/nomination	36	25.2
Compensation (Japanese-Canadians)	22	15.4
Ethnic vote	18	12.6
General election issues	12	8.4
General ethnic issues	12	8.4
Media coverage/discrimination	8	5.6
Immigration	7	4.9
Multiculturalism	6	4.2
Advocacy	4	2.8
Other	18	12.6
Total[a]	143	100.1

[a]Because of rounding, percentages do not total 100.

Table 5.16
Distribution of primary news events/issues, disability items

	Item	
Event/issue	N	%
Mentally disabled/right to vote	19	50
Access/voting procedures	7	18
Report of Standing Committee	5	13
Other	7	18
Total[a]	38	99

[a]Because of rounding, percentages do not total 100.

egories most frequently appearing concerned issues regarding the recruitment and nomination of ethnic candidates (the main news focus in 25 percent of the stories), the compensation package for Japanese-Canadians, announced by the federal government in September 1988 (15 percent of the news items) and the nature, magnitude and implications of the ethnic vote (almost 13 percent of the news). A surprisingly small number of items focused on immigration issues in relation to the election, and advocacy-focused issues were virtually invisible. The remaining news items were distributed among general election issues (8 percent), general ethnic issues (8 percent), media coverage and discrimination (6 percent), multiculturalism (referring to the passing of the *Multiculturalism Bill*, C-93, 4 percent) and other issues (where the primary focus of the item could not be coded in any of the above categories, 12.6 percent).

A media focus on the recruitment and nomination of ethnic candidates and on the presence of an ethnic vote (which together account for almost 38 percent of all the items) can be seen as one indicator of the growing attention given to the increasing role of ethnic groups in political parties and elections. Indeed, Stasiulis and Abu-Laban argue that the 1988 federal election was a "watershed election for ethnopolitics in Canada," marked chiefly by a new "aggressive pursuit of nominations" by members of ethnic groups, particularly within the Liberal party and in Toronto-area ridings (1990, 584–85). What is interesting to note is the particular frame given to ethnopolitics by the media. While a close interpretive or textual reading of the news items is beyond the scope of this particular study (though it would be an important complementary project), certain tendencies are evident.

The dominant frame, when writing about ethnopolitics, is that ethnic minorities constitute a unified, powerful political force that challenges traditional party structures and has the capacity to change the face of electoral politics. This "March of the Third Force" (as an article in *Toronto Life* labelled it in December 1988) was represented as an attempt by the ethnic community to claim a new place in the structures of power. Headlines such as "Ethnic Power Demands to Be Recognized" (Montreal *Gazette*, 2 June); "Ethnic Groups Grow Militant in Metro Nomination Battles" (*Globe and Mail*, 27 June); "Ethnic Candidates Storm Liberal Party" (*Globe and Mail*, 16 August) and "Ethnics' Power Play Shaking up Liberals" (*Toronto Star*, 24 April) are one indicator of the news frame established by the media. Ethnic groups constitute a bloc in political battles; their activities are defined by militance and conflict; their battles are primarily urban-centred (largely Toronto) and focused within the Liberal party. Particular attention is paid within the items on nominations to allegations of rigged voting, instant Liberals and stacked nomination meetings (summed up in a *Toronto Star* headline on 14 July as "nomination brawls"), overshadowing to a considerable extent any discussion of candidate platforms or party policies. The overarching frame here is a negative one, characterized by charges of misconduct, militancy and challenge to the status quo.

News items about the ethnic vote specifically focused on the non-differentiated unity of the various ethnic groups and the fact that the parties needed to court and capture that bloc vote. Story headlines such as "Charting the Ethnic Vote" (Montreal *Gazette*, 29 October), "Broadbent Policy Woos Ethnic Voters" (*Toronto Star*, 14 August), "New Department Meant to Woo Ethnic Vote" (*Ottawa Citizen*, 16 September), "Federal Politicians Court Ethnic Leaders" (Halifax *Chronicle-Herald*, 31 May) and "Candidates Courting Ethnic Vote" (*Vancouver Sun*, 27 June) are typical of this frame. Yet there are convincing arguments to show that ethnic groups do not vote as a bloc; nor do ethnopolitics appear to be changing the face of the political power structure. Zajc's study of ethnic candidates in the 1988 election demonstrates that they are nominated overwhelmingly in ridings with high ethnic constituencies and are therefore not changing the face of traditional French and Anglo-Celtic ridings (1990). Also, as Stasiulis and Abu-Laban note, the nomination meetings became a site not just for the expression of ethnic group versus Anglo-Celtic conflict; equally important was the expression of interethnic divisions through "differentiated ethnic lines of conflict" (1990, 591). Finally, one must question the success of ethnic activism in 1988 in changing the face of parliamentary representation; the number of elected MPs of ethnic origin dropped to 49 from the 1984 level of 51 (ibid., 595).

The third most frequently cited news focus concerned the compensation package for Japanese-Canadians. The event orientation of this focus was framed in three particular phases: items concerning the negotiations leading up to the settlement package (with particular emphasis on the impact of the pending election), items detailing the announcement of the compensation package by the federal government and items concerning the fallout of the settlement for other groups (with particular emphasis linking demands by the Ukrainian- and Chinese-Canadian communities to this event).

The primary news focus in items regarding persons with disabilities is distributed among four categories (table 5.16). It is striking that fully half of the news items dealt with the 17 October decision of the Federal Court of Canada to give persons with mental health disabilities confined to institutional care the right to vote (*Canadian Disability Rights Council* 1988). The event orientation of this item, as defined in the theoretical section of this study, and its constituting something new in election politics were the item's frame for entering the news. These news accounts were essentially focused on three phases: the court challenge brought by the Canadian Disability Rights Council, the ruling of the Federal Court and the mechanics involved in enumerating those with mental health disabilities in institutions and ensuring proper procedures at the poll. (It is interesting to note that while papers vary in the use of the terms "mentally disabled" and "mentally handicapped," the *Globe and Mail* was the only paper to still use the term "retarded." A particularly memorable headline, on the front page of the *Globe and Mail* for 22 October ran "Problems Plague Vote by Retarded, Institutions Warn" – immediately below the lead headline "Dangerous Psychopath Set Free with New Name, Immunity"!)

The second most frequently appearing category concerns questions of access to voting by persons with disabilities. These are consistently short items dealing with the logistics of voting. Most were news briefs announcing either advance poll locations and dates where those with physical disabilities could vote (along with other specially designated groups) or describing particular facilities (e.g., wheelchair ramps) available to enhance the access of persons with disabilities. In none of these items can one find references to organizations or individuals speaking on behalf of persons with disabilities about their needs.

The third category, representing 13 percent of the total number of items, concerns the August release of *No News Is Bad News* (Canada, House of Commons 1988), the report of the House of Commons Standing Committee on the Status of Disabled Persons, chaired by Tory MP Patrick Boyer. The items report on the release of the report and focus on the charges levelled against the media. Headlines such as "Media Ignore Disabled, Commons Report Charges" (*Calgary Herald*, 19 August), "Media Fails in Coverage of Disabled, MPs Report" (*Toronto Star*, 19 August) and "News Media Blamed for Unrealistic View of Disabled People" (*Globe and Mail*, 19 August) present a confrontational and conflict-based theme as the frame for understanding the issues.

The remaining items regarding persons with disabilities are located in the "other" news focus category in which there is a variety of unrelated issues.

Before turning to a summary of the main conclusions of this analysis, it is imperative to consider the viewpoints of members of groups for/of persons with disabilities and ethnic minorities to establish their perspectives on the question of media access during election campaigns. These views are summarized in the following section and are based on telephone interviews conducted in January 1991 with a selected number of organizations working on behalf of these groups (the complete interview list is located in the "Interviews" section).

Views from the Margin

As was noted earlier in the discussion of methodology, it was not the intention of this study to fully survey groups for/of persons with disabilities and ethnic minorities. Those interested in a more detailed survey of visible minority members may wish to examine two related studies for the Commission: one by Carolle Simard (1991), on visible minorities and their participation in the Canadian electoral system, and one by Daiva Stasiulis and Yasmeen Abu-Laban (1991), on ethnic candidates. Nevertheless, it was considered important to obtain a sense of the coverage from the perspective of those who feel its impact. The groups were first chosen by identifying organizations that had earlier appeared before the Commission or had made submissions. The list of contacts was then extended by asking these organizations to name others that might be interviewed. Fifteen interviews were conducted with representatives of various groups: ten for groups representing people with disabilities, and five for ethnic groups. The smaller number of ethnic groups interviewed is a reflection of the difficulty we encountered in identifying organized lobby groups that had mobilized around electoral issues.

The first question asked of all groups concerned their view of what the main issues of importance were to their organizations in the 1988 election. Organizations representing persons with disabilities cited four key issues:

- the Free Trade Agreement (in terms of its potential impact on social services, including health, UIC and the *Vocational Rehabilitation Act*);
- accessibility and voter registration (including issues regarding when and how people with disabilities can vote, problems caused by the illegality of proxy voting and the right of persons with mental health disabilities to vote);
- employment equity policies; and
- the Meech Lake Accord and its potential impact on social programs (including the consequences for national standards within those programs).

It is interesting to compare this list with those actually framed by the media as central in the coverage. As discussed earlier, election news coverage that involves persons with disabilities seldom refers to any larger election issues, including those prioritized by the organizations interviewed. The one area of overlap is the question of accessibility, which, as pointed out above, is a dominant focus in the news coverage.

The key issues defined by organizations for ethnic groups were as follows:

- the positions of all parties and candidates on policies of multiculturalism;
- immigration processes and policies;
- race relations and policies that might deal with racism;
- employment equity; and
- the Meech Lake Accord and the participation of ethnocultural communities in constitutional debates.

Again, we can see a disjuncture between what the groups themselves are defining as central and what is actually covered. In our review of election news research, it was noted that the media tend to allow the parties to define the issues of significance. Our evidence clearly establishes the inability of marginalized groups to carve a space for themselves in the dominant frame. In the previous discussion of primary news focus for items about ethnic groups (based on the results given in table 5.15), it was argued that the key issues were the nomination and recruitment of ethnic candidates, the compensation package for Japanese-Canadians and the implications of the ethnic vote – issues that would seem crucial to the interest of the parties (in the case of the compensation package, it was a clear vote-garnering strategy by the PCs on the eve of the election call). Issues like immigration, multiculturalism and advocacy measures (which include employment equity) are extremely low in their proportion of the coverage.

The second set of questions addressed in the interviews concerned organizations' perception of media coverage of the issues they saw as central. For both groups, there was a high level of dissatisfaction. Organizations representing persons with disabilities noted that there is little media attention at the national level to issues pertinent to their concerns. Coverage, they argued, tends to focus on local issues and largely concern soft news. Several spokespersons argued that when political candidates do address issues pertaining to people with disabilities, it is often ignored by the news media because it is not sufficiently dramatic. Technical considerations of access were also prominent among their complaints, including the low proportion of closed-captioned election news on television. The need to use alternative media (voice tapes, extra-large-print newsprint, etc.) was noted because of the failure of traditional media to make information sufficiently accessible.

The organizations representing ethnic groups argued that ethnic diversity is not reflected in election news coverage. Only one spokesperson, for the World Sikh Organization, felt coverage was fair in its treatment, although the volume of coverage was not regarded as adequate. Others argued that there were inherent biases in media coverage and that the minority point of view had little access to the media. There was general agreement that employment equity issues received inadequate coverage and that the media did little to examine the parties' platforms on race and ethnic issues. Specific criticism was directed at the televised leaders debates for their failure to consider issues pertaining to ethnic groups and for the absence of any minority journalists on the panel. One final comment of interest here was the observation that "once the election is over, the news media forget about ethnic voters."

When asked about the nature of their contact with media personnel during the election, the majority of spokespersons indicated contact was infrequent and usually a result of their own initiative. Six of the ten organizations representing persons with disabilities said the media did not initiate any contact, while others noted "a couple of telephone calls." Only one group, the Canadian Paraplegic Association, felt the media were "very good" at contacting them (this was generally in relation to a Human Rights Commission challenge). Six of these organizations engaged in routine strategies to increase their visibility in the press. This included issuing press releases, writing letters to the editor and arranging for interviews. The Coalition of Provincial Organizations of the Handicapped commented that they specifically attempted to express four areas of concern to the media (employment, independent living, transportation and human rights) but none was picked up as an issue in election coverage.

Representatives for ethnic groups also remarked on the failure of media to establish contact. The Canadian Ethnocultural Council noted that they initiated all contact, although the media did follow up on their press releases. Another noted that the media would approach them to "fill in the gaps" in stories being written. The Centre for Research, Action and Race Relations indicated that they were asked questions about ethnic candidates and ethnic voting, but not about issues of concern to ethnic minorities. The Urban Alliance on Race Relations commented that they were usually approached after something was said in the media, when their reaction was needed. Two of the organizations did not engage in any activities to initiate media contact, and one commented that print media offered a better chance of access because it lacked the funds necessary to offer radio and television "the glamorous images and sounds they need."

Finally, the organizations were asked if they had particular recommendations that could improve media practices in this area. It is interesting to note that at the top of the list for both groups was a recommendation regarding employment equity in the media. It is felt that coverage will not change until more journalists with disabilities and journalists from ethnic minorities are hired. As noted by Alice Basarke, for the World Sikh Organization, "discrimination is not the real problem, rather the ignorance of most journalists is central." In this regard, training sessions for all journalists, to sensitize them to the needs and concerns of these groups, was a high priority. Organizations for persons with disabilities also made technical suggestions, such as the increase of closed-captioned news broadcasts for those with hearing impairments and increased spacing between words in print news for people with visual impairments, to improve the access of these groups.

Some organizations focused on the role groups themselves can play in improving coverage. The Canadian Mental Health Association spoke of its stigma-stopper projects: when group members see a particularly offensive news item or ad, they are encouraged to contact the media and lodge formal complaints, write letters to the editor, contact the Human Rights Commission, etc. In a similar vein, the Urban Alliance on Race Relations spoke of the need to launch "pressure campaigns where ethnic groups and organizations sit down with media executives." The BC Coalition of the Disabled argued that groups must take the initiative with the media and cited the access guide (listing possible sources to contact) they prepared and distributed to media outlets. Finally, among both sets of organizations, there was a perception that the media need to establish formal guidelines and procedures on questions of language and balance, monitored by some form of ethics committee.

CONCLUSION: THE REPRODUCTION OF MARGINALIZATION

The objective of this study was to examine the interrelated issues of image and access in the news media as one mechanism for examining the inclusion of minority groups in the wider political process. The specific concern was to investigate the extent to which ethnic groups and persons with disabilities were integrated into the news frames of election campaigns. The evidence gathered through a content analysis of newspaper coverage of the 1988 federal election demonstrates that on a variety of dimensions, media coverage reflects and reproduces the marginal sociopolitical location of these groups.

The presentation of news about ethnic groups and persons with disabilities is characterized by scarcity, little visibility and low priority (as indicated by factors such as frequency of appearance, word length, headline size and location in the paper). The frame for election news coverage is characterized by little discussion of major election issues and policies and a reliance on bureaucratic voices over individual voices. There was a noticeable difference between the groups on the involvement of federal political sources; for the items regarding persons with disabilities, the three parties are virtually invisible. Two interpretations of this are possible: federal political parties either rank issues concerning disability very low on their campaign priority list and hence are not engaged in the kinds of activities that would draw media attention, or news media ignore those occasions when political engagement with disability issues or groups does take place. In fact, one could argue that both processes are probably at work.

For ethnic groups, the federal political voice was more visible and, indeed, was most visible for the Progressive Conservatives on every measure except political candidates. What is more important about this finding is that the PCs are more visible than ethnic organizations and ethnic individuals. The central news frame for ethnic election issues is set, in other words, by members of the dominant majority, and ethnic minorities enter in a subordinate role. This became clear with the evidence on the nature of the source role. In almost half of the news items about ethnic groups, their voice was judged incidental to the news, while the PCs and Liberals played the role of the primary definer, or originator, in over one-third of the items. This confirms what seems a general trend in election news coverage, wherein the major parties set the public agenda of issues.

The opposite was true for items about persons with disabilities. The relative absence of federal sources from the frame meant a greater role for organizations representing this group. Nevertheless, it is coupled with a higher degree of invisibility in the news in general; the overwhelming majority of references to persons with disabilities in election news are single, passing mentions.

Finally, the frame for news about ethnic groups and persons with disabilities was a restricted frame and, in each case, narrowed the scope of election issues. For ethnic groups, three topics dominated the coverage: the recruitment and nomination of ethnic candidates (especially for the Liberal party in Toronto-area ridings), the compensation package for Japanese-Canadians and the nature, magnitude and implications of the ethnic vote. For persons with disabilities, the frame was dominated by three issues: the court decision regarding the right to vote for those with mental health disabilities, questions of access to voting facilities and the release of a parliamentary report on media treatment of persons with disabilities (it is interesting to speculate whether the report would have received coverage if it had concerned something other than media treatment). Not only is this a restricted frame, but also it does not, as indicated in the interviews, fairly represent the range of electoral issues concerning the two groups. In fact, representatives from both groups felt blocked in their attempts to enter their concerns on the media agenda for debate.

This is not the forum to engage in a discussion of the probable effects or impact of media coverage. Nonetheless, it is important to consider the implications of the dominant framework of news about ethnic groups and persons with disabilities that the public receives. We have argued that it is a framework that essentially marginalizes the minority group's concerns and the minority group itself. There is also the question of the broader public and the media construction of the political agenda. In many senses, politics is a media construction; that is, the public's understanding of political information, issues, processes and priorities is mediated by the press. It is not that the media instruct the public how to think about political issues; it is that the public consensus about what is part of the political agenda is constructed, for the most part, by the media. For this reason, the role played by the media in the politics of exclusion and marginalization of different minority groups is crucial. Moreover, the public has little opportunity to resist or challenge the dominant news frame or, indeed, to construct an alternative understanding of the issues.

Our intention is not to suggest that journalists are out to distort our understanding of minority group positions; we suggested earlier that one must recognize that there are preferred news values and news sources that reflect organizational and professional dictates and work routines. What one can do, however, is point out the implications of these media practices for silencing particular voices and particular issues.

These consequences are played out across a range of subordinate social groups. It is therefore imperative that we begin to link our research on the marginalization of such groups as women, Aboriginal groups, the elderly, ethnic minorities and persons with disabilities during election campaigns to fully understand the parameters of political exclusion. In addition, we need to develop strategies for enhancing the access of these groups to participation in the media and for sensitizing media personnel to their concerns. Following are some recommendations based on the findings of this study. They are a beginning point only; the marginalization of these groups is not a creation of the media and cannot be redressed through media reform. One can, however, begin to widen the frame of news and attempt to ensure a more equitable place for minority groups within that frame.

RECOMMENDATIONS

Media Organizations

Although media organizations are outside the scope of intervention by the Royal Commission on Electoral Reform and Party Financing, and in recognition of arguments against a regulated or restricted press, there is clearly a need for media organizations to take proactive steps in the representation of ethnic groups and persons with disabilities. The Commission could play an important role in encouraging media organizations to consider the following recommendations:

1. Engage in proactive search and recruitment practices to increase the hiring of journalists from ethnic minorities and journalists with disabilities.
2. Commit resources to workshops and training sessions for journalists to sensitize them to the concerns of these groups. Organized through consultation with the appropriate organizations, these workshops would provide a routinized forum for access of minority group interests.
3. Establish formal guidelines on matters of language use in references to minority groups.
4. Establish an ethics committee and a complaints mechanism with specific reference to minority groups.

The Royal Commission on Electoral Reform and Party Financing

The Commission could play a key role in addressing three critical problem areas: the organizational infrastructure of minority groups, the inability of minority groups to establish their voice in the news, and technical and logistical difficulties experienced by particular groups. The following recommendations are seen as areas where the Commission could begin to address the unequal ability to communicate during elections:

1. The ability of minority groups to initiate and establish routine contact with media organizations is fundamentally determined by their organizational resources. The Commission needs to consider the viability of establishing funds and resources to assist these groups during election campaigns.
2. The Commission should consider the establishment of a broad-based federal mechanism to receive complaints from minority groups regarding questions of media coverage and access, and to convey these complaints to the appropriate media outlets.
3. The Commission needs to address the technical and logistical problems experienced by particular minority groups. For ethnic group candidates, the language-gap problem was raised as a difficulty for

some groups, particularly during enumeration. Depending on the nature of the disability, persons with disabilities experience serious problems in simply receiving information. The need for closed captioning in election news and election advertising on television, far greater attention to visual impairment in the publication of election materials and a national standard for facilities accessible to those with physical disabilities are key among the concerns of these groups.

APPENDIX
CODING SHEET

1. Topical Focus: a) Ethnic ☐
              b) Disabled ☐

2. Disabled item.

3. Date of Item: a) Day ————————————————————
            b) Month ————————————————————

4. Source of item:————————————————————————(press)

5. Genre of item:
  a) news report ☐
  b) news brief ☐
  c) news backgrounder ☐
  d) editorial ☐
  e) feature ☐
  f) opinion column ☐
  g) letter ☐
  h) photograph ☐
  i) editorial cartoon ☐
  j) other (specify) ————————————————————

6. Total number of words in item:————————————————————

7. Length of principal headline:
  a) one column in width ☐
  b) two columns in width ☐
  c) three columns in width ☐
  d) four columns in width ☐
  e) five columns or greater in width ☐

8. Placement of item by section:
  a) front page, first section ☐
  b) inner page, first section ☐
  c) front page, inner section ☐
  d) inner page, inner section ☐
  e) not known ☐

9. Production source of item:
   a) staff reporter(s) ☐
   b) staff editorialist ☐
   c) staff columnist ☐
   d) daily bureau ☐
   e) corporate news agency ☐
   f) CP news agency ☐
   g) special to the daily ☐
   h) no production source listed/other (specify) _____

10. Dateline of item:
    a) Ottawa ☐
    b) BC ☐
    c) Alberta ☐
    d) Saskatchewan ☐
    e) Manitoba ☐
    f) Ontario ☐
    g) Quebec ☐
    h) New Brunswick ☐
    i) Nova Scotia ☐
    j) PEI ☐
    k) Newfoundland ☐
    l) Yukon ☐
    m) NWT ☐
    n) no dateline by province given/other (specify) _____

11. Primary focus of item:
    a) national issue(s) ☐
    b) provincial issue(s) ☐
    c) local issue(s) ☐
    d) combination of above (specify) _____

12. Principal federal election issue(s) cited in item:
    a) Economy/Unemployment ☐
    b) Free Trade ☐
    c) National Unity ☐
    d) Social ☐
    e) Immigration ☐
    f) other (specify) ☐ _____
    g) no election issue cited ☐

13. Primary news topic cited in item: _____

14. Secondary news topic cited in item: _____

15. Primary focus of news topic by province:
    a) BC ☐
    b) Alberta ☐

c) Saskatchewan ❐
d) Manitoba ❐
e) Ontario ❐
f) Quebec ❐
g) New Brunswick ❐
h) Nova Scotia ❐
i) PEI ❐
j) Newfoundland ❐
k) Yukon ❐
l) NWT ❐
m) no provincial focus given/other (specify) _____

16. Primary focus of news topic by city:
    a) Vancouver ❐
    b) Edmonton ❐
    c) Calgary ❐
    d) Regina ❐
    e) Winnipeg ❐
    f) Toronto ❐
    g) Hamilton ❐
    h) Ottawa ❐
    i) Montreal ❐
    j) Quebec City ❐
    k) Fredericton ❐
    l) Halifax ❐
    m) Charlottetown ❐
    n) St. John's ❐
    o) no city focus/other (specify) _____

17. Federal political actor(s) cited and/or quoted in item:
    a) party as actor: PC ❐   Lib. ❐   NDP ❐   Other/Spec_____
    b) party leader: PC ❐   Lib. ❐   NDP ❐   Other/Spec_____
    c) party officials: PC ❐   Lib. ❐   NDP ❐   Other/Spec_____
    d) candidate(s):   PC ❐   Lib. ❐   NDP ❐   Other/Spec_____
    e) no federal political actor cited: ❐

18. Role of federal political actor(s) in generation of news item:
    a) originator(s) of news: PC ❐   Lib. ❐   NDP ❐
       Other: ❐ (specify)_____
    b) reaction to news: PC ❐   Lib. ❐   NDP ❐
       Other: ❐ (specify)_____
    c) incidental to news: PC ❐   Lib. ❐   NDP ❐
       Other: ❐ (specify)_____
    d) not applicable ❐

19. Organizations/actor(s) for designated group cited/quoted in item:
    a) organization _____
    b) organization _____

c) organization _____
d) organization _____
e) organization _____
f) human actors (number of mentions) _____

20. Role of organizations/actor(s) for designated group in generation of news item:

a) originator(s) of news lead: ☐ (specify) _____
_____

b) reaction to news lead: ☐ (specify) _____
_____

c) incidental to news lead: ☐ (specify) _____
_____

d) not applicable ☐

21. Other actors/institutions (i.e., non-party/non-designated group) cited or quoted in item:

a) institution _____
b) institution _____
c) institution _____
d) institution _____
e) institution _____
f) human actor (number of mentions) _____

22. Role of other actors/institutions (i.e., non-party/non-designated group) in generation of news item:

a) originator(s) of news: ☐ (specify) _____
b) reaction to news: ☐ (specify) _____
c) incidental to news: ☐ (specify) _____
d) not applicable: ☐

ACKNOWLEDGEMENTS

I would like to thank the following people who contributed to the completion of this report: Stuart Allen, who helped in the construction of the coding schedule and in the overview of news production studies; Lise Ballantyne, Cindy Carter, Carolyn Emblem, May Farah, Debi Guin and Heather Pyman, who helped in different stages of the project; and finally, Alan Frizzell, who provided invaluable assistance in the data analysis.

INTERVIEWS

All interviews were conducted by telephone.

Organizations Representing Persons with Disabilities

Barnes, Don, Newfoundland Association for Community Living, St. John's, Nfld.

Birrell, Margaret Priestley, Executive Director, BC Coalition of the Disabled, Vancouver, BC.

Fleming, Ellen, Executive Director, Hearing Society, Saint John, NB.

Graham, Mel, Coalition of Provincial Organizations of the Handicapped, Winnipeg, Man.

Lane, John, Executive Director (Manitoba Division), Canadian Paraplegic Association, Winnipeg, Man.

Lie-Nielsen, Anne, Executive Director, Council of the Disabled, Charlottetown, PEI.

Neubauer, Joanne, President, Handicapped Action Committee, Victoria, BC.

Pennington, Edward J., General Director, Canadian Mental Health Association, Toronto, Ont.

Roots, James, Executive Director, The Canadian Association of the Deaf, Ottawa, Ont.

Vincent, Danielle, Executive Director, Premier's Council on the Status of the Disabled, Fredericton, NB.

Organizations Representing Ethnic and Racial Minorities

Basarke, Alice, Executive Assistant, World Sikh Organization, Nepean, Ont.

Bouska, Bernard, Acting Director, Canadian Ethnocultural Council, Ottawa, Ont.

Head, Dr. Wilson, Urban Alliance on Race Relations, Toronto, Ont.

Kevany, Kathleen, London Cross Cultural Learner Centre, London, Ont.

Niemi, Fo, Centre for Research, Action and Race Relations, London, Ont.

ABBREVIATIONS

c.	chapter
F.T.R.	Federal Trial Reports
R.S.C.	Revised Statutes of Canada

BIBLIOGRAPHY

Abu-Laban, Baha, and Donald Mottershead. 1981. "Cultural Pluralism and Varieties of Ethnic Politics." *Canadian Ethnic Studies* 13 (3): 44–63.

Alberta Report. 1988. "Facing the Ethnic Factor." 6 June, 10–11.

Altheide, David L. 1976. *Creating Reality – How TV News Distorts Events*. Beverly Hills: Sage Publications.

Alvarado, Manuel, and John O. Thompson, eds. 1990. *The Media Reader*. London: BFI Publishing.

Becker, Howard S. 1967. "Whose Side Are We on?" *Social Problems* 14 (3): 239–47.

Biklen, Douglas. 1987. "Framed: Print Journalism's Treatment of Disability Issues." In *Images of the Disabled, Disabling Images,* ed. Alan Gartner and Tom Joe. New York: Praeger.

Black, Jerome H., and Christian Leithner. 1987. "Patterns of Ethnic Media Consumption: A Comparative Examination of Ethnic Groupings in Toronto." *Canadian Ethnic Studies* 19 (1): 21–41.

Bogdan, Robert, Douglas Biklen, Arthur Shapiro and David Spelkoman. 1982. "The Disabled: Media's Monster." *Social Policy* 13 (2): 32–35.

Brown, Joan C. 1977. *A Hit and Miss Affair – Policies for Disabled People in Canada.* Ottawa: Canadian Council on Social Development.

Burnet, Jean, and Howard Palmer. 1988. *Coming Canadians: An Introduction to a History of Canada's Peoples.* Toronto: McClelland and Stewart.

Canada. *Vocational Rehabilitation of Disabled Persons Act,* R.S.C. 1985, c. V-3.

Canada. House of Commons. Standing Committee on the Status of Disabled Persons. 1988. *No News Is Bad News.* Ottawa: Queen's Printer.

Canada. Multiculturalism and Citizenship Canada. 1982. *Visible Minorities and the Media Conference Report.* Ottawa: Minister of Supply and Services Canada.

———. 1983. *Race Relations and the Law.* Report of a symposium held in Vancouver, 22–24 April 1982. Ottawa: Minister of Supply and Services Canada.

———. 1989. *Operation of the Canadian Multiculturalism Act – Annual Report 1988–89.* Ottawa: Minister of Supply and Services Canada.

Canada. Secretary of State. 1986. *Profile of Disabled Persons in Canada.* Ottawa: Minister of Supply and Services Canada.

———. 1987. *Multiculturalism: Being Canadian.* Ottawa: Minister of Supply and Services Canada.

———. 1987–88. *Annual Report.* Ottawa: Minister of Supply and Services Canada.

———. 1988–89. *Annual Report.* Ottawa: Minister of Supply and Services Canada.

———. 1990. *Response to the Second Report of the Standing Committee on Human Rights and the Status of the Disabled – A Consensus for Action: The Economic Integration of Disabled Persons.* Ottawa: Secretary of State.

Canadian Broadcasting Corporation. 1985. *A Study on Multicultural Reflection in CBC Radio.* Ottawa: CBC.

Canadian Disability Rights Council v. Canada (1988), 21 F.T.R. 268.

Canadian Multiculturalism Council. 1988. *Reflections from the Electronic Mirror: Report of a National Forum on Multiculturalism in Broadcasting* held in Toronto 13–14 May. Ottawa.

Canadian Radio-television and Telecommunications Commission (CRTC). 1985. "A Broadcasting Policy Reflecting Canada's Linguistic and Cultural Diversity." Public Notice 1985–139. Ottawa: CRTC.

Caplan, Gerald, Michael Kirby and Hugh Segal. 1988. *Election: The Issues, the Strategies, the Aftermath.* Scarborough: Prentice-Hall Canada.

Clarke, Harold D., Allan Kornberg and Marianne Stewart. 1985. "Active Minorities: Political Participation in Canadian Democracy." In *Minorities and the Canadian State*, ed. Neil Nevitte and Allan Kornberg. Oakville: Mosaic Press.

Crepault, Michel, and Joanne McDermott. 1988. "The Representation of Disabled Persons in the French-Language Press in Quebec." Research study prepared for the Standing Committee on the Status of Disabled Persons. Ottawa.

Dahlie, Jorgen, and Tissa Fernando. 1981. *Ethnicity, Power and Politics in Canada.* Toronto: Methuen.

Deverell, Shelton Rita. 1986. *Equal Opportunities to Perform: A Study of the Role of Performers Who Are Members of Visible and Audible Minority Groups in Canadian Communications Media.* Toronto: ACTRA.

Driedger, Diane. 1989. *The Last Civil Rights Movement.* New York: St. Martin's Press.

Eliasoph, Nina. 1988. "Routines and the Making of Oppositional News." *Critical Studies in Mass Communication* 5:313–34.

Epstein, Edward Jay. 1973. *News from Nowhere – Television and the News.* New York: Random House.

Ericson, Richard V., Patricia Baranek and Janet B.L. Chan. 1987. *Visualizing Deviance: A Study of News Organizations.* Toronto: University of Toronto Press.

———. 1989. *Negotiating Control: A Study of News Sources.* Toronto: University of Toronto Press.

Erin Research. 1990. *The Portrayal of Gender in Canadian Broadcasting.* Report prepared for the CRTC. Ottawa: Minister of Supply and Services Canada.

Ferguson, Russell, et al. 1990. *Out There: Marginalization and Contemporary Cultures.* Cambridge: MIT Press.

Financial Post. 1988. "The Racist Bogey of 'Dual Loyalty.' " 26 March, 16.

Fishman, Mark. 1980. *Manufacturing the News*. Austin: University of Texas Press.

———. 1981. "Crime Waves as Ideology." In *The Manufacture of News: Social Problems, Deviance and The Mass Media*, ed. S. Cohen and J. Young. London: Constable.

Fletcher, Frederick J. 1987. "Mass Media and Parliamentary Elections in Canada." *Legislative Studies Quarterly* 12 (3): 341–72.

Frizzell, Alan, and Anthony Westell. 1985. *The Canadian General Election of 1984*. Ottawa: Carleton University Press.

Frizzell, Alan, Jon Pammett and Anthony Westell. 1989. *The Canadian General Election of 1988*. Ottawa: Carleton University Press.

Galtung, Johan, and Mari Ruge. 1965. "The Structure of Foreign News." *Journal of International Peace Research* 1:64–90.

———. 1981. "Structuring and Selecting News." In *The Manufacture of News: Social Problems, Deviance and the Mass Media*, ed. S. Cohen and J. Young. London: Constable.

Gans, Herbert J. 1979. *Deciding What's News*. New York: Vintage Books.

Gartner, Alan, and Tom Joe, eds. 1987. *Images of the Disabled, Disabling Images*. New York: Praeger.

Generations Research Inc. 1988. *The Portrayal of Canadian Cultural Diversity on Canadian Network Television – A Content Analysis*. Report prepared for the Secretary of State. Ottawa.

Ginzberg, Effie. 1987. *Power without Responsibility: The Press We Deserve*. Toronto: Urban Alliance on Race Relations.

Gitlin, Todd. 1980. *The Whole World Is Watching: Mass Media in the Making and Unmaking of the New Left*. Berkeley: University of California Press.

Glasgow University Media Group. 1982. *Really Bad News*. London: Writers and Readers.

Granzberg, Gary. 1983. *The Portrayal of Minorities by Canadian Television during the 1982 Prime-Time Season*. Report prepared for the Secretary of State. Ottawa.

Hall, Stuart. 1981. "A World at One with Itself." In *The Manufacture of News: Social Problems, Deviance and the Mass Media*, ed. S. Cohen and J. Young. London: Constable.

Hall, Stuart, Chas Critcher, Tony Jefferson, John Clarke and Brian Roberts. 1978. *Policing the Crisis: Mugging, the State, and Law and Order*. London: Macmillan.

Hartley, John. 1982. *Understanding News*. London: Methuen.

Hartley, John, and Martin Montgomery. 1985. "Representations and Relations: Ideology and Power in Press and TV News." In *Discourse and Communication*, ed. T.A. van Dijk. New York: Walter de Gruyter.

Hartman, Paul, and Charles Husband. 1974. *Racism and the Mass Media*. London: Davis-Poynter.

Indra, Doreen M. 1979. "South Asian Stereotypes in the Vancouver Press." *Ethnic and Racial Studies* 12 (2): 166–89.

Kallen, Evelyn. 1982–83. "Multiculturalism: Ideology, Policy and Reality." *Journal of Communication Studies* 17 (1): 51–53.

———. 1988. "The Meech Lake Accord: Entrenching a Pecking Order of Minority Rights." *Canadian Public Policy* 14 (Supplement): 107–20.

———. 1989. *Label Me Human: Minority Rights of Stigmatized Canadians*. Toronto: University of Toronto Press.

Karim, H. Karim. 1988. "Covering Refugees with Figures of Speech." *Content* (January/February): 30–31.

———. 1989a. "A Content Analysis of Newspapers, Academic Papers, Ethnocultural Briefs, Attitude Surveys, and Ministerial Correspondence." Ottawa: Multiculturalism and Citizenship, Policy and Research.

———. 1989b. "Multiculturalism in Public Discourse." *Language and Society* (Spring): 39–40.

Karim, H. Karim, and Gareth Sansom. 1990. *Ethnicity and the Mass Media in Canada: An Annotated Bibliography*. Ottawa: Multiculturalism and Citizenship, Policy and Research.

Kirschbaum, J.M., B. Heydenkorn, V. Mauko and P. Gaida. 1971. *Twenty Years of the Ethnic Press Association of Ontario*. Toronto: Ethnic Press Association.

Lam, Lawrence. 1980. "The Role of Ethnic Media for Immigrants: A Case Study of Chinese Immigrants and Their Media in Toronto." *Canadian Ethnic Studies* 12 (1): 74–92.

Longmore, Paul K. 1985. "A Note on Language and the Social Identity of Disabled People." *American Behavioral Scientist* 28 (3): 419–23.

Maclean's. 1988, "The Battle for Ontario." 3 October, 13–14.

———. 1988. "Election Fever." 19 September, 30–31.

———. 1988. "Memories of Shame." 3 October, 12.

———. 1988. "The Nation-Makers." 11 July, 8–11.

———. 1988. "Promises, Promises – Critics Assail the Tory Spending Spree." 26 September, 16.

————. 1988. "Questions in the Background." 14 November, 21–23.

————. 1988. "Righting History." 3 October, 10–11.

————. 1988. "Shuffling the Lineup." 26 September, 13.

————. 1988. "A Tory Crusade for the Immigrant Vote." 13 June, 10.

————. 1988. "The Tory 'Dead Zone.' " 6 June, 14.

Marlett, Nancy J., Robert S. Gall, et al., eds. 1984. *Dialogue on Disability: A Canadian Perspective. Volume I. The Service System.* Calgary: University of Calgary Press.

Media Research Inc. (PEAC). 1982. *The Presence and Portrayal of Non-whites in English Language Television Advertising in Canada.* Report prepared for the Secretary of State. Ottawa.

Miller, Randall M. 1985. "Ethnic Media." *Ethnic Forum* 5 (1–2): 52–65.

Molotch, Harvey, and Marilyn Lester. 1974. "News as Purposive Behavior: On the Strategic Use of Routine Events, Accidents, and Scandals." *American Sociological Review* 39 (1): 101–12.

Owaisi, Lateef, Zafar Bangash and Amina Syed. 1978. *Visible Minorities in Mass Media Advertising.* Report prepared for the Canadian Consultative Council on Multiculturalism. Ottawa: Minister of Supply and Services Canada.

Paletz, David, and Robert Entman. 1981. *Media, Power, Politics.* New York: Free Press.

Plancke, Julie. 1989. "Disabled Journalists: Empathy Overdue." *Content* (January/February): 21–24.

Rock, Paul. 1981. "News as Eternal Recurrence." In *The Manufacture of News: Social Problems, Deviance and the Mass Media,* ed. S. Cohen and J. Young. London: Constable.

Rubin, Bernard. 1983. "Mass Media Stereotyping and Ethnic and Religious Groups." *Nieman Reports* (Winter): 17–22.

Scanlon, Joseph. 1977. "The Sikhs of Vancouver: A Case Study of the Role of the Media in Ethnic Relations." In *Race, Ethnicity and Media: An Analysis of Media Reporting in the UK, Canada, and Ireland.* Paris: UNESCO.

Schlesinger, Philip. 1990. "Rethinking the Sociology of Journalism: Source Strategies and the Limits of Media-Centrism." In *Public Communication: The New Imperatives,* ed. M. Ferguson. Beverly Hills: Sage Publications.

Sigal, Leon V. 1978. "Defining News Organizationally: News Definitions in Practice." In *Women and the News,* ed. L.K. Epstein. New York: Hastings House.

Simard, Carolle. 1991. "Visible Minorities and the Canadian Political System." In *Ethno-cultural Groups and Visible Minorities in Canadian Politics: The Question of Access,* ed. Kathy Megyery. Vol. 7 of the research studies of the Royal Commission on Electoral Reform and Party Financing. Ottawa and Toronto: RCERPF/Dundurn.

Singer, Benjamin D. 1983. "Minorities and the Media: A Content Analysis of Native Canadians in the Daily Press." In *Communications in Canadian Society,* ed. B.D. Singer. Don Mills: Addison-Wesley.

Soderlund, Walter C., Walter I. Romanow, E. Donald Briggs and Ronald Wagenburg. 1984. *Media and Elections in Canada.* Toronto: Holt, Rinehart and Winston of Canada.

Spiller, Frank, and Kim Smiley. 1985. *Multiculturalism and Electronic Communications.* Ottawa: Francis Spiller Associates.

———. 1986. *Multicultural Broadcasting Canada.* Ottawa: Francis Spiller Associates.

Stasiulis, Daiva K. 1989. "Minority Resistance in the Local State: Toronto in the 1970s and 1980s." *Ethnic and Racial Studies* 2 (1): 63–83.

Stasiulis, Daiva K., and Frances Abele. 1989. "Canada as a 'White Settler Colony': What About Natives and Immigrants?" In *The New Canadian Political Economy,* ed. Wallace Clement and Glen Williams. Montreal: McGill-Queen's University Press.

Stasiulis, Daiva K., and Yasmeen Abu-Laban. 1990. "Ethnic Activism and the Politics of Limited Inclusion in Canada." In *Canadian Politics: An Introduction to the Discipline,* ed. Alain G. Gagnon and James Bickerton. Peterborough: Broadview Press.

———. 1991. "The House the Parties Built: (Re)constructing Ethnic Representation in Canadian Politics." In *Ethno-cultural Groups and Visible Minorities in Canadian Politics: The Question of Access,* ed. Kathy Megyery. Vol. 7 of the research studies of the Royal Commission on Electoral Reform and Party Financing. Ottawa and Toronto: RCERPF/Dundurn.

Sutherland, Allan T. 1981. *Disabled We Stand.* Bloomington: Indiana University Press.

Taras, David. 1990. *The Newsmakers.* Scarborough: Nelson Canada.

Toronto Life. 1988. "March of the Third Force." (December): 43–47ff.

Tuchman, Gaye. 1977. "The Exception Proves the Rule: The Study of Routine News Practice." In *Strategies for Communication Research,* ed. P.M. Hirsch, P.V. Miller and F.G. Kline. Beverly Hills: Sage Publications.

———. 1978. *Making News: A Study of the Construction of Reality.* New York: Free Press.

van Dijk, Teun A. 1988a. *News Analysis: Case Studies of International and National News in the Press.* Hillsdale: Lawrence Erlbaum Associates.

———. 1988b. *News as Discourse.* Hillsdale: Lawrence Erlbaum Associates.

Wilson, Clint C., and Felix Gutierrez. 1985. *Minorities and the Media – Diversity and the End of Mass Communications.* Beverly Hills: Sage Publications.

Zajc, Lydia. 1990. "The Ethnicity and Competitiveness of Ethnic Minority Nominees in the 1988 Federal Election." Montreal: McGill University.

Zybala, Stanley. 1982. "Problems of Survival for the Ethnic Press in Canada." *Polyphony* 4 (1): 15–31.

CONTRIBUTORS TO VOLUME 22

Robert Bernier   École nationale
     d'administration publique

Jean Charron   Université Laval
Christopher Dornan   Carleton University
William O. Gilsdorf   Concordia University
Robert A. Hackett   Simon Fraser University
Eileen Saunders   Carleton University

ACKNOWLEDGEMENTS

The Royal Commission on Electoral Reform and Party Financing and the publishers wish to acknowledge with gratitude the permission of the following to reprint and translate material:

Cambridge University Press; *Le Devoir*; Éditions du Boréal; Éditions Hurtubise HMH; Éditions Québec/Amérique; Éditions Stock, SA; Fédération professionnelle des journalistes du Québec; Le Jour, Division de Sogides ltée; *Legislative Studies Quarterly*; Les magazines Maclean Hunter Québec; Gaëtan Morin; Sweet & Maxwell.

Care has been taken to trace the ownership of copyright material used in the text, including the tables and figures. The authors and publishers welcome any information enabling them to rectify any reference or credit in subsequent editions.

~

Consistent with the Commission's objective of promoting full participation in the electoral system by all segments of Canadian society, gender neutrality has been used wherever possible in the editing of the research studies.

THE COLLECTED RESEARCH STUDIES*

* The titles of studies may not be final in all cases.

SYLVIA BASHEVKIN	Women's Participation in Political Parties
LISA YOUNG	Legislative Turnover and the Election of Women to the Canadian House of Commons
LYNDA ERICKSON	Women and Candidacies for the House of Commons
GERTRUDE J. ROBINSON AND ARMANDE SAINT-JEAN, WITH THE ASSISTANCE OF CHRISTINE RIOUX	Women Politicians and Their Media Coverage: A Generational Analysis

VOLUME 7
Ethno-cultural Groups and Visible Minorities in Canadian Politics: The Question of Access
Kathy Megyery, Editor

DAIVA K. STASIULIS AND YASMEEN ABU-LABAN	The House the Parties Built: (Re)constructing Ethnic Representation in Canadian Politics
ALAIN PELLETIER	Politics and Ethnicity: Representation of Ethnic and Visible-Minority Groups in the House of Commons
CAROLLE SIMARD, WITH THE ASSISTANCE OF SYLVIE BÉLANGER, NATHALIE LAVOIE, ANNE-LISE POLO AND SERGE TURMEL	Visible Minorities and the Canadian Political System

VOLUME 8
Youth in Canadian Politics: Participation and Involvement
Kathy Megyery, Editor

RAYMOND HUDON, BERNARD FOURNIER AND LOUIS MÉTIVIER, WITH THE ASSISTANCE OF BENOÎT-PAUL HÉBERT	To What Extent Are Today's Young People Interested in Politics? Inquiries among 16- to 24-Year-Olds
PATRICE GARANT	Revisiting the Voting Age Issue under the *Canadian Charter of Rights and Freedoms*

COMMISSION ORGANIZATION

CHAIRMAN
Pierre Lortie

COMMISSIONERS
Pierre Fortier
Robert Gabor
William Knight
Lucie Pépin

SENIOR OFFICERS

Executive Director	*Director of Research*
Guy Goulard	Peter Aucoin

Special Adviser to the Chairman
Jean-Marc Hamel

Research
F. Leslie Seidle,
  Senior Research Coordinator

Coordinators
Herman Bakvis
Michael Cassidy
Frederick J. Fletcher
Janet Hiebert
Kathy Megyery
Robert A. Milen
David Small

Assistant Coordinators
David Mac Donald
Cheryl D. Mitchell

Legislation
Jules Brière, Senior Adviser
Gérard Bertrand
Patrick Orr

Communications and Publishing
Richard Rochefort, Director
Hélène Papineau, Assistant
  Director
Paul Morisset, Editor
Kathryn Randle, Editor

Finance and Administration
Maurice R. Lacasse, Director

Contracts and Personnel
Thérèse Lacasse, Chief

EDITORIAL, DESIGN AND PRODUCTION SERVICES

ROYAL COMMISSION ON ELECTORAL REFORM AND PARTY FINANCING

Editors   Denis Bastien, Susan Becker Davidson, Ginette Bertrand, Louis Bilodeau, Claude Brabant, Louis Chabot, Danielle Chaput, Norman Dahl, Carlos del Burgo, Julie Desgagners, Chantal Granger, Volker Junginger, Denis Landry, André LaRose, Paul Morisset, Christine O'Meara, Mario Pelletier, Marie-Noël Pichelin, Kathryn Randle, Georges Royer, Eve Valiquette, Dominique Vincent.

LE CENTRE DE DOCUMENTATION JURIDIQUE DU QUÉBEC INC.

Hubert Reid, *President*

Claire Grégoire, *Comptroller*

Lucie Poirier, *Production Manager*
Gisèle Gingras, *Special Project Assistant*

Translators   Pierre-Yves de la Garde, Richard Lapointe, Marie-Josée Turcotte.

Technical Editors   Stéphane Côté Coulombe, *Coordinator*; Josée Chabot, Danielle Morin.

Copy Editors   Martine Germain, Lise Larochelle, Elisabeth Reid, Carole St-Louis, Isabelle Tousignant, Charles Tremblay, Sébastien Viau.

Word Processing   André Vallée.

Formatting   Typoform, Claude Audet; Linda Goudreau, *Formatting Coordinator.*

WILSON & LAFLEUR LTÉE

Claude Wilson, *President*

Printed and bound in Canada by
Best Gagné Book Manufacturers